D1766691

Drs. Sarah Pressman and Acacia Parks, award-winning leade
psychology and health, have curated a brilliant, evidence-ba~~~ ~~~~~~~ ~~~~ ~~~~
teachers feasible, engaging, and educational ways to introduce students to the basic
tenets of positive psychology. What sets this great book apart is the excellence,
thoughtfulness, and diversity of the interventions. There is something for everyone
here to help, heal, and lead students to flourishing and to the good life.

—**Elaine O'Brien, PhD, MAPP,** former Assistant Professor, Philadelphia College of
Osteopathic Medicine, Philadelphia, PA; Kinesiologist, with specialization in human
movement psychology; coauthor of *The Power of Play: Optimize Your Joy Potential;*
author of Splash Dance: What a Feeling! Aqua Fitness Meets Positive Psychology

Honestly, I'm excited to get my copy; I found so many things I want to use next
year! Each chapter is an ideal mix of experiential activities and the scholarship
behind them.

—**Cynthia L. S. Pury, PhD,** Professor, Department of Psychology, Clemson University,
Clemson, SC

If you're teaching or giving workshops on well-being, you hope to inspire a room full
of people to explore, discover, and learn. This book is the fuel to help you do just that.

—**Todd B. Kashdan, PhD,** Professor of Psychology, George Mason University, Fairfax, VA;
author of *The Upside of Your Dark Side* and *The Art of Insubordination: How to Dissent*
and Defy Effectively

Edited by two respected researchers in the field of positive psychology, this activity
book provides easy onboarding for those new to the teaching of positive constructs
while adding to the repertoire of those who are more seasoned in the field. As the
number of classes in positive psychology grows, the need for creative and varied
classroom activities grows as well. Pressman and Parks deliver exactly that with this
comprehensive and updated resource.

—**Jennifer Teramoto Pedrotti, PhD,** Associate Vice President for DEI Academic Initiatives,
California Polytechnic State University, San Luis Obispo

More Activities for Teaching Positive Psychology: A Guide for Instructors offers state-of-the-art activities based on the latest evidence-informed theories of the science of positive psychology. As a professor of positive psychology and cofounder of the first PhD and research-based master's degree programs in positive psychology, I give my absolute highest endorsement of this new volume to anyone teaching positive psychology in a university setting, as well as to those teaching and applying positive psychology in workplaces, schools, communities, therapy and coaching, and health and well-being care settings across the globe.

—**Stewart I. Donaldson, PhD,** Distinguished University Professor, Claremont Graduate University, Claremont, CA

The field is increasingly crowded with positive psychology textbooks, but *More Activities for Teaching Positive Psychology* stands out from the rest by offering experiments, activities, and exercises that help learners understand how and why positive psychology can be so powerful in their lives. Now with this new work, Pressman and Parks give us even more to love. The activities will be helpful not just for professors but also for researchers and practitioners to take the science of positive psychology beyond the classroom. Indispensable in a world where positivity is so sorely needed.

—**Judith T. Moskowitz, PhD, MPH,** Professor of Medical Social Sciences, Northwestern University, Feinberg School of Medicine, Evanston, IL

More Activities
for Teaching
Positive Psychology

More Activities for Teaching Positive Psychology

A GUIDE FOR INSTRUCTORS

EDITED BY

Sarah D. Pressman
Acacia C. Parks

AMERICAN PSYCHOLOGICAL ASSOCIATION

Published by
American Psychological Association
750 First Street, NE
Washington, DC 20002
https://www.apa.org

Order Department
https://www.apa.org/pubs/books
order@apa.org

Typeset in Meridien and Ortodoxa by Lumina Datamatics, India

Printer: Sheridan Books, Chelsea, MI
Cover Designer: Beth Schlenoff Design, Bethesda, MD

Library of Congress Cataloging-in-Publication Data

Names: Pressman, Sarah D., editor. | Parks, Acacia C., editor. | American
  Psychological Association.
Title: More activities for teaching positive psychology : a guide for
  instructors / edited by Sarah D. Pressman and Acacia C. Parks.
Description: Washington, DC : American Psychological Association, [2025] |
  Includes bibliographical references and index.
Identifiers: LCCN 2024006100 (print) | LCCN 2024006101 (ebook) | ISBN
  9781433839283 (paperback) | ISBN 9781433839290 (ebook)
Subjects: LCSH: Positive psychology. | Social psychology.
Classification: LCC BF204.6 .M667 2025 (print) | LCC BF204.6 (ebook) |
  DDC 150.19/88071—dc23/eng/20240325
LC record available at https://lccn.loc.gov/2024006100
LC ebook record available at https://lccn.loc.gov/2024006101

https://doi.org/10.1037/0000417-000

Printed in the United States of America

10 9 8 7 6 5 4 3 2 1

*From both editors, this book is dedicated to the two shining beacons of
positive psychology who shaped this field and our careers in it:
Professors Shane Lopez and Ed Diener. The planet is darker without your light.*

For my loves, Brian and Ian, who pack my days with every type of positivity.
—SARAH D. PRESSMAN

*For Cassie—you're every positive psychology activity wrapped
up into one small human. I love you big, and forever.*
—ACACIA C. PARKS

CONTENTS

*Indicates an activity that requires more than one lecture to complete (e.g., with a pre–post assessment, work to do at home). Note that many other activities can also be done across multiple classes, with many authors offering adjustments depending on how much time you have available.

CONTRIBUTORS

Justine R. Bautista, MA, Department of Social Ecology, University of California, Irvine, CA, United States

Elizabeth Blevins, PhD, Department of Psychology, Stanford University, Stanford, CA, United States

Kennedy M. Blevins, MA, Department of Psychological Science, University of California, Irvine, CA, United States

Jordan A. Booker, PhD, Department of Psychological Sciences, University of Missouri, Columbia, MO, United States

Kim Cameron, PhD, William Russell Kelly Professor (emeritus), Ross School of Business, University of Michigan, Ann Arbor, MI, United States

Arne Carlsen, PhD, Department of Leadership and Organizational Behaviour, BI Norwegian Business School, Oslo, Norway

John K. Coffey, PhD, School of Social and Behavioral Sciences, Arizona State University, Tempe, AZ, United States

Tamlin S. Conner, PhD, Department of Psychology, University of Otago, Dunedin, Otago, New Zealand

Jack R. H. Cooper, PhD, Department of Psychology, University of Otago, Dunedin, Otago, New Zealand

Marie P. Cross, PhD, Department of Biobehavioral Health, Pennsylvania State University, State College, PA, United States

Brittney R. Denson (Davis), PhD, RTI International, Research Triangle Park, NC, United States

Jessica E. Desrochers, MESc, Department of Psychology, Carleton University, Ottawa, ON, Canada

Jane E. Dutton, PhD, Department of Management and Organizations, University of Michigan, Ann Arbor, MI, United States

Robert A. Emmons, PhD, Department of Psychology, University of California, Davis, CA, United States

Barbara L. Fredrickson, PhD, Department of Psychology and Neuroscience, University of North Carolina at Chapel Hill, Chapel Hill, NC, United States

Matthew W. Gallagher, PhD, Department of Psychology, University of Houston, Houston, TX, United States

Emma L. Grisham, PhD, Department of Psychology and Neuroscience, Duke University, Durham, NC, United States

Samantha J. Heintzelman, PhD, Department of Psychology, Rutgers University, Newark, NJ, United States

Hidefumi Hitokoto, PhD, Department of Psychological Sciences, School of Humanities, Kwansei Gakuin University, Nishinomiya, Hyogo, Japan

Dacher Keltner, PhD, Department of Psychology, University of California, Berkeley, CA, United States

Margaret L. Kern, PhD, Centre for Wellbeing Science, The University of Melbourne, Parkville, Victoria, Australia

Patrick Klaiber, PhD, Department of Developmental Psychology, Tilburg University, Tilburg, North Brabant, The Netherlands

Laura P. Kohn-Wood, PhD, School of Education and Human Development, University of Miami, Coral Gables, FL, United States

Ashley L. Kuchar, PhD, Educational Psychology, The University of Texas at Austin, Austin, TX, United States

Jaime L. Kurtz, PhD, Department of Psychology, James Madison University, Harrisonburg, VA, United States

Kostadin Kushlev, PhD, Department of Psychology, Georgetown University, Washington, DC, United States

Sally Maitlis, PhD, Saïd Business School, University of Oxford, Oxford, Oxfordshire, United Kingdom

Ajit Singh Mann, MA, Quality of Life Research Center, Division of Behavioral and Organizational Sciences, Claremont Graduate University, Claremont, CA, United States

Hannah Masling, BA, Department of Psychology, Colorado College, Colorado Springs, CO, United States

Jeanne Nakamura, PhD, Quality of Life Research Center, Division of Behavioral and Organizational Sciences, Claremont Graduate University, Claremont, CA, United States

Kristin D. Neff, PhD, Department of Educational Psychology, University of Texas at Austin, Austin, TX, United States

S. Katherine Nelson-Coffey, PhD, School of Social and Behavioral Sciences, Arizona State University, Tempe, AZ, United States

Virginie Paquette, PhD (c), Department of Psychology, Université du Québec à Montréal, Montreal, QC, Canada

Kenneth I. Pargament, PhD, Department of Psychology, Bowling Green State University, Bowling Green, OH, United States

Sarah D. Pressman, PhD, Department of Psychological Science, University of California, Irvine, CA, United States

Patrick Robinson, MA, Quality of Life Research Center, Division of Behavioral and Organizational Sciences, Claremont Graduate University, Claremont, CA, United States

Laurie R. Santos, PhD, Department of Psychology, Yale University, New Haven, CT, United States

Stephen M. Schueller, PhD, Department of Psychological Science, University of California, Irvine, CA, United States

Kennon M. Sheldon, PhD, Department of Psychological Sciences, University of Missouri, Columbia, MO, United States

David K. Sherman, PhD, Department of Psychological and Brain Sciences, University of California, Santa Barbara, CA, United States

Zachary A. Silver, PhD, Department of Psychology, Occidental College, Los Angeles, CA, United States

Emiliana Simon-Thomas, PhD, Greater Good Science Center, University of California, Berkeley, CA, United States

Nancy L. Sin, PhD, Department of Psychology, University of British Columbia, Vancouver, BC, Canada

Jany St-Cyr, PhD Student, Laboratoire de Recherche sur le Comportement Social, Département de Psychologie, Université du Québec à Montréal, Montreal, QC, Canada

Margarita Tarragona, PhD, Centro ITAM de Estudios del Bienestar, Instituto Tecnológico Autónomo de México, Mexico City, Mexico

Guerdiana Thelomar, MSEd, PhD Student, Department of Educational and Psychological Studies, University of Miami, Coral Gables, FL, United States

Liudmila Titova, PhD, Department of Psychology, University of Washington, Seattle, WA, United States

Jeanne L. Tsai, PhD, Department of Psychology, Stanford University, Stanford, CA, United States

Yukiko Uchida, PhD, Institute for the Future of Human Society, Kyoto University, Kyoto, Japan

Robert J. Vallerand, PhD, Université du Québec à Montréal, Montreal, QC, Canada

Patty Van Cappellen, PhD, Social Science Research Institute, Duke University, Durham, NC, United States

Serena Wong, PhD, Department of Psychiatry, University of Western Ontario, London, ON, Canada

John M. Zelenski, PhD, Department of Psychology, Carleton University, Ottowa, ON, Canada

Joanne F. Zinger, PhD, Department of Psychological Science, University of California, Irvine, CA, United States

PREFACE

The first volume of *Activities for Teaching Positive Psychology* was created to provide instructors of positive psychology with a resource similar to those available for older areas of psychology, which have countless video libraries, case studies, and activity books. The positive reception of the first volume made it clear that this was a much-needed resource and that a second volume would be extremely welcome and highly useful to the growing number of instructors teaching well-being courses. Therefore, this second volume is intended to assist all of those professors who are looking for new content, activities, and pedagogical tools to keep their classes engaging and to help them stay up-to-date on new insights from the field. We also noted, at the start of the last book, that there was no other book that allowed positive psychology instructors to learn how to teach each topic, not from a generalist writing a single textbook but from an expert on that particular topic. We are pleased to say that while we have continued this tradition in this new volume, we have worked to broaden our contributor pool. In this book, we have included senior researchers as well as up-and-coming junior experts, leaders in the pedagogy and practice of positive psychology, and individuals from a range of countries around the world. We hope that by including a wide range of voices, we will represent the amazing diversity of the field.

The areas that you will encounter will be a range of new and old. Some of them were covered in the last volume, but via different types of activities; for example, as a topic exploration versus an in-class experiment, or a classic manipulation of a positive psychology theme versus a new and exciting application described in this book. We recognized that instructors might want more than one activity to illustrate a concept and/or may prefer a certain type of activity over another. As such, in this book, you will find new and engaging activities that you may never have considered before. To help you discover these activities more readily, in this edition, we have organized topics conceptually. As you will note in Volume 1, subjects were categorized as experiments, concept explorations, illustrations, and self-reflections. In this volume of the book, we have instead grouped the chapters thematically to make it easier for instructors to find the activities that match the assigned readings for the day (e.g., positive cognitions, relationships, interventions). We hope this is a simpler way to find the appropriate enrichment activity that highlights the construct each lecture is focused on. While content varies somewhat widely across different positive psychology books, we believe that by combining the two volumes of these teaching activities books, it will be possible to have an appropriate activity for almost every lecture you would want to deliver.

Another change from the last volume to this volume is the emphasis on experimentation. After receiving feedback from the users of the first book, we learned that students generally were more energized by the experimentally oriented activities that allowed them to collect data or see the effects of a theory in real time. That said, students still enjoyed a meaningful discussion on the importance of the topic, the value of the activity, future directions, and so forth. With this in mind, the vast majority of activities in this book are experiments, interventions, or similar manipulations with data collection partnered with an enjoyable set of prompts and readings that can aid in helping students understand and extract the key points of the activity. We also include far more appendices in this version, with instructions that you can edit as needed and print out as activity sheets to give to students to use in class. For example, you might have students use these sheets to fill out essays, do self-evaluations of well-being, or collect data. All of these can be turned in to you to aid your evaluations of student learning and participation.

Finally, you will note a lot of new content not found in the first volume. For example, there is a new and unique focus on research methods in positive psychology in the first section of the book. As you no doubt have noticed, science and scientists have been under attack of late thanks to growing misinformation, fake news, and a general distrust that grew during the COVID-19 pandemic. Thus, it has never been more important to partner the teaching of positive psychology with instructions on methodological rigor, critical thinking, and strong research approaches. Unfortunately, most positive psychology text-books do not have a methods section, nor do they focus on these topics. Thus, we hope that you will help take up the charge of ensuring our positive psychologists of the future are well-versed in these areas by adopting some of these brilliant activities into a few of your course lectures.

Between the two editors, we have over 25 years of experience teaching positive psychology courses, lecturing to the public, leading workshops, doing empirical and theoretical research in the field, building happiness applications, and translating this work for public and academic consumption. This experience helped us guide our superstar authors to create highly usable, informative, and helpful chapters that will truly transform your classroom. We know that this book will change how we teach positive psychology in the future for the better, and we hope the same is true for you.

ORGANIZATION

This book is organized into five sections according to the themes of the chapters. Each section starts with a brief introduction to the topics covered as well as some advice on how to approach those chapters. The first section includes the newest content to this book series and focuses on letting students try out a range of research methods and critical thinking activities, as well as one chapter that demonstrates ways to improve the quality of classroom discussions more broadly. In Section II, we consider numerous activities and interventions examining either improving well-being or understanding how to change your day/life/environment in a manner that improves well-being. Section III highlights a number of important positive cognitions such as hopeful expectations, meaning interpretations, passion assessments, and the important concept of flow. Next, Section IV looks at the critical themes of prosociality and positive social relationships. As was often said by the late, great positive psychologist Chris Peterson, "other people matter." Thus, we spend some time in this section offering you opportunities to engage your students on the value of social relationships and prosocial behavior, touching on putting these in different cultural and organizational frameworks. Related to this last point, the final section of the book (Section V) focuses on framing positive psychology in different contexts. As you likely know, well-being outcomes vary widely depending on numerous factors such as culture, geographic location, a range of demographic variables (e.g., socioeconomic status, age, sex), the environment, and health. This final section dips its toes into the wide range of critical contexts that interact with well-being, but, of course, there are numerous others to consider, and we hope that you do in discussions of these types of issues with your students.

HOW TO USE THIS BOOK

This book will be especially helpful in reducing feelings of burnout and disengagement in your students. The activities in the following pages will allow your students to connect with others in the classroom and with you (the instructor), and they will enable your students to act as scientists making their own exciting new discoveries about how positive psychology works. You won't have to rack your brain on how to engage students with a new topic when you can have a world expert do the work for you.

This book is packed with 30 chapters from skilled academics, each of whom crafted a new active learning experience that illustrates a seminal concept in positive psychology and is accompanied by content that will help you teach. This includes a succinct summary and background reading for each concept that you can use to teach students about the topics; detailed step-by-step instructions for running the activity; examples of what to say; detailed themes to raise in the discussions; and many supplementary handouts, videos, and assignments to round out your teaching. The active learning components involve discussions, making presentations, participating in a project, working with others, or even collecting data as a way of discovering/learning something. All of these approaches are well represented in this book, and we anticipate that implementing active learning into your course will change your course (and student outcomes) for the better. Most of these activities can be done over the span of one lecture, but a few will ask you to give students a week to work on something or ask you to strategically run an activity partnered with something going on in the real world (e.g., doing an activity before a big midterm). Activities that require longer than one lecture (e.g., due to at-home activities, self-monitoring, before and after assessments) are noted with an asterisk in the Table of Contents. As a result, it is important to read over any activities you hope to use well before you use them. This extra planning is worth it, as you will be dazzled by the creative exercises in this book and the incredible opportunities for your students to learn something using their own data and experiences. Concepts will truly stick in their minds, resulting in wonderful classroom environments and better learning outcomes. Finally, most chapters include some kind of assignment. These are typically designed to foster engagement and discussion in the classroom or to reinforce self-discovery about how the activity worked. Should you want exam questions and content-oriented testing materials, this should be easy to craft by using the background information provided in each chapter as well as the recommended readings each author has provided.

If you are an instructor with a preexisting positive psychology class, you can use this book by consulting the Table of Contents or the brief activity summaries in each chapter to find subjects that align with your curriculum. The authors have helpfully included a list of lecture topics that their activities can be easily integrated into in the Activity Setting section of each chapter. You can then incorporate these activities into your class plans to provide active learning in the classroom, assign them for students to complete outside of class, or even replace lecture material with something more interactive and discussion-based. You can also find many additional activities in the first book in this series (Froh & Parks, 2013) that may be of use. Additionally, as you will see in Section I of this book, we also include many areas not covered in the typical positive psychology textbook that can enhance your course, such as exciting new research methods that students can try out in your classroom, positive health and stress management ideas not discussed in most positive psychology texts, new areas of interest from the field of affective science, and important critical thinking topics.

For instructors who are brand new to the field or experienced experts creating a new well-being–oriented course that you are teaching for the first time, you may want to take a different approach. Using this book will allow you to make a unique course that will feel like your own as opposed to depending on someone else's syllabus and/or relying on a textbook order of topics to decide what and when to teach something. For you, we recommend reading over the introductions to each of the five sections of the book, and perhaps the synopsis of each individual activity, as a starting point. You could then design an entire course based on active learning activities first and then supplement these after the fact with readings and more standard lecture materials. You will find this easy to do, as each activity includes very specific instructions on how to introduce each topic, text on what to say to students (including some scripts), homework assignments, and more. An additional option you would have with this approach is making your course an open-materials course to save students the expense of buying a new textbook. As you will notice when reading these activities, authors provide required and optional readings (typically journal articles and freely available websites as well as online resources, e.g., videos) and only on occasion rely on books that would have to be purchased (although some of these are likely available in your school's library). Given the importance of spreading positive psychology to everyone—not only those with the means to buy textbooks—this can increase the accessibility of your course to a broader range of individuals.

Some of you reading this may simply be interested in applying positive psychology in your own lives and/or incorporating it into your workplace, your practice, coaching activities, or perhaps other nonpositive psychology courses that have overlap with this field. Reviewers of this book indicated that many of the included activities could be used to help teach research methods, social psychology, emotion, health psychology, environmental psychology, cognition, clinical psychology, industrial/organizational (I/O) psychology, introduction to psychology, and more. Given that there are many areas in psychology and connected fields without the depth of activities found here, we hope that this book will enrich many classrooms, clinics, workshops, and perhaps even just the day-to-day lives of some of our readers. For those of you in this category, we suggest, like the new instructors, that you peruse the Table of Contents for topics that jump out at you and that you read the first page or so of each chapter for those areas that catch your attention. Each chapter includes a brief upfront summary of the goals and tasks of the activity and can be readily skimmed to find sections that match your needs.

Finally, a few small pieces of advice as you guide individuals through these activities: First, because of expectancy effects, in some circumstances, you may want to avoid telling students what they are about to do and/or the intended outcomes, as these may alter the results or ruin the fun of the A-HA! moment that many activities produce. In these types of situations, we recommend that you simply tell students up front (at the start of the course or before the specific lecture) that you will be doing activities designed to help students do their best and have a successful academic experience and that they should enter these active learning experiences with open minds. You can also focus on the tasks at hand (e.g., today, we will be doing a writing exercise, a meditation, data collection) without describing the outcomes or big-picture topics that will arise from the activity. Please note: Many chapter authors have specific instructions for when certain readings should be done (in order to facilitate the correct learning experience), so pay attention to those instructions.

As you complete the activities in this book, you may encounter a number of factors that can influence how well they work. For example, some students may not enjoy certain activities, some interventions may not be effective, and sometimes, the opposite of the expected outcome may occur. In these cases, it is important to explain to students that not all interventions work equally well for everyone. This is why it is often recommended in positive psychology research to give participants in interventions a choice of activities that they can complete (e.g., Seligman et al., 2006). Thus, this can be brought up in your lectures along with the broader impact of individual differences (e.g., age, culture, personality) and activity features (e.g., the length of the activity) on activity effectiveness, as shown in Figure 1. There are many research studies that support the idea that some activities will work better for some people. We encourage you to discuss this in the classroom and to refer to the examples of culture-oriented activities in Section V of the book. No doubt, every student in your course will have the opportunity to learn something new about this interesting field and hopefully increase their well-being along the way. Printable versions of the worksheets and handouts in the chapter appendices in this book and direct links to the resources in the Online Materials sections can be found on the APA website at https://www.apa.org/pubs/books/more-activities-teaching-positive-psychology.

FIGURE 1. The Positive Activity Model

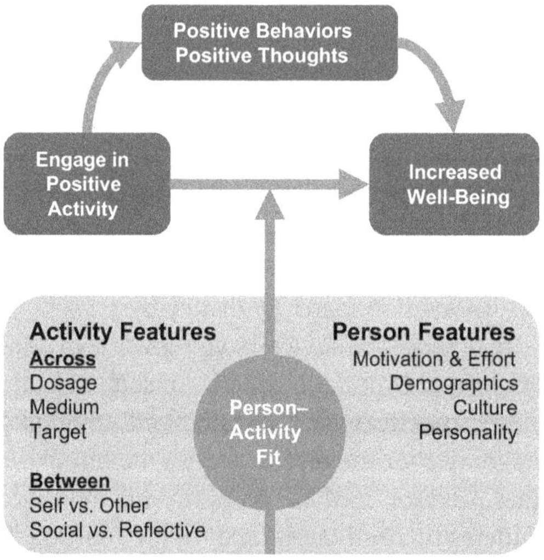

Note. Adapted from "How Do Simple Positive Activities Increase Well-Being?," by S. Lyubomirsky and K. Layous, 2013, *Current Directions in Psychological Science, 22*(1), p. 58 (https://doi.org/10.1177/0963721412469809). Copyright 2013 by SAGE Publications. Adapted with permission.

ACKNOWLEDGMENTS

We are grateful to Marie Cross for her painstaking proofreading, writing support, and helpful feedback on the book manuscript. We also must mention our gratitude to the incredible Shane Lopez. Shane taught Acacia everything she needed to know about book proposal writing and contract negotiation. He was also responsible for shepherding Sarah more deeply into the field of positive psychology and was a valued mentor and friend. Without him, this book would not exist. We miss you every day, Shane. Most importantly, we are eternally grateful to our all-star lineup of authors for spending the time working on this book. It is because of your willingness to help, and your dedication to showing students the best parts of positive psychology via your expertise, that this book exists. We are endlessly grateful that even during a global pandemic, you were willing to spend the time to craft these gorgeous activities that will enrich the lives of so many. This message of thanks is especially sent out to those of our authors who were willing to contribute a second time to this book series, including Barb Fredrickson, Bob Emmons, Ken Sheldon, Ken Pargament, Jane Dutton, and one of our coeditors, Sarah D. Pressman. We are so fortunate to get to work with people like you who truly embody the best parts of positive psychology.

REFERENCES

Froh, J., & Parks, A. C. (2013). *Activities for teaching positive psychology: A guide for instructors*. American Psychological Association. https://doi.org/10.1037/14042-000

Lyubomirsky, S., & Layous, K. (2013). How do simple positive activities increase well-being? *Current Directions in Psychological Science*, *22*(1), 57–62. https://doi.org/10.1177/0963721412469809

Seligman, M. E. P., Rashid, T., & Parks, A. C. (2006). Positive psychotherapy. *American Psychologist*, *61*(8), 774–788. https://doi.org/10.1037/0003-066X.61.8.774

LIVING THE RESEARCH: POSITIVE PSYCHOLOGY METHODS, APPLICATIONS, AND CRITICAL ANALYSIS IN THE CLASSROOM

INTRODUCTION: LIVING THE RESEARCH: POSITIVE PSYCHOLOGY METHODS, APPLICATIONS, AND CRITICAL ANALYSIS IN THE CLASSROOM

In the first section, we lead you through topics that were not touched on in the first edition of this book—*Research Methods in Positive Psychology and Improving Positive Psychological Science*—both inside and outside of the classroom. This section features expert authors who will lead instructors and students through several exciting activities. When I (Dr. S. Pressman) teach positive psychology, I like to lead with research methods. While not always the most exciting part of psychology for some students, it provides them with essential grounding on how to understand many studies in the field and, importantly, demystifies how to do research. Having an early lecture focused on ways to assess well-being is a great way to get students thinking, and the activities included will give you lots of concepts and activities to make this section of your class very active and fun.

First, focused more on helping *you*, the instructor, we start with a chapter applying positive psychology to enrich your classroom environment via conversation pods. Read this activity prior to the start of the semester or quarter, and use the lesson to create an invaluable sense of belonging, social connection, and engagement throughout the time you teach your course.

Next, we explore critical concepts from affective science and how they connect to important positive psychology theories such as the broaden-and-build theory. You and your students are then guided through the value of studying positive facial expressions (i.e., smiling) as a key measure in positive psychology research. Next, students get the chance to use their own writing samples with both computerized and qualitative approaches to learn about how you can glean important well-being insights on topics like positive emotions and personal growth from their own personal life stories (or from publicly available narratives). These are all eye-opening chances for students to do the work themselves as researchers while discovering key aspects of well-being assessment.

Finally, and critically, in this age of misinformation, clickbait news, and companies trying to make money off of happiness without using best practices from research, we are so pleased to have public and social media experts, as well as well-being app researchers, create exercises for students that will teach them how to evaluate the positive psychology stories they see in the news, as well as how to critically appraise the many positive psychology–themed apps on the market these days. These critical thinking/application exercises would be wonderful activities to include at the end of your course when students are ready to take what they have learned from you and apply it to the real world.

1

Conversational Pods

Enriching the Learning of Positive Psychology Through Dialogue and Connection

Margarita Tarragona

This chapter describes how to implement conversational pods, or small discussion groups, to make learning positive psychology more meaningful and to foster positive interpersonal relationships between students in positive psychology courses.

CONCEPT

This activity combines the author's expertise in positive psychology, therapy, and coaching to improve the classroom experience by focusing on the importance of conversation, personal narratives, and dialogue. This perspective has led to the creation of conversational pods, which are semistructured conversational formats that are an important element of positive psychology classes. This activity is perfect for the first day (or week) of class to generate a feeling of connection and belonging among students, as well as to encourage the likelihood of engaging classroom discussions throughout the semester or quarter.

MATERIALS NEEDED

There is no need for any special materials. All we need are people who are willing to talk and listen to each other after experimenting with a positive psychology activity or intervention.

https://doi.org/10.1037/0000417-001
More Activities for Teaching Positive Psychology: A Guide for Instructors, S. D. Pressman and A. C. Parks (Editors)

ACTIVITY SETTING

It is ideal for the conversation pods to leave the classroom and go to other spaces to talk, especially somewhere outdoors, if the weather and the learning context permit it. If possible, it is a good idea to have some distance between the different groups so each pod can have a sense of privacy, but the setting can be adapted to what the educational setting allows and what is practical, depending on the size of the group and the characteristics of the location. Participants should not take notes or record their interactions; the goal is to be fully present in the conversation in the small group.

ACTIVITY DURATION

The length of the small group conversation can vary; we normally devote between 15 and 20 minutes to it.

BACKGROUND AND INSTRUCTIONS

Throughout my career, I have combined teaching positive psychology and being a therapist and coach. My experience as a practitioner has taught me about the importance of conversation and dialogue as ways of generating new possibilities in people's lives, as well as how our personal narratives shape our identity. My interest in conversational and narrative processes has influenced the way I work with students in positive psychology courses, especially in terms of the application of positive interventions in their lives, and it has led me to include conversational pods, a semistructured conversational format, as an important element of positive psychology classes.

The idea that conversation can be a central part of positive psychology courses is based on several concepts from narrative psychology and positive psychology:

- The importance of putting experiences into words: Harry Goolishian, the founder of collaborative therapy, used to say, "I never know what I mean until I say it" (Anderson & Gehart, 2012, p. 39). When we talk about our behaviors and emotions, when we articulate them to share them, they become clearer.

- Creating a collaborative learning community, a learning environment in which students work in groups, "mutually searching for understanding, solutions, or meanings, or creating a product: Collaborative learning activities vary widely, but most center on students' exploration or application of the course material, not simply the teacher's presentation or explication of it" (Smith & MacGregor, 1992, p. 11). In this case, students apply positive psychology interventions individually and explore their meaning together in their conversational pods.

- Dialogue can help create knowledge: Anderson (2000) said that in order to have a dialogue, there needs to be space for all voices; that is, all the participants need to feel that they belong in that conversation; to know that they can exchange thoughts, opinions, and feelings; and that, when this happens, new meanings are generated in the process.

- Relationships and conversations mutually construct each other (Anderson, 2000): Having a conversation with someone can strengthen our connection to that person, and that closeness can, in turn, allow another meaningful conversation to take place.

- Narrative identity: Conversation is the primary way through which we tell our stories. McAdams (2022, Vocabulary section), one of the most prominent researchers of personal stories, defines narrative identity as "an internalized and evolving story of the self" that gives the person a sense of unity and purpose in their life. When students apply positive psychology and then share the stories of what it was like for them to do this, it can be easier for them to internalize those experiences, make them more meaningful, and integrate them into their sense of who they are.

There are many concepts from positive psychology that come to life when students participate in conversational pods:

- Mattering: Prilleltensky and Prilleltensky (2021) defined mattering as the need to feel valued and the need to add value. When students regularly share their experiences in their small groups and each member is heard by the others, they feel appreciated, and they realize they have something to contribute. They experience mattering.

- Positivity resonance: Brown and Fredrickson (2021) defined positivity resonance as coexperienced positive affect, and their research shows that it is very important in the development of social bonds and caring communities. Students often share moments of laughter, gratitude, and fun when they are in their conversational pods, and they identify them as moments of positivity resonance.

Conversational pods are not a positive psychology intervention. Rather, they are a way of processing any positive psychology activity in a learning environment. Working with small discussion groups or pods is very simple. It consists of having students regularly talk with a small group or conversational pod about their experience of implementing a positive intervention.

In my undergraduate positive psychology class at Instituto Tecnológico Autónomo de México, we meet weekly. In each session, we study a positive psychology topic; for example, positive emotions, flow experiences, grit, the relationship between money and happiness, mindfulness, and so forth. As an assignment at the end of each class, during the upcoming week, students have to implement a positive intervention related to the theme we have studied. When we meet for the next class the following week, students go into their small groups to discuss their experiences of doing the positive intervention before we move on to the new area of the course. Figure 1.1 illustrates this sequence.

Positive Psychology Interventions as Experiments

I call the assigned positive interventions "experiments with a no. of 1." I like to present positive intervention assignments as experiments because I want to invite students to be curious about their experiences and not to think of positive psychology activities as recipes, nor think that they succeed or fail if the activity has a certain effect on them. Also, importantly, because research shows that not all interventions work for everyone, there has to be a good fit between the person and the activity (Layous et al., 2014).

The experiments that students implement and later discuss with their pod are well-known positive interventions, like writing a gratitude journal (Bono et al., 2004), offering active-constructive responses to good news (Gable et al., 2006), spending money on other people (Aknin et al., 2020), meditating for 10 minutes every day (Fredrickson et al., 2017), and 10 other activities over the semester.

Instructions for Conversational Pods

How to Set Up the Conversational Pods

1. On the first day of class, randomly assign students to groups of four or five participants. Research shows that a maximum of five people allows for meaningful dialogue in group discussions (Fay et al., 2000).

2. Tell students that once they are assigned to a small group, they stay in the same group, or conversational pod, throughout the semester or for the duration of the course. This allows them to forge personal relationships with the members of their pod and to create a climate of psychological safety.

3. During their first meeting as a small group, students choose a name for their pod and later share it with the whole class. This is fun, and it helps to begin to create a sense of belonging.

FIGURE 1.1. Timing of Conversations in Pods

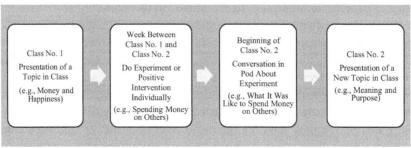

Guidelines for Interaction in the Conversational Pods

There are three basic guidelines for the pod's conversations.:

1. "What happens in Vegas, stays in Vegas": Even though students will discuss their experiences doing positive interventions, and these will likely be pleasant, it is still important to commit to confidentiality within the group. Students agree that they will not share what pod members say with anyone outside the pod.

2. The pass rule: Systemic therapist and dialogue facilitator Roth (1993) said that to have a productive conversation, it is important to have a noncoercive environment and the right to pass. If a member of the group is asked a question and they don't want to answer it, they can simply say, "I pass." They don't need to offer any explanation, and other group members should not insist on getting a response. This allows people to be in control of what they share about themselves.

3. Manage time correctly: This ensures that every pod member who wants to talk gets a chance to do so.

In my experience, these guidelines help create an environment in which students feel comfortable talking. I have never had a student refuse to participate in these conversational activities, but if this were to happen, I would prioritize their well-being and would not pressure them to participate in the small group discussions.

What Students Should Discuss in the Conversational Pods

The prompts that guide their discussion and get the conversation going are

- What was it like for you to do this experiment (positive intervention)?
- What did it make you think?
- What did it make you feel?
- What ideas from the class did you continue to think about during the week?

DISCUSSION

When the positive psychology course ends, students have to write a reflection paper about what they have learned. Most of them spontaneously speak about their experience in the conversational pods as a very meaningful one, and many refer to it as a highlight of the class.

For example, one student wrote the following:

This class helped me open up more with other people, which had been hard for me at the university. I feel that I have created good relationships in this class.

Another student said,

I began to get a sense of what each person in the group was like and to imagine their reactions to each of the exercises . . . I also felt perfectly trusting that I could share all the details of what an activity had been like for me.

Someone else commented,

> It is cool and useful to listen to different people talk about their experiences, their feelings, and what they have gone through because, many times, when we listen to others, we realize things that we cannot figure out on our own.

Yet another participant wrote about his experience talking with the members of his pod:

> It was a way of connecting with their human side. We were able to talk about what we felt and how we are virtuous in some ways. I felt that I got to know them much better, that I knew intimate aspects of them that only their closest friends get to appreciate. Frankly, I thought it was incredible.

Perhaps what best illustrates the effect of working with conversational pods is a scene I saw on the last day of class: Students met with their small group for the last time and came back to the classroom. When I turned toward the door, I saw two young men, members of a pod, heartfully embracing each other as they said goodbye. To me, this showed the quality of the connection they had developed. As one student wrote in her final reflection, "We started this course as strangers, and we leave as friends."

REFERENCES

Aknin, L. B., Dunn, E. W., Proulx, J., Lok, I., & Norton, M. I. (2020). Does spending money on others promote happiness?: A registered replication report. *Journal of Personality and Social Psychology, 119*(2), e15–e26. https://doi.org/10.1037/pspa0000191

Anderson, H. (2000). *Supervision as a collaborative learning community* (pp. 7–10). American Association for Marriage and Family Therapy Supervision Bulletin.

Anderson, H., & Gehart, D. (Eds.). (2012). *Collaborative therapy: Relationships and conversations that make a difference.* Routledge. https://doi.org/10.4324/9780203944547

Bono, G., Emmons, R. A., & McCullough, M. E. (2004). Gratitude in practice and the practice of gratitude. In P. A. Linley & S. Joseph (Eds.), *Positive psychology in practice* (pp. 464–481). Wiley. https://doi.org/10.1002/9780470939338.ch29

Brown, C. L., & Fredrickson, B. L. (2021). Characteristics and consequences of co-experienced positive affect: Understanding the origins of social skills, social bonds, and caring, healthy communities. *Current Opinion in Behavioral Sciences, 39,* 58–63. https://doi.org/10.1016/j.cobeha.2021.02.002

Fay, N., Garrod, S., & Carletta, J. (2000). Group discussion as interactive dialogue or as serial monologue: The influence of group size. *Psychological Science, 11*(6), 481–486. https://doi.org/10.1111/1467-9280.00292

Fredrickson, B. L., Boulton, A. J., Firestine, A. M., Van Cappellen, P., Algoe, S. B., Brantley, M. M., Kim, S. L., Brantley, J., & Salzberg, S. (2017). Positive emotion correlates of meditation practice: A comparison of mindfulness meditation and loving-kindness meditation. *Mindfulness, 8*(6), 1623–1633. https://doi.org/10.1007/s12671-017-0735-9

Gable, S. L., Gonzaga, G. C., & Strachman, A. (2006). Will you be there for me when things go right? Supportive responses to positive event disclosures. *Journal of Personality and Social Psychology, 91*(5), 904–917. https://doi.org/10.1037/0022-3514.91.5.904

Layous, K., Chancellor, J., & Lyubomirsky, S. (2014). Positive activities as protective factors against mental health conditions. *Journal of Abnormal Psychology, 123*(1), 3–12. https://doi.org/10.1037/a0034709

McAdams, D. P. (2022). Self and identity. In R. Biswas-Diener & E. Diener (Eds.), *Noba textbook series: Psychology.* DEF Publishers. http://noba.to/3gsuardw

Prilleltensky, I., & Prilleltensky, O. (2021). *How people matter: Why it affects health, happiness, love, work, and society.* Cambridge University Press. https://doi.org/10.1017/9781108979405

Roth, S. (1993). Speaking the unspoken: A work-group consultation to reopen dialogue. In E. Imber-Black (Ed.), *Secrets in families and family therapy* (pp. 268–291). W. W. Norton.

Smith, B. L., & MacGregor, J. T. (1992). What is collaborative learning? In A. S. Goodsell (Ed.), *Collaborative learning: A sourcebook for higher education* (pp. 9–22). National Center on Postsecondary Teaching, Learning and Assessment, Pennsylvania State University.

2

Authentic Embodied Positive Emotions

An Experiential Introduction to the Broaden-and-Build Theory

Patty Van Cappellen and Barbara L. Fredrickson

In this activity, students will (a) mentally relive a negative emotion and then mentally relive a positive emotion following prompts, (b) reflect on and share the differences between their experiences reliving negative versus positive emotions, and (c) engage in a class discussion following prompts from the instructor to cultivate a firsthand understanding of the broaden-and-build theory of positive emotions.

CONCEPT

Affective science is vital for understanding a central active ingredient in positive psychology interventions (PPIs): positive emotions. This activity introduces students to the broaden-and-build theory of positive emotions and helps students understand how positive and negative emotions differ. The discussion highlights that experiences of positive emotions do not just live in our heads. To be the active ingredient of PPIs, positive emotions must be authentic, contextually appropriate, and resonate throughout our whole being.

https://doi.org/10.1037/0000417-002
More Activities for Teaching Positive Psychology: A Guide for Instructors, S. D. Pressman and A. C. Parks (Editors)

MATERIALS NEEDED

- Text instructions (for the prompts to relive a negative and positive emotion and the questions to ask students) included below.
- Writing/recording materials (e.g., paper, laptops) or a physical or virtual whiteboard for sharing content with the class.
- The suggested prepared PowerPoint presentation in the Online Materials section at the end of the chapter.

ACTIVITY SETTING

We recommend carrying out this activity during an in-person class or a synchronous online video platform (e.g., Zoom) lecture. We recommend only running this activity in synchronous classes since active participation is needed for the discussion portion. We suggest teaching this material when you first introduce students to the study of emotions and positive emotions, particularly the broaden-and-build theory, or when discussing how interventions in positive psychology work.

ACTIVITY DURATION

We suggest using one class period (i.e., 50 minutes) that opens with this activity as a springboard for teaching students about the broaden-and-build theory of positive emotions and/or the positive activity model of PPIs.

SUGGESTED READINGS

- Instructors' suggested reading before the activity: Students should not read this article before the activity in order to better experience the exercise without being influenced by this new knowledge. However, this is a recommended reading after the activity to consolidate students' learning:
  - Fredrickson (2013)
- Recommended reading for students before the activity to show why it is useful to learn about the science of emotions and positive emotions when studying positive psychology and PPIs:
  - Gander et al. (2020)
  - Lyubomirsky and Layous (2013)
- Optional reading for students after the activity for additional enrichment:
  - For students who want to go further on emotion regulation strategies: Gross (2015)

- For students who want to go further on the interpersonal benefits of sharing positive emotions with others versus experiencing positive emotions solo: Fredrickson (2016).

- For students who want to go further on cross-cultural considerations of what it means to be happy: Oishi et al. (2013).

- For students who want to go further on ways that we can tune up the enjoyment of PPIs: Van Cappellen et al. (2020).

BACKGROUND AND INSTRUCTIONS

How Is Affective Science Relevant to Positive Psychology?

Although PPIs have generally been shown to be effective (Sin & Lyubomirsky, 2009), not every positive activity that a person performs will increase their well-being. To understand when a PPI will work and why it sometimes does not, it helps to understand the "active ingredients" that contribute to their success; that is, the circumstances that need to be present to build well-being. The positive activity model adapted from Lyubomirsky and Layous (2013) suggests that a central active ingredient in PPIs is positive emotions. Indeed, positive actions lead to positive emotions, thoughts, and behaviors, as well as needs satisfaction, which in turn enhance well-being. That said, there are important characteristics of the person, features of the activities, and other factors that influence the extent to which specific activities have the potential to elicit such important positive emotions and ultimately build well-being.

Advances in affective science provide a solid foundation to understand both the specificity and variety of positive emotions. Indeed, as the proposed activity will exemplify, positive emotions are not simply the feel good symmetrical opposite of negative emotions. Rather, they have their own specific functions (more on this later). They also come in more shades than the single positive emotion included in Ekman's six basic emotions (happiness) or the high-energy ones measured through popular surveys, like the Positive And Negative Affect Schedule (e.g., enthusiasm, pride, inspiration). Other, quieter positive emotions, such as gratitude and awe, are the primary focus of many PPIs (e.g., gratitude journaling, time in nature). Many positive emotions are also directly associated with virtuous behaviors (Kruse et al., 2014; Stellar et al., 2017), positive interpersonal processes (Algoe, 2019), and spirituality (Van Cappellen et al., 2021), which correspond to some of the building blocks that enable human flourishing.

What Is an Emotion? A Brief Introduction

To better understand positive emotions, we start by giving a definition of what an emotion is (Keltner & Gross, 1999; Levenson, 1999; Shiota, in press). Emotions are multifaceted mind and body responses to a change in an individual's environment that they appraise (interpret) in a certain way. The multifaceted responses correspond to subjective experience, expressive behavior (e.g., facial, bodily, verbal), and peripheral physiological responses (e.g., heart rate, respiration). Emotions further affect thoughts and behaviors and are central to any psychological model of the human mind. In this chapter, we unpack some elements of this definition.

Emotions arise when we, as individuals, face a notable change in our current situation, which can be either out in the world or in our minds (e.g., via memories, mental speculations, ruminations). When a person registers a change in their current situation—either consciously or unconsciously—their knowledge, unique traits, cultural background, and personal histories combine to guide their attention and interpretation of those circumstances in ways that may be both universally human and individually idiosyncratic to varying degrees. That interpretative lens (aka appraisal) shapes which emotions unfold (Frijda et al., 1989; Moors et al., 2013).

Once an emotion unfolds, it resonates throughout the human body: It changes a person's facial expressions, physiology, posture, and vocal intonation, all in loosely coupled ways. What you subjectively perceive as a feeling state is only one facet of this multifaceted response. Expressing emotions does not stop at verbal or written expression; it also encompasses the nonverbal (Keltner et al., 2019). Being attuned to the fully embodied experience of emotion and to your subtly shifting bodily sensations can help you be in better touch with your genuine and authentic emotions (Füstös et al., 2013; Nummenmaa et al., 2014).

Differences Between Positive and Negative Emotions: Introduction to the Broaden-and-Build Theory of Positive Emotions

Instructors

We suggest that you read this section before the activity but that you do not share this information with your students just yet. The proposed activity is meant to provide your students with an idea of how emotions feel from a first-person perspective (providing the definition of emotion will help them notice and organize their experience) and to encourage them to experience firsthand how positive and negative emotions differ. Your goal is to first convey these ideas experientially and then reinforce them didactically.

The broaden-and-build theory of positive emotions (Fredrickson, 1998) posits that positive emotions have different effects over the short and long terms compared with negative emotions. Over the short term, negative emotions narrow the scope of attention to help individuals act in the moment in ways that have been adaptive to our human ancestors in similar situations (which may or may not be adaptive in the present day; Basso et al., 1996; Fredrickson & Branigan, 2005). By contrast, positive emotions broaden the scope of attention (e.g., seeing the big picture, noticing more of what is going on around us), thought–action repertoires (e.g., wanting to do many different things, creativity), and social mindsets (e.g., feelings of oneness with others).

Over the long term, repeated brief moments of positive emotions (and the accompanying broadened mindsets) add up to build a person's durable resources—stronger relationships (Algoe et al., 2013; Fredrickson et al., 2008), better physical and mental health (Fredrickson et al., 2021; Kok et al., 2013), new knowledge and skills (Ouweneel et al., 2012; Tugade et al., 2004)—that can help them in the face of hard times later on. For example, by experiencing frequent positive emotions, we build up our psychological well-being and our capacity for resilience (Cohn et al., 2009; Gloria & Steinhardt, 2016). While negative emotions evolved to help humans respond to immediate threats, repeated experiences of negative emotions do not compound to spur growth and resilience.

ACTIVITY INSTRUCTIONS

You should now introduce the relived emotion exercise by noting that memories can spark authentic emotions. To allow students' own autobiographical memories to surface, we note when instructions are best conveyed in a gentle voice, akin to a guided meditation. That is, following each of the two relived emotion activities, we suggest instructors return to the voice they typically use when leading classroom discussions. You will find what you should read to students in italics. Please also note the pause and long pause instructions, which should last approximately 15 seconds and 45 seconds, respectively.

1. First, ask students to mentally relive a negative emotion. Please read the following text slowly, pausing regularly so that students have time to reflect. This first part should take approximately 5 minutes.
   Take a moment right now to identify and then relive in your mind a time when you were so frustrated or angry that you felt like you could explode. Think back to that moment and build a picture of it in your mind: Where were you? Who were you with? What had just happened? As you begin to build a mental picture of this event, relive how you felt at the time and let that feeling grow a bit, just for these few moments (long pause). Now, gently notice what stands out in your experience:

   • What had just happened? What triggered your emotion? (pause)

   • How does your body feel? (pause)

   • How does your face feel? (pause)

   • What thoughts come to mind? (pause)

   • What does this feeling make you want to do? (pause)

   • Now thinking about this emotion: If you had to feel this way repeatedly, what do you think the impact would be in your life (e.g., your health, your social life)? (pause)

2. Discussion: Repeat the questions above (all but the first, for privacy reasons) not in that gentle meditation voice but in your normal class

discussion voice. Ask students to share responses in spontaneous popcorn style (i.e., rapid sharing of responses one after the other) while you underscore key features of the definition of emotions in general. Allow 5 minutes for this part.

3. Next, ask students to relive a positive emotion. Again, be sure that you go through the below instructions slowly enough to allow students to generate ideas. (Note: Always do this activity with a negative emotion first and then a positive emotion to ensure that students end the exercise feeling better than when they started.)

Next, take a moment to identify and then relive in your mind a time when you were so happy or delighted that you felt you could jump for joy or just sit and smile. Think back to that moment and build a picture of it in your mind: Where were you? Who were you with? What had just happened? As you begin to build a mental picture of this event, relive how you felt at the time and, again, let that feeling grow a bit (long pause). Now, gently notice what stands out in your experience:

- What had just happened? What triggered your emotion? (pause)
- How does your body feel? (pause)
- How does your face feel? (pause)
- What thoughts come to mind? (pause)
- What does this feeling make you want to do? (pause)
- Now thinking about this emotion: If you had to feel this way repeatedly, what do you think the impact would be in your life (e.g., for your health or for your social life)? (pause)

4. Ask students (with the whole class, or you can divide the class into smaller groups and then have one person report for each group) about differences between their experiences reliving negative versus positive emotions. Allow 10 to 15 minutes for this part. Note what you noticed from your perspective as their instructor watching them (e.g., their softer faces, smiles). Use this opportunity to map their reported experiences onto key differences between negative and positive emotions.

5. For topics not yet covered, see the Discussion section below. This provides follow-up questions and suggests instructional comments to help students recognize key attributes of emotions and differences between positive and negative emotions. Use the remaining time for this discussion and to more fully present the broaden-and-build theory of positive emotions.

DISCUSSION

You can use some or all of these discussion questions and the suggested instructional comments below each question to relate the experiential activity to the didactic teaching of key points.

1. "How easy was it to find a past positive and negative experience to relive? Was one easier to retrieve than the other?"
   Instructors: Positive could be easier because they are more plentiful in daily life (this asymmetry is called positivity offset) or negative could be easier because they are more intense and attention grabbing (this asymmetry is called negativity bias).

2. "Without entering into too much detail, very generally, what was happening in the environment and did it differ between positive and negative emotions?"
   Instructors: Care is needed here to preserve student privacy and dignity, and you may also choose to skip this question. The point here is to have students realize that a foundational appraisal is whether the person's new circumstances are in some way "good for me" or "bad for me"—this core interpretation charts the path toward a positive versus negative emotion. It helps students understand what we are talking about when we say a "positive" or "negative" emotion.

3. "Did you experience a difference in the number and kind of thoughts you had? Were they more or less beneficial or wanted?"
   Instructors: After a negative emotion, some may report thoughts that are very much focused on the trigger of that emotion or that are generally narrow. After a positive emotion, some may report more creativity, thinking about the broad aspects of the situation or of their life (supporting meaning-making). Along with the next question, these responses can be connected back to the broaden aspect of the broaden-and-build theory.

4. "Did the emotions make you want to do one thing in particular? Or did they open up lots of ideas for possible next actions?"
   Instructors: Sometimes, for positive emotions, lots of possible actions come to mind rather than a specific one (e.g., fight, flee), which is more typical of negative emotions. Plus, positive emotions may not necessarily prompt us to take any outward action in that moment (e.g., savoring, learning). This part supports the broaden aspect of the broaden-and-build theory: Positive emotions have been shown to broaden the scope of action urges, whereas negative emotions narrow that same set of urges. The logic of a narrowed action urge with a negative emotion is to prepare the mind and body for a specific and immediate action that may have aided our ancestors' survival within moments of threat to life or limb.

5. "What do you think the impact in your life (e.g., for your health, for your social life) would be if you had to feel negative versus positive emotions repeatedly?"
   Instructors: This helps students envision that emotions, although fleeting, can have compounding effects over time if experienced frequently. This part supports the build aspect of the broaden-and-build theory: Whereas negative emotions tend to promote quick actions that are thought to have helped human ancestors survive clear and present danger, positive emotions are not

like that. The benefits of positive emotions to human ancestors are thought to have been more cumulative and gradual by prompting learning and growth. Notable to the build portion of this theory is that it is explicitly longitudinal. While the experience of positive emotions in any particular moment is, by definition, fleeting, those fleeting moments of broadened awareness are hypothesized to have cumulative consequences (akin to the time scale of the benefit of eating your vegetables), ultimately building an individual's consequential, enduring, and adaptive resources.

In addition, you may want to point out that it is the frequency, not the intensity or duration, of positive emotions that predicts benefits to health and well-being over time. A steady diet of mild, short-lived positive emotions adds up over time to create more resilience and resourcefulness. This distinction is important when implementing a PPI: One should not try to be maximally happy for long periods of time but instead cultivate frequent, authentic opportunities to experience positive emotions, often mild and always fleeting.

6. "Do you think people can have different emotional reactions to the same trigger? One person feeling positive and one person feeling negative? How do we explain such differences?"
Instructors: You can point out that someone's unique traits, personal history, and cultural background that have uniquely shaped them will, in turn, shape how they interpret their environment and, therefore, which emotion unfolds. This is also true for how we let our emotions unfold (think about the multifaceted responses) and how we regulate our emotions (see Gross, 2015, to go further with the materials and learn about emotion regulation). For example, culture (e.g., East vs. West) or religious affiliation can influence the kind of emotions people value and seek out. You might refer to Jeanne Tsai's work on affect valuation theory (see activity in Chapter 25, this volume and Tsai et al., 2006) and on religion (Vishkin, 2021).

7. "What are some shortcomings of the ideas we've just discussed? What aspect(s) of your experience do you feel is not adequately captured in these theories? Or what's missing that you wish we knew more about?"
Instructors: This question is meant to engage students' critical thinking more than to present new knowledge. You can ask students to come up with ideas for the kind of research they wish existed (and encourage them to find out if that did not come out!).

8. "How do you think mixed emotions fit in? What are they, and what value (ancestral or present-day) might they hold?"
Instructors: This last question is also meant to engage students' critical thinking more than to present new knowledge. This question is a wild card if you want to keep the conversation going after students are done generating responses to the previous question. We suggest that one aspect missing from this discussion is the consideration of mixed emotions. For example, we can be in situations where we feel sad and happy at the same time, such as when we watch a movie and feel moved (Hanich et al., 2014).

ASSIGNMENT

Some suggested questions for students to consolidate knowledge (to be given after the activity as an at-home assignment, in class as a 1-minute paper, or as questions for a virtual discussion board):

- How would you define an emotion?
- What are the main differences between positive and negative emotions?
- Can you summarize the broaden-and-build theory of positive emotions in a few lines?
- How might knowledge of emotion theory help you construct better PPIs?

ONLINE MATERIALS

- See separate PowerPoint with slides including definitions, the activity step-by-step, and the broaden-and-build theory of positive emotions (https://tinyurl.com/MATPPchap2)

- Greater Good Science Center (2021)

- Templeton World Charity Foundation (2020)

REFERENCES

Algoe, S. B. (2019). Positive interpersonal processes. *Current Directions in Psychological Science, 28*(2), 183–188. https://doi.org/10.1177/0963721419827272

Algoe, S. B., Fredrickson, B. L., & Gable, S. L. (2013). The social functions of the emotion of gratitude via expression. *Emotion, 13*(4), 605–609. https://doi.org/10.1037/a0032701

Basso, M. R., Schefft, B. K., Ris, M. D., & Dember, W. N. (1996). Mood and global–local visual processing. *Journal of the International Neuropsychological Society, 2*(3), 249–255. https://doi.org/10.1017/S1355617700001193

Cohn, M. A., Fredrickson, B. L., Brown, S. L., Mikels, J. A., & Conway, A. M. (2009). Happiness unpacked: Positive emotions increase life satisfaction by building resilience. *Emotion, 9*(3), 361–368. https://doi.org/10.1037/a0015952

Fredrickson, B. L. (1998). What good are positive emotions? *Review of General Psychology, 2*(3), 300–319. https://doi.org/10.1037/1089-2680.2.3.300

Fredrickson, B. L. (2013). Positive emotions broaden and build. *Advances in Experimental Social Psychology, 47*, 1–53. https://doi.org/10.1016/B978-0-12-407236-7.00001-2

Fredrickson, B. L. (2016). Positivity resonance as a fresh, evidence-based perspective on an age-old topic. In L. F. Barrett, M. Lewis, & J. M. Haviland-Jones (Eds.), *Handbook of Emotions* (4th ed., pp. 847–858). Guilford Press.

Fredrickson, B. L., Arizmendi, C., & Van Cappellen, P. (2021). Same-day, cross-day, and upward spiral relations between positive affect and positive health behaviours. *Psychology & Health, 36*(4), 444–460. https://doi.org/10.1080/08870446.2020.1778696

Fredrickson, B. L., & Branigan, C. (2005). Positive emotions broaden the scope of attention and thought–action repertoires. *Cognition and Emotion, 19*(3), 313–332. https://doi.org/10.1080/02699930441000238

Fredrickson, B. L., Cohn, M. A., Coffey, K. A., Pek, J., & Finkel, S. M. (2008). Open hearts build lives: Positive emotions, induced through loving-kindness meditation, build consequential personal resources. *Journal of Personality and Social Psychology, 95*(5), 1045–1062. https://doi.org/10.1037/a0013262

Frijda, N. H., Kuipers, P., & Ter Schure, E. (1989). Relations among emotion, appraisal, and emotional action readiness. *Journal of Personality and Social Psychology, 57*(2), 212–228. https://doi.org/10.1037/0022-3514.57.2.212

Füstös, J., Gramann, K., Herbert, B. M., & Pollatos, O. (2013). On the embodiment of emotion regulation: Interoceptive awareness facilitates reappraisal. *Social Cognitive and Affective Neuroscience, 8*(8), 911–917. https://doi.org/10.1093/scan/nss089

Gander, F., Proyer, R. T., Hentz, E., & Ruch, W. (2020). Working mechanisms in positive interventions: A study using daily assessment of positive emotions. *The Journal of Positive Psychology, 15*(5), 633–638. https://doi.org/10.1080/17439760.2020.1789698

Gloria, C. T., & Steinhardt, M. A. (2016). Relationships among positive emotions, coping, resilience and mental health. *Stress and Health, 32*(2), 145–156. https://doi.org/10.1002/smi.2589

Greater Good Science Center. (2021, June 11). *Barbara Fredrickson: Positive emotions open our mind* [Video]. YouTube. https://www.youtube.com/watch?v=Z7dFDHzV36g

Gross, J. J. (2015). Emotion regulation: Current status and future prospects. *Psychological Inquiry, 26*(1), 1–26. https://doi.org/10.1080/1047840X.2014.940781

Hanich, J., Wagner, V., Shah, M., Jacobsen, T., & Menninghaus, W. (2014). Why we like to watch sad films. The pleasure of being moved in aesthetic experiences. *Psychology of Aesthetics, Creativity, and the Arts, 8*(2), 130–143. https://doi.org/10.1037/a0035690

Keltner, D., & Gross, J. J. (1999). Functional accounts of emotions. *Cognition and Emotion, 13*(5), 467–480. https://doi.org/10.1080/026999399379140

Keltner, D., Sauter, D., Tracy, J., & Cowen, A. (2019). Emotional expression: Advances in basic emotion theory. *Journal of Nonverbal Behavior, 43*(2), 133–160. https://doi.org/10.1007/s10919-019-00293-3

Kok, B. E., Coffey, K. A., Cohn, M. A., Catalino, L. I., Vacharkulksemsuk, T., Algoe, S. B., Brantley, M., & Fredrickson, B. L. (2013). How positive emotions build physical health: Perceived positive social connections account for the upward spiral between positive emotions and vagal tone. *Psychological Science, 24*(7), 1123–1132. https://doi.org/10.1177/0956797612470827

Kruse, E., Chancellor, J., Ruberton, P. M., & Lyubomirsky, S. (2014). An upward spiral between gratitude and humility. *Social Psychological & Personality Science, 5*(7), 805–814. https://doi.org/10.1177/1948550614534700

Levenson, R. W. (1999). The intrapersonal functions of emotion. *Cognition and Emotion, 13*(5), 481–504. https://doi.org/10.1080/026999399379159

Lyubomirsky, S., & Layous, K. (2013). How do simple positive activities increase well-being? *Current Directions in Psychological Science, 22*(1), 57–62. https://doi.org/10.1177/0963721412469809

Moors, A., Ellsworth, P. C., Scherer, K. R., & Frijda, N. H. (2013). Appraisal theories of emotion: State of the art and future development. *Emotion Review, 5*(2), 119–124. https://doi.org/10.1177/1754073912468165

Nummenmaa, L., Glerean, E., Hari, R., & Hietanen, J. K. (2014). Bodily maps of emotions. *Proceedings of the National Academy of Sciences of the United States of America, 111*(2), 646–651. https://doi.org/10.1073/pnas.1321664111

Oishi, S., Graham, J., Kesebir, S., & Galinha, I. C. (2013). Concepts of happiness across time and cultures. *Personality and Social Psychology Bulletin, 39*(5), 559–577. https://doi.org/10.1177/0146167213480042

Ouweneel, E., Le Blanc, P. M., Schaufeli, W. B., & van Wijhe, C. I. (2012). Good morning, good day: A diary study on positive emotions, hope, and work engagement. *Human Relations, 65*(9), 1129–1154. https://doi.org/10.1177/0018726711429382

Shiota, M. N. (in press). Theories of basic and discrete emotions. In A. Scarantino (Ed.), *Routledge handbook of emotion theory*. Routledge.

Sin, N. L., & Lyubomirsky, S. (2009). Enhancing well-being and alleviating depressive symptoms with positive psychology interventions: A practice-friendly meta-analysis. *Journal of Clinical Psychology, 65*(5), 467–487. https://doi.org/10.1002/jclp.20593

Stellar, J. E., Gordon, A. M., Piff, P. K., Cordaro, D., Anderson, C. L., Bai, Y., Maruskin, L. A., & Keltner, D. (2017). Self-transcendent emotions and their social functions: Compassion, gratitude, and awe bind us to others through prosociality. *Emotion Review, 9*(3), 200–207. https://doi.org/10.1177/1754073916684557

Templeton World Charity Foundation. (2020, April 28). *Understanding everyday love* [Video]. YouTube. https://www.youtube.com/watch?v=UWnqREJFrYk.

Tsai, J. L., Knutson, B., & Fung, H. H. (2006). Cultural variation in affect valuation. *Journal of Personality and Social Psychology, 90*(2), 288–307. https://doi.org/10.1037/0022-3514.90.2.288

Tugade, M. M., Fredrickson, B. L., & Barrett, L. F. (2004). Psychological resilience and positive emotional granularity: Examining the benefits of positive emotions on coping and health. *Journal of Personality, 72*(6), 1161–1190. https://doi.org/10.1111/j.1467-6494.2004.00294.x

Van Cappellen, P., Catalino, L. I., & Fredrickson, B. L. (2020). A new micro-intervention to increase the enjoyment and continued practice of meditation. *Emotion, 20*(8), 1332–1343. https://doi.org/10.1037/emo0000684

Van Cappellen, P., Edwards, M. E., & Fredrickson, B. L. (2021). Upward spirals of positive emotions and religious behaviors. *Current Opinion in Psychology, 40*, 92–98. https://doi.org/10.1016/j.copsyc.2020.09.004

Vishkin, A. (2021). Variation and consistency in the links between religion and emotion regulation. *Current Opinion in Psychology, 40*, 6–9. https://doi.org/10.1016/j.copsyc.2020.08.005

3

Duchenne Smiles

Windows to the Soul

Kennon M. Sheldon

This activity will teach students about what factors may affect happiness and how Duchenne smiles express that happiness.

CONCEPT

Duchenne smiles are smiles that involve the whole face—including the upper cheek and eye muscles, not just the mouth muscles. In comparison with social smiles, Duchenne smiles seem to glow, showing observers that the smiler is experiencing genuine positive emotion. Thus, people who often display Duchenne smiles are likely to be happier people, in general. Furthermore, given what we know about what causes happiness, they may even be more moral, virtuous, and eudaimonically motivated people. This activity allows students to test these ideas and to learn about (a) what factors may affect happiness and (b) how Duchenne smiles express that happiness.

MATERIALS NEEDED

Each student will need to receive a sheet of paper with a picture of a person's face on it and questions to rate about that face below (these can be copied from Appendix 3.1). There are two different versions of the face, which will be randomly assigned to students. Both versions are of the same person's face, but the faces vary in their expressions: social smile or Duchenne smile. These stimuli/

https://doi.org/10.1037/0000417-003
More Activities for Teaching Positive Psychology: A Guide for Instructors, S. D. Pressman and A. C. Parks (Editors)

questions could also be hosted online (e.g., in Qualtrics, Google Docs), which would also enable easy data collection about class results.

ACTIVITY SETTING

This is a good activity when considering the nature and functions of positive emotion or when discussing nonverbal expressions of emotion. It can also be an appropriate activity when discussing eudaimonic well-being, theorized to be expressed by frequent Duchenne smiles.

The activity would probably be easiest in a single in-person class because the instructor can mix up the two versions of the form and pass them out. The instructor would collect the completed forms and either tabulate the data then and there or report the results in a later class. The activity could also be done asynchronously, for example, if the two forms were instantiated as two separate blocks in an online survey and if students were randomly assigned to one or the other block. This would require the instructor to program the two versions of the form into one survey and then send a link to students.

ACTIVITY DURATION

This activity can be done in a single lecture and will take approximately 10 to 15 minutes. The activity involves students forming a quick impression and then making five ratings, followed by a few minutes for results tabulation and discussion.

SUGGESTED READINGS

No preliminary reading is required by students—in fact, it is best if they are naïve to the topic of Duchenne smiles. For students interested in learning more about this topic following the activity, I recommend the articles below.

Optional readings for after the activity:

- Sheldon, Corcoran, and Sheldon (2021)
- Sheldon, Corcoran, and Trent (2021)

BACKGROUND AND INSTRUCTIONS

In the in-person class version of the activity, start by saying,

> Today, we'll consider the topic of happiness and well-being from a different angle: in terms of how people appear, not in terms of how they rate their emotions. This is important because people may sometimes be self-deceived in their happiness ratings—maybe they want to believe they are happier than they

are or that they are less happy than they are. Today's question is: "Can we tell how happy people are just by looking at them?"

Pass out the mixed stack of forms, face down. Ask students not to turn over their form until you tell them to (this will keep them from thinking too much before the activity starts). When everybody is ready, say,

> Please turn over your form. Take a minute to think about the person in the picture at the top of the form. How are they feeling? How would you feel about them? Then, look down and rate each of the descriptors of the person. What impression does the person make on you?

Give them a few minutes to make the five ratings.

If you would like to look at the data with your class in real time, you can also have students use a classroom data collection app like iClicker or TopHat to report their results during an in-person class (or Zoom polls, Qualtrics, etc., for online learning). You would ask students to transfer their five ratings to the app (answering either A1–A5 or B1–B5, depending on the form letter at the top of their page). The advantage of doing this is that the means could be instantly tabulated for comparison in that class. As noted above, the activity could also be done remotely or asynchronously by sending students a link to a survey that randomly assigns them to one form or another. Later, a description could be uploaded to the course management system (like Canvas) that presents the introduction (as described earlier in this chapter), the background (as described next), and the results. Then, students might be assigned a discussion activity based on the results.

After in-class data collection, give background on the Duchenne smile concept (including images of Duchenne and non-Duchenne smilers as well as the muscles of the face involved in these smiles). First identified by French physiologist Claude Duchenne in the late 1900s, Duchenne smiles activate both the zygomatic major muscle, which raises the corners of the mouth, and the orbicularis oculi muscle, which raises the cheeks and crinkles the eyes. Duchenne smiles are associated with genuine enjoyment and are usually spontaneous. This contrasts with non-Duchenne smiles, which activate only the zygomatic major (mouth to cheek) muscles (Ekman et al., 1990). Non-Duchenne smiles are often intentional and typically serve as social signals, conveying acquiescence, respect, politeness, and the like. It can be difficult to interpret the meaning of social (non-Duchenne) smiles; as such, they are often referred to as fake smiles (i.e., due to their lack of signaling true positive emotion). You might also tell students that many studies have used archival data of people's photographs to make inferences about those people. For example, Harker and Keltner (2001) showed that coded Duchenne smiling within female college students' yearbook photos predicted important later life outcomes for those women (e.g., higher future well-being, increased likelihood of marrying, more satisfying marriages 30 years later). Students might consider this as they examine pictures of themselves, perhaps in their online profiles or posts!

At this point, you might pause to concretely illustrate the distinction between the two smiles with students. You could have them pair up and practice producing both non-Duchenne smiles and Duchenne smiles with each other. Ask students which one is more difficult to produce. Students should realize that non-Duchenne smiles are more easily produced and are more common. In contrast, research has shown that Duchenne smiles are harder to produce because they seem to require genuine mirth and positive feelings. Duchenne smiles also take more work and are more tiring because they activate more muscles. The instructor might also ask questions such as, "Do you think Duchenne smiles happen while laughing?" Maybe only during belly laughs, you might suggest. Or, "Can Duchenne smiles happen even when we are only smiling contentedly at a loved one?" Probably—the positive emotions expressed by Duchenne smiles do not always have to be intense.

Then, you could deepen the picture. Recently, Sheldon, Corcoran, and Sheldon (2021) provided an evolutionary interpretation of the function of Duchenne smiles, arguing that they evolved as honest signals of chronic positive affect. Honest signals are characteristics that are hard to fake, like the extravagant tail of the male peacock, which signals health. The most impressive peacocks must be that healthy to produce that tail. Sheldon, Corcoran, and Sheldon's (2021) argument was that happy people are in a psychologically healthy condition, which they signal in part by the frequent Duchenne smiles they display. Duchenne smiles are hard to fake because you must feel that good to produce them. As a result, people who are not feeling good have difficulty producing them. Because happiness is associated with virtuous, eudaimonic, or prosocial personality styles (Sheldon & Lyubomirsky, 2021), Duchenne smiles might ultimately signal the good character of the smiler—providing a "window into their souls." The evolutionary function of Duchenne smiles, according to Sheldon, Corcoran, and Sheldon (2021), is to alert perceivers to the virtuous behaviors and motivations of the smiler, to create a sense of connection between smilers and perceivers, and to elicit more cooperation from perceivers.

In a concrete demonstration of the character-signaling idea, Sheldon, Corcoran, and Trent (2021) collected 64 head-and-shoulder images for study, all of them Catholic priests in priestly regalia, mostly from church websites. Thirty-two of the images were of priests who were later convicted of sex crimes, taken from a national database. The other 32 were matched controls of the priests who replaced the convicted priests at their own churches (the two groups looked about the same age). Multiple student samples randomly rated the 64 images as to (a) how happy each priest looked and (b) how likely it was that they were one of the sex offenders (participants read that half the images were of convicted offenders). The consistent finding was that participants could identify the sex offenders at a much greater than chance rate because the sex offenders looked less happy (a mediational finding). Sheldon, Corcoran and

Trent (2021) argued that even though the pictures were taken before the offending priests' convictions, the priests had likely already descended into an unhealthy way of thinking and/or behaving, which showed on their faces. Participants could use facial information, including Duchenne smiles, to infer this (see Sheldon, Corcoran, & Sheldon, 20121, for more theoretical background).

After introducing these ideas, you could proceed to test five hypotheses using the ratings of the class. The hypotheses to test:

1. Targets displaying Duchenne smiles are rated as experiencing more positive emotion at that moment (Question 1), compared with targets displaying social or neutral smiles. This would support the often-demonstrated link between Duchenne smiles and momentary positive emotion.

2. Targets displaying Duchenne smiles should also be rated as happier people (Question 2) compared with the other groups. This would support the less-established link between Duchenne smiles and inferences of the smiler's general state of happiness.

3. Targets displaying Duchenne smiles should be rated as more trustworthy (Question 3). This would support the proposed link between Duchenne smiles and inferences of the smiler's honesty and virtuous intentions.

4. Targets displaying Duchenne smiles should be rated as more honest (Question 4). This would support the proposed link between Duchenne smiles and inferences of the smiler's honesty and virtuous intentions.

5. Finally, students should rate themselves as more willing to cooperate with targets displaying Duchenne smiles (Question 5). This would replicate a frequent finding in the Duchenne smile literature, namely, that people are more willing to behave cooperatively with Duchenne smilers (i.e., not defect against them in a prisoner's dilemma).

DISCUSSION

Discussion might be initiated by summarizing the results and what they are claimed to mean. It is likely that the hypotheses will be supported in the data collected from your students, which you could use to reiterate the points made earlier. However, it is also possible that some of them will not be supported. This can lead to fruitful discussion: Why not? Is it due to inadequate sample size and power? Or to a reluctance by people to make very general inferences from a single image? (beyond "they look happy at this moment"). Or maybe the images aren't convincing examples of the two types of smiles? On the other hand, perhaps the honest signaling theory is simply wrong—if so, what does it miss or leave out?

To illustrate the latter possibility, one study described in *How to Spot a Liar: Experts Uncover the Signs of Deception—Can You See Them?* found that exaggerated Duchenne smiles were associated with lying. How might this complicate things? Perhaps Duchenne smiles are easier to produce intentionally than typically supposed. If so, this might evidence an evolutionary arms race in which dishonest personalities learn to well-simulate Duchenne smiles, requiring new learning by perceivers to tell the difference between real and simulated Duchenne smiles. Or perhaps liars are not simulating Duchenne smiles—perhaps they are taking genuine delight in fooling perceivers? This might be another ingenious strategy in the evolutionary competition between cooperators and defectors.

Instructors might wrap up the discussion by inviting students to pay more attention to the role of smiling in social life, including both Duchenne and non-Duchenne smiling. Can they simulate Duchenne smiles when they want to? What about the other people with whom the student interacts?

APPENDIX 3.1: Rating Task Forms

Your name/ID_____

RATING TASK: FORM A

Please look at the image below. What kind of person is this? After studying the image for a few seconds, answer the questions below by circling a number for each one.

1 = none; 2 = a little; 3 = some; 4 = much; 5 = very much

1. How much positive emotion are they feeling? 1 2 3 4 5
2. How happy is this person overall? 1 2 3 4 5
3. How trustworthy is this person? 1 2 3 4 5
4. How honest is this person? 1 2 3 4 5
5. Would you cooperate with this person? 1 2 3 4 5

RATING TASK: FORM B

Your name/ID_____

Please look at the image below. What kind of person is this? After studying the image for a few seconds, answer the questions below by circling a number for each one.

1 = none; 2 = a little; 3 = some; 4 = much; 5 = very much

1. How much positive emotion are they feeling? 1 2 3 4 5
2. How happy is this person overall? 1 2 3 4 5
3. How trustworthy is this person? 1 2 3 4 5
4. How honest is this person? 1 2 3 4 5
5. Would you cooperate with this person? 1 2 3 4 5

A printable version of this appendix can be downloaded from the APA website at https://www.apa.org/pubs/books/more-activities-teaching-positive-psychology.

─────────────

Note. Adapted from "Individual Differences in the Recognition of Enjoyment Smiles: No Role for Perceptual–Attentional Factors and Autistic-Like Traits," by V. Manera, M. Del Giudice, E. Grandi, and L. Colle, 2011, *Frontiers in Psychology, 2,* Article 143 (https://doi.org/10.3389/fpsyg.2011.00143). CC BY 4.0.

REFERENCES

Ekman, P., Davidson, R. J., & Friesen, W. V. (1990). The Duchenne smile: Emotional expression and brain physiology: II. *Journal of Personality and Social Psychology, 58*(2), 342–353. https://doi.org/10.1037/0022-3514.58.2.342

Harker, L., & Keltner, D. (2001). Expressions of positive emotion in women's college yearbook pictures and their relationship to personality and life outcomes across adulthood. *Journal of Personality and Social Psychology, 80*(1), 112–124. https://doi.org/10.1037/0022-3514.80.1.112

Manera, V., Del Giudice, M., Grandi, E., & Colle, L. (2011). Individual differences in the recognition of enjoyment smiles: No role for perceptual–attentional factors and autistic-like traits. *Frontiers in Psychology, 2,* Article 143. https://doi.org/10.3389/fpsyg. 2011.00143

Sheldon, K. M., Corcoran, M., & Sheldon, M. (2021). Duchenne smiles as honest signals of chronic positive affect. *Perspectives on Psychological Science, 16*(3), 654–666. https://doi.org/10.1177/1745691620959831

Sheldon, K. M., Corcoran, M., & Trent, J. (2021). The face of crime: Apparent happiness differentiates criminal and non-criminal photos. *The Journal of Positive Psychology, 16*(4), 551–560. https://doi.org/10.1080/17439760.2020.1805500

Sheldon, K. M., & Lyubomirsky, S. (2021). Revisiting the pie chart and sustainable happiness model: Happiness can be successfully pursued. *The Journal of Positive Psychology, 16*(2), 145–154. https://doi.org/10.1080/17439760.2019.1689421

4

Exploring Language as an Unobtrusive Measure of Positive Psychosocial Characteristics

Margaret L. Kern

The goal of this activity is to explore the ways that writing samples can be used to covertly capture psychosocial functioning.

CONCEPT

Much of psychological research relies upon self-report measures, which directly ask participants to reflect upon and respond to a structured set of statements or questions. While useful, such measures are also prone to numerous biases. Language is central to modern human life, both reflecting and forming our emotions, thoughts, beliefs, attitudes, and cultures. This activity allows students to explore and reflect upon their own language and how language can complement self-report measures to capture human emotion, thoughts, perspectives, and behaviors relevant to positive psychology and other types of research.

Learning Outcomes

- Identify the limitations and biases associated with self-report measures.
- Apply manual and automatic approaches to analyze qualitative data.

https://doi.org/10.1037/0000417-004
More Activities for Teaching Positive Psychology: A Guide for Instructors, S. D. Pressman and A. C. Parks (Editors)

- Evaluate the benefits and limitations of closed-vocabulary approaches.
- Recognize ways that language reflects and impacts upon human experiences.

MATERIALS NEEDED

Ask students to bring two samples of their writing to class, such as a set of their recent posts on social media, text messages, or a piece of writing. A short sample (~50 words or one paragraph equivalent) should be printed or written out. A second, longer sample (~500 words or one to two pages of text) should be in electronic format (e.g., Word or text document, pdf) on an internet-connected tablet or laptop they will use in the activity.

Print one copy of the word lists (Appendix 4.1) and reporting worksheet (Appendix 4.2) per person. You will also need three different colors of highlighters or pens per group (for online modalities, Google Docs or similar works using three different text highlighter colors).

ACTIVITY SETTING

This activity is intended to be an experiential classroom learning activity, which involves a combination of guided discussion and active textual analysis. The directions here are for a face-to-face setting, but the activity can easily be adjusted for online classes using Google Docs or a similar shared text-based document for the analysis and breakout rooms during the group-based work. Discussions occur with the whole class, with the analytic portion occurring in groups of four to five students, providing an opportunity for collaborative learning. This activity can be taught alongside lectures on research methods, measurements of well-being, linguistics, or similar.

ACTIVITY DURATION

The activity is best run during a class period, with 10 minutes for the initial discussion on self-report measures and language, 10 minutes manually working through the shorter text samples in groups, 5 minutes of whole class interim discussion, 5 minutes automatically analyzing the text samples in groups, and 15 minutes of final discussion (45 minutes total).

SUGGESTED READINGS

- Kern et al. (2019)
- Kern et al. (2016)

No readings are required before the activity, as the activity aims to have students experience and gain insights into the power of language without preconceived ideas. Following the activity, students should be encouraged to read the following resources.

- Recommended reading for students after the activity:
  - Kern et al. (2016)

- Additional optional readings for those interested in language-coding methodology:
  - Eichstaedt et al. (2021)
  - Pennebaker (2011)
  - Pennebaker et al. (2015)

BACKGROUND AND INSTRUCTIONS

This activity gives students the opportunity to play with coding qualitative data, first manually and then using the Linguistic Inquiry Word Count (LIWC) program to code the data automatically. The goal of this activity is to see what is possible with natural language-processing approaches (both manual and automatic) and to recognize some of the limitations of automatic data analysis.

1. To prepare for the session, ask students to select or compile two writing samples. One should be printed or written out and be about 50 words in length (equivalent to one paragraph). The second should be an electronic version and be about 500 words in length (equivalent to one to two pages of text). This might be an essay they have written, a combination of social media posts or text messages, a diary entry, or any other text they are willing for a few classmates to see. Note that students should not put a lot of thought into selecting a sample but should choose texts they have easy access to and which they wrote themselves—the text is simply for the activity, not to be graded. As such, students should NOT edit the text, even if there are misspellings, emoticons, swear words, and so forth. Invite students to be as creative as they desire in selecting the text samples.

2. In class, note that studies in the social sciences tend to use self-report measures to study different phenomena. However, self-report measures also have numerous limitations. Invite students to reflect and share limitations and problems that can occur with self-report measures.

    a. Common issues to bring up with students include (a) response scale biases (where respondents restrict their answers to specific regions of the scale), (b) social desirability biases (where respondents adjust their responses to portray themselves in a positive light), (c) halo effects (where responses to one characteristic flow on to other characteristics), (d) guessing the purpose of the research (where participants guess at the purpose of the research and adjust their responses to either fit the hypotheses of the study or purposely try to corrupt the data through false responses), and (e) privacy concerns (in which participants are concerned over the privacy of their response and answer in ways that align with the expectations of whoever they think will see their response).

b. Ask students what types of issues might be especially present in studies of positive psychology constructs that are self-reported. Common issues to consider include (a) the tendency in many cultures for participants to present themselves as happier than they are, (b) stigmas around mental health-related issues, (c) language and concepts that are grounded in Western perspectives that may misalign with people from other cultures or worldviews, and (d) conceptualizing well-being based on academic models that misalign with layperson conceptualizations of well-being.

3. Next, ask students to consider the role that language plays in their lives, including specific examples of ways that language reflects or forms daily experiences.

a. Have students reflect upon positive versus negative language and the effect that different uses might have had on their experiences. For example, maybe they criticized a friend who reacted negatively, leading to an argument. Or perhaps they encouraged a friend, leading to a greater sense of connection.

b. Ask for specific examples of how positively and negatively oriented language affected their personal experiences. Encourage students to think about not only the words themselves but how the words made them feel.

4. Next, note that studies find that language can be used as an unobtrusive measure of different psychological characteristics, such as emotions, thoughts, beliefs, and values. In the online space, our language acts as a digital footprint, leaving traces of our persona in the virtual world. We might try to create a specific persona through our language, but that still becomes how others perceive us. This experiential activity provides a simplistic example of how we can use language to study human emotions, thoughts, and characteristics.

5. Break students into groups of four or five. Give each group the word list (Appendix 4.1) and three colored pens/highlighters (or if online, instruct students to use three different highlighting colors).

6. Tell the students that the word list contains three different dictionaries or sets of words that represent the categories of positive emotions, friend words, and personal pronouns. Note that these are just sample lists, that other words might fit in the category, and that students are free to highlight words with the same color if they belong to that group. Instruct students to work

through each group member's printed/written text sample, highlighting words that fit into the three dictionaries, using a different color for each dictionary. Then, count how many times each dictionary was used in their own sample and for the group as a whole, recording personal and group summary responses in Appendix 4.2, Part 1.

7. Have each group report the number of dictionary occurrences for their group and ask for any observations about the activity or results.

   a. Note that this is a way of manually identifying psychological content in text. Also acknowledge that this is a very lengthy process, and while it might work well for short pieces of text, it would become time consuming for long pieces of text.

8. Note that we can use computers to automate the coding of data, allowing much larger text samples to be analyzed across a much broader set of topics. Some approaches are closed-vocabulary approaches, which involve a computer identifying words from preconceived dictionaries, like the three dictionaries used before. Others are open-vocabulary approaches, in which the computer program identifies clusters of words from the data (see the Discussion section and the readings for details and examples).

   a. A starting place for automatically analyzing data is to create a word cloud, which visualizes the most frequently used words in a set of text. Go to the website https://www.wordle.net. Install the Wordle software (for Windows or Mac, respectively). Once installed, enter the set of text, run the program, and see the visual image that arises. This provides a sense of the words that are used in the set of text.

9. Returning to their groups, students will next analyze their longer electronic text using the LIWC trial tool (https://www.liwc.app/demo) and the LexHub lexicon tool (http://lexhub.org/wlt/lexica.html) on their digital internet-connected device.

   a. Begin with Wordle. Enter the longer piece of writing into Wordle and see what words appear in the visual diagram, providing an overall visual indication of the writing.

   b. Next, use the LIWC demo. Students should copy and paste their longer piece of writing into the text box, indicate what type of writing it is, and run the analysis, recording their results on the handout (Appendix 4.2, Part 2). Note that the results give a percentage across several main categories, compared with the average for that category with the type of writing noted (more detailed analyses are available with the full LIWC software, but this provides a freely available demonstration).

   c. Next, using the LexHub lexicon tool, students should again enter their longer piece of writing in Step 1. In Step 2, select "AgeGender," "Hedonometer," and "PERMA," then click "Run analysis." Again, students should record the results on the handout (Appendix 4.2, Part 3). If time remains, the group should discuss any reactions to the results or the process, noting any observations or reflections on the handout (Appendix 4.2, Part 4).

10. Returning to the main group, discuss the results, insights, or questions that arose, and any challenges or observations that occurred.

   a. Some key points to include are consideration of which categories were most common in their writing and how that depends on the type of writing, the potential implications of looking at different aspects of well-being, and the challenge of making sense of the results without further visualizations. Often, with this work, visualizations are necessary to really make sense of the pattern of findings—images can nicely summarize a lot of words. Also note that often, there are low correlations between self-report and text-based language, suggesting that the two are capturing two different aspects of the self (i.e., the perceived self vs. the presented self).

   b. As part of the discussion, consider what ethical issues might be involved with analyzing different language samples. For instance, what if the data reveal that a person is struggling with severe mental health issues? What if the person is purposely constructing a specific image in their writing? How might making assumptions about people based on their language be a poor indication of functioning? Natural language might better capture a person's thoughts and emotions than a self-report measure.

DISCUSSION

These two activities aim to demonstrate that emotions, social aspects, and behaviors can appear in textual data. Unlike self-report measures, which incorporate at least some degree of reflection and thought, language reveals many of our subconscious thoughts, beliefs, attitudes, and emotions (Eichstaedt et al., 2021; Kern et al., 2016). This can range from straightforward positive and negative emotions to more complex psychosocial constructs (Kosinski et al., 2016).

There is a significant body of literature that has studied emotions, social aspects, and behaviors through qualitative analyses (Braun & Clarke, 2006). This is important work, which has gathered linguistic data, manually identified themes, and provided considerable insights related to personality and related areas. However, such approaches are very time-intensive, like in the first manual coding activity. While automated approaches require supervision and care in interpreting the results, such approaches provide tools to speed up the coding process, allowing the processing of greater amounts of qualitative information in shorter periods of time (Eichstaedt et al., 2021).

This activity draws upon closed-vocabulary approaches (see Eichstaedt et al., 2021; Kern et al., 2016, for discussions of closed- and open-vocabulary approaches), in which text is scanned for words appearing on a preconceived set of words (i.e., the dictionaries). This can occur through manual coding of textual data, which is time consuming but successfully provides a deep understanding of the qualitative data collected (e.g., Braun & Clarke, 2006). Closed-vocabulary approaches expand upon this by automating the identification of key themes appearing in the qualitative data. The first activity draws on a limited number of categories, which are expanded in the automated version (and increase further with the full LIWC software).

Still, closed-vocabulary approaches can miss many of the nuances that occur in human language (Eichstaedt et al., 2021). Open-vocabulary approaches, where various themes and categories that occur in the data can be identified (e.g., see the activity written by Booker, Chapter 5, this volume), can better represent the underlying psychosocial constructs that are there, but they require more data and provide messier solutions. Ultimately, it is the combination of closed- and open-vocabulary approaches that can help us use language as an unobtrusive measure of human thoughts, emotions, attitudes, beliefs, and behaviors (Eichstaedt et al., 2021). Such measures do not replace traditional self-reporting. Indeed, the results arising from self-report data and automatic analysis often bring up different insights, as they look at different parts of the data. It is like two people looking at a globe from two different sides—both people would describe a real part of the world, but the descriptions would differ based on their perspective. In the same way, self-report data and automatic data analysis provide different insights on the same data. Unobtrusive data provide a helpful complement and expand opportunities for collecting data representing the whole human experience, including aspects that go beyond conscious awareness. As the area of computational social science rapidly advances, it is exciting to think about what might be possible as data scientists work with social scientists to create cutting-edge ways of making sense of textual data.

ASSIGNMENT

Following the session, instruct students to read the suggested readings noted above. Have them reflect on the writing samples they and their group members chose and what insights arose through the analyses and discussions. Ask students to briefly reflect upon insights that arose from the activity, benefits and limitations of using language as an unobtrusive measure of psychosocial constructs, and ethical aspects that might be relevant to the use of such data.

APPENDIX 4.1: Word Lists for Manual Data Coding

Positive emotion word		Friend word	Personal pronoun
☺	Passion*	Accomplice*	He
Admir*	Peaceful	Acquaint*	He's
Ador*	Playful	Ally	He's
Agree*	Please*	Babe*	Her
Alright	Pleasur*	Best friend*	Hers
Amaze*	Polite popular	Bestie	Herself
Amazing	Positive	Besties	Hes
Appreciate*	Pretty	Bf	Him
Approv*	Proud	Bff*	Himself
Awesome	Radiant	Boyfriend*	His
Bless*	Ready	Bud	I
Bliss*	Reassure*	Buddies	I'd
Calm	Rejoice*	Buddy*	I'll
Cheerful	Relax*	Chap	I'm
Cheery	Resolv*	Chum	I've
Contented	Respected	Chums	Idk
Contentment	Reward*	Classmates	I don't know
Creative	Rich	Classmate	Im
Delicious*	Romantic	Clique*	Ive
Eager	Safe	Colleague*	Let's
Eagerly	Satisfy*	Coma*	Lets
Ease*	Scrumptious*	Compadre*	Me
Engag*	Sentimental*	Companion*	Mine
Enjoy*	Sexy	Comrad*	My
Enthus*	Silly	Confidant*	Myself
Excellent	Smart	Contact*	Oneself
Excited	Sociability	Crew	Our
Fabulous	Sociable	Cutie*	Ours
Fair	Special	Date	Ourselves
Fantastic	Splendid	Dawg*	She
Fine	Strong	Dear	She'd
Flirtatious	Successful	Dude*	She'll
Free	Sunny	Ex-bf*	She's
Fun	Superb*	Ex-boyfriend*	Shes
Gentle	Superior	Ex-gf*	Thee
Glad	Supported	Ex-girlfriend*	Their*
Good	Surprised	Fellow	Them
Gorgeous	Sweet	Fellows	Themself
Graceful	Talent*	Fiancé	Themselves
Grand	Thankful	Follower*	They
Grateful	Thoughtful	Friend*	They'd

Positive emotion word		Friend word	Personal pronoun
Great	Toleran*	Gang	They'll
Haha	Tranquil*	Gangs	They've
Happ*	Trusted	Gf*	Thine
Healthy	Trustworthy	Girlfriend*	Thou
Heartfelt	Upbeat	Honey	Thy
Helpful	Useful	Hottie	U
Honoured	Valuabl*	Lover*	Ur
Humor*	Vigor*	Mate	Us
Humour*	Vigour*	Mates	We
Important	Virtue*	Neighbor	We'd
Impress*	Virtuo*	Neighbour	We'll
Interested	Warm	Pal	We're
Keen*	Wealth*	Pals	We've
Kind	Well	Partner*	Y'all
Laugh	Well-being	Possee	Y'alls
Liked	Wellness	Roommate*	Ya
Lol	Win	Roomie*	You
Love*	Wisdom	Schoolmate	You'd
Lucky	Wise	Sidekick*	You'll
Magnific*	Wonderful	Soulmate*	You're
Neat	Worthwhile	Squad	You've
Nice	Wow*	Sweetheart*	Yours truly, yours
Ok	Yay*	Sweetie*	Yourself
Okay	Yum	Sympathy*	Yourselves
Optimistic			

Note. This is just a sample of words for each category, adapted from the LIWC dictionaries (Pennebaker et al., 2015)—feel free to count other words that fit within the category when counting occurrences in your language sample. An asterisk indicates variant word endings (e.g., happ* includes happy, happiness, happier). Some common misspellings/abbreviations are also included. LIWC = Linguistic Inquiry Word Count.

A printable version of this appendix can be downloaded from the APA website at https://www.apa.org/pubs/books/more-activities-teaching-positive-psychology.

APPENDIX 4.2: Handout for Recording Manual and Automatic Codes

PART 1: MANUAL HAND CODING

Text source	Positive emotion	Friend word	Pronoun
Personal text			
Group text			

PART 2: LIWC ONLINE CODING: GENERAL CODES

Type of text: _____

Traditional LIWC dimension	Your text	Average for type of writing
I-words (I, me, my)		
Positive tone		
Negative tone		
Social words		
Cognitive processes		
Allure		
Moralization		
Summary variables		
Analytic		
Authentic		

Note. LIWC = Linguistic Inquiry Word Count.

PART 3: LEXHUB CATEGORIES

Lexicon	Category	Personal score	Group score
Hedonometer	Hedonometer		
PERMA	Achievement		
PERMA	Disengagement		
PERMA	Engagement		
PERMA	Lack_of_Achievement		
PERMA	Lack_of_Meaning		
PERMA	Meaning		
PERMA	Negative_Emotions		
PERMA	Negative_Relationships		
PERMA	Positive_Emotions		
PERMA	Relationships		
AgeGender	Age		
AgeGender	Gender		

Note. PERMA = positive emotions, engagement, relationships, meaning, and accomplishment.

PART 4: OBSERVATIONS AND REFLECTIONS

Provide any observations or reflections you might have on the process of automatically analyzing textual information. There are no right or wrong answers, but we encourage you to consider any insights that have arisen through the analytic process.

A printable version of this appendix can be downloaded from the APA website at https://www.apa.org/pubs/books/more-activities-teaching-positive-psychology.

REFERENCES

Braun, V., & Clarke, V. (2006). Using thematic analysis in psychology. *Qualitative Research in Psychology, 3*(2), 77–101. https://doi.org/10.1191/1478088706qp063oa

Eichstaedt, J. C., Kern, M. L., Yaden, D. B., Schwartz, H. A., Giorgi, S., Park, G., Hagan, C. A., Tobolsky, V. A., Smith, L. K., Buffone, A., Iwry, J., Seligman, M. E. P., & Ungar, L. H. (2021). Closed- and open-vocabulary approaches to text analysis: A review, quantitative comparison, and recommendations. *Psychological Methods, 26*(4), 398–427. https://doi.org/10.1037/met0000349

Kern, M. L., McCarthy, P. X., Chakrabarty, D., & Rizoiu, M.-A. (2019). Social media-predicted personality traits and values can help match people to their ideal jobs. *Proceedings of the National Academy of Sciences of the United States of America, 116*(52), 26459–26464. https://doi.org/10.1073/pnas.1917942116

Kern, M. L., Park, G., Eichstaedt, J. C., Schwartz, H. A., Sap, M., Smith, L. K., & Ungar, L. H. (2016). Gaining insights from social media language: Methodologies and challenges. *Psychological Methods, 21*(4), 507–525. https://doi.org/10.1037/met0000091

Kosinski, M., Wang, Y., Lakkaraju, H., & Leskovec, J. (2016). Mining big data to extract patterns and predict real-life outcomes. *Psychological Methods, 21*(4), 493–506. https://doi.org/10.1037/met0000105

Pennebaker, J. W. (2011). The secret life of pronouns. *New Scientist, 211*(2828), 42–45. https://doi.org/10.1016/S0262-4079(11)62167-2

Pennebaker, J. W., Boyd, R. L., Jordan, K., & Blackburn, K. (2015). *The development and psychometric properties of LIWC2015*. University of Texas at Austin.

5

How Can Life Stories Provide Insights for Positive Psychology?

Jordan A. Booker

In this activity, students will engage with life stories (their own or an available set to review). This activity provides opportunities to make links between study approaches with life stories and topics in positive psychology.

CONCEPT

Storytelling is a natural activity that could be used to focus students toward reflecting on past experiences and can help students make important connections with different course concepts that include the ways storytelling approaches can be assets to daily life. Since the 1980s, the science of life storytelling has expanded widely, focusing on topics central to positive psychology: connections between forms of storytelling and the ways people incorporate happiness in their lives, the importance of storytelling in the face of trauma and distress for resilience, how integrating lived experiences through storytelling promotes ego and identity development, and ways that certain forms of storytelling or salient life stories complement well-being.

This activity can be centered on experiences related to positive psychology or complement lectures centered on positive development, adaptive cognitive schemas, constructive forms of personality, and a focus on stories as methods of capturing and rating human experiences.

https://doi.org/10.1037/0000417-005
More Activities for Teaching Positive Psychology: A Guide for Instructors, S. D. Pressman and A. C. Parks (Editors)

MATERIALS NEEDED

Either a pencil/pen and paper (or provided worksheet) or a computer with a word processing application. If additional materials for in-class engagement are assigned, working from a laptop would be ideal.

ACTIVITY SETTING

This activity could be completed before class as a home assignment or during the class period. This activity could be done in person or remotely. If students are asked to provide a life story, they will be responding to a narrative prompt. Their response could be written locally (e.g., pen and paper; Word or text document) or provided through an online survey (e.g., Qualtrics) or discussion assignment format through a course management system (e.g., Blackboard, Canvas). We recommend that if collecting responses for this activity through a survey or course management system, you also provide private options for responding so that students' names are not tied to their responses and/or their responses are initially masked from peers.

ACTIVITY DURATION

Though the timing is flexible, providing 15 to 30 minutes of total dedicated class time could give ample space for students to engage with life stories in a constructive and fulfilling way. If students were asked to reflect on and write a life story during class, it would be helpful to provide 10 to 15 minutes for them to first complete that activity. If students had already prepared their own life story or reviewed a separate example, they may need less class time to prepare for discussion or other activities with peers. There is flexibility in the source of life stories for this activity. Students could be asked to privately reflect on and organize an autobiographical narrative or could work from instructor-provided narrative examples. Either approach could be followed by a broader class discussion on how these stories point to themes in positive psychology (e.g., positive feeling states, aspects of character or morals, stories highlighting resilience).

SUGGESTED READINGS

Though a class activity centered on life stories could be successfully carried out without required reading, familiarizing students with an article presenting concepts about narratives and life stories, as well as why it is valuable to study life stories, would be helpful in orienting them to class activities.

- Recommended reading before class:
  - Adler et al. (2017)

- Supplemental readings of narrative-centered empirical studies that reinforce the relevance of narrative science for topics in positive psychology. These articles could reinforce the relevance of life story research for questions in areas of personality differences (e.g., evidence of differences in storytelling approaches between people), developmental issues (e.g., the role of age in narrative findings, ties with identity development), and research methods (e.g., the importance of certain narrative prompts, the importance of cross-sectional and longitudinal study designs).
  - J. J. Bauer and McAdams (2010)
  - Booker, Wesley, and Pierre (2021)
  - McLean and Lilgendahl (2008)

BACKGROUND AND INSTRUCTIONS

Humans are natural storytellers. We use stories to make sense of experiences across the day, to organize different happenings across the major chapters of our life stories, and to pass along information with others (Bruner, 1990, 1991; Fivush, 2011; McAdams, 1995, 2001). The stories of our lives that we build and share provide important opportunities to form meaning from our experiences and develop a consistent view of ourselves—a narrative identity—that reflects who we were in the past, how the past informs who we are in the present, and how our current standing shapes where we can go in the future (J. J. Bauer et al., 2008; McAdams, 2018; McAdams & McLean, 2013). The ways people develop, refine, and maintain a well-integrated and consistent narrative identity reflect psychological health, resilience, and well-being (e.g., Adler, 2012; Booker, Fivush, & Graci, 2022; McLean, Syed, et al., 2020). Further, the ways people express narrative identity in their life stories are placed within intersecting areas of developmental, cognitive, personality, clinical, social, and cultural psychology. Hence, there can be different topical entry points for incorporating life storytelling as a method to reinforce subject areas in positive psychology.

Complex and integrative storytelling capacities take time to fully emerge (Fivush, 2011; Fivush et al., 2017; Habermas & Bluck, 2000; Reese, 2009). Autobiographical storytelling is shaped by the storage and later retrieval of accessible and relevant events and details (P. J. Bauer, 2002, 2015). People differ in the ways they express dimensions of narrative identity, like how elaborative they are and the extent to which they emphasize communal values during storytelling (Adler et al., 2016; Booker, Brakke, Sales, & Fivush, 2022; Booker & Graci, 2021; Guo et al., 2016; McAdams & Pals, 2006). Further, multiple facets of culture play pronounced roles in how and when stories are shared, with norms of storytelling shaping expectations for what counts as a "good story" and how different expressions of narrative identity may be relevant for meaning-making and functioning in people's lives (Booker, Brakke, & Pierre, 2022; McLean, Delker, et al., 2020; Syed, 2021; Syed & Azmitia, 2008; Syed & McLean, 2021). Life storytelling as a research method is well-situated for topics in positive psychology and the ways positive psychology is related to other domains of behavioral science. Many correlational or longitudinal measures of interest to narrative researchers tend to involve well-being, character, personal fulfillment, and functioning (Adler, 2012; Adler & Poulin, 2009; J. J. Bauer & McAdams, 2010; Booker, Ell, et al., 2022; Booker et al., 2020; Booker, Hernandez, et al., 2022; McLean, Syed, et al., 2020; Waters & Fivush, 2015).

Class activities could take different forms to find different ways of making issues of autobiographical storytelling and ways of studying storytelling—as a method and means of studying themes in positive psychology—tangible for students.

Ideas for Students' Life Storytelling During Class

One approach, centered on in-class engagement, involves presenting students with one or more life story prompts and giving them time to respond to that prompt through a written narrative during the class period. You may encourage students to try to provide about two or three paragraphs in their response. For student comfort, you could provide multiple prompts for students to select from. Appendices 5.1–5.3 present three possible topics: experiences during the college transition, a self-defining memory, and a high-point experience in life. These prompts represent both common experiences for college adults (Booker, Hernandez, et al., 2022) and additional issues that have been successfully and comfortably used with college populations in the past (McAdams, 2008; J. Singer et al., 2007). These represent a small subset of possible subjects. Additional topics can be selected from approaches like the broader Life Story Interview or tailored given relevant experiences for students. One example derives from the impacts of the COVID-19 pandemic on students' lives (Booker, Ell, et al., 2022). Further, if you were interested in attempting a positive mood induction with students—a small activity that may bolster positive emotion experiences in the moment—having students reflect on high-point experiences (Appendix 5.3) or other events involving gratitude or opportunities for growth in their lives are promising.

There are also commonly used follow-up questions that could give students opportunities to reflect on how their stories involved certain feelings or felt important to them, based on the self-defining memory task, which can be found on Dr. Jefferson Singer's website (http://www.self-definingmemories.com/;

Blagov & Singer, 2004; J. Singer et al., 2007; J. A. Singer et al., 2013). The positive emotions students endorse in important life stories are related to higher endorsements of adjustment and lower reports of distress (Blagov & Singer, 2004), and questions like these could be connected to other topics focused on personal strengths and assets. After students have the chance to provide an autobiographical narrative, you could also move toward a discussion making connections with other subjects in the course (e.g., How might the event they shared take on a different meaning for them 5 years from now? What were things that were easier or harder to recall? Were they completely confident in their details? Did this feel like the amount of detail they provided or the ways they emphasized positive or negative feelings was typical of how they usually shared stories with others?).

There are important ethical concerns about whether and how to incorporate student-provided life stories in the classroom. Students may not feel comfortable sharing aspects of their lives with peers or instructors, and some shared events may inadvertently involve intrusive or legally relevant details that could lead to distress for students. Even having students enter stories into an anonymous discussion board may not fully avoid these concerns. To limit possible ethics issues, the use of separate life story examples from other public domains, like StoryCorps, may be ideal for in-class activities. Students could still review, work with, and discuss such publicly available stories in meaningful ways. Selected stories could involve storytellers from similar backgrounds or from other important backgrounds: children, adult peers outside of college contexts, and so on.

Ideas for Student Storytelling at Home

If you expect that students would feel more comfortable providing life stories in private, you could assign a narrative prompt response as an at-home assignment. Again, students could be given multiple prompts to select from in responding and could complete follow-up items on emotions elicited from the events and the importance/significance of the event. You could also provide students with a precursor activity to encourage thinking about their storytelling and confidence in organizing and sharing life stories. A brief storytelling self-efficacy scale is provided in Appendix 5.4 (Booker, 2021). This scale asks about different facets of storytelling that are often of interest to narrative researchers (e.g., confidence in providing a well-detailed or organized story, comfort sharing a life story with a stranger). Though a self-report of self-efficacy differs from the ways narrative researchers manually rate stories for certain dimensions, these self-appraisals could be relevant for class connections in cognitive and personality topics, and endorsements of personal confidence and self-efficacy are relevant to psychological adjustment and well-being (e.g., Zajacova et al., 2005). If there is interest in assessing students' insights following these at-home activities, it may provide more comfort for students if instructors collect a separate reflection and discussion piece on their experience of storytelling and thinking purposefully on stories rather than grading their life stories based on specific characteristics or a rubric. Given the intimacy of some life stories, students may become stressed about having aspects of their lives rated for being "good enough" for class.

Ideas for Students Rating Available Life Stories From Others

A third option, one that could be adapted for in-class or at-home formats, involves presenting students with existing narratives and providing them with opportunities to practice narrative coding approaches—ways they can practice assigning certain values or characteristics to part of or a total life story using an existing set of instructions or a *coding manual.* For this approach, it may help to assign a reading by prominent narrative researchers on common approaches to defining, collecting, and studying narrative responses in psychology (Adler et al., 2017; McAdams & McLean, 2013). It is recommended to use a set of low-risk and publicly accessible life stories for an activity like this rather than stories collected from the class or other groups around campus, which can be identified even with efforts to mask names and some locations. The StoryCorps website has a growing repository of publicly available life stories collected from citizens representing different backgrounds and addressing a variety of topics (https://storycorps.org/ stories/). You could assign one or more stories for groups of students to work together to review and rate one or more narrative identity dimensions. An accessible coding approach—reflecting prominent dimensions of motivation and reasoning from narrative identity research (McLean, Syed, et al., 2020)—has been presented in Appendix 5.5. This involves two tally-based rating approaches for capturing motivational dimensions of agency (broad motivations for personal success, assertiveness, and control) and communion (broad motivations on love, care, and engagement with others). These motivations reflect broad human drives for personal and interpersonal success. This rating scheme focuses on specific themes that may be expressed in the life story, and a sum score is formed given how many themes are identified in the story (here, scores could range from 0 to 4). Differences in these motivational dimensions of storytelling have been associated with psychological adjustment and well-being. Broadly, people who tend to express more agency and communion in their life stories tend to endorse greater well-being and functioning in the moment and over time (Booker, Ell, et al., 2022; Booker, Fivush, & Graci, 2022).

Depending on your class aims, these activities could lead to discussions on the relevance of life storytelling and narrative approaches with well-being and broader personal assets. You could also situate this activity in the context of personality, cognitive, or developmental topics. For example, developmentally, we expect adults to be better equipped to reflect on and make sense of broad motivations that explain their behaviors and reasoning in an earlier life event (Booker, Fivush, & Graci, 2022; Fivush et al., 2017). Still, you may see considerable variability across a group of example life stories, reflecting differences in personality. After students try these rating approaches, class discussions could center on broader take-aways and connections to other themes/topics in the course.

DISCUSSION

Life stories are relevant for positive psychology and other related domains of psychology, and having students engage with their own or others' life stories can reinforce important points about positive feelings, well-being, character, and personal assets. Some of the following discussion prompts could follow up in-class activities or be used for at-home student reflections.

Sample questions for at-home reflection or an in-class group discussion:

- Even though storytelling about typical life events might be something we take for granted, how do you see storytelling as something that can be an asset or resource for people—something that could help them appreciate uplifting events, show resilience in the face of difficult events, and make sense of different experiences?

- There are arguments that time is important for storytelling in a few major ways: It takes time for skills in storytelling to fully develop; also, people's stories can change over time, and how they draw meaning and insight from experiences can change over time.

  - How do you think an attempt at sharing a story like this would look different for a 10-year-old version of you? How well do you think you could have brought in details or focused on important goals for your life as a child? How might these changes be important as you continue deciding on who you are as a person and the values and morals that are important for your everyday life?

  - In contrast, think of the major takeaways from the event you shared. How do you think your major takeaway might be different if you were reflecting on this same event 10 years from now? Would this event be as important to you? Do you think you would feel the same way about it? If you were organizing this experience differently, how might it still be a valuable resource for you and the way you understand how you got to that point in life?

- Were there other people prominently featured in your story—people who were carrying out important actions or whose conversations and feelings you also focused on? What do you think it might say about you and your focus on relationships when you tend to focus more on your interactions with others and on your relationships with others when you remember past events, especially when those relationships made a positive impact on you?

Sample questions for in-class reflection following nomothetic ratings of other storytelling sources (e.g., StoryCorps):

- If you had to guess which stories were from people who felt especially happy and/or fulfilled with their lives, which stories would you point to? What stood out to you about these stories and how they were presented?

- Were there any stories that seemed to point to valuable aspects of character from storytellers—ways people mentioned showing gratitude, courage, forgiveness, honesty, kindness, etc.? How important were these mentions of character for the story? Were they a driving force for actions that occurred or broader insights storytellers shared about their lives?

- Across different cultures, there are broad scripts, or expected actions and milestones, that people should be achieving at different points in life—events like graduation, moving out of the family home, and starting work by certain points. Did you see evidence of some of these major milestones in the stories you reviewed? Did the milestones that were relevant for different people seem to differ given major developmental differences, like what adolescents focused on compared with younger adults compared with middle adults, etc.? How did events stand out? Why might reaching these milestones be so important to how people understand themselves and feel about their lives?

- While there are some ways that people are expected to show broader tendencies of storytelling as a reflection of personality (e.g., expressing more detail often, using more deep reasoning while recollecting events), the ways people organize and share stories can also differ based on the emotional tone of the story and whether the event was more positive or more negative. Did you notice a difference between clearly positive events and clearly negative ones? If so, which events did people seem to provide more details and go into further depth on? How did people express broader takeaways and insights for their lives across different types of events? How might these differences across positive and negative life events each be helpful for people or helpful in making sense of their lives?

ONLINE MATERIALS

The StoryCorps website includes a repository of publicly accessible life stories aimed at preserving a rich breadth of human experiences. These stories could provide good examples for students to think about life stories purposefully (https://storycorps.org/stories/).

Jefferson Singer's website, focused on self-defining memories, includes relevant readings about the self-defining memory paradigm and materials for presenting the self-defining memory task to others (http://www.self-definingmemories.com/).

A revised version of the Life Story Interview, which includes multiple narrative prompts relevant for adult storytellers, has been organized by Dan P. McAdams and can be found through his research team's website (https://sites.northwestern.edu/thestudyoflivesresearchgroup/).

APPENDIX 5.1: Example Narrative Prompt 1—The College Transition

The entry to college is a major transition for many individuals, involving changes in people's obligations, roles, and time demands. Below, we will ask you to write about your college transition experience, detailing what aspects of that transition stood out (or continue to stand out) to you.

Please reflect on how the college transition has been for you (or how the transition was if you feel as if it is more distant now).

Describe your experience in a few sentences. What are the first things that come to mind about your college transition experience? What are your thoughts and feelings about the college transition? How do you understand your college transition, reflecting on it now? Is there any lesson or bottom line you take away from your college transition experience now?

A printable version of this appendix can be downloaded from the APA website at https://www.apa.org/pubs/books/more-activities-teaching-positive-psychology.

APPENDIX 5.2: Example Narrative Prompt 2—The Self-Defining Memory

I'd like you to recall a special kind of personal memory called a self-defining memory. A self-defining memory has the following attributes:

- It is at least 1 year old.

- It is a memory from your life that you remember very clearly and that still feels important to you even as you think about it.

- It is a memory about an important enduring theme, issue, or conflict from your life. It is a memory that helps explain who you are as an individual and might be the memory you would tell someone else if you wanted them to understand you in a profound way.

- It is a memory linked to other similar memories that share the same theme or concern.

- It may be a memory that is positive or negative, or both, in how it makes you feel. The only important aspect is that it leads to strong feelings.

To understand best what a self-defining memory is, imagine you have just met someone you like very much and are going for a walk together. Each of you is very committed to helping the other get to know the "real you." You are not trying to play a role or to strike a pose. While, inevitably, we say things that present a picture of ourselves that might not be completely accurate, imagine that you are making every effort to be honest. During the conversation, you describe a memory that you feel powerfully conveys how you have come to be the person you currently are. It is precisely this memory, which you tell the other person and simultaneously repeat to yourself, that constitutes a self-defining memory.

A printable version of this appendix can be downloaded from the APA website at https://www.apa.org/pubs/books/more-activities-teaching-positive-psychology.

APPENDIX 5.3: Example Narrative Prompt 3—High-Point Memory

Please describe a scene, episode, or moment in your life that stands out as an especially positive experience. This might be the high-point scene of your entire life or else an especially happy, joyous, exciting, or wonderful moment in the story.

Please describe this high-point scene in detail. What happened, when and where, who was involved, and what were you thinking and feeling? Also, please say a word or two about why you think this moment was so good and what the scene may say about who you are as a person.

A printable version of this appendix can be downloaded from the APA website at https://www.apa.org/pubs/books/more-activities-teaching-positive-psychology.

APPENDIX 5.4: Possible Precursor Activity—Autobiographical Storytelling Self-Efficacy Scale

CONFIDENCE IN STORYTELLING

For many people, sharing stories about their lives is a routine experience. This goes for both the mundane events (e.g., "How was your day?") and the larger, important events we recall (e.g., "What is an event that helps explain who you are today?"). However, there can be differences in how confident people are in being able to share life stories.

The following items ask you about your confidence in organizing, framing, and finding meaning in life stories. Please indicate how confident you are with each of the following types of storytelling. There are no right or wrong answers.

0	10	20	30	40	50	60	70	80	90	100
Cannot do at all					*Moderately can do*			*Highly certain can do*		

SHARING PERSONALLY MEANINGFUL STORIES OF YOUR LIFE

1. Share a meaningful life story that includes much detail about what happened and what you were thinking and feeling.

2. Share a meaningful life story that has clear organization, with details going from beginning to middle to end, without needing to make side notes or getting offtrack.

3. Share a meaningful life story that establishes connections between what happened in that past event and who you are as an individual today.

4. Share a meaningful life story that showcases your personal goals, assertiveness, and control over the situation.

5. Share a meaningful life story that showcases goals for connecting with others, being emotionally close with others, and being supported by close others.

6. Share a meaningful life story that shows ways you have grown as an individual following that experience.

7. Share a meaningful life story that shows new insights or values because of your experience with that event.

8. Share a meaningful life story that could be ended with positive closure and resolution.

9. Share a meaningful life story with a loved one or someone close to you.

10. Share a meaningful life story with a stranger or acquaintance you do not know well.

A printable version of this appendix can be downloaded from the APA website at https://www.apa.org/pubs/books/more-activities-teaching-positive-psychology.

APPENDIX 5.5: Rating Stories for Agency and Communion

Narrative researchers, and particularly researchers interested in how people express life stories as an aspect of personality—or what is called narrative identity—tend to rate life stories for broad characteristics or dimensions. These include ways of structuring life stories with organization and rich details, ways of framing stories that mention emotions and goals, and ways people make connections between their life events and who they are as individuals—they integrate reasoning and meaning.

Existing approaches for rating expressions of motivation and broad human needs in life stories is by capturing aspects of *agency*—goals for getting ahead in life—and *communion*—goals for getting along with others. These are two of the broadest fundamental needs in the human experience (McAdams et al., 1996). One approach for rating life stories for expressions of agency and communion is to use a checklist of certain themes that might be mentioned that fit with how we define these goals. Researchers have used criteria that fit with broader definitions of agency and communion to determine how people emphasize these different motives in their life stories. There are four broad categories for each type of motive and goal. A scoring approach is to rate whether each theme is absent (0) or present (1) within a story and then sum the total of agentic themes (max score of 4) and the total of communion themes (max score of 4).

Agentic themes, centered on power, control, independence, and achievement:

- *Self-mastery*—working toward personal improvement and autonomy.

- *Status*—mentions of status and position, particularly an accomplished status.

- *Achievement/responsibility*—meeting challenges and goals for oneself, being competent.

- *Empowerment*—receiving support for power and decisions from the surrounding environment.

Communal themes, centered on love, intimacy, sharing, belonging, and care:

- *Love/friendship*—recognizing positive relationship bonds and feelings toward close others.

- *Dialogue*—focus on engaging in reciprocal discussions with others, particularly (but not limited to) when sharing intimate or important details.

- *Care/help*—focus on warmth, altruism, and support toward others in need and/or receiving care from others.

- *Community*—feeling belonging to a group that is greater than oneself or one's immediate interactions (e.g., feeling community with a neighborhood or a larger social group).

Agency score = the tally of present agentic themes (0–4).
Communion score = the tally of present communal themes (0–4).

A printable version of this appendix can be downloaded from the APA website at https://www.apa.org/pubs/books/more-activities-teaching-positive-psychology.

REFERENCES

Adler, J. M. (2012). Living into the story: Agency and coherence in a longitudinal study of narrative identity development and mental health over the course of psychotherapy. *Journal of Personality and Social Psychology, 102*(2), 367–389. https://doi.org/10.1037/a0025289

Adler, J. M., Dunlop, W. L., Fivush, R., Lilgendahl, J. P., Lodi-Smith, J., McAdams, D. P., McLean, K. C., Pasupathi, M., & Syed, M. (2017). Research methods for studying narrative identity: A primer. *Social Psychological & Personality Science, 8*(5), 519–527. https://doi.org/10.1177/1948550617698202

Adler, J. M., Lodi-Smith, J., Philippe, F. L., & Houle, I. (2016). The incremental validity of narrative identity in predicting well-being: A review of the field and recommendations for the future. *Personality and Social Psychology Review, 20*(2), 142–175. https://doi.org/10.1177/1088868315585068

Adler, J. M., & Poulin, M. J. (2009). The political is personal: Narrating 9/11 and psychological well-being. *Journal of Personality, 77*(4), 903–932. https://doi.org/10.1111/j.1467-6494.2009.00569.x

Bauer, J. J., & McAdams, D. P. (2010). Eudaimonic growth: Narrative growth goals predict increases in ego development and subjective well-being 3 years later. *Developmental Psychology, 46*(4), 761–772. https://doi.org/10.1037/a0019654

Bauer, J. J., McAdams, D. P., & Pals, J. L. (2008). Narrative identity and eudaimonic well-being. *Journal of Happiness Studies, 9*(1), 81–104. https://doi.org/10.1007/s10902-006-9021-6

Bauer, P. J. (2002). Long-term recall memory: Behavioral and neuro-developmental changes in the first 2 years of life. *Current Directions in Psychological Science, 11*(4), 137–141. https://doi.org/10.1111/1467-8721.00186

Bauer, P. J. (2015). Development of episodic and autobiographical memory: The importance of remembering forgetting. *Developmental Review, 38,* 146–166. https://doi.org/10.1016/j.dr.2015.07.011

Blagov, P. S., & Singer, J. A. (2004). Four dimensions of self-defining memories (specificity, meaning, content, and affect) and their relationships to self-restraint, distress, and repressive defensiveness. *Journal of Personality, 72*(3), 481–511. https://doi.org/10.1111/j.0022-3506.2004.00270.x

Booker, J. A. (2021). *Autobiographical Storytelling Self-Efficacy Scale* [Unpublished manuscript]. Department of Psychological Sciences, University of Missouri.

Booker, J. A., Brakke, K., & Pierre, N. (2022). It's time to make more goals so I can keep pushing: Hope, growth, and well-being among young Black women. *Emerging Adulthood, 10*(4), 876–890. https://doi.org/10.1177/21676968221089179

Booker, J. A., Brakke, K., Sales, J. M., & Fivush, R. (2022). Narrative identity across multiple autobiographical episodes: Considering means and variability with well-being. *Self and Identity, 21*(3), 339–362. https://doi.org/10.1080/15298868.2021.1895301

Booker, J. A., Ell, M., Fivush, R., Greenhoot, A. F., McLean, K. C., Wainryb, C., & Pasupathi, M. (2022). Early impacts of college, interrupted: Considering first-year students' narratives about COVID and reports of adjustment during college shutdowns. *Psychological Science, 33*(11), 1928–1946. https://doi.org/10.1177/09567976221108941

Booker, J. A., Fivush, R., & Graci, M. E. (2022). Narrative identity informs psychological adjustment: Considering three themes captured across five time points and two event valences. *Journal of Personality, 90*(3), 324–342. https://doi.org/10.1111/jopy.12668

Booker, J. A., Fivush, R., Graci, M. E., Heitz, H., Hudak, L. A., Jovanovic, T., Rothbaum, B. O., & Stevens, J. S. (2020). Longitudinal changes in trauma narratives over the first year and associations with coping and mental health. *Journal of Affective Disorders, 272,* 116–124. https://doi.org/10.1016/j.jad.2020.04.009

Booker, J. A., & Graci, M. E. (2021). Between- and within-person differences in communion given gender and personality. *Personality and Individual Differences, 183,* 111–117. https://doi.org/10.1016/j.paid.2021.111117

Booker, J. A., Hernandez, E., Talley, K. E., & Dunsmore, J. C. (2022). Connecting with others: Dispositional and situational relatedness during the college transition. *Journal of Social and Personal Relationships, 39*(2), 198–220. https://doi.org/10.1177/02654075211034566

Booker, J. A., Wesley, R., & Pierre, N. (2021). Agency, identity development, and subjective well-being, among undergraduate students at a central United States university. *Journal of College Student Development, 62*(4), 488–493. https://doi.org/10.1353/csd.2021.0049

Bruner, J. (1990). *Acts of meaning.* Harvard University Press.

Bruner, J. (1991). The narrative construction of reality. *Critical Inquiry, 18*(1), 1–21. https://doi.org/10.1086/448619

Fivush, R. (2011). The development of autobiographical memory. *Annual Review of Psychology, 62*(1), 559–582. https://doi.org/10.1146/annurev.psych.121208.131702

Fivush, R., Booker, J. A., & Graci, M. E. (2017). Ongoing narrative meaning-making within events and across the life span. *Imagination, Cognition and Personality, 37*(2), 127–152. https://doi.org/10.1177/0276236617733824

Guo, J., Klevan, M., & McAdams, D. P. (2016). Personality traits, ego development, and the redemptive self. *Personality and Social Psychology Bulletin, 42*(11), 1551–1563. https://doi.org/10.1177/0146167216665093

Habermas, T., & Bluck, S. (2000). Getting a life: The emergence of the life story in adolescence. *Psychological Bulletin, 126*(5), 748–769. https://doi.org/10.1037/0033-2909.126.5.748

McAdams, D. P. (1995). What do we know when we know a person? *Journal of Personality, 63*(3), 365–396. https://doi.org/10.1111/j.1467-6494.1995.tb00500.x

McAdams, D. P. (2001). The psychology of life stories. *Review of General Psychology, 5*(2), 100–122. https://doi.org/10.1037/1089-2680.5.2.100

McAdams, D. P. (2008). Personal narratives and the life story. In O. P. John, R. W. Robins, & L. A. Pervin (Eds.), *Handbook of personality: Theory and research* (3rd ed., pp. 242–262). Guilford Press.

McAdams, D. P. (2018). Narrative identity: What is it? What does it do? How do you measure it? *Imagination, Cognition and Personality, 37*(3), 359–372. https://doi.org/10.1177/0276236618756704

McAdams, D. P., Hoffman, B. J., & Mansfield, E. D. (1996). Themes of agency and communion in significant autobiographical scenes. *Journal of Personality, 64*(2), 339–377. https://doi.org/10.1111/j.1467-6494.1996.tb00514.x

McAdams, D. P., & McLean, K. C. (2013). Narrative identity. *Current Directions in Psychological Science, 22*(3), 233–238. https://doi.org/10.1177/0963721413475622

McAdams, D. P., & Pals, J. L. (2006). A new Big Five: Fundamental principles for an integrative science of personality. *American Psychologist, 61*(3), 204–217. https://doi.org/10.1037/0003-066X.61.3.204

McLean, K. C., Delker, B. C., Dunlop, W. L., Salton, R., & Syed, M. (2020). Redemptive stories and those who tell them are preferred in the U.S. *Collabra: Psychology, 6*(1), Article 39. https://doi.org/10.1525/collabra.369

McLean, K. C., & Lilgendahl, J. P. (2008). Why recall our highs and lows: Relations between memory functions, age, and well-being. *Memory, 16*(7), 751–762. https://doi.org/10/fhf5mz

McLean, K. C., Syed, M., Pasupathi, M., Adler, J. M., Dunlop, W. L., Drustrup, D., Fivush, R., Graci, M. E., Lilgendahl, J. P., Lodi-Smith, J., McAdams, D. P., & McCoy, T. P. (2020). The empirical structure of narrative identity: The initial Big Three. *Journal of Personality and Social Psychology, 119*(4), 920–944. https://doi.org/10.1037/pspp0000247

Reese, E. (2009). The development of autobiographical memory: Origins and consequences. *Advances in Child Development and Behavior, 37*, 145–200. https://doi.org/10.1016/S0065-2407(09)03704-5

Singer, J. A., Blagov, P., Berry, M., & Oost, K. M. (2013). Self-defining memories, scripts, and the life story: Narrative identity in personality and psychotherapy. *Journal of Personality, 81*(6), 569–582. https://doi.org/10.1111/jopy.12005

Singer, J., Rexhaj, B., & Baddeley, J. (2007). Older, wiser, and happier? Comparing older adults' and college students' self-defining memories. *Memory, 15*(8), 886–898. https://doi.org/10.1080/09658210701754351

Syed, M. (2021). *Where are race, ethnicity, and culture in personality research?* PsyArXiv. https://doi.org/10.31234/osf.io/m57ph

Syed, M., & Azmitia, M. (2008). A narrative approach to ethnic identity in emerging adulthood: Bringing life to the identity status model. *Developmental Psychology, 44*(4), 1012–1027. https://doi.org/10.1037/0012-1649.44.4.1012

Syed, M., & McLean, K. C. (2021). *Who gets to live the good life? Master narratives, identity, and well-being within a marginalizing society.* PsyArXiv. https://doi.org/10.31234/osf.io/4pjuf

Waters, T. E. A., & Fivush, R. (2015). Relations between narrative coherence, identity, and psychological well-being in emerging adulthood. *Journal of Personality, 83*(4), 441–451. https://doi.org/10.1111/jopy.12120

Zajacova, A., Lynch, S. M., & Espenshade, T. J. (2005). Self-efficacy, stress, and academic success in college. *Research in Higher Education, 46*(6), 677–706. https://doi.org/10.1007/s11162-004-4139-z

Who Can I Trust?

Evaluating Sources of Information Related to Happiness

Zachary A. Silver and Laurie R. Santos

This activity will teach students how to critically evaluate popular media articles about positive psychology.

CONCEPT

In a world saturated with information related to happiness and well-being, it can be difficult to discern between trustworthy science and pseudoscience, which should be ignored. In this classroom activity, students will develop and practice the process of critically evaluating the source and content of positive psychology information published in popular media to distinguish between genuine science and pseudoscience.

MATERIALS NEEDED

Students will need a pen or pencil as well as the supplied evaluation checklist and sample excerpts (see Appendices 6.1 and 6.2).

https://doi.org/10.1037/0000417-006
More Activities for Teaching Positive Psychology: A Guide for Instructors, S. D. Pressman and A. C. Parks (Editors)

ACTIVITY SETTING

This activity can be completed in class or as an out-of-class assignment. Given the importance of developing the skills needed to interpret media coverage of positive psychology results, this activity will be most effective if assigned either as part of a research methods unit in a course or toward the end of a course as an introduction to strategies for applying positive psychology knowledge to the real world. This activity is suitable for students who have a basic understanding of the psychological research process. For students who have not previously completed an introduction to psychology or research methods course, teachers should consider defining the research vocabulary (e.g., sample size, correlational design).

ACTIVITY DURATION

Depending on the duration of the discussion, the in-class portion of the activity can be completed in 30 to 60 minutes. The optional at-home assignment will require 20 to 30 minutes. This activity can also be completed in asynchronous classroom models; to adapt the activity for asynchronous learning, the in-class discussion portion of the activity can be substituted for an online discussion facilitated through discussion board posts using learning management software.

SUGGESTED READINGS

- Suggested readings for before the activity:
  - Jhangiani et al. (2019)
  - Greifeneder et al. (2021)

BACKGROUND AND INSTRUCTIONS

Given the increase in the prevalence of positive psychology in popular culture, the media is now ripe with recommendations for how to become happier. But which of these countless recommendations are based on solid scientific evidence? This classroom activity aims to build the skills needed to critically evaluate the scientific validity of podcasts, blogs, and other popular publications that make claims about the science of happiness.

In class, teachers can distribute the sample source excerpts to students (see Appendix 6.2). These sample sources are fictitious articles that can be rated based on the criteria outlined in Appendix 6.1. Please note that there are two possible ways to distribute these excerpts to students: Display the excerpts individually on a PowerPoint presentation or distribute a worksheet containing all six excerpts simultaneously. Alternatively, rather than using the Appendix 6.2 examples, you could invite students to bring in their own sources from the news and share them with the class to evaluate together or in small groups.

Divide students into groups (we recommend groups of three to five students) and instruct them to read and evaluate these sample sources. Each student group should collectively score a source on a scale of 1 to 10 based on the evaluation criteria provided in the handout. Each group can then share their rating and the reasons behind it with the full class using a classroom poll (for online options, consider Zoom, Qualtrics, and Poll Everywhere; for offline options, students can submit their ratings via notecards).

After students complete their initial ratings of the sample sources, distribute the "Who can I trust" handout to students (see Appendix 6.1). This document features a list of criteria students can use to evaluate the validity of different sources. Students should review this document and become familiar with the key indicators of real science versus pseudoscience. After reviewing the document, instruct students to return to their groups and reassess their ratings. In a second round of polling, students will provide a new rating for each source. The instructor can then compare students' pre- and postratings and use any changes as a starting point for an in-class discussion.

For a presentation component, instruct students to explain (a) the specific claims made by the sample source, (b) the key criteria relevant to their rating of the source, (c) how their opinion of the source changed after reading the evaluation checklist, and (d) how readers should interpret the source in the context of this evaluation.

DISCUSSION

With widespread misinformation online, pressure for clickable headlines, and limited attention spans of readers reducing the ability to allow for subtle nuances in science communication, it has never been as important to teach students to be thoughtful consumers of news coverage and online information (West & Bergstrom, 2021). In-class discussion should emphasize these types of points and the importance of determining whether a given source is trustworthy. Possible discussion questions include, "Why is it necessary that we adhere to such rigid criteria when evaluating scientific claims about happiness?" or "What can we do as consumers of scientific information to promote accurate evaluations and interpretations of scientific claims?"

Additionally, discussions may highlight the challenges readers and consumers of scientific information face when determining whether an article, blog, or podcast is trustworthy. Example questions for this portion of the discussion include, "Which criterion was the most difficult to assess in the sample sources we evaluated in class?" or "How should we evaluate scientific claims when sources are ambiguous or when certain information essential to a source's evaluation is unavailable?"

Ideally, the in-class discussion should highlight the unfortunate reality that a large portion of the information available in popular media related to increasing happiness does not meet the criteria for trustworthiness. Thus, the final topic of the discussion ought to center on how people should deal with potentially inaccurate or untrustworthy information. Possible discussion questions for this final portion may include, "How would you respond to a friend or family member sharing an untrustworthy article on social media?" or "What are some strategies you might recommend to others to help them tell the difference between trustworthy science and untrustworthy pseudoscience?" Note for instructors: See Greifeneder et al. (2021) for an overview of how misinformation spreads and how to best correct it.

ASSIGNMENT

Following the in-class activity and discussion, students can complete an optional at-home assignment. In this assignment, instruct students to monitor their social media feeds and news articles for content related to increasing happiness. Ask students to find one trustworthy source and one nontrustworthy source and to explain why they categorized these sources as such using the criteria discussed in class. Finally, students should complete a written response in which they have an opportunity to reflect on their experience evaluating these sources. These written reflections should prompt students to contemplate what they found challenging about the exercise, what they found most surprising when evaluating sources, and how they plan to use the skills they developed in this activity to improve their scientific literacy in the future.

APPENDIX 6.1: Checklist for Evaluating Scientific Communication

When evaluating scientific claims, it is important to consider a variety of factors, including information related to the researchers' backgrounds, where the research was published, and how the research was conducted. Note that some articles may present information that is not based on research but rather opinions. Such articles should be interpreted with skepticism, as we cannot trust scientific claims that are not grounded in research. The subsections below detail many of the key considerations when evaluating information related to happiness reported in popular media. In addition to the suggestions provided in this chapter, there are many freely available sources that provide additional guidance on how to evaluate sources (Columbia University Libraries, 2020; Kipnis & Baer, 2023; Purdue Writing Lab, 2018).

WHO IS THE AUTHOR?

When evaluating the validity of scientific claims, it is essential to recognize whether the author of the reported research has sufficient credentials and background to justify the claims they make in their research. More specifically, in the field of positive psychology, look for authors who hold advanced degrees in psychology or related fields and conduct their research either in university settings or through well-established government research bodies, such as the National Institutes of Health. Avoid sources authored by individuals who do not have an explicitly scientific background or who are not affiliated with reputable research entities, for example, universities. Note that private entities, for instance, corporations, often employ scientists to conduct research on their behalf. When evaluating research funded by these private entities, carefully consider whether the background of the company or the researcher represents a conflict of interest. For example, if you find a study funded by the dairy milk industry that claims that frequent milk intake can increase happiness, it would be advisable to approach this research with skepticism, as the origin of the research represents a potential conflict of interest.

WHO PUBLISHED THE RESEARCH?

Blogs, videos, podcasts, and other popular media sources that discuss happiness often refer to specific empirical research studies in their content. When determining whether these sources can be trusted, you should also determine where the research being discussed was originally published. Reputable popular media sources will likely disclose this information (e.g., an experiment published in *Psychological Science*), while less reputable sources may omit this information entirely. Always question sources that do not disclose where the research they describe was originally published, as this might indicate that the claims made in the source are not based on research but rather the author's opinion. Additionally, just as an author may have a conflict of interest that could bias their research, publications may also have conflicts of interest that impact what they publish and how they interpret research. For instance, if a religious website publishes an article exploring how prayer can increase happiness, carefully consider whether this publication may introduce some degree of bias. For this reason, it is essential to refer back to the original research to avoid any inaccurate representations of the findings.

Once you know where the research being discussed was originally published, your next step is to determine whether the publication mentioned is reputable. One critical factor that determines the reputability of a publication is whether the experiments described were subject to *peer review*—a process where experts in the field collectively determine whether a submitted research study is suitable for publication. Peer-reviewed research is categorically considered more trustworthy than non-peer-reviewed research. If research is not subject to peer review, you, as a reader, do not have any way to verify that the research was collected, analyzed, and interpreted accurately.

WAS THE RESEARCH WELL-DESIGNED/CONDUCTED?

For this phase of evaluation, it is usually necessary to find the original source of the research (i.e., the original publication) rather than the popular media source (i.e., the news article, blog, podcast), as popular science media does not always give you the level of detail needed to know whether a study was well-designed. Once you have determined that the author of the research is qualified and that the research is published in an acceptable journal, the next step in deciding whether a research finding is trustworthy is to critically evaluate the components of the scientific research article itself. The criteria described here are not exhaustive but represent a good starting point for scientific considerations specific to research related to happiness. See the Suggested Readings section for additional information on research design considerations.

Sample Size and Representativeness

How many participants took part in the study? Look for samples larger than 100 participants as a general guideline. Next, ensure that the participants who comprise the sample are representative of the claims made in the article. For instance, if the article asserts that a proposed intervention increases happiness in all adults, ensure that the experiments include a diverse sample of adults. If the sample does not align with the claims, the authors' interpretations of their findings should not be taken at face value.

Design Concerns

Research that explores scientific strategies for increasing happiness often involves an experimental intervention to one group of participants and compares their postintervention happiness to a control group—a second group of participants who did not experience the intervention. Ideally, any research that discusses an intervention should include a control. A secondary consideration concerns whether the control and experimental groups are aware of the intervention and their relative participation. Well-conducted studies usually make sure that participants are not aware of which group (experimental vs. control) they are in—they are thus considered blind to condition. Studies in which participants are not blind to condition often have two problems with their results. The first problem is the *placebo effect*—an effect in which participants in the experimental group may show improvements in well-being not because the intervention has a true causal effect on their happiness but instead because they expect to experience improvements to their well-being as a result of the intervention. A second potential problem is the *nocebo effect*—an effect in which participants in a control group expect that they will not experience any improvement to their happiness. If participants in the control group are aware they are assigned to a control group, they may show little change in their well-being, not because the intervention did not have a positive causal effect but because they did not expect to show any improvements due to their status as a control. Optimally, participants will be assigned to either the control or experimental condition randomly. This technique, known as random assignment to condition, minimizes the likelihood that factors outside of the experimental manipulation could lead to changes in the dependent variable being measured. Unfortunately, random assignment to conditions is not always possible. For example, consider a group of researchers who want to design an intervention to explore whether participating in a meditation program improves positive emotion. Ideally, these researchers would compare the positive emotion of a group of participants who completed the intervention (experimental group) to a group that did not complete the intervention (control group), and participants would be randomly assigned to one of these two different conditions. However, it may be difficult—or in some cases unethical—to recruit participants who will not receive the intervention. For this reason, researchers sometimes use what is known as a waitlist control condition such that both groups of participants eventually receive the intervention, but one group (the waitlisted group) receives the intervention at a later time than the experimental group and can thus serve as a control group until they receive the intervention. Waitlist control designs enable researchers to deliver their interventions to all participants they recruit, which can alleviate some of the ethical concerns associated with withholding an intervention or treatment from a group of participants. The downside to waitlist control designs is that participants are not blind to the conditions of the experiment, as they are aware of their status either in the experimental group or on the waitlist. Further, such studies often include some bias because they tend to include only individuals who *want* to learn how to meditate (or be happier, etc.), which means the sample may not be representative of all types of people.

Experimental Versus Correlational Designs

When interpreting the claims made by scientific research, it is essential to consider whether the claims are appropriate for the type of research conducted. Experimental designs involve the manipulation of an independent variable (e.g., the presence or absence of a gratitude intervention) and its impact on a dependent variable (e.g., a self-reported well-being score; see the Suggested Readings section for a more detailed description of experimental designs). Experimental designs enable researchers to infer a causal link between the independent variable and the dependent variable (e.g., individuals who participated in a gratitude intervention might show a larger increase in positive emotion compared with individuals who did not participate in the intervention; thus, the researchers could conclude that participating in the gratitude intervention caused more positive emotion). Correlational designs do not involve the manipulation of a variable but instead explore the naturally occurring relationship between two variables (e.g., individuals who naturally express more gratitude might show higher levels of positive emotion; see the Suggested Readings section for more detailed descriptions). Notably, correlational designs do not suggest a causal link between the two variables being measured. Often, popular media sources misinterpret the results of correlational studies and incorrectly report that one variable caused a change in the other variable. The findings of correlational studies are still valuable and worth considering because they document natural relationships between variables, but as a consumer of scientific information, it is vital to discern between experimental and correlational designs and to not falsely attribute a causal link between variables in correlational studies.

A NOTE ON SUMMATIVE MEDIA

If the source in question is not about a specific research finding but rather a summary of a topic (e.g., a blog or podcast covering a range of information), it is essential to refer back to the original source material and evaluate the authors' credentials for each research finding. In other words, for articles, blogs, and podcasts that summarize research, carefully examine the criteria listed above for each source summarized in the article, blog, or podcast. If this information is not available, consider this a signal that the article, blog, or podcast may not be trustworthy.

A printable version of this appendix can be downloaded from the APA website at https://www.apa.org/pubs/books/more-activities-teaching-positive-psychology.

APPENDIX 6.2: Sample Excerpts

The excerpts below are fictitious examples of how you might encounter scientific information related to happiness reported in popular media. For each example, refer to the checklist in Appendix 6.1 to determine whether the reporting can be trusted.

Please consider this table as a tool to try applying the evaluations above on your own, scoring each category from 1 (*worst*) to 10 (*best*).

Criteria	Question to evaluate	Score (1–10)	Note and comment
Author	Is the author qualified to write about positive psychology? Does the author have an explicitly scientific background? Is the author affiliated with a reputable research entity?		
Publication	Is the publication reputable? Is the publication peer-reviewed?		
Research	Was the research well-designed? Was there a control group? Were participants randomly assigned to groups? Was the sample size large enough? Were the participants representative of the population? Was the research conducted using an experimental design?		
Conclusions	Are the conclusions supported by the evidence? Are the conclusions overstated or exaggerated? Are there any alternative explanations for the findings?		

To better understand the impact of skiing on happiness, we reached out to professional skier Simon Red, who conducted a survey of 25 male skiers' happiness before and after a day on the slopes. They found that skiers were, on average, 11% happier after a day of skiing compared with their happiness scores before skiing.

—The SkiCast Podcast

Psychologist Ernest Purple and colleagues designed an experiment to explore whether participation in a 6-week meditation course would decrease stress in college students. The researchers recruited 200 students; they assigned 100 students to complete a fall session of the course and the remaining 100 students to a waitlist. These waitlisted students would eventually complete a spring session of the course. Compared with the waitlisted students, the students participating in the meditation course showed significant reductions in their stress levels.

—Meditation Monthly

Psychologist Frankfort Green conducted an independent survey of students in their class at Fake University and found a strong correlation between the number of recent romantic partners and overall happiness. Professor Green published the results on their personal website and told us that their results represent an exciting next step in understanding how relationships impact mental health.

—Relationships Podcast

A team of researchers at Northeastern Rhode Island University collected information about the exercise and sleep habits of 25 college students. They found a strong correlation between the students' average hours of exercise and average hours of sleep. Thus, we now know that frequent exercise causes us to get more sleep.

—The SleepCast

A team of researchers at Northeastern Connecticut University carried out an experiment to determine if listening to jazz music reduces stress in college students. The researchers randomly assigned 100 students to listen to jazz music each day for 30 days and 100 students to listen to other types of music during that same duration. Participants in both groups reported their levels of stress both before and after their music-listening intervention. The results from this experiment, published in *Psychological Science*, suggest that the genre of music may play a key role in stress reduction, as students who listened to jazz reported a significantly larger reduction in stress relative to the students who listened to other genres of music.

—Music Cognition Magazine

An experimental study conducted by the Cotton Growers' Association of America found that participants who wore clothing made from 100% organic cotton reported statistically significantly higher levels of positive emotion and significantly lower levels of stress compared with a control group who wore clothing made of polyester and other synthetic fibers.

—Textiles and Science

A printable version of this appendix can be downloaded from the APA website at https://www.apa.org/pubs/books/more-activities-teaching-positive-psychology.

REFERENCES

Columbia University Libraries. (2020). *Evaluating online sources.* https://library.columbia.
edu/libraries/undergraduate/evaluating_web.html

Greifeneder, R., Jaffe, M., Newman, E., & Schwarz, N. (2021). *The psychology of fake news:
Accepting, sharing, and correcting misinformation.* Taylor & Francis.

Jhangiani, R. S., Chiang, I. A., Cuttler, C., & Leighton, D. C. (2019). Experimental design.
In R. S. Jhangiani, I. A. Chiang, C. Cuttler, & D. C. Leighton (Eds.), *Research methods in
psychology* (4th ed.). Kwantlen Polytechnic University. https://kpu.pressbooks.pub/
psychmethods4e/chapter/experimental-design/

Kipnis, D., & Baer, A. (2023). *Research guides: Evaluating online sources: A toolkit.* Rowan
University. https://libguides.rowan.edu/EvaluatingOnlineSources

Purdue Writing Lab. (2018). *Evaluating digital sources.* https://owl.purdue.edu/owl/
research_and_citation/conducting_research/evaluating_sources_of_information/
evaluating_digital_sources.html

West, J. D., & Bergstrom, C. T. (2021). Misinformation in and about science. *Proceedings of
the National Academy of Sciences of the United States of America, 118*(15), Article
e1912444117. https://doi.org/10.1073/pnas.1912444117

7

Evaluating Positive Psychology Apps

Justine R. Bautista and Stephen M. Schueller

Students will be asked to evaluate a positive psychology app after 1 week of use based on several different factors, then present their evaluation of the app to the class.

CONCEPT

As the number of health apps (i.e., software applications, especially common on mobile devices) continues to grow, many people, especially young people, have used these resources. In fact, 69% of 14- to 22-year-olds in the United States have reported using an app to promote their mental health or wellness (Rideout et al., 2021). Although app stores provide average consumer ratings, these ratings do not speak to aspects of the app's quality, such as the scientific evidence supporting it or whether it uses evidence-based principles. As consumers of products like these and students learning positive psychology, being able to critically evaluate these products may benefit students in an increasingly digital world. This activity is designed to teach students about how to evaluate positive psychology apps and make a recommendation on the use of a specific app after rigorously evaluating it.

https://doi.org/10.1037/0000417-007
More Activities for Teaching Positive Psychology: A Guide for Instructors, S. D. Pressman and A. C. Parks (Editors)

MATERIALS NEEDED

Students will need a mobile device to access the positive psychology app of their choice. They should also have access to the internet, either through a data plan or WiFi, in order to test the app before their presentation. For the presentation, students will need an electronic device such as a laptop, desktop computer, or tablet with a suitable program for creating a presentation, like PowerPoint. Devices with screen recording capacity can help students share examples of interactions with the app.

ACTIVITY SETTING

This activity will be completed mostly at home with in-class discussion and presentation. Student testing and evaluation of apps will occur outside of the classroom, while presentations and discussions will take place during class time. This activity is suitable for both in-person and virtual learning. We initially envisioned it for a class of approximately 30 students, which, when organized into groups of six, allows for a manageable 2.5-hour presentation session, with each group allotted approximately 20 to 30 minutes for their presentation. For larger classes, adjustments may be made. In virtual settings, parallel presentation tracks may be useful, as breakout rooms would allow multiple groups to present simultaneously. Extending presentation periods across multiple class sessions and forming larger groups are also options to accommodate larger class sizes. Students could also prerecord their presentations for students to watch on their own time, or the instructor could select a subset of student videos for discussion purposes.

ACTIVITY DURATION

Upon choosing an app to focus on, students will be instructed to test the app for 1 week and take notes about their use. In our experience, such use might take about 30 to 60 minutes, spread across multiple sessions throughout the week. As the activity is written, each student presentation should take about 20 minutes, with additional time (~10 minutes) for discussion. If this is too much time for your class (because of a large class size), you might consider having students submit recordings and then play excerpts of presentations to encourage class discussion at a later point.

SUGGESTED READINGS

- Recommended readings for before the activity:
  - Bates et al. (2018)
  - Jake-Schoffman et al. (2017)
  - Wykes et al. (2019)

- Optional readings for after the activity:
  - Eisenstadt et al. (2021)
  - Gál et al. (2021)
  - Goldberg et al. (2022)

BACKGROUND AND INSTRUCTIONS

Instructors should orient both themselves and their students by providing guidance on evaluation metrics and categories to consider when evaluating an app. Three primary evaluation dimensions are (a) credibility, (b) user experience, and (c) data security and privacy. We provide a list of potential apps below, but instructors might also construct their own list based on resources made available to students on campuses or specific topics that are covered in other portions of the class (e.g., gratitude, mindfulness, journaling, tracking apps). In teaching this assignment, we recommend that instructors use a sample app separate from the list provided to students to both teach the concepts related to evaluation (i.e., credibility, user experience, and data security and privacy) and provide an example of the presentation.

Students will be provided with a list of apps. Our recommendations for apps include Happify, Merrier, Headspace, Think Up, and SuperBetter. We also encourage you to feel free to recommend other apps to your students. However, it is important to keep in mind that keeping a list of options should allow students to form clusters with other students who have used the same app. These apps include those that are directly or loosely based on positive psychology principles, popular apps many students might have used, and some apps with direct empirical support (i.e., Happify, Headspace, and SuperBetter). As technology advances and apps continue to be developed, this list may change over time.[1] This list may also change depending on resources that a university may have (e.g., free subscriptions). Instructors should also consider apps that are available across multiple platforms, including the App Store, Google Play, and Samsung Store, and may survey the class prior to the assignment start date to determine if there are common apps students are using. We recommend using apps of varying quality (i.e., those with research support and those without, those with a good user experience and those with a poor user experience) so students have diverse experiences reviewing apps and facilitating discussion of these key points. In our list of apps, for example, Happify, Headspace, and SuperBetter are high-quality apps on the basis of their existing support by research evidence and positive user experience.

As a brief review of published findings supporting the effectiveness of these apps, Happify has been evaluated in both controlled trials (e.g., Hunter et al., 2019; Parks et al., 2018) and through naturalistic observations (e.g., Carpenter et al., 2016). Headspace has been subjected to multiple small yet promising

---

[1] This list was generated in 2022.

controlled trials demonstrating benefits in well-being and mental health (e.g., Fish & Saul, 2019; Howells et al., 2016) and improvements in mindfulness (e.g., Rosen et al., 2018). SuperBetter has had two controlled trials showing benefits for depression (Roepke et al., 2015) as well as concussion symptoms, which the game underlying the app was initially designed to address (Worthen-Chaudhari et al., 2017). Merrier and ThinkUp do not have research studies evaluating their benefits. These studies, however, also demonstrate some of the challenges when evaluating apps. Some apps, yet not many (Larsen et al., 2019), might have studies conducted on the app itself. Others might draw on indirect scientific evidence, that is, results of studies supporting the interventions on which the app is based. In these cases, it is useful to evaluate whether the indirect scientific evidence draws from well-established treatments, including those considered evidence-based practices or recommended by practice guidelines for particular outcomes. It is also best that students have a foundational knowledge of research methods and evaluation, so employing this activity in a setting with a research methods course prerequisite would be most effective. If you find that your students are relatively new to research evaluation, consider referencing supplementary material such as Silver and Santos (Chapter 6, this volume), which provides guidance on distinguishing between trustworthy science and pseudoscience. This is not to say this is an easy process, but it provides good opportunities to discuss aspects of research design, study quality, and interpretation of findings, which can be generalized to other topics in your course. This knowledge will also empower students to critically assess the scientific validity of the information they encounter during the app evaluation process.

Students should consider the following concepts when evaluating the app, posing these questions to guide themselves into forming a decision about the app's effectiveness in each category:

1. Credibility
   - Does the app have direct scientific evidence, that is, research studies that support its effectiveness? Are studies conducted either by third parties or with external collaborators?
   - Does the app have indirect scientific evidence, that is, is it founded on evidence-based interventions?
   - Does the development team include subject matter experts in its intervention strategy? Where are these subject matter experts represented on the project team (i.e., founder, leadership role, employee, advisor)?
   - Does the app provide clear, measurable, and specific targets?
   - What do consumers say about the app?

2. User experience
   - Is the app functional and enjoyable for users?
   - How easy is it to use the app?

- How easy is it to learn to use the app?
- Is the app visually appealing?
- Is the technology interesting?

3. Data security and privacy
   - How does the app address data entered by users?
   - Does the privacy policy from developers follow ethical standards?
   - How does the app describe its use as an intervention resource?

Students will then begin working on their presentation, where they will focus on five key features of the app. These features include:

1. General overview of the app
2. Overview of the intervention or target goal of the app
3. Credibility
4. User experience
5. Data security and privacy

When presenting the app, students should provide a clear overview of the app, including its available features, overall goal, and the area of positive psychology that the app is intended to address. Furthermore, the student should outline their evaluation of the key metrics introduced by the instructor. Based on their findings, students should offer a rating in each area of credibility, user experience, and data security and privacy as either acceptable, questionable, or unacceptable. Students can think about these ratings as a recommendation, with "acceptable" being an app they would recommend (green light), "questionable" being an app that the user should evaluate before proceeding (yellow light), and "unacceptable" being an app they would encourage people not to use (red light).

Credibility

Students should determine what scientific evidence supports the app either directly (evidence-based) or indirectly (evidence-informed). Research studies supporting the app are often presented on the app's website, or the name of the app can be used as a search term in a literature review. It is worth noting that estimates suggest that only approximately 3% of apps are evidence-informed and only 1% are evidence-based, that is, that they have at least one study directly evaluating the effectiveness of the app (Larsen et al., 2019). Therefore, most apps that students evaluate will not have scientific support. Many companies may use research that supports the overall goal of the app, that is, that interventions can reduce anxiety, or from products that have other goals, that is, an app can help support weight loss but a new product is focused on improving mental health. An app with no direct or indirect scientific evidence should be considered "unacceptable." An app with some indirect scientific evidence but no direct scientific evidence would most likely be "questionable." An app with strong direct scientific evidence (i.e., high-quality empirical support) would most likely be "acceptable." Other aspects of credibility might influence the rating, including who developed the app, the feasibility of target outcomes, and consumer feedback. However, these aspects should contribute to the determination of "acceptable" versus "questionable."

User Experience

Students should assess the user experience, including how easy the app is to use or learn to use, its visual and functional design, and how engaging it is. User experience may be based on their personal experience using the app as well as others, including app store reviews, media articles, and/or academic research. User experience can also address whether there are considerations for diverse audiences and populations, including aspects such as accessibility or cultural relevance. User experience incorporates elements that might be more subjective and vary between students, for example, aesthetic appeal and what features they find more engaging. However, some more objective elements can help guide recommendations of "unacceptable," "questionable," or "acceptable." "Unacceptable" apps would be those that have significant technical glitches or features (or lack of features) that inhibit repeated use of the app. "Questionable" apps would be those with complicated user interfaces or those that would be difficult to use for specific groups. "Acceptable" apps would be those that adopt universal design principles that make them easy to use and have features that promote long-term engagement.

Security and Privacy

Students assess issues of data security and privacy, including reviewing the app's privacy policy and terms of service, to determine what happens to data entered into the app and, while using the app, considering what type of data users provide. "Unacceptable" apps would be those that lack a data security and privacy policy or do not provide sufficient information to know what happens to one's data. "Questionable" apps would be those that provide some details regarding data security and privacy but in generality rather than specifics (e.g., stating the data will be shared with third parties but not identifying what type of data, what third parties, or for what purposes). "Acceptable" apps would be those that have well-described data security and privacy policies and conform to industry standards (like Service Organization Control Type 2 [SOC2] certification that addresses cybersecurity compliance, or Health Insurance Portability and Accountability Act of 1996 [HIPAA] which addresses sensitive patient health information, for apps that interface with health systems). For further determinations between "questionable" and "acceptable," students may also refer Wykes et al., 2019, for considerations regarding the ethics and privacy of the app.

Overall Assessment

Upon completing their evaluation, students should provide an overall assessment (yes/no) on whether they would recommend the app to someone interested in using a positive psychology app. This assessment should come from a holistic assessment of the app, considering credibility, user experience, and security and privacy. Apps that score as "unacceptable" in any category would likely result in a no; however, apps need not receive "acceptable" in all categories to warrant a yes. Students should consider how different categories might offset each other (i.e., an app with an excellent user experience might be recommended even with questionable credibility). Students should justify their recommendation while also reflecting on their relative weighting of each category. In providing their overall assessment, students should be able to demonstrate knowledge of the app, including aspects related to their assessment and an ability to answer questions pertaining to their review and assessment.

DISCUSSION

Although it may not always be the case, presentations from students should reflect results from past research, which instructors are highly encouraged to discuss with the class. It is important to note that developers also may not place a heavy emphasis on privacy and data security policies, which are especially concerning in apps that house patient data in their platform. Prior literature has highlighted a lack of transparency in most apps regarding issues of privacy and security, formal regulation of data handling, and data sharing with third parties, breaching the confidentiality of sensitive patient data disclosed in the app (Minen et al., 2018; O'Loughlin et al., 2019). While engaging in this project, students may find similar issues when doing research on app privacy and security.

As a multitude of untested positive psychology apps exist, students can benefit from an understanding of how to evaluate these tools and common issues among them. For example, among apps that contain scientific language in their description, very few can link to actual published research studies (Larsen et al., 2019; Marshall et al., 2020). In fact, a scarce number of apps actually have research studies supporting them, with one study estimating that less than 4% of mental health apps are evidence-based (Sucala et al., 2017). As such, when evaluating credibility, many students may not find many—or any— studies directly supporting the effectiveness of an app. Credibility and user experience tend to be unrelated (Neary & Schueller, 2018). This suggests that many evidence-based apps have poor user experience, and many apps with good user experience may not be evidence-based.

In light of the aforementioned issues associated with mental health apps, students may benefit from exploring app review platforms. One Mind PsyberGuide, a web-based platform for app evaluations, provides a set of metrics aimed at helping consumers make informed decisions about the mental health apps they choose to download (Neary & Schueller, 2018). Instructors and students may use this platform to evaluate apps within this project and beyond.

Student presentations can facilitate class discussion regarding comparisons of apps as well as quality standards in positive psychology apps. These discussions may include strategies and resources for finding information about apps; considerations of different information sources and strength of evidence; trade-offs and considerations between different aspects, like credibility versus user experience; and debates about what apps may be reasonable to recommend and for what purposes (e.g., populations, disorders, settings, contexts). Sample discussion questions can be found in Appendix 7.2. Additionally, the rubric for grading the presentation can be found in Appendix 7.1.

APPENDIX 7.1: Digital Health Presentation

Student Name:

Presentation Date:

Presentation Topic:

Grade: [Student Score]____/30

Graded Categories:

- Presentation is of appropriate length (20–30 minutes) and provides opportunities for questions and discussion by the class: 3 points.
  1 = insufficient length, too brief; 2 = somewhat inappropriate; 3 = appropriate.

- Presentation provides a clear overview of the product: 4 points.

- Presentation provides an overview of a health domain or problem that the product aims to solve: 2 points.

- Presentation covers the issue of credibility (What scientific evidence, either direct or indirect, supports the digital health product?): 5 points.
  0 = not addressed; 1 = insufficient; 3 = moderately addressed; 5 = fully addressed.

- Presentation covers issues of user experience (How usable/easy to use is the product? What are considerations for diverse audiences/populations?): 5 points.
  0 = not addressed; 1 = insufficient; 3 = moderately addressed; 5 = fully addressed.

- Presentation covers the issue of data security and privacy (Are there actual or hypothetical privacy concerns? Did the presentation consider the terms of service or privacy policy?): 5 points.
  0 = not addressed; 1 = insufficient; 3 = moderately addressed; 5 = fully addressed.

- Clarity of the presentation: The presentation is well-organized and there is sufficient use of visual aids, for example, slides or demonstration videos: 4 points.

- Capacity to answer questions: The presenter is able to respond to questions: 2 points.

Topic	Possible points	Points received
Length	3	
Overview of product	4	
Overview of health area	2	
Credibility	5	
User experience	5	
Data security and privacy	5	
Clarity	4	
Questions	2	
Total	30	

Feedback will be provided on the following areas:

Summary and synthesis:

Positives:

Areas for improvement:

Conclusions:

A printable version of this appendix can be downloaded from the APA website at https://www.apa.org/pubs/books/more-activities-teaching-positive-psychology.

APPENDIX 7.2: Sample Discussion Questions

1. How did you find the information they used to evaluate the quality of the app? What information was hard to find?
2. How did you go about evaluating the app?
3. What aspects of an app are most important to consider and why?
4. What are the warning signs for an app that should not be recommended for use?
5. Would you use this app long-term? Why or why not?
6. Would you recommend it to other people, and if so, for what?

A printable version of this appendix can be downloaded from the APA website at https://www.apa.org/pubs/books/more-activities-teaching-positive-psychology.

REFERENCES

Bates, D. W., Landman, A., & Levine, D. M. (2018). Health apps and health policy: What is needed? *JAMA, 320*(19), 1975–1976. https://doi.org/10.1001/jama.2018.14378

Carpenter, J., Crutchley, P., Zilca, R. D., Schwartz, H. A., Smith, L. K., Cobb, A. M., & Parks, A. C. (2016). Seeing the "big" picture: Big data methods for exploring relationships between usage, language, and outcome in internet intervention data. *Journal of Medical Internet Research, 18*(8), Article e241. https://doi.org/10.2196/jmir.5725

Eisenstadt, M., Liverpool, S., Infanti, E., Ciuvat, R. M., & Carlsson, C. (2021). Mobile apps that promote emotion regulation, positive mental health, and well-being in the general population: Systematic review and meta-analysis. *JMIR Mental Health, 8*(11), Article e31170. https://doi.org/10.2196/31170

Fish, M. T., & Saul, A. D. (2019). The gamification of meditation: A randomized-controlled study of a prescribed mobile mindfulness meditation application in reducing college students' depression. *Simulation & Gaming, 50*(4), 419–435. https://doi.org/10.1177/1046878119851821

Gál, É., tefan, S., & Cristea, I. A. (2021). The efficacy of mindfulness meditation apps in enhancing users' well-being and mental health related outcomes: A meta-analysis of randomized controlled trials. *Journal of Affective Disorders, 279*, 131–142. https://doi.org/10.1016/j.jad.2020.09.134

Goldberg, S. B., Lam, S. U., Simonsson, O., Torous, J., & Sun, S. (2022). Mobile phone-based interventions for mental health: A systematic meta-review of 14 meta-analyses of randomized controlled trials. *PLOS Digital Health, 1*(1), Article e0000002. https://doi.org/10.1371/journal.pdig.0000002

Howells, A., Ivtzan, I., & Eiroa-Orosa, F. J. (2016). Putting the 'app' in happiness: A randomised controlled trial of a smartphone-based mindfulness intervention to enhance wellbeing. *Journal of Happiness Studies, 17*(1), 163–185. https://doi.org/10.1007/s10902-014-9589-1

Hunter, J. F., Olah, M. S., Williams, A. L., Parks, A. C., & Pressman, S. D. (2019). Effect of brief biofeedback via a smartphone app on stress recovery: Randomized experimental study. *JMIR Serious Games, 7*(4), Article e15974. https://doi.org/10.2196/15974

Jake-Schoffman, D. E., Silfee, V. J., Waring, M. E., Boudreaux, E. D., Sadasivam, R. S., Mullen, S. P., Carey, J. L., Hayes, R. B., Ding, E. Y., Bennett, G. G., & Pagoto, S. L. (2017). Methods for evaluating the content, usability, and efficacy of commercial mobile health apps. *JMIR mHealth and uHealth, 5*(12), Article e190. https://doi.org/10.2196/mhealth.8758

Larsen, M. E., Huckvale, K., Nicholas, J., Torous, J., Birrell, L., Li, E., & Reda, B. (2019). Using science to sell apps: Evaluation of mental health app store quality claims. *npj Digital Medicine, 2*(1), Article 18. https://doi.org/10.1038/s41746-019-0093-1

Marshall, J. M., Dunstan, D. A., & Bartik, W. (2020). Clinical or gimmickal: The use and effectiveness of mobile mental health apps for treating anxiety and depression. *The Australian and New Zealand Journal of Psychiatry, 54*(1), 20–28. https://doi.org/10.1177/0004867419876700

Minen, M. T., Stieglitz, E. J., Sciortino, R., & Torous, J. (2018). Privacy issues in smartphone applications: An analysis of headache/migraine applications. *Headache, 58*(7), 1014–1027. https://doi.org/10.1111/head.13341

Neary, M., & Schueller, S. M. (2018). State of the field of mental health apps. *Cognitive and Behavioral Practice, 25*(4), 531–537. https://doi.org/10.1016/j.cbpra.2018.01.002

O'Loughlin, K., Neary, M., Adkins, E. C., & Schueller, S. M. (2019). Reviewing the data security and privacy policies of mobile apps for depression. *Internet Interventions, 15*, 110–115. https://doi.org/10.1016/j.invent.2018.12.001

Parks, A. C., Williams, A. L., Tugade, M. M., Hokes, K. E., Honomichl, R. D., & Zilca, R. D. (2018). Testing a scalable web and smartphone based intervention to improve depression, anxiety, and resilience: A randomized controlled trial. *International Journal of Wellbeing, 8*(2), 22–67. https://doi.org/10.5502/ijw.v8i2.745

Rideout, V., Peebles, A., & Robb, M. B. (2021). *Coping with COVID-19: How young people use digital media to manage their mental health.* Common Sense Media and Hope Lab.

Roepke, A. M., Jaffee, S. R., Riffle, O. M., McGonigal, J., Broome, R., & Maxwell, B. (2015). Randomized controlled trial of SuperBetter, a smartphone-based/internet-based self-help tool to reduce depressive symptoms. *Games for Health Journal, 4*(3), 235–246. https://doi.org/10.1089/g4h.2014.0046

Rosen, K. D., Paniagua, S. M., Kazanis, W., Jones, S., & Potter, J. S. (2018). Quality of life among women diagnosed with breast cancer: A randomized waitlist controlled trial of commercially available mobile app-delivered mindfulness training. *Psycho-Oncology, 27*(8), 2023–2030. https://doi.org/10.1002/pon.4764

Sucala, M., Cuijpers, P., Muench, F., Cardo , R., Soflau, R., Dobrean, A., Achimas-Cadariu, P., & David, D. (2017). Anxiety: There is an app for that. A systematic review of anxiety apps. *Depression and Anxiety, 34*(6), 518–525. https://doi.org/10.1002/da.22654

Worthen-Chaudhari, L., McGonigal, J., Logan, K., Bockbrader, M. A., Yeates, K. O., & Mysiw, W. J. (2017). Reducing concussion symptoms among teenage youth: Evaluation of a mobile health app. *Brain Injury, 31*(10), 1279–1286. https://doi.org/10.1080/02699052.2017.1332388

Wykes, T., Lipshitz, J., & Schueller, S. M. (2019). Towards the design of ethical standards related to digital mental health and all its applications. *Current Treatment Options in Psychiatry, 6*(3), 232–242. https://doi.org/10.1007/s40501-019-00180-0

Using Smartphones to Teach About Self-Report Bias and Accuracy in Well-Being Research

Kostadin Kushlev and Hannah Masling

Students will estimate their phone screen time and then use their smartphones to measure their objective screen time in order to see if subjective and objective measures of screen time are similarly related to well-being.

CONCEPT

Does screen time make us unhappy? Most of what we know about the relationship between screen time and well-being is based on people's self-reported, subjective estimates of their screen time (Orben & Przybylski, 2019; Twenge & Campbell, 2019). Self-reports are often biased, but when bias is systematic, people can still be accurate in their self-reports relative to other people (Mathieu & Gosling, 2012). If everybody underestimates their screen time, for example, self-reports may still accurately reflect how much time a person spends on their phone relative to others. At the end of this activity, students will have an understanding of when it is appropriate to use self-reports to understand the relationship between behavior and well-being.

https://doi.org/10.1037/0000417-008
More Activities for Teaching Positive Psychology: A Guide for Instructors, S. D. Pressman and A. C. Parks (Editors)

MATERIALS NEEDED

Students will need a smartphone to track and measure their screen time.

ACTIVITY SETTING

The activity best takes place in class. While some components of the activity can be completed independently—including students estimating, measuring, and reporting their screen time—the group discussion requires a collaborative setting, like a classroom or Zoom call. This activity can fit well when teaching positive psychology topics, such as research methods in positive psychology, social media and well-being, and digital technology and happiness.

ACTIVITY DURATION

This activity should take 30 minutes. Part 1—estimating, measuring, and reporting students' screen time—should take around 5 minutes. Part 2 (discussion) should take up to 25 minutes. Depending on the instructor's preference, Parts 1 and 2 can be completed in one class session or across two class sessions to allow the instructor to calculate the means and correlations between classes.

SUGGESTED READINGS

- Recommended reading for before the activity:
  - Mathieu and Gosling (2012)
- Recommended reading for after the activity:
  - Ellis et al. (2019)

BACKGROUND AND INSTRUCTIONS

It is well-established that people tend to overestimate how happy they will feel in the future after a positive event (Gilbert & Wilson, 2007). But if everybody overestimates their future happiness, then rank-ordering people, even based on their biased affective forecasts, will still give us an accurate picture of who is actually going to experience more or less happiness in the future (Mathieu & Gosling, 2012). We can apply this same concept of relative accuracy based on systematically biased self-reports to screen time and its relationship to happiness.

Instructors can introduce this activity by posing the question of whether self-reporting is an accurate way to measure screen time. If not, can we trust the existing research on the relationship between screen time and well-being, which is based primarily on self-reports of screen time (Orben & Przybylski, 2019; Twenge & Campbell, 2019)?

After introducing the activity, the instructor will initiate Part 1 by administering an online survey. In the survey, students will first subjectively estimate their screen time and then report their objective screen time as measured by their phones. The survey also includes a measure of positive and negative affect: The Scale of Positive and Negative Experiences (Diener et al., 2010). We provide a template for this survey in the Online Materials section. Instructions and YouTube videos demonstrating the measurement process are linked in the survey. These instructions for each operating system are also available in Appendix 8.1.

In Part 2 of this activity, the instructor will first calculate the means for both estimated and smartphone-measured screen time and display this to the class (see Figure 8.1). Based on past research, we know that people underestimate their phone use (Ellis et al., 2019). These effects are especially pronounced when estimating the number of notifications and phone pickups, but they also apply to screen time. Thus, students' objective measurements of their screen time should, on average, be higher than their subjective estimates. By visualizing this discrepancy between objective and subjective estimates, the instructor can introduce the concept of systematic bias (see Figure A8.2A, also provided as a handout for students in Appendix 8.2).

How is systematic bias different from random measurement error? To answer this question, the instructor will calculate the correlation between the subjective estimates and objectively measured screen time and display this to the class. Being systematically biased means that although people's estimates are not valid measures of the construct, those estimates may still be accurate relative to those

FIGURE 8.1. Subjective Estimates of Screen Time (in Hours/Day) Tend to Be Lower Than Objective Measures

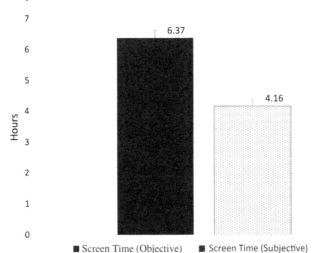

Note. Error bars represent error of the mean. Data from Tibbetts et al. (2021).

of others (Mathieu & Gosling, 2012). Thus, even though people are inaccurate in estimating their true screen time, they can still be accurate in how much time they spend on their phones compared with others. For example, Jim's estimate of his screen time is 4 hours when his actual screen time is 5 hours, whereas Mary's estimate is 3.5 hours when her actual screen time is 4.5 hours. Even though both Jim and Mary are inaccurate in their estimates in the absolute sense, their estimates are accurate relative to each other, as they correctly show that Jim uses his phone more than Mary. Instructors can illustrate this concept of relative accuracy by visualizing the correlation between subjective and objective estimates (in previous research, this correlation was $r = .48$, $p < .001$; Ellis et al., 2019). Alternatively, instructors can show the rank-order correlation between the list of students ordered by subjective and objective measures, which should also be large and positive.

What does this mean for the validity of the existing research on happiness and screen time? To answer this question, the instructor will display a visualization of the correlations of both objective and subjective reports of screen time with an indicator of well-being, such as positive affect. Figures B2 and B3 present the expected correlations of positive affect with subjective and objective measures of screen time, respectively. The weak relationship shown in both figures is consistent with past research showing that screen time is about as weakly related to well-being as eating potatoes (Orben & Przybylski, 2019).

It is always better to use the most valid measure of a given construct. Thus, whenever possible, we should opt to obtain objective measures of screen time. If we have to rely on subjective estimates, however, the validity of our results would depend on the goals of our research. If the goal is to find out how much time people truly spend on their phones, using subjective measures would result in inaccurate results. If, however, the goal is to see how screen time relates to happiness, subjective estimates may be an acceptable measure so long as people are indeed systematically biased.

DISCUSSION

Instructors can stimulate discussion on the validity of self-reports of screen time (Figure 8.1) with the following questions:

1. Are subjective estimates of screen time valid measures of screen time? Because validity refers to the extent to which a measure captures the true value of a construct, the answer is no.

2. If researchers wanted to know how much time people actually spend on their phones, should they use people's subjective measures of screen time?

3. Would the subjective estimates be positively or negatively correlated with the objective reports?

Next, to stimulate discussion on the concept of relative accuracy (Figure B2), instructors may consider the following questions:

1. How would the correlation between objective and self-reported screen time change if people were blindly guessing their screen time versus systematically underestimating it? This question can drive students to realize that the correlation between any variable and random error (noise) is always zero.

2. Would the correlation between objective and self-reported screen time change if people were systematically overestimating their screen time to the same extent as they were underestimating it? Some students may have the incorrect intuition that the sign of the correlation would change, but systematic bias should result in a positive correlation regardless of whether people are systematically underestimating or overestimating.

3. If researchers wanted to see how screen time is related to some other variable, such as gender, personality traits, or stress, would using the subjective estimates be an acceptable substitute for the objective measures?

Finally, instructors should consider broadening the discussion to include the wider implications of this activity for measurement in positive psychology. Though subjective well-being is, by definition, a subjective state, researchers have developed a variety of non-self-report measures of well-being, such as analyzing facial expressions or asking friends and family to report how happy a person is. When should researchers use such non-self-report measures of subjective well-being? Imagine, for example, that people from Country A and Country B are, objectively speaking, equally happy. People from Country A, however, systematically overreport their happiness, and people from Country B underreport their happiness. If a researcher wants to investigate the relationship between income and happiness within each country, the results should be valid because the bias is systematic. Conversely, if a researcher wants to compare how happy people in those two countries are, they will need to find a measure that is not biased in opposite directions within each country. In short, this activity can be used to stimulate discussion around the validity of a range of findings in positive psychology.

ONLINE MATERIALS

All additional online materials, including instructional videos and a Qualtrics survey template, are available on Open Science Framework at https://tinyurl.com/MATPPchap8-1.

Videos are also available on YouTube:

- iOS screen time measure instruction video: https://tinyurl.com/MATPPchap8-2
- Android screen time measure instruction video: https://tinyurl.com/MATPPchap8-3

APPENDIX 8.1: Screen Time Measuring Instructions

iOS (iPhone) Screen Time Measuring Instructions:

- Open the Settings app and click on Screen Time.
- Click on See All Activity, below the bar graph.
- Click on Week, as opposed to Day, at the top of the page.
- With your finger over the bar graph showing Daily Average, swipe once to the right to see the bar graph showing Last Week's Average.
- Record the number under Last Week's Average, above the bar graph, in the survey. This number is the average daily screen time from last week.

Android Screen Time Measuring Instructions:

- Open the Settings app and click on Digital Wellbeing & parental controls.
- Click on the bar graph icon in the top right corner of the page.
- Record the number in the center of the screen, under Daily Average Screen Time. This number is the average daily screen time from last week.

A printable version of this appendix can be downloaded from the APA website at https://www.apa.org/pubs/books/more-activities-teaching-positive-psychology.

APPENDIX 8.2: Activity Figures

The figures illustrate the difference between absolute and relative accuracy. Even though subjective estimates of screen time tend to be, on average, lower than objectively measured screen time (Figure A8.2A), both subjective and objective screen time are similarly related to positive affect (Figures A8.2B and A8.2C).

FIGURE A8.2A. Subjective Estimates of Screen Time (in Hours/Day) Tend to Be Lower Than Objective Measures

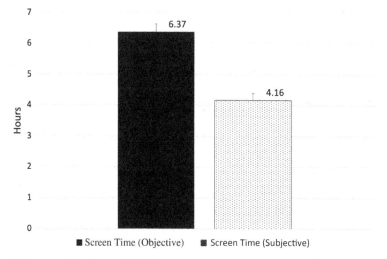

Note. Data from Tibbetts et al. (2021).

FIGURE A8.2B. Relationship Between Subjective Estimates of Phone Screen Time and Positive Affect (Scale of Positive and Negative Experiences)

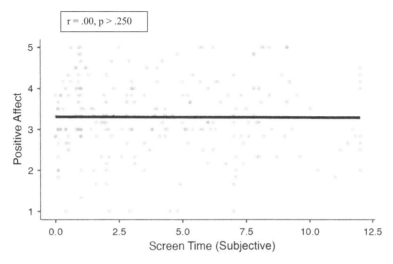

Note. Data from Tibbetts et al. (2021).

FIGURE A8.2C. Relationship Between Objective Measures of Phone Screen Time and Positive Affect (Scale of Positive and Negative Experiences)

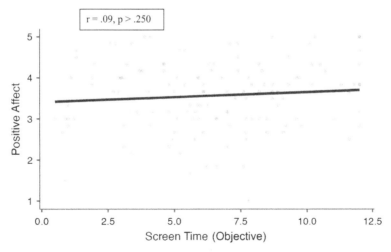

Note. Data from Tibbetts et al. (2021).

A printable version of this appendix can be downloaded from the APA website at https://www.apa.org/pubs/books/more-activities-teaching-positive-psychology.

REFERENCES

Diener, E., Wirtz, D., Tov, W., Kim-Prieto, C., Choi, D., Oishi, S., & Biswas-Diener, R. (2010). New well-being measures: Short scales to assess flourishing and positive and negative feelings. *Social Indicators Research, 97*(2), 143–156. https://doi.org/10.1007/s11205-009-9493-y

Ellis, D. A., Davidson, B. I., Shaw, H., & Geyer, K. (2019). Do smartphone usage scales predict behavior? *International Journal of Human–Computer Studies, 130*, 86–92. https://doi.org/10.1016/j.ijhcs.2019.05.004

Gilbert, D. T., & Wilson, T. D. (2007). Prospection: Experiencing the future. *Science, 317*(5843), 1351–1354. https://doi.org/10.1126/science.1144161

Mathieu, M. T., & Gosling, S. D. (2012). The accuracy or inaccuracy of affective forecasts depends on how accuracy is indexed: A meta-analysis of past studies. *Psychological Science, 23*(2), 161–162. https://doi.org/10.1177/0956797611427044

Orben, A., & Przybylski, A. K. (2019). The association between adolescent well-being and digital technology use. *Nature Human Behaviour, 3*(2), 173–182. https://doi.org/10.1038/s41562-018-0506-1

Tibbetts, M., Epstein-Shuman, A., Leitao, M., & Kushlev, K. (2021). A week during COVID-19: Online social interactions are associated with greater connection and more stress. *Computers in Human Behavior Reports, 4*, Article 100133. https://doi.org/10.1016/j.chbr.2021.100133

Twenge, J. M., & Campbell, W. K. (2019). Media use is linked to lower psychological well-being: Evidence from three datasets. *Psychiatric Quarterly, 90*(2), 311–331. https://doi.org/10.1007/s11126-019-09630-7

II

CHANGING AND TRACKING PSYCHOLOGICAL WELL-BEING

INTRODUCTION: CHANGING AND TRACKING PSYCHOLOGICAL WELL-BEING

This section focuses on some of the more classic interventions and experiments you will find in positive psychology textbooks, as well as many new activities that will help you highlight important concepts in standard lectures. These chapters will be easy to integrate into the typical course given that they match well on to classic topics such as strengths, awe, gratitude, mood, and spirituality. We anticipate that many of these activities will have robust effects on student well-being and will be highly impactful; for this reason, we suggest doing at least one as early as possible in the course (to convince students you have something special to offer), and one or more right at the end (to leave them on a powerful note). One thing to consider is that some of these activities will require homework,[1] mood tracking, or out-of-class activities, so we recommend that you read over the activities well in advance so that you can position them during the appropriate time of the week (e.g., on a Friday so that students can collect data over the weekend) and that you allot enough class time for the activity. These types of activities work well as assignments that happen regularly throughout the course (e.g., self-experimentation papers constituting 10% of the final grade; ask them to do one every 2–3 weeks). Importantly, prior to doing the activities in this section, recall Figure 1 in the prologue to this book, which discusses factors that influence the effectiveness of positive psychology activities and interventions. This will be an important figure to come back to as you go through this section since not all activities will work equally well for all of your students.

In this section, your students will first be invited to enhance their levels of gratitude in a new and powerful way: by expressing gratitude to someone who is no longer around to thank. Next, students will explore the power of awe to change feelings of connection and humility, followed by a related experiential

---

[1] Note that we mark an asterisk in the Table of Contents on activities that will require discussion in more than one lecture.

exercise on the impressive well-being benefits of nature, even when observed on video or in nearby places. Students will also have their first opportunity to meditate by drawing on and reliving a sacred experience from a treasure trove of favorite memories. The next three exercises focus on having students better understand how they can take advantage of positive psychology constructs to improve their day-to-day life. The first activity invites students to attempt a difficult task—planning a perfectly happy day—something that they will soon discover is impossible and thus is a great A-HA! moment to invite your students to experience early in your course. This could, however, easily be complemented by the next activity on uplifts, or the daily positive experiences that we have. It is easy to miss those, despite them being more common than attention-grabbing stressors, but the secret is to learn to notice them more, and this exercise invites students to do so. Finally, we end this section with a classic strengths-discovery exercise, where students learn about their signature strengths, accompanied by a helpful activity and discussion on how students can integrate those into their daily lives and futures. We expect that several of these activities could easily be the highlight of your course, and the only hard thing you will find is how to decide which ones to use.

9

The Virtual Gratitude Visit

Robert A. Emmons

The Virtual Gratitude Visit (VGV) is an activity that involves expressing gratitude to a person who is not physically present by using the empty chair technique.

CONCEPT

Gratitude visits are typically conducted in person. But what if the person you are grateful to is no longer alive or otherwise unavailable? The use of VGV is recommended in those instances, as well as for people who cannot profit from the existing interventions requiring writing or perhaps those who prefer to express their gratitude verbally.

MATERIALS NEEDED

Two chairs, paper, and a pencil/pen to write about the experience.

ACTIVITY SETTING

The activity can be performed in your own home or in another setting where you feel comfortable and have some degree of privacy. This activity works well for both in-person and online teaching.

https://doi.org/10.1037/0000417-009
More Activities for Teaching Positive Psychology: A Guide for Instructors, S. D. Pressman and A. C. Parks (Editors)

ACTIVITY DURATION

The activity requires 30 minutes of in-class instruction and description of the exercise, 10 minutes of role-playing, and then 30 minutes at home where the activity is performed.

SUGGESTED READING

Recommended reading for before the activity:

- D. J. Tomasulo (2019)

BACKGROUND AND INSTRUCTIONS

Have you ever had the desire to thank a person who has touched your life in a special way, but you never did so? What if that person is no longer around? This activity provides you with the opportunity to say thank you even if the other person is not physically present.

For this activity, two chairs are arranged: one for the expresser or sender of gratitude and the second (auxiliary) empty chair for the receiver of the gratitude (the unavailable other). The expresser arranges the chairs in a way that symbolically depicts the relationship. You may place the chairs close to each other, far apart, side by side, or one behind the other. Having swum in the waters of academia all my life, I have always been intrigued by the variety of ways in which professors arrange the chairs and desks in their offices. It is not random. The chairs' arrangement sets the emotional tone for the encounter, a procedure modeled after standard therapeutic practices, especially those incorporating elements of psychodramas. A psychodrama is an emotionally expressive therapeutic technique with foundations in experiential forms of therapy. The participant is asked to reenact specific scenes or past experiences in the context of meaningful personal relationships. The method allows the person to recognize and express feelings that they could not express during a previous time in their life. The VGV was designed by positive psychologist Dan Tomasulo, and much of the description here is based on a publication (D. J. Tomasulo, 2019). While you may think of virtual as a world created by a computer, virtual here is something that exists in the mind, in essence, without a physical presence but appears to be present. You will be imagining the presence of an important person or being who will not be physically present during the activity; thus, it is virtual.

The expresser sits in his or her chair and expresses gratitude and appreciation toward the imagined other in the empty chair. Typically, the person looks at the empty chair directly and expresses the imagined individual statements of appreciation. To give an example of an exchange, the expresser may say,

> Dad, I appreciated that you always volunteered to coach me in Little League and took the time to take us on family vacations every summer. You made sure we

spent time together, and even as I got older and more independent, you always showed an interest in what I was doing.

Following this (and perhaps several other statements deepening the expression of gratitude), the expresser reverses roles and becomes the receiver. In doing so, the expresser responds as if the gratitude had just been expressed to him or her. In the above example, the expresser reversed roles and became his dad and responded,

> It was not an easy decision to quit my job to stay home and raise you. But I am so glad that it worked out for us financially. Spending time with you was one of my favorite things to do. I am so proud of the man you've become and so grateful to be your dad.

The expresser then returns to the original chair, saying a closing remark to the empty chair. This ends the enactment. I have used this technique in online classes I have taught with students of all ages, and they describe it as extraordinarily powerful and meaningful. I have also tried it out myself. You cannot genuinely endorse a practice that you yourself have not experienced! Therefore, I recommend you try this activity yourself before you assign it.

The full set of instructions for the homework activity is available in Appendix 9.1, but I recommend first explaining the concept and going over some examples in class prior to having students try it at home on their own. Please see the Discussion section for some possible talking points, research examples, and ideas on whom to express gratitude toward. Speaking to an empty chair may feel a little awkward at first. That is to be expected! Do not let this deter you. In fact, you may actually feel more comfortable with the other person not present. Research shows that we often worry about how our expressions of thanks are received and fear that the receiver will feel embarrassed by them (Kumar & Epley, 2018).

DISCUSSION

Gratitude is the awareness that we have benefitted from the actions of another person or agent. It is one of the deepest touch points of human existence. Gratitude is the recognition of all that holds us in the web of life and all that has made it possible to have the moment we are experiencing. Science has revealed that the practice of gratitude generates a positive ripple effect through every area of our lives, potentially satisfying some of our deepest yearnings—our desire for happiness, our pursuit of better relationships, and our ceaseless quest for inner peace, health, wholeness, and contentment. Gratitude widens the perceptual field and helps us to see the big picture of the opportunities in it. If we have learned anything from the science of gratitude (and we have learned a lot!), it is that there is no flourishing, no resilience, and no thriving without the capacity to give thanks. Simply stated, gratitude works! It heals, energizes, and changes lives (Emmons, 2013, 2016).

Gratitude is more, though, than a tool for self-improvement. Gratitude is a way of life. As an essential element of human flourishing, it is critical to harmonious functioning, an amplifier of goodness in oneself, the world, and others. Empirical research conducted into the nature and effects of gratitude over the last 2 decades has uncovered numerous beneficial consequences of experiencing and expressing gratitude. Study after study declares its benefits for psychological, physical, relational, and spiritual flourishing. People who live gratefully are more generally appreciative of the positive in themselves, others, and the world. Not only does gratitude enhance physical health, lead to better coping, and foster resilience, but grateful feelings also increase other positive emotions and life satisfaction, and, perhaps most uniquely, gratitude facilitates the development and maintenance of friendships (Algoe et al., 2020; Armenta et al., 2022; Gallagher et al., 2021; Russell et al., 2023).

The VGV exercise is powerful as it is in the context of relationships where the power and potency of gratitude (or lack thereof) is most clearly exhibited. Gratitude is the fuel that keeps relationships going and growing every day, preventing them from sputtering and conking out. The essence of gratitude is living in a vital awareness of the good that has been done for us day in and day out. The VGV allows us to express our gratitude to a significant person, even if that person is no longer accessible to us. When we are grateful, we are moved by the wish to return the good that we have received. Nothing is more characteristic of gratitude than this, and perhaps there is nothing as frustrating as being blocked in the desire to thank others by making a reciprocating gift that is adequate to the one we have received (Kronman, 2017). Research by O'Connell et al. (2017) focused on the enhanced power of expressing gratitude to others. They compared a gratitude journal group (reflection only) to a similar group that also verbally expressed their gratitude (expression + reflection). The researchers found an advantage to expressed gratitude over and above the private, reflection condition or the control group. In the expressing-to-others group, negative emotions and depression decreased, which provided greater emotional balance. The authors concluded that other-oriented gratitude is enhanced when it is outwardly expressed (O'Connell et al., 2017). This research moves away from sole written expression to a powerful form of verbal expression to another. The VGV employs this essence of verbal expression to others by using an empty chair in the way of a psychodramatic role-play.

The VGV is extremely valuable for at least one other reason: It highlights both the intention of the giver and the perceived receptivity of the receiver. Helping us imagine how another person might receive expressions of thanks may make us better receivers ourselves. Empirical research has shown that people underestimate both the positive impact of expressing gratitude and the surprise that such expressions have on the recipient (Kumar & Epley, 2018).

As an intervention, gratitude has been at the core of the positive psychology movement. One of the first positive interventions studied was the gratitude visit, where participants wrote and delivered letters of gratitude to people whom they felt they had not adequately thanked (Seligman et al., 2005). One of the more frequently used exercises for gratitude is the gratitude letter and visit. Expressing gratitude to others can have a significant effect on health and happiness. Previous research has studied the effect of the *gratitude letter*: a letter in which gratitude is expressed to another person. A study by Lyubomirsky et al. (2011) found that compared with their nonmotivated counterparts, motivated participants reported improved overall well-being and fewer depressive symptoms at the end of the intervention. In addition, motivated participants also showed improved well-being at the 6-month follow-up and reductions in depressive symptoms at the 9-month follow-up (Lyubomirsky et al., 2011; see also Seligman et al., 2005).

It may be useful to compare the gratitude letter to the VGV, for they share some similarities. The instructions for the letter can be found in Appendix 9.2.

In comparison with other interventions, those who performed the gratitude visit were found to be the least depressed and the happiest of all the participants. Gratitude has also been found to enhance self-esteem (McCullough et al., 2002), life satisfaction (Kashdan et al., 2006), prosocial behavior (Wood et al., 2008), and interpersonal relationships (Algoe et al., 2020; Tsang, 2007), and it was noted by Lyubomirsky et al. (2005) as one of the leading interventions that can contribute to sustainable happiness.

The traditional methods and research on the gratitude letter and visit can be modified and restyled with the VGV. First, most evidence-based interventions concerning gratitude involve writing and reading through the use of journals and letters and sharing of the same. As O'Connell et al. (2017) highlighted, expressive writing is only one means by which a therapeutic improvement can happen. Since the VGV uses an enactment of feelings of gratitude in role-plays with an empty chair, it liberates the technique from a written procedure. This unscripted enactment has the potential to reap the benefits of expressing gratitude toward others yet can be accomplished without them present. Drama therapy (D. Tomasulo & Szucs, 2015), psychodrama (Fong, 2006), and role-playing (Nikzadeh & Soudani, 2016) are all methodologies that have been shown to offer emotional benefits (Kipper & Ritchie, 2003). Additionally, the usefulness of the VGV as a nonreading and nonwriting intervention could have tremendous value for the more than 775 million adults in the world who are illiterate ("List of Countries by Literacy Rate," 2017). Interventions that can address the need to deliver the advantages of expressing gratitude to these typically underrepresented individuals deserve research and application attention.

Second, the delivery of a gratitude letter as initially intended involves the availability of a live recipient. As the VGV uses role-playing with an empty chair to enact a gratitude visit, the activity can include others who are unavailable. This significantly broadens the applicability of the technique. More specifically, using this empty chair approach may be helpful in four ways:

1. The person one has gratitude for may no longer be living, and an enactment would be one way to activate the positive effects of the relationship.

2. The person may be alive yet unavailable. As an example, it may be a person from childhood who has moved or a friend with whom one has lost contact.

3. As internal family systems have shown, there may be parts of ourselves that we have gratitude toward (e.g., a time when we had more resilience, grit,

joy in our lives). An enactment with these parts may be helpful in activating strength from another memory point in time. Role-playing allows this type of intrapsychic exploration of gratitude to take place.

4. Expressing gratitude toward a higher power or entity through an enactment may be particularly helpful. Research has shown that gratitude to God and other spiritual beings are frequently experienced emotions.

The VGV is highly promising, but to date, its effects have not been systematically studied or quantified. Therefore, the need for randomized controlled trials on its effectiveness is important, especially as compared with the more traditional letter/visit and gratitude journaling.

The famous humanitarian Dr. Albert Schweitzer (1955; as cited in Anderson, 1955) once said, "At times our own light goes out and is rekindled by a spark from another person. Each of us has cause to think with deep gratitude of those who have lighted the flame within us" (p. 7). This activity allows you to reflect on the person who lit your flame.

ASSIGNMENT

Here are some questions (also in Appendix 9.1) that students can reflect on following the exercise. They can write down their reactions immediately after the home activity, which then can be shared in a subsequent class session:

1. What is something that stood out to you about this exercise?

2. What is something that you will remember and take away from this exercise?

3. What aspects of the VGV were difficult or uncomfortable for you? Why?

4. Has this exercise helped you think differently about gratitude or the person to whom you expressed your thanks?

5. A prominent neuroscientist recently said, "The intentional practice of gratitude could have significant positive implications for the harmony of the human civilization, from interpersonal relationships to international diplomacy" (Henning et al., 2017, Neuroscientist section). Do you agree or disagree with this statement? Why? Can you draw a connection between your personal practice of the VGV and the interpersonal harmony that is described in this quote?

ONLINE MATERIALS

- An antidote to dissatisfaction: https://tinyurl.com/MATPPchap9-1
- An experiment in gratitude: The science of happiness: https://tinyurl.com/MATPPchap9-2
- Ben-Shahar & Tomasulo (2017)
- Seligman (2009)
- D. J. Tomasulo (2012)

APPENDIX 9.1: Instructions for Student Take-Home Activity

This activity allows you to express your gratitude to someone you can no longer thank. They may have passed away, or you may have lost touch with them. Think about what you would like to say to them in preparation for this activity. There is no need to prepare anything else.

Get two chairs and arrange them in a way that represents your relationship with the person. They can be close together, far apart, side by side, or one behind the other.

Once you are happy with the setup, sit in one chair and express your gratitude and appreciation to the imagined person in the empty chair. Look directly at the empty chair and tell the imagined person what you are grateful for. For example, you might say,

> Dad, I appreciated that you always volunteered to coach me in Little League and took the time to take us on family vacations every summer. You made sure we spent time together, and even as I got older and more independent, you always showed an interest in what I was doing.

Follow this with any other statements of gratitude you have for the person.

Once you are finished, switch roles and become the receiver. Now respond as if the gratitude had just been expressed to you. Become the person you are thanking and say what you think they would say. In the above example, the dad might reply,

> It was not an easy decision to quit my job to stay home and raise you. But I am so glad that it worked out for us financially. Spending time with you was one of my favorite things to do. I am so proud of the man you have become and so grateful to be your father.

Return to your original chair and say a closing remark to the empty chair. Writing reflections on the activity:

1. What is something that stood out to you about this exercise?

2. What is something that you will remember and take away from this exercise?

3. What aspects of the VGV were difficult or uncomfortable for you? Why?

4. Has this exercise helped you think differently about gratitude or the person to whom you expressed your thanks?

5. A prominent neuroscientist recently said, "The intentional practice of gratitude could have significant positive implications for the harmony of the human civilization, from interpersonal relationships to international diplomacy" (Henning et al., 2017, Neuroscientist section). Do you agree or disagree with this statement? Why? Can you draw a connection between your personal practice of the VGV and the interpersonal harmony that is described in this quote?

Note. Data from Tomasulo (2019).

A printable version of this appendix can be downloaded from the APA website at https://www.apa.org/pubs/books/more-activities-teaching-positive-psychology.

APPENDIX 9.2: Gratitude Letter Instructions (as a Point of Comparison With the VGV)

Call to mind someone who did something for you for which you are extremely grateful but to whom you never expressed your deep gratitude. This could be a relative, friend, teacher, or colleague. Try to pick someone who is still alive and could meet you face-to-face in the next week. It may be most helpful to select a person or act that you haven't thought about for a while—something that isn't always on your mind.

Now, write a letter to one of these people, guided by the following steps:

- Write as though you are addressing this person directly ("Dear _____").

- Don't worry about grammar or spelling.

- Describe in specific terms what this person did, why you are grateful to this person, and how this person's behavior affected your life. Try to be as concrete as possible.

- Describe what you are doing in your life now and how you often remember their efforts.

- Try to keep your letter to roughly one page (around 300 words).

Next, you should try, if at all possible, to deliver your letter in person, following these steps:

- Plan a visit with the recipient. Let that person know you'd like to see them and have something special to share, but don't reveal the exact purpose of the meeting.

- When you meet, let the person know that you are grateful to them and would like to read a letter expressing your gratitude; ask that they refrain from interrupting until you're done.

- Take your time reading the letter. While you read, pay attention to their reaction as well as your own.

- After you have read the letter, be receptive to their reaction and discuss your feelings together.

- Remember to give the letter to the person when you leave.

A printable version of this appendix can be downloaded from the APA website at https://www.apa.org/pubs/books/more-activities-teaching-positive-psychology.

REFERENCES

Algoe, S. B., Dwyer, P. C., Younge, A., & Oveis, C. (2020). A new perspective on the social functions of emotions: Gratitude and the witnessing effect. *Journal of Personality and Social Psychology, 119*(1), 40–74. https://doi.org/10.1037/pspi0000202

Anderson, E. (1955). *The world of Albert Schweitzer: A book of photographs.* Harper & Brothers.

Armenta, C. N., Fritz, M. M., Walsh, L. C., & Lyubomirsky, S. (2022). Satisfied yet striving: Gratitude fosters life satisfaction and improvement motivation in youth. *Emotion, 22*(5), 1004–1016. https://doi.org/10.1037/emo0000896

Ben-Shahar, T., & Tomasulo, D. (2017). *Happier TV* [Video]. YouTube. https://www.youtube.com/watch?v=Vkk_Db_3Jww

Emmons, R. A. (2013). *Gratitude works! A twenty-one day program for creating emotional prosperity.* Jossey-Bass.

Emmons, R. A. (2016). *The little book of gratitude.* Gaia.

Fong, J. (2006). Psychodrama as a preventative measure: Teenage girls confronting violence. *Journal of Group Psychotherapy, Psychodrama & Sociometry, 59*(3), 99–108. https://doi.org/10.3200/JGPP.59.3.99-108

Gallagher, S., Creaven, A. M., Howard, S., Ginty, A. T., & Whittaker, A. C. (2021). Gratitude, social support and cardiovascular reactivity to acute psychological stress. *Biological Psychology, 162*, Article 108090. https://doi.org/10.1016/j.biopsycho.2021.108090

Henning, M., Fox, G. R., Kaplan, J., Damasio, H., & Damasio, A. (2017). A potential role for mu-opioids in mediating the positive effects of gratitude. *Frontiers in Psychology, 8*, Article 868. https://doi.org/10.3389/fpsyg.2017.00868

Kashdan, T. B., Uswatte, G., & Julian, T. (2006). Gratitude and hedonic and eudaimonic well-being in Vietnam war veterans. *Behaviour Research and Therapy, 44*(2), 177–199. https://doi.org/10.1016/j.brat.2005.01.005

Kipper, D. A., & Ritchie, T. D. (2003). The effectiveness of psychodramatic techniques: A meta-analysis. *Group Dynamics: Theory, Research, and Practice, 7*(1), 13–25. https://doi.org/10.1037/1089-2699.7.1.13

Kronman, A. T. (2017). *Confessions of a born-again pagan.* Yale University Press.

Kumar, A., & Epley, N. (2018). Undervaluing gratitude: Expressers misunderstand the consequences of showing appreciation. *Psychological Science, 29*(9), 1423–1435. https://doi.org/10.1177/0956797618772506

List of countries by literacy rate. (2021, April). In *Wikipedia, the free encyclopedia.* https://en.wikipedia.org/wiki/List_of_countries_by_literacy_rate

Lyubomirsky, S., Dickerhoof, R., Boehm, J. K., & Sheldon, K. M. (2011). Becoming happier takes both a will and a proper way: An experimental longitudinal intervention to boost well-being. *Emotion, 11*(2), 391–402. https://doi.org/10.1037/a0022575

Lyubomirsky, S., Sheldon, K. M., & Schkade, D. (2005). Pursuing happiness: The architecture of sustainable change. *Review of General Psychology, 9*(2), 111–131. https://doi.org/10.1037/1089-2680.9.2.111

McCullough, M. E., Emmons, R. A., & Tsang, J. A. (2002). The grateful disposition: A conceptual and empirical topography. *Journal of Personality and Social Psychology, 82*(1), 112–127. https://doi.org/10.1037/0022-3514.82.1.112

Nikzadeh, E., & Soudani, M. (2016). Evaluating the effectiveness of drama therapy by psychodrama method on psychological well-being and false beliefs of addicts. *Review of European Studies, 8*(3), 148–155. https://doi.org/10.5539/res.v8n3p148

O'Connell, B. H., O'Shea, D., & Gallagher, S. (2017). Feeling thanks and saying thanks: A randomized controlled trial examining if and how socially oriented gratitude journals work. *Journal of Clinical Psychology, 73*(10), 1280–1300. https://doi.org/10.1002/jclp.22469

Russell, P. S., Frackowiak, M., Cohen-Chen, S., Rusconi, P., & Fasoli, F. (2023). Induced gratitude and hope, and experienced fear, but not experienced disgust, facilitate COVID-19 prevention. *Cognition and Emotion, 37*(2), 196–219. https://doi.org/10.1080/02699931.2022.2157377

Seligman, M. E. P. (2009). *The gratitude visit* [Video]. YouTube. https://www.youtube.com/watch?v=iptEvstz6_M

Seligman, M. E. P., Steen, T. A., Park, N., & Peterson, C. (2005). Positive psychology progress: Empirical validation of interventions. *American Psychologist, 60*(5), 410–421. https://doi.org/10.1037/0003-066X.60.5.410

Tomasulo, D. J. (2012). *Virtual gratitude visit* [Video]. YouTube. https://www.youtube.com/watch?v=izGmSvOmYXc

Tomasulo, D. J. (2019). The Virtual Gratitude Visit (VGV): Using psychodrama and role-playing as a positive intervention. In L. E. van Zyl & S. Rothmann, Sr. (Eds.), *Positive psychological intervention design and protocols for multi-cultural contexts* (pp. 405–413). Springer. https://doi.org/10.1007/978-3-030-20020-6_18

Tomasulo, D., & Szucs, A. (2015). The ACTing cure: Evidence-based group treatment for people with intellectual disabilities. *Dramatherapy, 37*(2–3), 100–115. https://doi.org/10.1080/02630672.2016.1162824

Tsang, J. (2007). Gratitude for small and large favors: A behavioral test. *The Journal of Positive Psychology, 2*(3), 157–167. https://doi.org/10.1080/17439760701229019

Wood, A. M., Joseph, S., & Maltby, J. (2008). Gratitude uniquely predicts satisfaction with life: Incremental validity above the domains and facets of the five factor model. *Personality and Individual Differences, 45*(1), 49–54. https://doi.org/10.1016/j.paid.2008.02.019

10

Awe Outing

Emiliana Simon-Thomas and Dacher Keltner

Dedicate a 15-minute outing to delving into your sense of wonder and curiosity about what you see, hear, and take in with your senses, as if you are encountering the world around you for the very first time.

CONCEPT

People most often experience awe as an energizing, inspiring, and uplifting emotion when they are in novel, physically vast, and expectation-defying contexts. Awe often comes with neck tingles and feelings of warmth and expansion around the chest and is expressed with raised eyebrows and a partly open-mouthed "wow." With deliberate intention, people can feel awe anyplace—even about mundane and ordinary things, such as walking in a city, listening to music, or seeing seasonal changes in foliage. The awe outing is a way to evoke awe by approaching day-to-day experiences with more inquiry, openness, and observation. Awe experiences promote interpersonal humility and connectedness and motivate moral behaviors, and the overall propensity for awe predicts greater well-being in life.

MATERIALS NEEDED

No materials other than time and space are needed for an awe outing. If you are going to do this as a group activity, you will need to choose an indoor (e.g., library, art gallery or studio, exhibit space) or outdoor (e.g., courtyard, plaza,

https://doi.org/10.1037/0000417-010
More Activities for Teaching Positive Psychology: A Guide for Instructors, S. D. Pressman and A. C. Parks (Editors)

campus walking path) destination. If students are going to do this on their own, they will need to print Appendix 10.1 with the instructions and take it with them. If you plan to do a virtual awe outing, you will need to select an awe-eliciting video and secure equipment to project the video on the largest available screen.

ACTIVITY SETTING

The most promising setting for an awe outing is outdoors where there is some nature—parks, areas with trees and lawns, or gardens—away from the reminders and pressures of everyday demands. While it is easier to evoke awe during outings immersed in unfamiliar terrain, it is also possible to conduct an awe outing indoors or at a frequently visited site. Awe outings can be done alone or together in groups. It is even possible to do an awe outing virtually, by watching an awe-inspiring video.

ACTIVITY DURATION

In principle, leading an awe outing takes 25 minutes: 5 minutes for introduction and getting to a designated location, 15 minutes to traverse and explore the location with an undistracted sense of open-minded inquisitiveness, and 5 minutes to debrief and return to the classroom location. A virtual awe outing can take less time (e.g., 15 minutes), as awe-eliciting video segments are often 5 minutes long.

SUGGESTED READINGS

- Recommended readings for before the activity:
  - The Science of Awe White Paper from the Greater Good Science Center: https://tinyurl.com/MATPPch10-1
  - Monroy and Keltner (2023)
  - Sturm et al. (2022)
- Optional readings for after the activity:
  - Piff et al. (2015)
  - Six Ways to Incorporate Awe Into Your Daily Life: https://tinyurl.com/MATPPch10-2
  - Anderson et al. (2018)

BACKGROUND AND INSTRUCTIONS

Awe is the feeling of being in the presence of something incredible that challenges our understanding of the world, like a full moon brimming over the horizon, crashing waves in front of an endless sea, or the fruits of someone's extraordinary creativity, courage, or kindness. When people feel awe, they may use other words to describe the experience, such as wonder, amazement, surprise, or transcendence. It is the easiest to feel awe in newer surroundings, where aspects of the physical space are grand, surprising, and unfamiliar—in places that have two key features: vastness and novelty. But with the right outlook, we can experience awe in almost any setting, turning routine moments into flashes of inspiration and wonder.

The first step to adopting an outlook of awe is to ask: What is mysterious or novel about whatever is in front of me right now? No matter where you are, you can evoke awe by purposefully noticing whatever is coming into your senses (e.g., humid air, angular urban skyline, the fragrance of cut grass) and inquiring into what seems impossibly complex or unknown about the different things you see (e.g., How does planetary weather work? How many people built this city and what was there and how did it look before? How does grass keep growing and why does my brain recognize this smell?).

The second step is to adopt a calm, welcoming stance—to embrace and admire the vast unknown. Infusing an outing with awe can turn ordinary time into a series of awe-inspiring moments filled with delightful, humbling surprises.

Sometimes, it can feel like we are at the center of our own universe, fixated on our personal concerns without much regard for other people or outside issues. Experiencing awe can lift us out of this self-focused mindset, stirring feelings of wonder and inspiration by reminding us that we are a part of something larger than ourselves and that our true interests actually go beyond self-focused concerns.

PAST RESEARCH ON AWE

Researchers define *awe* as a response to things that we perceive as vast and that challenge the typical ways that we interpret and understand the world (Monroy & Keltner, 2023). Research suggests that experiencing awe not only enhances happiness and physical health but also reduces feelings of entitlement and increases generosity.

While there's no single explanation for why humans experience awe, a leading idea is that awe fosters humility, which can reduce fear and aggression, unite collective responses in the face of potential threats, and smooth conflictual dynamics related to social hierarchy and power.

It may seem as though to experience awe, we must travel to distant lands, but there are many opportunities closer to home—we just need to seek them out and adopt the outlook to notice them. The awe outing practice helps you do just that.

Studies suggest that feeling awe has a way of lifting people outside of their usual routine and connecting them with something greater and more significant (Monroy & Keltner, 2023). This sense of broader connectedness and purpose can help relieve negative moods and enhance happiness, and it can also make people more generous as they become less focused on themselves. Evoking feelings of awe may be especially helpful when you feel bogged down by day-to-day hassles.

In one study of the effects of awe outings on well-being (Sturm et al., 2022), a group of older adult volunteers was randomly assigned to take 15-minute walking awe outings (like this activity) every week for 8 weeks. Another comparison group was instructed to take regular 15-minute walks every week for 8 weeks. The awe walkers felt more joy, compassion, and appreciation during their walks and also felt more compassionate and less distressed in daily life. Selfie photos that they took during their awe walks showed bigger, more robust smile expressions, and the awe walkers positioned themselves lower down in the camera frame—an indication of having a "smaller self," a sign of humility which is associated with kind and helpful behavior.

In another study, one group of people stood in a grove of towering eucalyptus trees and gazed up for 1 minute; a second comparison group looked up at a plain concrete wall, also for a full minute (Piff et al., 2015). Afterward, a member of the research team "accidentally" spilled a bunch of pens on the ground. People who had looked up at the trees reported feeling awe and offered more help (they picked up more pens); they also reported being less materialistic, self-focused, and entitled to preferential treatment (Piff et al., 2015).

For the great scientist Albert Einstein, awe and wonder are the sources of what is best about humans: our capacity to create art, to do science, and to discover things about the world. Brief awe practices like the awe outing support this thinking that experiences of awe lead to more rigorous thought, deeper curiosity, a more spacious sense of time, and healthier minds and bodies.

Before sending students off (with the full set of Awe Outing instructions listed in Appendix 10.1), you should recommend locations for them to go to (see ideas below) and remind them to put their mobile devices out of reach or only use them for awe-related photos. It might help to take three deep breaths (6-second inhale, 7-second exhale) as a group beforehand and encourage everyone to take this kind of breath again if they find themselves distracted from their awe outing, for example, if thoughts about their everyday duties and concerns come to mind. You could say,

> For this awe outing, please give yourself more time and space than you usually would to observe, wonder, and ask big questions in your mind. Try to immerse yourself in inquiry about the mystery and beauty of things, like "How does this leaf exist?" and notice when you might be experiencing awe. If you get distracted, that's okay; just take a deep breath, 6 seconds in and 7 seconds out, and try again to look closely, listen carefully, feel deeply, and inquire about what is around you.

RECOMMENDED LOCATIONS FOR AWE OUTINGS

Here are some specific ideas for awe outing destinations to suggest to your students.

Natural Settings

- a local park or garden
- a hilltop with panoramic views
- a path or trail lined with tall trees
- the shore of an ocean, lake, river, or waterfall
- a clear night when you can see the stars
- a place where you can watch a sunset or sunrise

Urban Settings

- a yard, low-traffic sidewalk, or school playground
- the top of a skyscraper, or look up in an area dense with tall buildings
- a historic monument
- a part of your city that you've never explored before
- a large ballpark or stadium
- a city art locale and explore different galleries
- botanical gardens or a zoo to see plants and animal species you've never seen before
- go around with no destination in mind and see where it takes you

Indoor Settings

- a library
- a gallery or hallway with art on the walls
- a planetarium or aquarium
- a historic mansion, cathedral, or opera house
- go slowly around a museum, giving your full attention to each piece

Virtual Setting

- To conduct a video-based awe outing, check out the 360° virtual awe outing listed in the Online Materials section.

DISCUSSION

Here are some questions that might help promote a classroom discussion after the awe outing:

- What are some examples of awe experiences that you have had?

- Why do you think people feel awe in the first place? Can you think of an advantage that experiencing awe might provide that makes it helpful to human survival?

- What does awe feel like? Did you experience any notable physical sensations?

- Does awe impact your thinking? Did you notice any new kind of understanding or have any special thoughts or cool ideas?

- Does awe change how you feel about yourself, other people, or your social connections—both close others and humanity at large?

- What are the benefits of awe?

- How can we cultivate awe in our daily lives?

- What are the challenges of conducting awe research?

- What arc some future directions for awe research?

Research on awe is still in its early stages, and there are a number of limitations that need to be addressed in future studies. One limitation is that the majority of awe research has been conducted in Western cultures. It is important to replicate these findings in other cultures to see if awe feels the same for people with non-Western cultural backgrounds (Nakayama et al., 2020). Another limitation is that most research in this area has focused on short-term effects. It is important to conduct longitudinal studies to see if the effects of awe persist over time. Additionally, most research on awe has used self-report measures. It is important to use physiological and behavioral measures to validate self-report measures of awe.

Despite these limitations, the research on awe is promising. As discussed earlier in this chapter, awe has been shown to have a number of benefits for psychological and physical well-being. Awe can promote humility, compassion, prosocial behavior, and creativity. It can also increase feelings of trust, belonging, and common humanity, and reduce stress, anxiety, and depression. As research in this area continues, we can expect to learn more about the benefits of awe and how to cultivate it in our daily lives.

You might end your class discussion with some possible new directions for the field of awe research. You could ask your students to generate their own ideas of where the field should go based on the readings they did before class and their experience with the awe walk. Alternatively, here are some potential examples that you could raise:

- explore the cultural dimensions of awe
- investigate the long-term effects of awe
- develop physiological and behavioral measures of awe
- examine the effects of awe on different populations, such as children, older adults, and people with mental health conditions
- study the mechanisms by which awe exerts its effects
- develop interventions to promote awe

Research in these areas will help us to better understand the nature and effects of awe. This knowledge can be used to develop interventions to promote awe in individuals and communities. Awe has the potential to make the world a more compassionate, creative, and sustainable place.

ASSIGNMENT

Open Writing Reflection

Briefly describe the last three experiences in your life where you felt awe. Include details like where you were, whether you were with other people (who?) or alone, what time of day it was, what inspired awe, and how you felt in your body and mind. Then take the quiz at the following link: https://greatergood.berkeley.edu/quizzes/take_quiz/awe. Write down your score and a few ideas for what you could do to increase your levels of awe.

ONLINE MATERIALS

- Greater Good Science Center (GGSC) awe topic page: https://greatergood.berkeley.edu/topic/awe
- How Nature Helps Us Heal: https://greatergood.berkeley.edu/article/item/how_nature_helps_us_heal
- Eight Reasons Why Awe Makes Your Life Better: https://greatergood.berkeley.edu/article/item/eight_reasons_why_awe_makes_your_life_better
- How Awe Transforms the Body and Mind video: https://greatergood.berkeley.edu/video/item/how_awe_transforms_the_body_and_mind
- GGSC awe quiz: https://greatergood.berkeley.edu/quizzes/take_quiz/awe
- Greater Good in Action (GGIA) awe outing: https://ggia.berkeley.edu/practice/awe_walk
- GGIA awe video: https://ggia.berkeley.edu/practice/awe_video
- GGIA awe story: https://ggia.berkeley.edu/practice/awe_story
- GGIA awe narrative: https://ggia.berkeley.edu/practice/awe_narrative
- YouTube link to virtual awe outing in Muir Woods: https://tinyurl.com/MATPPch10-muir

APPENDIX 10.1: Awe Outing

Please take this instruction sheet with you and go somewhere outdoors. While the key to this exercise is that you can experience awe anywhere, you are more likely to experience it in places that are vast, surprising, or unfamiliar. That said, the key to eliciting awe is adopting the right frame of mind: noticing whatever is coming into your senses, being curious about what is unknown, and welcoming calm. Some possible ideas are to go to a natural setting (e.g., the shore of a body of water, a mountain, somewhere you can see the sunrise/sunset), an awe-inspiring urban setting (e.g., the top of a skyscraper, a historic monument, a botanical garden, or just somewhere new), or beautiful indoor settings (e.g., an aquarium, a cathedral, a gallery).

Before you start, turn off your cell phone. Cell phones (and other digital devices) can be distracting and draw your attention away from what's happening around you. Even better, don't bring your phone with you at all so that you won't be tempted to check it. During your awe outing, try to approach what you see, hear, smell, or otherwise sense with freshness, imagining that you're encountering it for the first time. Then follow these steps:

- Take a deep breath in. Count to six as you inhale and seven as you exhale. Feel the air move through your nasal passages and hear the sound of your breath. Come back to this breath throughout your awe outing.

- As you get going, feel the ground beneath your body and the air on your skin, listen to surrounding sounds, and smell what is wafting from anything nearby.

- Shift your awareness so that you are open to what is around you, to things that are vast, impressively complex, unexpected, unexplainable, or that surprise and delight you.

- Take another deep breath in. Again, count to six as you inhale and seven as you exhale.

- Let your attention be open in exploration for what inspires awe. Is it a wide landscape? The tiny patterns of light and shadow? An appliance or piece of furniture? Let your attention move from the vast to the small.

- Let your inner voice ask far-fetched questions: What is new, unknown, or unexplored about what is around you?

- Continue your awe outing and, every so often, bring your attention back to your breath. Count to six as you inhale and seven as you exhale. Notice—really notice—the multitude of sights, sounds, smells, and other sensations that are dancing through your awareness that often go undetected or even suppressed.

Once you get in the habit of taking outings like this, you may be struck by how frequently you have opportunities to experience awe—they are practically infinite.

As you move through your day, take note of the moments that bring you wonder, give you goosebumps, or make your chest feel broader; these are your opportunities for awe. They may be in your neighborhood, in front of art, listening to music, or doing something together with other people. By seeking and noting your experiences of awe that stir humility and wonder, you may discover that they point you toward what you're supposed to do while you're here on Earth.

ASSIGNMENT: OPEN WRITING REFLECTION

Briefly describe the last three experiences in your life where you felt awe. Include details like where you were, whether you were with other people (who?) or alone, what time of day it was, what inspired awe, and how you felt in your body and mind. Then take the quiz at the following link: https://greatergood.berkeley.edu/quizzes/take_quiz/awe. Write down your score and a few ideas for what you could do to increase your levels of awe.

A printable version of this appendix can be downloaded from the APA website at https://www.apa.org/pubs/books/more-activities-teaching-positive-psychology.

REFERENCES

Anderson, C. L., Monroy, M., & Keltner, D. (2018). Awe in nature heals: Evidence from military veterans, at-risk youth, and college students. *Emotion, 18*(8), 1195–1202. https://doi.org/10.1037/emo0000442

Monroy, M., & Keltner, D. (2023). Awe as a pathway to mental and physical health. *Perspectives in Psychological Science, 18*(2), 309–320. https://doi.org/10.1177/17456916221094856

Nakayama, M., Nozaki, Y., Taylor, P. M., Keltner, D., & Uchida, Y. (2020). Individual and cultural differences in predispositions to feel positive and negative aspects of awe. *Journal of Cross-Cultural Psychology, 51*(10), 771–793. https://doi.org/10.1177/0022022120959821

Piff, P. K., Dietze, P., Feinberg, M., Stancato, D. M., & Keltner, D. (2015). Awe, the small self, and prosocial behavior. *Journal of Personality and Social Psychology, 108*(6), 883–899. https://doi.org/10.1037/pspi0000018

Sturm, V. E., Datta, S., Roy, A. R. K., Sible, I. J., Kosik, E. L., Veziris, C. R., Chow, T. E., Morris, N. A., Neuhaus, J., Kramer, J. H., Miller, B. L., Holley, S. R., & Keltner, D. (2022). Big smile, small self: Awe walks promote prosocial positive emotions in older adults. *Emotion, 22*(5), 1044–1058. https://doi.org/10.1037/emo0000876

11

Happiness Is in Our Nature

Exploring Predicted and Emotional Responses to the Natural Environment

Jessica E. Desrochers and John M. Zelenski

Students will take time to appreciate the well-being benefits of easily accessible nature.

CONCEPT

This activity asks students to experience nearby or virtual nature and explores possible underestimates of affective benefits. It demonstrates how physical environments can influence well-being, introduces the idea of affective forecasting errors (i.e., incorrectly predicting one's future emotions; T. D. Wilson & Gilbert, 2005), and could be scaled up to a more meaningful positive psychology intervention with personal and possible environmental benefits.

MATERIALS NEEDED

Questionnaire (see Appendix 11.1 for worksheets or Qualtrics questionnaire in the Other Online Materials section) and videos (see Video Links).

ACTIVITY SETTING

This activity can be completed in a couple of ways. The easiest, shortest, and most self-contained version (nature videos) works in a classroom with video capability or fully online (see Qualtrics Survey Format file). A longer and potentially more

https://doi.org/10.1037/0000417-011
More Activities for Teaching Positive Psychology: A Guide for Instructors, S. D. Pressman and A. C. Parks (Editors)

effective version involves sending students out into nearby nature (e.g., park, river, pond, garden). Pleasant effects of nature—real or virtual—are quite robust, but the forecasting errors may be less generalizable. Forecasting errors for broad positive and negative affect in actual nearby nature have been previously found (Nisbet & Zelenski, 2011). When running this activity in our own classroom, we found forecasting error underestimates were limited to awe in videos and only when the video was quite awesome. This activity fits in modules about emotions (inducing positive emotions and some potential consequences), thinking (i.e., judgments via the affective forecasts), or social/environmental influences (nature as a physical or virtual context).

ACTIVITY DURATION

The in-class or online version of this activity can take as little as 10 minutes. Larger classes may need more time or technology, for example, online polls or clickers, to compute class averages (optional); follow-up discussion time is flexible. For a version with actual nature, 5 minutes of class time instruction and questionnaire distribution is followed by homework asking students to spend 10 to 15 minutes in nearby nature. If you are lucky enough to be close to some pleasant nature on campus, it could even work as an immediate short field trip; here, we recommend instructing silence for the group during the nature experience. For online classes, the instructions could be delivered live or recorded with either nature videos or homework to spend time in real nature. In a follow-up class after the homework or group activity, another 10 to 30 minutes can be used to compile mood reports and to discuss.

SUGGESTED READINGS

These optional readings are best completed after the activity because prior knowledge about the benefits of nature and forecasting errors could influence responses:

- Nisbet and Zelenski (2011)
- Capaldi et al. (2015) [open access]

BACKGROUND AND INSTRUCTIONS

Connecting with nature is broadly associated with better moods and other positive outcomes like a sense of meaning in life, prosociality, and awe. Supportive research includes surveys showing that nearby greenspace predicts higher life satisfaction (e.g., White et al., 2013), momentary *experience sampling* where being in GPS-identified greenspaces predicts high levels of momentary happiness (MacKerron & Mourato, 2013), and experimental manipulations where actual nature and virtual representations (images, videos) produce increases in pleasant emotions and decreases in unpleasant emotions (McMahan & Estes, 2015). The specific emotion of awe is commonly elicited by natural phenomena (Shiota et al., 2007), even while mundane nature consistently prompts pleasantness and fascination (for a more in-depth look at awe, see the "Awe Outing" activity from Simon-Thomas and Keltner, Chapter 10, this volume). People's subjective sense of connection with nature, as an individual difference, is also positively correlated with a wide range of well-being indicators (Capaldi et al., 2014; Pritchard et al., 2020).

Most theoretical explanations for the strong link between nature and well-being refer to *biophilia*, the idea that people have an innate need to associate with other life forms and lifelike phenomena (E. O. Wilson, 1984). This need is thought to stem from a long evolutionary history where (pre-)humans lived in natural environments (cf. urban communities) and that humans flourished when finding environments full of other life. In essence, our attraction to healthy nature is based on drives that helped our ancestors survive and thrive.

Although modern urban living environments come with some clear benefits in terms of safety and comfort, the mismatch with our more natural ancestral environments may yield costs, too. It is easy to avoid close contact with nature by default in contemporary daily life, and our disconnection from nature seems to be growing over time (Kesebir & Kesebir, 2017). This necessarily diminishes the direct benefits we could enjoy from more frequent contact with nature, but it might also shift perspectives and experiences in a way that makes people fail to appreciate what they are missing. This idea was supported in studies where Canadian students first predicted how they would feel after a short walk in nearby nature and then reported their actual moods following the walks (Nisbet & Zelenski, 2011). The results suggested an affective forecasting error, where students underestimated the mood boosts of the nature walks, on average. Predictions about future emotions help guide decisions (i.e., toward things anticipated to be more pleasant; T. D. Wilson & Gilbert, 2005), so underestimating mood boosts could result in less time in nature, further disconnecting people from nature and its benefits in an unfortunate downward cycle. On a more optimistic note, adding a mindfulness instruction to short nature walks seemed to boost the students' sense of connection with nature (Nisbet et al., 2019). Ultimately, when people spend more time in nature, they are likely to enjoy better moods and a closer subjective connection with nature, both of which are also associated with more sustainable behavior (see Kasser, 2017; Mackay & Schmitt, 2019; Whitburn et al., 2020).

The proposed activity exposes students to nature, which is expected to boost their moods; it also tests possible affective forecasting errors. To complete the activity, the students will carry out the following steps (see Figure 11.1 for a

FIGURE 11.1. Visual Representation of the Steps of the Activity for the Students

| Prenature Experience Affect | Forecasted (Anticipated) Affect | Nature Exposure | Postnature Affect |

visual representation of the steps of the activity). The questionnaires can be provided to students as hard copy worksheets, through clicker (poll) questions in the classroom, or through a Qualtrics survey (or other survey methods; see Appendix 11.1 and links for questionnaire, worksheets, or Qualtrics Survey Format file).

- First, the students are asked about their current feelings to gather their baseline affect.

- Next, the students are asked to estimate how they think they will feel after a nature exposure using the same affect items. To allow for fair predictions, let students know what to expect with a brief description (e.g., "a short nature video" or "a 15-minute walk in the campus garden").

- The students are then exposed to nature. This can be through either real nature exposure or virtual nature. Research shows that real nature exposure is consistently better at improving moods than virtual nature (Browning et al., 2020; McMahan & Estes, 2015); however, this does not discount the benefits of virtual nature exposure. In real nature exposure, students can be asked to go out into nearby nature as a homework assignment (to be revisited next class), or a short class field trip can be done during class time. The real nature exposure can be greenspaces, such as parks or walking trails. For virtual nature, the students can be exposed to nature videos. We have included two links to nature videos in the Video Links section at the end of the chapter, but feel free to substitute similar others (BBC nature documentary trailers are often awesome, and http://explore.org offers a variety of live and highlight webcam videos for mundane nature observations). Our two linked videos are either described as amazing nature (compilation of videos of animals from a high-quality nature documentary) or mundane nature (video is a compilation of everyday wildlife, like birds, squirrels, frogs, turtles, rabbits, and fish). Either video works alone; they could also be compared to highlight awe being induced more by extraordinary nature. Students can be exposed to virtual nature in the classroom, or the videos can be embedded in online surveys.

- Right after the nature experience—or possibly during, if they are experiencing actual nature—ask students to report their feelings again using the same measure.

- The comparison of their initial feelings (i.e., baseline affect) with their post-nature feelings can indicate mood boosts due to nature exposure (if postnature feelings are more positive). Similarly, comparing anticipated, or forecasted, feelings with postnature feelings may indicate a forecasting error (e.g., the students may underestimate how they would feel in nature if their postnature moods are higher than their anticipated mood scores). The simplest version of this comparison uses the short form of the mood questionnaire (i.e., three items: pleasant, tense, and amazed), and individual students simply compare their own ratings on individual items over time.

- If there are time and resources for more calculations, a longer mood/forecast questionnaire can be used to compute averages across similar items (pleasant affect, unpleasant affect, and awe; see Appendix 11.1 for details) and across students. The students can individually compare their own ratings over time to facilitate discussion or complete the writing assignment prompts. We have also provided a Qualtrics Survey Format file that can be used to collect all student ratings together quickly if they have access to smartphones or computers. The data can be exported and transferred to a spreadsheet or statistics program to produce means quickly. Similarly, a Google Sheet or Microsoft Excel cloud file accessed via OneDrive can allow the students to enter their own scores (i.e., preexperience, anticipated, and postexperience). Finally, paired sample (within-person) *t* tests could be used to test the statistical significance of mean differences across two time points—this may be more applicable in larger groups. If using paper and pencil worksheets, consider presenting the class mean levels on another day, as hand computations will take some time.

- Finally, a discussion or writing assignment can prompt students to reflect on the activity (see the Assignment section for discussion or assignment questions). To discuss the results of the assignment, the instructor could ask students to consider their personal scores, compute, and show means for the class as a whole, or use the example results slides (see the Other Online Materials section; Figure 11.2). Figure 11.2 is an example bar chart of the affective forecasting error reported by Nisbet and Zelenski (2011) and shows the difference in positive affect between forecasters and experiencers by the walking routes (outdoor nature vs. indoor tunnels). For the results using videos, example figures from our online class are available in the Other Online Materials section. If discussing the figures (examples or real), instructors can show that a nature exposure not only shows a boost in mood (i.e., pre to post differences in affect) but also has an affective forecasting error (i.e., differences from

FIGURE 11.2. The Affective Forecasting Error of Indoor and Outdoor Walks

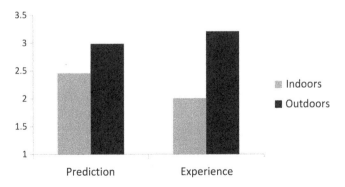

Note. Adapted from "Underestimating Nearby Nature: Affective Forecasting Errors Obscure the Happy Path to Sustainability," by E. K. Nisbet and J. M. Zelenski, 2011, *Psychological Science, 22*(9), p. 1103 (https://doi.org/10.1177/0956797611418527). Copyright 2011 by SAGE Publications. Adapted with permission.

forecasted to postaffect scores), where people underestimated their moods following their experience in nature. Discussion could deal with why people generally underestimate the emotional benefits of nature exposure and how to incorporate more nature in their everyday life.

• There is a possibility that the expected results do not occur in the instructor's classroom data. In these circumstances, a comparison between the classroom's data and previous research—for instance, those from Nisbet and Zelenski (2011)—could be shown. With this, further discussion could deal with why they believe their results do not align with previous research. Potential reasons include (a) the class size, which could affect the experience or magnify the role of idiosyncratic variation in smaller groups; (b) the type/quality of nature exposure (virtual or real; differently defined natural environments; see the Discussion section); and (c) the students' engagement with the task and possible distractions.

DISCUSSION

The activity is expected to result in students feeling better (e.g., more pleasant, less tense) postnature exposure, no matter the type, and potentially underestimating how good the nature experience will make them feel (see Figure 11.2). When choosing the nature exposure, it is useful to consider the different types of nature and how it is consumed. Across nature exposure research, there are many ways nature is defined, such as urban greenspaces, wild unmanaged nature, blue spaces (i.e., lakes, oceans), countryside, tree canopies, and plants, to name a few. Research suggests that different types of nature may not be consistently associated with substantially different mood effects (or perhaps that the effects are nuanced and complicated). For example, in a meta-analysis, wild and managed nature exposure had similar effects on mood (McMahan & Estes, 2015). With that said, it appears that some wild natural environments are preferred to others. For example, lakes, mountains, and beaches are typically preferred over swamps and marshes, though having more familiarity with a particular environment seems to boost appreciation for it, too (Mangone et al., 2021). When it comes to the exposure type, real nature is consistently better at increasing positive affect than simulated nature (e.g., images, videos, virtual reality; Browning et al., 2020; McMahan & Estes, 2015). The exposure method may also be important when using virtual nature experiences. For example, when Yeo et al. (2020) compared the impact of three different types of virtual nature exposures, (a) high-definition television; (b) 360° virtual reality video; and (c) computer-generated virtual reality nature, on affect scores, they found that negative affect was decreased across all three types of nature exposure, but the difference across exposure types was not significant. However, even though each exposure type increased positive affect, computer-generated virtual reality nature exposure had the greatest improvement over either the TV or 360° video. This suggests that some types of virtual nature exposure, like virtual reality, may be best for increasing affect.

This activity relies on relatively brief nature exposures, and it may be possible to amplify the positive effects by repeating them over time. Although lasting and meaningful well-being change is challenging to facilitate, some nature-based interventions appear promising. For example, Canadians who committed to spending 30 minutes a day in nature over the course of 30 days (i.e., the 30 × 30 Nature Challenge) reported lasting improvements in their emotions and stronger connections with nature at the end (though this study did not have a control group; Nisbet, 2015).

There are clearly individual and contextual differences in people's ability to experience nature. For example, location or disability might hinder access to actual nature. Virtual nature can help here, though it is also worth noting that nature's benefits appear for nearby and modest examples, such as urban bird feeders, small gardens, urban trees, and so forth (Capaldi et al., 2015). Additionally, the biophilic design approach tries to mirror elements of nature in built spaces, for example, by using natural materials (e.g., wood grain, water features), natural imagery (e.g., decorative leaves or ivy), natural proportions and forms (e.g., more curves, fractals), or windows to actual nature (Kellert & Calabrese, 2015). Using these principles, along with urban planning that includes more natural spaces, might help reap some of nature's benefits more easily in contemporary day-to-day life.

Of course, some nature is genuinely unpleasant, and these types of nature will not boost moods. For example, many people dislike snakes and spiders, which are common targets for phobias. Similarly, dangerous, damaged, and polluted natural environments are displeasing. Aversion to dangerous nature can be seen as a mirror of biophilia. That is, very similar to the idea that people evolved to associate with healthy, life-giving nature, we also evolved to avoid unhealthy and dangerous elements in nature (E. O. Wilson, 1984). Ancestors with these inclinations were more successful. Some aversion to unappealing nature can be averted by considering broader ecosystems (e.g., spiders have an important role). Fortunately, most natural environments are full of life and pleasant, particularly the environments we are likely to encounter in contemporary developed societies.

At a broader level, nature activities may also benefit the environment. Previous research has examined subjective and physical connections with nature in association with sustainable behaviors. In meta-analytic work, Mackay and Schmitt (2019) showed that those who felt more connected to nature were more likely to engage in proenvironmental behaviors, both in correlational and experimental studies (though the experimental meta-analysis was less robust). As people spend more time in nature, they seem more inclined to take actions that protect the environment (Nisbet, 2015; Richardson et al., 2020; Zelenski et al., 2015). Additionally, review articles have explored links between happiness and environmentalism (Kasser, 2017; Zelenski & Desrochers, 2021). There is a small but robust positive correlation, but the causal direction(s) remains unclear. Said another way, it may be that happiness (potentially from nature) increases sustainable action or that doing sustainable actions boosts happiness.

Proenvironmental behaviors can be seen as prosocial behaviors, and research suggests that positive emotions can be both a cause and a consequence of prosociality (Zelenski & Desrochers, 2021). As is commonly the case, more research is needed to understand the reasons for clear associations between happiness, time in nature, and environmentalism. As concern over climate change grows, some people worry to the point of significant eco anxiety. Early hints from research and anecdotes suggest that connecting with nature by spending time in it and taking actions to protect it may help buffer eco anxiety, in addition to producing positive emotions.

Even with the robust relationship between nature exposure and positive mood boosts, the research in this field is not without limitations. For one, the research on affective forecasts of nature exposures has received little attention. As of today, there is only a single published research project that is limited to two natural environments (Nisbet & Zelenski, 2011) and an unpublished dissertation (Crawford, 2020) that shows more mixed results. Thus, the confidence in these forecasting conclusions is lower than the generally positive effects of nature due to the lack of replication efforts and minimal stimulus sampling. Efforts toward replicating and extending the affective forecasting research on nature exposure could speak to human disconnection from nature and potential implications for promoting nature contact for mood improvements through different types of nature exposure (i.e., real and virtual exposure; different types of natural environments).

ASSIGNMENT

Nature often makes people feel better. Additionally, people sometimes underestimate how much of a mood boost they experience when spending time in nature—whether actual or virtual. For the assignment, please (discuss or) write a short essay about your experience today and how it fits the research.

For example, you might consider:

- Did the nature (video) make you feel better? Did you anticipate this mood boost accurately? How much do your predictions about future moods guide your choices?

- Do you think there is potential to incorporate more nature into your day-to-day life? What can you do as an individual, and what kinds of systemic changes might help?

- If the nature (video) did not make you feel any better, why do you think this is? Do you think this particular (online) context matters? Are you just "not a nature person"? Are there variations that might work better for you? What about people who are different from you?

- Most people find the majority of examples of nature pleasant; why do you think this is? How can you reconcile this with elements of nature that are typically less pleasant (e.g., spiders, decay)?

- Does spending time with nature make you more inclined to protect it? Do you worry about nature, given climate change and human population growth? Are there nature-related experiences that might benefit both nature and your well-being?

Video Links for the Activity

- Mundane Nature: https://tinyurl.com/MATPPChap11-3
- Awesome Nature: https://tinyurl.com/MATPPchap11-4

Other Online Materials

- Qualtrics Survey file (https://tinyurl.com/MATPPchap11; to import if you have a Qualtrics account)
- paper and pencil worksheets
- example results figures in PowerPoint (from other students) can be found at https://tinyurl.com/MATPPchap11-2

APPENDIX 11.1: Affect and Forecasting Questionnaires

Note for instructors: These affect and forecasting questionnaires are ad hoc, yet similar to other adaptations from widely used adjective rating scales. Feel free to use other published scales or shorten versions of scales examining affect/mood. When creating the activity for your class, you can provide questionnaires as hard copies (see worksheet), clicker (poll) questions in class (by using the items below), or use Qualtrics (or other survey methods; see our Qualtrics Survey Format file found at https://tinyurl.com/Ch11nature). When choosing the method of the questionnaire, take into account the method of nature experience. For example, it may be easier for a student to bring a hard copy questionnaire with them when they experience real nature, but it may be easier to use Qualtrics surveys with embedded nature videos for a virtual nature experience.

COMPLETED BOTH BEFORE AND JUST AFTER NATURE EXPOSURE

Current Feelings

Please use the following adjectives to rate how you are feeling right now.

Not at all	A little	Moderately	A lot	Very much
1	2	3	4	5

1. Pleasant*
2. Interested

3. Happy
4. Sad
5. Tense*
6. Afraid
7. Amazed*
8. Awe
9. Wonder

COMPLETED JUST BEFORE THE NATURE EXPOSURE

Anticipated Feelings

In a moment, you will watch a short nature video or take a walk in the campus garden. Please rate how you think you will feel in the last moments of this activity.

Not at all	A little	Moderately	A lot	Very much
1	2	3	4	5

1. Pleasant*
2. Interested
3. Happy
4. Sad
5. Tense*
6. Afraid
7. Amazed*
8. Awe
9. Wonder

A short version of this questionnaire includes only the items with asterisks and requires no additional scoring—those individual items represent pleasant, unpleasant, and awed feelings.

If using the full scale, compute an average of ratings for Items 1–3 (pleasant), 4–6 (unpleasant), and 7–9 (awe) to assess these feelings more robustly. Create separate scores for baseline, forecasts, and postnature affect.

Feel free to explore other face-valid mood items, for instance "relaxed" or "fascinated," especially if you use actual local nature. Nature's impacts on mood tend to be broad (many different feelings, but also depending somewhat on context), though forecasting errors have not been studied as thoroughly.

A printable version of this appendix can be downloaded from the APA website at https://www.apa.org/pubs/books/more-activities-teaching-positive-psychology.

REFERENCES

Browning, M. H. E. M., Shipley, N., McAnirlin, O., Becker, D., Yu, C.-P., Hartig, T., & Dzhambov, A. M. (2020). An actual natural setting improves mood better than its virtual counterpart: A meta-analysis of experimental data. *Frontiers in Psychology, 11,* Article 2200. https://doi.org/10.3389/fpsyg.2020.02200

Capaldi, C. A., Dopko, R. L., & Zelenski, J. M. (2014). The relationship between nature connectedness and happiness: A meta-analysis. *Frontiers in Psychology, 5,* Article 976. https://doi.org/10.3389/fpsyg.2014.00976

Capaldi, C. A., Passmore, H.-A., Nisbet, E., Zelenski, J., & Dopko, R. (2015). Flourishing in nature: A review of the benefits of connecting with nature and its application as a well-being intervention. *International Journal of Wellbeing, 5*(4), 1–16. https://doi.org/10.5502/ijw.v5i4.449

Crawford, M. R. (2020). *Affective forecasting: Predicting the influence of nature on well-being* [Doctoral dissertation, University of British Columbia]. UBC Theses and Dissertations. https://open.library.ubc.ca/collections/ubctheses/24/items/1.0395435

Kasser, T. (2017). Living both well and sustainably: A review of the literature, with some reflections on future research, interventions and policy. *Philosophical Transactions of the Royal Society of London. Series A: Mathematical, Physical, and Engineering Sciences, 375*(2095), Article 20160369. https://doi.org/10.1098/rsta.2016.0369

Kellert, S., & Calabrese, E. (2015). *The practice of biophilic design.* https://www.biophilic-design.com

Kesebir, S., & Kesebir, P. (2017). A growing disconnection from nature is evident in cultural products. *Perspectives on Psychological Science, 12*(2), 258–269. https://doi.org/10.1177/1745691616662473

Mackay, C. M. L., & Schmitt, M. T. (2019). Do people who feel connected to nature do more to protect it? A meta-analysis. *Journal of Environmental Psychology, 65,* Article 101323. https://doi.org/10.1016/j.jenvp.2019.101323

MacKerron, G., & Mourato, S. (2013). Happiness is greater in natural environments. *Global Environmental Change, 23*(5), 992–1000. https://doi.org/10.1016/j.gloenvcha.2013.03.010

Mangone, G., Dopko, R. L., & Zelenski, J. M. (2021). Deciphering landscape preferences: Investigating the roles of familiarity and biome types. *Landscape and Urban Planning, 214,* Article 104189. https://doi.org/10.1016/j.landurbplan.2021.104189

McMahan, E. A., & Estes, D. (2015). The effect of contact with natural environments on positive and negative affect: A meta-analysis. *The Journal of Positive Psychology, 10*(6), 507–519. https://doi.org/10.1080/17439760.2014.994224

Nisbet, E. K. (2015). *Answering nature's call: Results of the 2015 David Suzuki Foundation's 30×30 nature challenge.* https://davidsuzuki.org/wp-content/uploads/2017/09/results-2015-david-suzuki-foundation-30x30-nature-challenge.pdf

Nisbet, E. K., & Zelenski, J. M. (2011). Underestimating nearby nature: Affective forecasting errors obscure the happy path to sustainability. *Psychological Science, 22*(9), 1101–1106. https://doi.org/10.1177/0956797611418527

Nisbet, E. K., Zelenski, J. M., & Grandpierre, Z. (2019). Mindfulness in nature enhances connectedness and mood. *Ecopsychology, 11*(2), 81–91. https://doi.org/10.1089/eco.2018.0061

Pritchard, A., Richardson, M., Sheffield, D., & McEwan, K. (2020). The relationship between nature connectedness and eudaimonic well-being: A meta-analysis. *Journal of Happiness Studies, 21*(3), 1145–1167. https://doi.org/10.1007/s10902-019-00118-6

Richardson, M., Passmore, H. A., Barbett, L., Lumber, R., Thomas, R., & Hunt, A. (2020). The green care code: How nature connectedness and simple activities help explain pro-nature conservation behaviours. *People and Nature, 2*(3), 821–839. https://doi.org/10.1002/pan3.10117

Shiota, M. N., Keltner, D., & Mossman, A. (2007). The nature of awe: Elicitors, appraisals, and effects on self-concept. *Cognition and Emotion, 21*(5), 944–963. https://doi.org/10.1080/02699930600923668

Whitburn, J., Linklater, W., & Abrahamse, W. (2020). Meta-analysis of human connection to nature and proenvironmental behavior. *Conservation Biology, 34*(1), 180–193. https://doi.org/10.1111/cobi.13381

White, M. P., Alcock, I., Wheeler, B. W., & Depledge, M. H. (2013). Would you be happier living in a greener urban area? A fixed-effects analysis of panel data. *Psychological Science, 24*(6), 920–928. https://doi.org/10.1177/0956797612464659

Wilson, E. O. (1984). *Biophilia*. Harvard University Press. https://doi.org/10.4159/9780674045231

Wilson, T. D., & Gilbert, D. T. (2005). Affective forecasting. *Current Directions in Psychological Science, 14*(3), 131–134. https://doi.org/10.1111/j.0963-7214.2005.00355.x

Yeo, N. L., White, M. P., Alcock, I., Garside, R., Dean, S. G., Smalley, A. J., & Gatersleben, B. (2020). What is the best way of delivering virtual nature for improving mood? An experimental comparison of high definition TV, 360° video, and computer generated virtual reality. *Journal of Environmental Psychology, 72*, Article 101500. https://doi.org/10.1016/j.jenvp.2020.101500

Zelenski, J. M., & Desrochers, J. E. (2021). Can positive and self-transcendent emotions promote pro-environmental behavior? *Current Opinion in Psychology, 42*, 31–35. https://doi.org/10.1016/j.copsyc.2021.02.009

Zelenski, J. M., Dopko, R. L., & Capaldi, C. A. (2015). Cooperation is in our nature: Nature exposure may promote cooperative and environmentally sustainable behavior. *Journal of Environmental Psychology, 42*, 24–31. https://doi.org/10.1016/j.jenvp.2015.01.005

12

The Treasure Chest

An Immersive Guided Imagery Meditation on Sacred Moments

Serena Wong and Kenneth I. Pargament

This activity invites students to immerse themselves in a brief guided meditation that explores memories of spiritual significance to them. They select one sacred moment from their past to relive, drawing comfort, love, and meaning from it before returning the memory to their metaphorical treasure chest.

CONCEPT

Sacred moments are brief periods in which one experiences transcendence, boundlessness, ultimacy, deep interconnectedness, and spiritual emotions. These can be a powerful resource in times of high stress. In this activity, students will relive a sacred experience via a meditation with a metaphorical treasure chest and reflect on the nature of this experience. This topic may be presented as one example of a spiritual resource for coping with life's difficulties. Sacred moments can also be integrated into broader discussions about spirituality, religion, and well-being or mental health.

MATERIALS NEEDED

Paper and pens.

https://doi.org/10.1037/0000417-012
More Activities for Teaching Positive Psychology: A Guide for Instructors, S. D. Pressman and A. C. Parks (Editors)

ACTIVITY SETTING

This activity is suited for quiet spaces that will allow for uninterrupted meditation. Both online and in-person formats have been supported in studies. There is no limit to the number of participants, so long as they can hear the facilitator speak. When presenting the activity online, it is helpful to have students mute themselves during the meditation and subsequently turn on their videos and microphones for discussion. Depending on group size, discussions can occur in smaller breakout rooms of three people each and/or with the group in its entirety.

ACTIVITY DURATION

Ten minutes for the meditation plus 20 to 30 minutes for discussion.

SUGGESTED READINGS

- Required reading for before the activity:
  - Pargament et al. (2014)[1]
- Optional enrichment readings:
  - Magyar-Russell et al. (2022)
  - Pargament et al. (2016)
  - Wilt et al. (2019)
  - Wong et al. (2018)

BACKGROUND AND INSTRUCTIONS

Sacred moments are brief periods of time in which one may experience transcendence, boundlessness, ultimacy, deep interconnectedness, and spiritual emotions (Pargament et al., 2014). They represent a powerful spiritual resource that individuals can tap into during times of trouble (Pargament, 2011; Wong et al., 2018). Sacred moments are linked with better mental health and psychological adjustment in different contexts, such as in a therapeutic relationship (Pargament et al., 2014), caregiving relationship (Wong & Pargament, 2018), when individuals are going through spiritual or religious struggles (Wilt et al., 2019), or across various time points in daily life (Magyar-Russell et al., 2022). Most recently, Wong and Pargament (2021) developed and evaluated a psychospiritual well-being program designed to cultivate sacred moments for college students in which higher levels of personal growth and spiritual growth were reported immediately after participating in the program. Instructions are provided here to facilitate discussion and the treasure chest meditation.

---

[1] Excerpts from this article may be used in lieu of the full reading to cater to students' reading levels and interest in empirical psychological studies.

- Ask students the following questions:
  - According to Pargament et al.'s (2014) research article, what are sacred moments?
  - What did the researchers find about the perceived effects of sacred moments?
  - Where else do you think sacred moments can take place?

- Invite students to participate in the treasure chest meditation using the following script (see Appendix 12.1; the time estimate is 10 minutes for this portion of the activity).

Note for educators prior to beginning: When offering guided meditations, it is helpful to practice timing and reading the script at a quieter volume, just loud enough so that everyone can hear your words. You may consider amplification through a microphone if you are managing a large group. The tone of delivery can be conversational. The rhythm for guided meditations is often measured, with longer pauses between paragraphs, and your rate of speech may be a beat slower than your usual pace.

Script

Let's take a moment to reflect on a sacred moment of our own. In these next few minutes, I will walk you through a guided meditation. You are all invited to participate in this experience. However, you can choose not to meditate today. If you have unwanted memories of bad events when you close your eyes, you might find this activity inappropriate for you at this time. Instead, you might focus on my voice with your eyes open through this activity. You are welcome to do whatever feels safe for you. Now, let's begin.

Just breathe. Settle into your seat with your hands resting comfortably and your feet touching the floor. You can close your eyes if you feel comfortable doing so. Otherwise, feel free to settle your gaze on a space that's close to you.

Allow your attention to begin to turn inward. You can always return to your breath when you feel lost or your mind wanders. In. Out. Remember, there is no right or wrong way of doing this exercise. Just breathe. (pause)

See if you can picture a treasure chest in your mind. This sealed treasure chest contains your most precious memories. Consider the size of your treasure chest—how big is it? How heavy? Perhaps your chest is made of wood, wicker, or lined with fabric. Notice its colors and how it sits in your mind.

Now imagine unsealing and opening your treasure chest. Inside this box are your memories. Here are your life's treasured moments, collected in one place—as snapshots or moving pictures. You begin sifting through your chest of memories.

As you move through your memories, see if you can find one sacred moment. Maybe you had a special encounter with another person, maybe you were outdoors, maybe you heard a piece of music, or maybe you were doing something seemingly ordinary. In any case, it is a moment in time that feels set apart from the others, when you connected with something greater than yourself. Perhaps it's a moment that lifted you up. A moment that feels time-less. A moment that opened your heart to something really real. A moment of deep connection. Perhaps, as you hold this moment in your mind, the edges of it even glow.

Now imagine the essence of this moment washing over you and into you. Warmly enveloping you into this sacred memory. Drawing you into your sacred moment. Perhaps you are wholly absorbed into this scene.

In your sacred moment, notice what's ahead of you, behind you, around you. Recall the sounds of this moment. The temperature. Any tastes, fragrances, or movements in the scene. Breathe in this sacred moment and draw what you need from it—whether it be comfort, meaning, or love. Take in all that you need. Continue to be in this sacred space for the next couple of minutes. (pause)

Now that you have been filled by this moment, allow yourself to let go of it until next time. It will always be there for you. You can return to your treasure chest at any time. Now gently turn your attention outward, into the room, into the present, and all through your body. When you feel ready, open your eyes.

- Encourage students to spend 5 minutes writing responses to the following prompts (see Appendix 12.2 for a printable worksheet):

  1. What was in your treasure chest? Please feel free to write or doodle what you envisioned.

  2. What makes a moment sacred to you? More specifically, what types of emotions could be involved in these moments? What kinds of thoughts might come up when you are having a sacred moment?

  3. How does your response to Question 2 compare with Pargament et al.'s (2014) conceptualization of sacred moments? What are some similarities and differences between your view of sacred moments and Pargament's?

  4. If you had a hard time finding a sacred moment, what do you think might have gotten in the way?

- Optional step: Place the students in groups of three to process their experi-ences using these prompts.

- With the whole group, invite students to share about their sacred moments. Thank each student for sharing. The facilitator may want to comment on how it feels to hear these moments being shared aloud.

- Inclusivity consideration: Some students may not identify with having spiritual or religious dimensions to their lives. The term "sacred" may not resonate with them, or it may even evoke a negative reaction if they have experienced religious or spiritual trauma. Instructors are encour-aged to pause if they notice students struggling with the word "sacred." Brainstorming with these students for a substitute word that reflects their cherished, life-affirming experiences is encouraged. Examples of words that are less likely to invoke religious or spiritual connotations include "elevated," "epic," "glorious," "awe-inspiring," or "majestic." To promote sensitivity and respect for everybody's experiences, instructors should include the alternative terms that were accepted by these students in the meditation and discussion of sacred moments.

DISCUSSION

A healthy spirituality may be essential to eudaimonic well-being (Pargament et al., 2016). It may serve as a life-affirming force during times of trouble, adding layers of meaning, beauty, and depth to our existence. Indeed, religious and spiritual resources have been tied to beneficial outcomes, including longevity (McCullough et al., 2000) and improved mental health (Pargament, 2011). Cultivating sacred moments is another way to enjoy the fruits of the spiritual dimension, regardless of one's identification along the continuum of belief and nonbelief. Several mental health and well-being interventions featuring sacred moments have yielded promising results (Goldstein, 2007; McCorkle et al., 2005; Wong, 2021). Moreover, we are only beginning to observe how sacred moments may lead to growth and the resolution of spiritual struggles over time. Ripe for further empirical study and experience, sacred moments may also inspire memorable discussions in the classroom.

Having had the opportunity to share their sacred moments, it may be helpful for students to discuss the common qualities sacred moments seem to have. They may be encouraged to reflect upon what aspects of sacred moments bring them beyond merely "good" times. It is important to note that there are no right or wrong answers when it comes to students' experiences. Students may also be asked if any of Pargament et al.'s (2014) theorized qualities resonate with them and their sacred moment. According to Pargament et al. (2014), sacred moments have the following qualities:

- *Transcendence:* Extraordinary in nature or set apart from everyday life; something greater than yourself.
- *Boundlessness:* Unforgettable, timeless, or infinite; reaching beyond ordinary boundaries.
- *Deep interconnectedness:* A close bond with someone or a group of people in which you are seen and fully embraced.
- *Ultimacy:* Arriving at a profound truth about yourself and life.
- *Spiritual emotions:* For example, awe, uplift, gratitude, compassion.

Instructors may also find it fruitful to ask students how they think we can cultivate or experience sacred moments more fully in our lives. Under what conditions do we think sacred moments are most likely to occur? For example, Pargament et al. (2014) noted that some participants reported feeling tension prior to the sacred moment. Feelings of trust and security in the relationship also seem to pave the way for sacred moments to occur between people.

On the other hand, certain conditions may make it harder for people to access their sacred moments. Potential barriers to accessing the sacred include trauma and anxiety (Wong & Pargament, 2017). Subsequent discussion may ensue about ways we can navigate through these barriers. It may be helpful here for instructors to normalize the experience of struggling to find a sacred moment and reassure the class that people can experience this for all sorts of reasons. Sometimes, we can feel pressured to choose a moment, so much so that we cannot decide on a single one. Other times, we might feel sad because we think we do not have any sacred memories, or perhaps such memories are hard to retrieve in the moment even though we know we had them. Trying to recall a sacred moment with someone who has recently departed from our lives or who has been a source of ambivalent feelings could also elicit emotions of loss or sadness. During the meditation, those carrying trauma were invited to keep their eyes open and focus on the sound of the instructor's voice instead of engaging with the exercise. If someone indicates that images of a traumatic nature resurfaced with their eyes closed, instructors can gently inquire about ways to help the person feel safer in class rather than asking questions about the trauma. Some ways to help a person feel safer in the present include opening one's eyes, naming the colors of objects in the vicinity, and having a sip of water. A referral to a counselor or psychologist may also be appropriate if the individual appears to be in distress. Ultimately, we encourage students to consider whatever difficulties they may have had in finding a sacred moment as a natural part of spiritual or self-exploration. It is okay to be at a place in one's journey where it is hard to see the sacred. Journaling about one or two daily experiences that elicited a sense of meaning or joy may be helpful for those who wish to identify potential sacred moments. Furthermore, some people may not be able to "see" images in their mind. It may be difficult to visualize scenes using our mind's eye. Fortunately, difficulty visualizing does not preclude individuals from having sacred moments or revisiting them. It may be helpful for students who do not visualize to hear that this guided meditation represents only one way of accessing sacred moments. They may be encouraged to brainstorm with their peers other ways to get in touch with what is sacred to them. For example, some students might benefit from looking at a photograph or bringing an object that is sacred to them.

The healing nature of sacred moments is another topic worthy of discussion. It is important for instructors to note that empirical evidence regarding the effects of sacred moments is limited at this time, but several studies have supported the favorable potential of cultivating sacred moments. Students might be asked why and how revisiting sacred moments could be helpful during times of stress. As a spiritual coping resource, sacred moments may represent a way to center and soothe oneself. They may serve as powerful core memories that bolster individuals in turmoil. They may also act as a counterweight to traumatic experiences. As trauma renders psychological damage, the wisdom from sacred moments may guide healing and remind them of what makes life worth living. Students may be invited to return to their treasure chests with more memories to cultivate. Finally, as a segue into the assignment, it may be worth processing with students how it felt for them to hear about other people's sacred moments. What we have noticed from listening to people's sacred moments is a cascade effect of vicarious sacred experiences in the listener. Thus, the sharing of sacred moments may be meaningful for both speakers and their witnesses. Those who are privileged to hear about a person's most precious memories may similarly feel awe and uplift.

ASSIGNMENT

Responses to these writing prompts can be completed individually (see Appendix 12.3):

1. What was it like for you to hear about other people's sacred moments? What kinds of thoughts and feelings did you have?

2. What are some examples of sacred qualities that have occurred in your life? The sacred qualities include transcendence, boundlessness, deep interconnectedness, ultimacy, and spiritual emotions.

3. What are some research questions about sacred moments that could be developed? For example, you might have hypotheses about specific predictors and consequences of sacred moments or how different populations might experience sacred moments.

APPENDIX 12.1: Treasure Chest Meditation

Note for educators: When offering guided meditations, it is helpful to practice timing and reading the script at a quieter volume, just loud enough so that everyone can hear your words. You may consider amplification through a microphone if you are managing a large group. The tone of delivery can be conversational. The rhythm for guided meditations is often measured, with longer pauses between paragraphs, and your rate of speech may be slightly slower than your usual pace.

Script

Let's take a moment to reflect on a sacred moment of our own. In these next few minutes, I will walk you through a guided meditation. You are all invited to participate in this experience. However, you can choose not to meditate today. If you have unwanted memories of bad events when you close your eyes, you might find this activity inappropriate for you at this time. Instead, you might focus on my voice with your eyes open through this activity. You are welcome to do whatever feels safe for you. Now, let's begin.

Just breathe. Settle into your seat with your hands resting comfortably and your feet touching the floor. You can close your eyes if you feel comfortable doing so. Otherwise, feel free to settle your gaze on a space that's close to you.

Allow your attention to begin to turn inward. You can always return to your breath when you feel lost or your mind wanders. In. Out. Remember, there is no right or wrong way of doing this exercise. Just breathe. (pause)

See if you can picture a treasure chest in your mind. This sealed treasure chest that contains your most precious memories. Consider the size of your treasure chest—how big is it? How heavy? Perhaps your chest is made of wood, wicker, or lined with fabric. Notice its colors and how it sits in your mind.

Now imagine unsealing and opening your treasure chest. Inside this box are your memories. Here are your life's treasured moments, collected in one place—as snapshots or moving pictures. You begin sifting through your chest of memories.

As you move through your memories, see if you can find one sacred moment. Maybe you had a special encounter with another person, maybe you were outdoors, maybe you heard a piece of music, or maybe you were doing something seemingly ordinary. In any case, it is a moment in time that feels set apart from the others, when you connected with something greater than yourself. Perhaps it's a moment that lifted you up. A moment that feels timeless. A moment that opened your heart to something really real. A moment of deep connection. Perhaps, as you hold this moment in your mind, the edges of it even glow.

Now imagine the essence of this moment washing over you and into you. Warmly enveloping you into this sacred memory. Drawing you into your sacred moment. Perhaps you are wholly absorbed into this scene.

Notice what's ahead of you, behind you, around you in this moment. Recall the sounds of this moment. The temperature. Any tastes, fragrances, or movements in the scene. Breathe in this sacred moment and draw what you need from it, whether it be comfort, meaning, or love. Take in all that you need. Continue to be in this sacred space for the next couple of minutes. (pause)

Now that you have been filled by this moment, allow yourself to let go of it until next time. It will always be there for you. You can return to your treasure chest at any time. Now gently turn your attention outward, into the room, into the present, and all through your body. When you feel ready, open your eyes.

A printable version of this appendix can be downloaded from the APA website at https://www.apa.org/pubs/books/more-activities-teaching-positive-psychology.

APPENDIX 12.2: Treasure Chest Meditation—Reflection Prompts

1. What was in your treasure chest? Please feel free to write or doodle what you envisioned.

2. What makes a moment sacred to you? More specifically, what types of emotions could be involved in these moments? What kinds of thoughts might come up when you are having a sacred moment?

3. How does your response to Question 2 compare with Pargament et al.'s (2014) conceptualization of sacred moments? What are some similarities and differences between your view of sacred moments and Pargament's?

4. If you had a hard time finding a sacred moment, what do you think might have gotten in the way?

A printable version of this appendix can be downloaded from the APA website at https://www.apa.org/pubs/books/more-activities-teaching-positive-psychology.

APPENDIX 12.3: Treasure Chest Meditation—Assignment

1. What was it like for you to hear about other people's sacred moments? What kinds of thoughts and feelings did you have?

2. What are some examples of sacred qualities that have occurred in your life? The sacred qualities include transcendence, boundlessness, deep interconnectedness, ultimacy, and spiritual emotions.

3. What are some research questions about sacred moments that could be developed? For example, you might have hypotheses about specific predictors and consequences of sacred moments or how different populations might experience sacred moments.

A printable version of this appendix can be downloaded from the APA website at https://www.apa.org/pubs/books/more-activities-teaching-positive-psychology.

REFERENCES

Goldstein, E. D. (2007). Sacred moments: Implications on well-being and stress. *Journal of Clinical Psychology, 63*(10), 1001–1019. https://doi.org/10.1002/jclp.20402

Magyar-Russell, G., Pargament, K. I., Grubbs, J. B., Wilt, J. A., & Exline, J. J. (2022). The experience of sacred moments and mental health benefits over time. *Psychology of Religion and Spirituality, 14*(2), 161–169. https://doi.org/10.1037/rel0000394

McCorkle, B. H., Bohn, C., Hughes, T., & Kim, D. (2005). "Sacred moments": Social anxiety in a larger perspective. *Mental Health, Religion & Culture, 8*(3), 227–238. https://doi.org/10.1080/13694670500138874

McCullough, M. E., Hoyt, W. T., Larson, D. B., Koenig, H. G., & Thoresen, C. (2000). Religious involvement and mortality: A meta-analytic review. *Health Psychology, 19*(3), 211–222. https://doi.org/10.1037/0278-6133.19.3.211

Pargament, K. I. (2011). *Spiritually integrated psychotherapy: Understanding and addressing the sacred.* Guilford Press.

Pargament, K. I., Lomax, J. W., McGee, J. S., & Fang, Q. (2014). Sacred moments in psychotherapy from the perspectives of mental health providers and clients: Prevalence, predictors, and consequences. *Spirituality in Clinical Practice, 1*(4), 248–262. https://doi.org/10.1037/scp0000043

Pargament, K. I., Wong, S., & Exline, J. J. (2016). Wholeness and holiness: The spiritual dimension of eudaimonics. In V. Joar (Ed.), *Handbook of eudaimonic well-being* (pp. 379–394). Springer. https://doi.org/10.1007/978-3-319-42445-3_25

Wilt, J. A., Pargament, K. I., & Exline, J. J. (2019). The transformative power of the sacred: Social, personality, and religious/spiritual antecedents and consequents of sacred moments during a religious/spiritual struggle. *Psychology of Religion and Spirituality, 11*(3), 233–246. https://doi.org/10.1037/rel0000176

Wong, S. (2021). *Cultivating sacred moments: Evaluating a pilot program to foster psychospiritual wellbeing* [Doctoral dissertation, Bowling Green State Univsersity]. ProQuest Dissertations and Theses Global.

Wong, S., & Pargament, K. I. (2017). Seeing the sacred: Fostering spiritual vision in counselling. *Journal of Counselling and Spirituality, 36*(1–2), 51–69. https://doi.org/10.2143/CS.36.1.3285226

Wong, S., & Pargament, K. I. (2018, August). Carpe momentum: Sacred moments as a predictor of wellbeing for family caregivers. In P. T. P. Wong (Chair), *Scholarship papers session* [Paper presentation]. 10th Biennial International Meaning Conference, Vancouver, Canada.

Wong, S., & Pargament, K. I. (2021, November). Cultivating sacred moments: Evaluating a pilot program to foster psychospiritual wellbeing. In S. S. Ahmad (Chair), *Cultivating religiosity and spirituality (R/S): Spiritual bypass and external locus of control as barriers to better mental health* [Paper presentation]. Association for Behavioural and Cognitive Therapies 2021 Virtual Convention.

Wong, S., Pargament, K. I., & Faigin, C. (2018). Sustained by the sacred: Religious and spiritual resources for resilience in adulthood and aging. In B. Resnick, L. P. Gwyther, & K. Roberto (Eds.), *Aging: Concepts, research, and outcomes* (pp. 191–214). Springer. https://doi.org/10.1007/978-3-030-04555-5_10

13

Is It Possible to Design and Live a Perfectly Happy Day?

Jaime L. Kurtz

Students are asked to design their "perfect day" and attempt to live that day. Afterward, they reflect on what they prioritized during this day and what they might change.

CONCEPT

Research suggests that we have many blind spots that can hinder our happiness and that excessively monitoring how happy we feel at any given moment can actually detract from our happiness (Mauss et al., 2011; Wilson & Gilbert, 2005). This activity brings these concepts to life by having students spend a day trying to deliberately make themselves happy. The perfect day assignment is best used alongside topics of hedonic adaptation, affective forecasting, self-knowledge, and/or with a discussion of the conscious pursuit of happiness.

MATERIALS NEEDED

Students will need a paper and pencil or a computer in order to concretely map out their perfect day in advance, as well as to complete the worksheet afterward. Students will also need a copy of the worksheet in Appendix 13.1.

https://doi.org/10.1037/0000417-013
More Activities for Teaching Positive Psychology: A Guide for Instructors, S. D. Pressman and A. C. Parks (Editors)

ACTIVITY SETTING

Ideally, this will be briefly explained in the classroom but actually conducted completely independently, in the students' real lives, outside of the classroom.

ACTIVITY DURATION

The activity takes about 10 minutes to explain. Then, ideally, students will have a free day in which to perform this assignment in between class meetings. If this is not possible, consider adapting the exercise to "the perfect afternoon" or even "the perfect hour."

SUGGESTED READINGS

- Before-the-activity readings: I do not recommend any readings prior to this activity since it is best if students approach the activity naively.

- After-the-activity enrichment articles: The first by Ford and Mauss (2014) accessibly highlights the downsides of consciously pursuing happiness. The second brief reading, by Wilson and Gilbert (2005), is a good overview of affective forecasting and decision making. Finally, you might consider using Chapter 14 of this book (Klaiber and Sin) as a follow-up activity focused on small moments of happiness and their effects on well-being, which is a natural next step after this learning exercise.
  - Ford and Mauss (2014)
  - Wilson and Gilbert (2005)

BACKGROUND AND INSTRUCTIONS

This activity allows students to explore their intuitions about what makes them happy and then see their intuitions play out in real time. With a little reflection, students should be able to come up with an idea of what their perfect day should look like. Therefore, it is best that they approach this activity naively, without having done any specific background readings beforehand.

- The instructor explains that students are to design a perfect day that maximizes their happiness but also one that they are reasonably able to live out in their current circumstances (meaning that it may not be feasible for them to see their families or romantic partners. Some of them may need to do this on a day when they have class, work, or other constraints. The challenge is to make whatever day they choose as perfect as it possibly can be).
  - The instructor should be deliberate about using the word "perfect" (this can later lead to an interesting discussion about how the pressure to craft a perfect day can detract from natural enjoyment). However, instructors

should not explicitly require students to monitor their happiness levels throughout the day (this often happens naturally, which can be an enlightening realization).

- Specifically, students are to plan what they will do and who they will spend their time with from the time they wake up until they go to sleep.
  - Instructors may encourage students to use a day planner or an online calendar to map out exactly what their day will look like. However, some students will want their perfect day to be lived spontaneously, without a lot of preplanning. Given this, instructors may want to suggest, but not require, structured planning.
  - Another idea is for instructors to ask students to provide a broad idea of what their perfect day will hopefully look like. It could be organized around specific themes, such as social connection, rest, or achievement. This will allow for more spontaneity as the day plays out.

- On their own, students attempt to live out that day.

- Soon after—ideally the next day—students look back on their day and write a reflection. See Appendix 13.1 for a list of effective prompts and discussion points.

- When the class meets next, begin with a discussion of the perfect day. Instructors can also use the questions provided in Appendix 13.1 to guide discussion. You might ask students to raise their hands if their perfect day included common themes such as getting extra sleep, shopping, spending time with friends, eating a favorite food, watching a movie, or doing schoolwork. You might ask what themes you missed and then open the topic up for discussion.
  - This may also lead to a conversation about what research shows does make people happy (e.g., socializing) and what generally does not (e.g., shopping for oneself vs. buying gifts for others; Dunn et al., 2008; Sandstrom & Dunn, 2014).

- If it does not arise naturally, ask if anyone felt excessive pressure to feel happy on this day and how that affected their experience. This may be a good time to introduce research on the paradoxical effects of consciously pursuing happiness (e.g., Mauss et al., 2011) and connect it to students' experiences of pursuing perfection.

- If the activity is presented early in the course, a second option is to have students return to their perfect day reflections toward the end of the course and determine if they would now change anything, given what they learned.

DISCUSSION

Research suggests that we are all imperfect predictors of what makes us happy. Surely, we do often get it right; we intuitively know that eating ice cream will be pleasurable, while getting the flu will be dreadful. But this exercise can effectively demonstrate that we also make numerous everyday errors when predicting what will make us happy per important work on affective forecasting errors (Wilson & Gilbert, 2005). Simply put, *affective forecasting* is the process of predicting one's future feelings. These predictions are important because they often drive one's decisions; a student may choose a specific major, Greek organization, roommate, or romantic partner because they think it will eventually lead them to happiness. Unfortunately, we are all prone to systematic errors when making these predictions. For example, the happiness that follows from a success or a material purchase often does not last as long as we think it will (Dunn et al., 2011; Gilbert et al., 1998). On the other hand, a brief social interaction with a stranger or money spent on someone else tends to bring us more happiness than we expect (Dunn et al., 2008; Sandstrom & Dunn, 2014; Sun et al., 2020).

The truths of affective forecasting errors often reveal themselves in discussions of the perfect day. Students may note that the exercise made them more aware of their own specific blind spots as they see them play out in their real lives. For example, students may comment on how they thought their perfect day should involve a lot of naps, catching up on their favorite TV programs, or other passive, solitary leisure activities, but then they realize they actually felt much happier while spending time with friends, going to the gym, or doing something more active and social. These realizations can lead to interesting discussions of why and when we make these sorts of errors. For example, students may want to discuss the cultural myths that glorify passive forms of leisure ("I need some me-time"; e.g., Csikszentmihalyi & LeFevre, 1989). Or they may note the powerful forces of marketing that made them automatically assume that happiness could be found while shopping (Dunn et al., 2011).

Another line of research establishes that the conscious, effortful pursuit of happiness can be highly counterproductive (e.g., Mauss et al., 2011). The perfect day activity also drives this point home (and this is why it is important to call it the perfect day, not merely a nice day or a happy day). Students often remark that they found themselves excessively monitoring their happiness in a way that felt unnatural and distracting. Moreover, the perfect day can often be disappointing. Students comment on being frustrated with aspects of life that interfered with their goal. This includes having to deal with school or work or minor inconveniences like bad weather. Some even cite interpersonal consequences, like being annoyed with friends who were not fully cooperating with their plans for the perfect day. This can reinforce the point that an excessive focus on one's own happiness can be highly self-centered (Mauss et al., 2012).

Having said that, based on past classroom experiences, the perfect day is an enjoyable and beneficial activity for students. While most of this evidence is anecdotal, in one introductory-level positive psychology course ($N = 26$), at the end of the semester, students responded to two questions about this activity, using a 1 (*not at all*) to 7 (*very much*) Likert scale. For the question "How enjoyable was this activity?" the mean was 5.92 ($SD = 1.59$). For the question "How useful was this activity, in terms of your well-being?" the mean was 5.30 ($SD = 1.02$).

As with many positive psychology activities, students vary in their reactions to the perfect day assignment. Personality certainly plays a role; optimists may be best able to see an ordinary day as being full of possibilities for happiness, while pessimists might find it difficult to craft a perfect day in imperfect conditions (e.g., having to go to work on their perfect day, planning a hike only to have it rain). This is an opportunity to discuss the idea of finding small moments of happiness in one's daily life, even if the broader circumstances are not ideal.

Ultimately, from this assignment, we conclude that the perfect day may not be feasible and that this framework creates unrealistic expectations and too much self-focus. The instructor can use this assignment to underscore a broad point: The lesson of positive psychology is not that a person should strive to be happy all of the time.

APPENDIX 13.1: Worksheet for the Perfect Day

BEFORE THE ACTIVITY

Think about what would constitute a perfect day (afternoon/hour) for you, one that you could realistically experience right now. What would this day look like? What would you do on your perfect day (afternoon/hour)? You might choose to map it out very carefully, with specific activities to be done at specific times from morning to night. Or, you might prefer a more spontaneous approach. The level of detail is up to you. However, please indicate some of the key places, people, and activities you plan to engage in.

_____
_____
_____
_____
_____
_____
_____
_____

Before class meets again, attempt to live that day (afternoon/hour). As soon as possible afterward, complete the next set of questions.

AFTER THE ACTIVITY

Instructions: As soon as possible after your perfect day, answer the following questions. Prepare to discuss in class.
What did you plan to do on your perfect day?

_____
_____
_____

How much concrete planning did you do ahead of time?

_____

_____

_____

Did the day go as expected? Why or why not? Consider both internal reasons (e.g., your own thoughts and feelings) and external reasons (e.g., your schedule, other people).

_____

_____

_____

What were some of the high points of the day? What were the low points?

_____

_____

_____

What would you most like to change?

_____

_____

_____

Did you notice yourself monitoring how happy you felt as you went about your day? Did you pressure yourself to be happy? If so, how do you think this affected your experience of your perfect day?

_____

_____

_____

A printable version of this appendix can be downloaded from the APA website at https://www.apa.org/pubs/books/more-activities-teaching-positive-psychology.

REFERENCES

Csikszentmihalyi, M., & LeFevre, J. (1989). Optimal experience in work and leisure. *Journal of Personality and Social Psychology, 56*(5), 815–822. https://doi.org/10.1037/0022-3514.56.5.815

Dunn, E. W., Aknin, L. B., & Norton, M. I. (2008). Spending money on others promotes happiness. *Science, 319*(5870), 1687–1688. https://doi.org/10.1126/science.1150952

Dunn, E. W., Gilbert, D. T., & Wilson, T. D. (2011). If money doesn't make you happy then you probably aren't spending it right. *Journal of Consumer Psychology, 21*(2), 115–125. https://doi.org/10.1016/j.jcps.2011.02.002

Ford, B. Q., & Mauss, I. B. (2014). The paradoxical effects of pursuing positive emotion: When and why wanting to feel happy backfires. In J. Gruber & J. T. Moskowitz (Eds.), *Positive emotion: Integrating the light sides and dark sides* (pp. 363–381). Oxford University Press. https://doi.org/10.1093/acprof:oso/9780199926725.003.0020

Gilbert, D. T., Pinel, E. C., Wilson, T. D., Blumberg, S. J., & Wheatley, T. P. (1998). Immune neglect: A source of durability bias in affective forecasting. *Journal of Personality and Social Psychology, 75*(3), 617–638. https://doi.org/10.1037/0022-3514.75.3.617

Mauss, I. B., Savino, N. S., Anderson, C. L., Weisbuch, M., Tamir, M., & Laudenslager, M. L. (2012). The pursuit of happiness can be lonely. *Emotion, 12*(5), 908–912. https://doi.org/10.1037/a0025299

Mauss, I. B., Tamir, M., Anderson, C. L., & Savino, N. S. (2011). Can seeking happiness make people unhappy? Paradoxical effects of valuing happiness. *Emotion, 11*(4), 807–815. https://doi.org/10.1037/a0022010

Sandstrom, G. M., & Dunn, E. W. (2014). Social interactions and well-being: The surprising power of weak ties. *Personality and Social Psychology Bulletin, 40*(7), 910–922. https://doi.org/10.1177/0146167214529799

Sun, J., Harris, K., & Vazire, S. (2020). Is well-being associated with the quantity and quality of social interactions? *Journal of Personality and Social Psychology, 119*(6), 1478–1496. https://doi.org/10.1037/pspp0000272

Wilson, T. D., & Gilbert, D. T. (2005). Affective forecasting: Knowing what to want. *Current Directions in Psychological Science, 14*(3), 131–134. https://doi.org/10.1111/j.0963-7214.2005.00355.x

14

Uplifts in Daily Life

Patrick Klaiber and Nancy L. Sin

Students will create their personal list of uplifts (daily positive events), which they will track for 2 days alongside the positive emotions experienced during the uplifts. This activity will prompt students to reflect on the frequency and types of uplifts they typically experience in daily life and the potential influences of these uplifts on their well-being.

CONCEPT

Uplifts are minor events in daily life, such as having dinner with friends, engaging in a hobby, or hiking. These experiences reflect transactions with one's environment and often result in upticks in positive emotions. Surprisingly, these uplifts are more common than daily stressors or negative events. This activity aims to encourage students to notice and reflect on uplifts in their daily lives and to highlight the potential benefits of these positive events for psychological, social, and physical well-being.

MATERIALS NEEDED

For the initial in-class portion of the activity, each student will need a pen or pencil and a printed worksheet to create their personal list of uplifts (Appendix 14.1). The activity can be adapted for an online format by providing students with an electronic file. It may be helpful for students to set reminders on their mobile phones for two consecutive evenings to prompt them to complete the worksheet.

https://doi.org/10.1037/0000417-014
More Activities for Teaching Positive Psychology: A Guide for Instructors, S. D. Pressman and A. C. Parks (Editors)

ACTIVITY SETTING

This activity is designed as an in-person classroom activity, but it can be adapted for remote learning. Students should create their personal uplift scale during class time, followed by at least 2 days of uplift tracking. Results and insights from the uplift tracking can be discussed in class, in addition to reflection through a short writing assignment. This activity best fits with topics like positive activity interventions, positive emotions, and savoring.

ACTIVITY DURATION

The in-class introduction to the activity will take approximately 10 to 15 minutes, and the uplift tracking, which students will do on their own, is expected to take less than 5 minutes each day for 2 days. Discussion of the uplift tracking results during class may require 15 to 30 minutes. Furthermore, if students are assigned to complete the writing assignment, they may need up to 60 minutes to respond to the writing prompts.

SUGGESTED READINGS

- Before the activity: In the week leading up to the class activity, it is recommended that students read the following article to learn about the concept of daily positive events and their implications for health:
  - Sin et al. (2015)

- After the activity: This is an optional reading that students can be instructed to read soon after they complete 2 days of uplift tracking. This article—which describes individual differences in daily positive events—can help students formulate their thoughts in preparation for an in-class discussion and/or writing assignment:
  - Klaiber et al. (2022)

BACKGROUND AND INSTRUCTIONS

Uplifts (also called daily positive events or pleasant events) are minor events in daily life, such as spending time in nature or sharing a laugh with a co-worker. These experiences often result in upticks in positive emotions when they occur (Klaiber et al., 2022). In national studies of the daily lives of American adults, uplifts are reported on an average of 72% to 75% of days—much more frequently than daily stressors (which occur on about 40% of days; Sin & Almeida, 2018). Uplifts vary widely in their characteristics, depending on the person and their social roles and responsibilities. In particular, most uplifts are positive social interactions (e.g., laughing with friends), yet some people—for instance, older adults—experience more uplifts in solitude (e.g., spending time in nature). People who juggle multiple social roles (e.g., work, family, and volunteering responsibilities) find that these roles bring more stressors as well as more opportunities for positive experiences. Importantly, uplifts and their attendant increases in psychological and social well-being are known to be protective for health, including better sleep quality and longer sleep duration (e.g., Sin et al., 2020); lower levels of inflammation (Sin et al., 2015); and steeper, more adaptive diurnal cortisol slopes (Sin et al., 2017).

This classroom activity is designed to encourage students to notice and reflect on uplifts in their daily lives and to highlight the potential benefits of these positive events for psychological, social, and physical well-being. Inspired by Fordyce's (1977) happiness program, students are instructed to create a personal list of eight uplifts that they usually enjoy and that typically might happen every day or several times a week for them. For 2 days, students will then rate their daily uplifts and corresponding positive emotions in the evening. In a subsequent class session, students will be encouraged to reflect on and discuss the insights from their uplift tracking activity. The practice of attending to uplifts is in line with the social media trend of embracing glimmers, which are described by TikTok creators as micromoments that lead to feelings of joy, calm, awe, safety, belonging, or other positive emotions (Balao, 2023).

We now turn to the instructions for this activity. For each student, distribute a copy of the uplift tracking sheet entitled My Personal Uplifts Scale (Appendix 14.1). Instruct students to create a list of eight positive events that occur fairly often in their everyday lives and that they typically find enjoyable (e.g., spending time with close friends, taking a leisurely walk, engaging in a hobby, recreational sports). To aid students in generating their list of uplifts, show an example of a completed worksheet (Appendix 14.2).

Students should then be instructed to pick 2 days on which they will track their uplifts and emotions prior to the next class, when the results of this activity will be discussed. In the evenings, before going to bed on those 2 days, students will indicate whether each of the uplifts occurred and how positive they felt during these events. The uplift tracking sheet also has an "Other uplifts" category to allow students to record miscellaneous positive events that were not on their list of eight uplifts. Students should continue to engage in their daily routines as usual in order to gain insight into their typical exposure and emotional responses to uplifts.

Intervention Option

If desired, the uplift tracking activity could be extended to include a within-person intervention: Students could spend 2 days tracking their natural patterns of uplifts, followed by several additional days of intentionally noticing, seeking out, and/or creating opportunities for uplifts. For example, students can select one or several specific uplift(s) to actively create or seek out, like spending time with friends, reading for pleasure, or trying out new recipes. Students should be provided with additional printouts of the uplift tracking sheet and should be instructed to circle or highlight the uplifts that they will intentionally engage in for the intervention. The instructor can suggest behavioral strategies for creating positive events, including planning the event in advance (e.g., scheduling a time and place) and inviting others to join, if applicable.

Class Discussion

After finishing the uplift tracking activity, students will be asked to bring the completed worksheets to the next class and/or to complete the writing assignment before the next class session. Discussion prompts are provided in the Assignment section. For an in-class discussion, the instructor may choose to utilize interactive polling (using live polling tools e.g., Mentimeter, Poll Everywhere, Slido, Zoom Whiteboard) in which students can share their experiences with the uplift tracking activity with their classmates. For interactive polling, prompts must be inputted into the polling website or application before class, and then the instructor will share a link with students during class so they can submit responses using their laptops or other mobile devices. Students can be asked to respond to prompts such as, "What emotions did you feel during your uplifts? (e.g., happy, grateful, excited, relaxed)" and "In one word or phrase, describe your most positive uplift during the activity tracking period." The responses can be displayed in real time on the classroom screen using various layouts (e.g., word cloud layout). For online classes that meet on Zoom, students can use the Whiteboard feature to write their responses to the prompts and to upvote and/or comment on their classmates' responses (e.g., by drawing circles, check marks, hearts). Based on previous research as well as pilot testing for this teaching activity, students are likely to experience multiple uplifts each day, and these uplifts are expected to produce noticeable boosts in positive emotions and other aspects of well-being (e.g., social connectedness, vitality). Further research findings and background information that can help instructors lead the classroom discussion are provided in the Discussion section.

DISCUSSION

Major life events (e.g., bereavement, job loss) have long been known to produce substantial and enduring impacts on mental and physical health. Yet, minor events—including uplifts and stressors—occur frequently in everyday life and may accumulate over time to influence long-term health and well-being. In the past half-century, a number of studies have used checklists (e.g., Hassles and Uplifts Scale by DeLongis et al., 1982; Pleasant Events Schedule by MacPhillamy & Lewinsohn, 1982) to track the occurrence and pleasantness of uplifts. Early research demonstrated that people who engage in more frequent uplifts tend to have lower severity of depressive symptoms (Lewinsohn & Libet, 1972) and greater happiness (Fordyce, 1977). This work has built the foundation for behavioral activation therapy, which utilizes positive events to combat depression and increase psychological well-being (Cuijpers et al., 2007; Mazzucchelli et al., 2010). In addition, research in positive psychology suggests that positive activities can serve as modifiable targets for interventions to enhance positive affect and ameliorate psychological distress (Wen et al., 2020). This classroom activity illustrates these concepts by encouraging students to observe the proximal effects of uplifts on emotions and reflect on the ways that uplifts can be incorporated into real-world strategies or programs to enhance well-being.

While engaging in more positive events may seem like an easy way to improve psychological well-being, many people face significant barriers. Engaging in positive events is effortful and requires a variety of resources, including motivation, energy, time, opportunity, social networks, and money. Structural factors—for instance, education, wealth, occupational class, and race and ethnicity—can influence access to resources, leading to social disparities in optimism and life satisfaction (Boehm et al., 2015). For example, communities of color and people with lower socioeconomic status tend to experience fewer positive events compared with people who are White and/or higher in socioeconomic status (Sin & Almeida, 2018). Furthermore, people with a depressive disorder tend to report fewer positive events but not reduced emotional benefits when positive events occur (Bylsma et al., 2011). These barriers are important to keep in mind when discussing the results of the activity with students. Furthermore, environmental factors can influence how many and what types of positive events people experience. Restrictions in daily life—such as the stay-at-home mandates early in the COVID-19 pandemic—led to more socially distanced uplifts, including positive remote social interactions and more positive events in nature (see Chapter 11, this volume, for more information on positive experiences in nature and also Klaiber et al., 2021). Personality also influences one's likelihood of experiencing uplifts: People with higher extraversion or openness to experience tend to have more uplifts than people with lower levels of these traits (Klaiber et al., 2022).

With regard to emotional responses to positive events, both stable person-level differences (e.g., personality, age) and contextual factors (e.g., factors that change moment-to-moment or day-to-day) can contribute to how much enjoyment is derived from positive experiences. For example, people higher in neuroticism show larger increases in positive emotions on days when uplifts occur than people lower in neuroticism (Klaiber et al., 2022). Also, younger adults experience greater declines in negative emotions in response to daily uplifts compared with middle-aged and older adults (Klaiber et al., 2021). Aspects of one's day are known to influence how much one benefits from uplifts. For instance, after nights of longer sleep, positive events are more likely to occur and produce relatively larger increases in positive emotions (Sin et al., 2020).

While uplifts usually result in increases in positive emotions, the specific emotions evoked can depend on the person and the characteristics of the positive event. Going for a walk in nature is likely to instill feelings of calmness, whereas attending a party with friends is more likely to prompt high arousal positive emotions, for example, excitement. There are also personality differences in the types of positive emotions that people experience (Klaiber et al., 2021). People with higher levels of openness to experience tend to feel more surprised during positive events, whereas people higher in extraversion tend to feel more proud during positive events.

Uplifts can have a variety of psychological, social, and physical benefits that extend beyond simply feeling good (Sin & Almeida, 2018). For example, some interpersonal uplifts can foster relationships by stimulating feelings of social connectedness. Uplifts that are challenging, stretch one's abilities, or involve small wins—such as learning a new language, training for a race, honing one's musical skills, or accomplishing tasks that advance personal goals—may lead to an enhanced sense of control, mastery, and greater self-esteem (Zautra et al., 2005). Uplifts may also buffer against the harms that arise from stress, for instance, reducing physical symptoms on stressful days (e.g., Bono et al., 2013).

This activity might raise the question of how students can maximize the benefits of positive events in their daily lives. To increase the positive effects of uplifts, people may consider engaging in a variety of different uplifts to maintain the freshness and meaning of these activities, as well as selecting activities that fit well with their personal preferences, strengths, and values (Wen et al., 2020). It is also recommended that people play an active part in creating their uplifts and not passively waiting for them to occur. Actively seeking out positive events has been shown to improve well-being and alleviate depressive symptoms by evoking positive emotions in daily life (Cuijpers et al., 2007; Mazzucchelli et al., 2010). Fewer social ties, work and family demands, and low motivation can be barriers that limit an individual's ability to encounter and enjoy positive events. To overcome these barriers, students can be intentional in selecting a variety of potential uplifts, spanning solitary as well as social experiences and higher energy (e.g., biking) as well as lower energy activities (e.g., reading). Students can also schedule these events in advance and enlist family and friends to take part in the positive experiences.

CONCLUSION

In contrast to the concept of stressors, most psychology students will have little or no exposure to empirical research and practical applications of uplifts. Uplifts occur more frequently than do daily hassles, contribute to enhanced positive emotions, and can promote psychological, social, and physical health. This teaching activity will help students gain insights into their daily uplifts and reflect on ways they might inject more positive experiences into their everyday lives. In doing so, students will obtain a more comprehensive picture of the richness of daily life events that impact health and well-being.

ASSIGNMENT

Prompts for a Writing Assignment or Classroom Discussion

Please think back to the days on which you tracked your uplifts and answer the following questions:

1. Did you detect any patterns in your daily uplifts? Did you feel differently during uplifts in solitude versus with other people? Which uplifts occurred more or less frequently than you had expected, and why?

2. Did the uplifts enhance your positive emotions in the moment? Why or why not?

3. What kind of emotions did you experience during or following the uplifts?

4. Besides emotions, have you noticed any other changes stemming from your uplifts?

5. In the future, what can you do to notice, enjoy, and create more opportunities for uplifts in your life?

6. For the intervention option only: Did you observe any differences on the days you were instructed to actively seek out uplifts compared with the days when you simply tracked your uplifts? Was it easy to engage in more uplifts in your daily life?

APPENDIX 14.1: My Personal Uplifts Scale

List your top uplifts below. For 2 days, indicate whether each uplift occurred and how positive you felt during the experience, using the following scale: 0 = *not positive at all*; 1 = *a little positive*; 2 = *moderately positive*; 3 = *very positive*.

	Day 1		Day 2	
My top uplift	Occurred? (y/n)	How positive did you feel during this event?	Occurred? (y/n)	How positive did you feel during this event?
1		0–1–2–3		0–1–2–3
2		0–1–2–3		0–1–2–3
3		0–1–2–3		0–1–2–3
4		0–1–2–3		0–1–2–3
5		0–1–2–3		0–1–2–3
6		0–1–2–3		0–1–2–3
7		0–1–2–3		0–1–2–3
8		0–1–2–3		0–1–2–3
Other uplifts		0–1–2–3		0–1–2–3

A printable version of this appendix can be downloaded from the APA website at https://www.apa.org/pubs/books/more-activities-teaching-positive-psychology.

APPENDIX 14.2: Example of a Completed Uplifts Scale

My top uplift	Day 1		Day 2	
	Occurred? (y/n)	How positive did you feel during this event?	Occurred? (y/n)	How positive did you feel during this event?
1. Going for a run	y	0-1-②-3	n	0-1-2-3
2. Playing the guitar	n	0-1-2-3	n	0-1-2-3
3. Listening to a podcast	n	0-1-2-3	y	⓪-1-2-3
4. Playing computer games	n	0-1-2-3	y	0-①-2-3
5. Going to the club	n	0-1-2-3	n	0-1-2-3
6. Watching a show with my partner	y	0-1-2-③	n	0-1-2-3
7. Visiting my grandmother	n	0-1-2-3	n	0-1-2-3
8. Eating ice cream	y	0-1-②-3	n	0-1-2-3
Other uplifts: Going on a date	n	0-1-2-3	y	0-1-2-③

A printable version of this appendix can be downloaded from the APA website at https://www.apa.org/pubs/books/more-activities-teaching-positive-psychology.

REFERENCES

Balao, N. (2023). A "glimmer" is the opposite of a trigger and many TikTok creators are embracing it. *In the Know.* https://www.intheknow.com/post/a-glimmer-is-the-opposite-of-a-trigger-and-tiktok-creators-are-embracing-it/#:~:text=%E2%80%9CBasically%20a%20glimmer%20is%20the,life%20feels%20so%20much%20sweeter.%E2%80%9D

Boehm, J. K., Chen, Y., Williams, D. R., Ryff, C., & Kubzansky, L. D. (2015). Unequally distributed psychological assets: Are there social disparities in optimism, life satisfaction, and positive affect? *PLOS ONE, 10*(2), Article e0118066. https://doi.org/10.1371/journal.pone.0118066

Bono, J. E., Glomb, T. M., Shen, W., Kim, E., & Koch, A. J. (2013). Building positive resources: Effects of positive events and positive reflection on work stress and health. *Academy of Management Journal, 56*(6), 1601–1627. https://doi.org/10.5465/amj.2011.0272

Bylsma, L. M., Taylor-Clift, A., & Rottenberg, J. (2011). Emotional reactivity to daily events in major and minor depression. *Journal of Abnormal Psychology, 120*(1), 155–167. https://doi.org/10.1037/a0021662

Cuijpers, P., van Straten, A., & Warmerdam, L. (2007). Behavioral activation treatments of depression: A meta-analysis. *Clinical Psychology Review, 27*(3), 318–326. https://doi.org/10.1016/j.cpr.2006.11.001

DeLongis, A., Coyne, J. C., Dakof, G., Folkman, S., & Lazarus, R. S. (1982). Relationship of daily hassles, uplifts, and major life events to health status. *Health Psychology, 1*(2), 119–136. https://doi.org/10.1037/0278-6133.1.2.119

Fordyce, M. W. (1977). Development of a program to increase personal happiness. *Journal of Counseling Psychology, 24*(6), 511–521. https://doi.org/10.1037/0022-0167.24.6.511

Klaiber, P., Wen, J. H., DeLongis, A., & Sin, N. L. (2021). The ups and downs of daily life during COVID-19: Age differences in affect, stress, and positive events. *The Journals of Gerontology. Series B, Psychological Sciences and Social Sciences, 76*(2), e30–e37. https://doi.org/10.1093/geronb/gbaa096

Klaiber, P., Wen, J. H., Ong, A. D., Almeida, D. M., & Sin, N. L. (2022). Personality differences in the occurrence and affective correlates of daily positive events. *Journal of Personality, 90*(3), 441–456. https://doi.org/10.1111/jopy.12676

Lewinsohn, P. M., & Libet, J. (1972). Pleasant events, activity schedules, and depressions. *Journal of Abnormal Psychology, 79*(3), 291–295. https://doi.org/10.1037/h0033207

MacPhillamy, D. J., & Lewinsohn, P. M. (1982). The pleasant events schedule: Studies on reliability, validity, and scale intercorrelation. *Journal of Consulting and Clinical Psychology, 50*(3), 363–380. https://doi.org/10.1037/0022-006X.50.3.363

Mazzucchelli, T. G., Kane, R. T., & Rees, C. S. (2010). Behavioral activation interventions for well-being: A meta-analysis. *The Journal of Positive Psychology, 5*(2), 105–121. https://doi.org/10.1080/17439760903569154

Sin, N. L., & Almeida, D. M. (2018). Daily positive experiences and health: Biobehavioral pathways and resilience to daily stress. In C. D. Ryff & R. F. Krueger (Eds.), *The Oxford handbook of integrative health science* (pp. 154–172). Oxford University Press. https://doi.org/10.1093/oxfordhb/9780190676384.013.10

Sin, N. L., Graham-Engeland, J. E., & Almeida, D. M. (2015). Daily positive events and inflammation: Findings from the National Study of Daily Experiences. *Brain, Behavior, and Immunity, 43*, 130–138. https://doi.org/10.1016/j.bbi.2014.07.015

Sin, N. L., Ong, A. D., Stawski, R. S., & Almeida, D. M. (2017). Daily positive events and diurnal cortisol rhythms: Examination of between-person differences and within-person variation. *Psychoneuroendocrinology, 83*, 91–100. https://doi.org/10.1016/j.psyneuen.2017.06.001

Sin, N. L., Wen, J. H., Klaiber, P., Buxton, O. M., & Almeida, D. M. (2020). Sleep duration and affective reactivity to stressors and positive events in daily life. *Health Psychology, 39*(12), 1078–1088. https://doi.org/10.1037/hea0001033

Wen, J. H., Lyubomirsky, S., & Sin, N. L. (2020). Positive activity interventions targeted to improve depressive symptoms. In S. I. Donaldson, M. Csikszentmihalyi, & J. Nakamura (Eds.), *Positive psychological science* (2nd ed., pp. 225–245). Routledge. https://doi.org/10.4324/9780203731833-17

Zautra, A. J., Affleck, G. G., Tennen, H., Reich, J. W., & Davis, M. C. (2005). Dynamic approaches to emotions and stress in everyday life: Bolger and Zuckerman reloaded with positive as well as negative affects. *Journal of Personality, 73*(6), 1511–1538. https://doi.org/10.1111/j.0022-3506.2005.00357.x

15

Learning to Use Your Strengths Daily

Joanne F. Zinger

In this activity, students complete a self-report strengths assessment, learn what their top signature strengths are (per the assessment results), and discuss how they might apply those strengths in their everyday lives.

CONCEPT

In this activity, students complete the values in action (VIA) character strengths assessment to identify their top five signature strengths, which are personal characteristics contributing to their happiness without diminishing others' happiness. They reflect on past instances of using these strengths, explore how they might apply them in various aspects of their lives, and discuss potential future endeavors that align with their signature strengths. This activity introduces students to the concept of character strengths and empowers them to utilize their unique strengths for personal and professional growth. The assignment can be conducted in various settings and is suitable for many types of classes as it encourages students to understand and harness their strengths, fostering well-being and self-awareness as a learning outcome.

https://doi.org/10.1037/0000417-015
More Activities for Teaching Positive Psychology: A Guide for Instructors, S. D. Pressman and A. C. Parks (Editors)

MATERIALS NEEDED

Students will need a computer, tablet, or phone with access to the internet to complete the free online VIA character strengths assessment (https://www.viacharacter.org/). Instructors will need a computer or tablet with access to the internet and a projector to show a short video clip. Alternatively, if the video clip cannot be shown during class, the instructor should watch the video before class and summarize the content (see Appendix 15.1 for a summary of the clip).

ACTIVITY SETTING

This activity can be conducted: (a) completely in the classroom, (b) using a combination of in the classroom and at home, (c) primarily at home, or (d) in an online environment.

- Completely in the classroom: If the instructor is not pressed for time in the course, completing the entire activity during class is a nice "break" from traditional instructor-led lecturing and will be an engaging, active-learning experience for the students.

- Combination of in the classroom and at home: In this option, the concept will be introduced during one class session. Then, students will complete tasks at home, and a discussion will take place during the following class session. As such, this option spans two class sessions.

- Primarily at home: In this option, the topic will be introduced in class, and then students will complete the remaining tasks at home.

- Online environment: This activity could easily be completed in an online environment by using prerecorded videos and allowing for discussion on a course message board or in breakout Zoom sessions.

This activity will fit well in (a) a positive psychology course when covering strengths and/or individual differences, (b) a personality course when covering the intersection of positive psychology and personality psychology, (c) an industrial/organizational psychology course when covering the use of a strengths-based approach in the workplace, (d) an introduction to psychology course when covering individual differences and/or positive psychology, and/or (e) an internship placement course where students are learning to apply their skills and competencies in a professional environment.

ACTIVITY DURATION

This activity takes 45 to 60 minutes to complete. However, the amount of actual class time spent on this activity can be reduced to 25 to 30 minutes (or even 5–10 minutes) by having students complete some (or most) components at home.

This activity can be completed in one class period or broken up across two class periods.

SUGGESTED READINGS

- Before the activity, students should read the section of their positive psychology textbook that discusses strengths or workplace well-being. If the course is being taught without a textbook (or in a nonpositive psychology course), an open-access chapter that includes an introduction to the concept of strengths assessments, such as this suggested reading, would also work:
  - Emmons (2023)

- The following articles may be assigned as additional or optional enrichment readings to enhance the quality of the discussion:
  - Linley et al. (2010)
  - Merritt et al. (2019)
  - Schutte and Malouff (2019)
  - Schutte and Malouff (2021)

BACKGROUND AND INSTRUCTIONS

In addition to studying positive emotions and positive institutions, positive psychology also studies positive traits. One way to conceptualize positive traits is through the examination of *character strengths*, which are personal characteristics that contribute to a person's happiness without diminishing the happiness of others; these include strengths like creativity, bravery, kindness, fairness, and gratitude. We all possess at least a few of these strengths, although the strengths we possess vary from person to person. The idea of character strengths was first proposed by Donald Clifton (Hodges & Clifton, 2004), with a great deal of later work on the topic developed by positive psychologists Chris Peterson and Martin Seligman (Peterson & Seligman, 2004). They argued that there are 24 different signature strengths; any given person is likely to be strong on some of them and weak on others, but we all have at least a few signature strengths that we are naturally good at. Furthermore, in order for us to be as happy as possible and to make the world a happier place, it is argued that we should find out what our strengths are and try to use them as often as possible. So, if we are already naturally good at something, we should put ourselves in situations where we can use the strengths that we already have to do our best work, improve our lives, and improve the lives of those around us. For more information on the history of strengths research and assessment, as well as different approaches to measuring strengths, please refer to most positive psychology textbooks for further background information (e.g., Lopez et al., 2018, Chapter 3); Seligman (2004)—especially Part II: Strengths and Virtues—is also an excellent resource. These materials will be useful when crafting your introduction to the activity detailed in the following steps:

Step 1: Provide an overview of the concept of signature strengths. This step should be completed in class.

Step 2: Show the following brief video clip, entitled, "How VIA Signature Strengths Can Enhance Your Life": https://www.youtube.com/watch? v=mklZ93lAv-w&t=9s&ab_channel=VIAStrengths. If you, the instructor, are unable to show this clip in class, you should describe/summarize its contents; please see Appendix 15.1 for a summary of this video clip. This step should be completed in class.

Step 3: To generate some curiosity, show a PowerPoint slide with all 24 signature strengths (https://tinyurl.com/38kfyfsb) and ask students to guess which one they think they are the strongest at. Students should either (a) share their answer electronically (e.g., Poll Everywhere, Google Forms, Kahoot!), (b) share their answer with the person sitting next to them, or (c) quietly write their answer down. This step should be completed in class.

Step 4: Direct students to the VIA Character Strengths website (https://www. viacharacter.org/survey/surveys/takesurvey); they will need to create a (free) account on this website before completing the survey.[1] After completing the survey, students should save their results by screenshotting or copying/pasting the results page. This step may be completed in class or at home.

Step 5: Students should spend some time reflecting on their results and answering the questions on the signature strengths handout (see Appendix 15.2). This step may be completed in class or at home.

Step 6: Have students share examples of a behavior they exhibited in the past in which they utilized one of their top five strengths. This step may be completed in class or at home (i.e., as a reflection essay or as a message board post).

Step 7: Have students share ideas about specific activities they could intentionally engage in, jobs/careers they could pursue, and/or tasks at their current

[1] Note that this activity could work equally well with other strengths measures, such as the CliftonStrengths assessment (formerly called StrengthsFinder; https://www.gallup.com/ cliftonstrengths/en/253868/popular-cliftonstrengths-assessment-products.aspx; Rath, 2007), but some of these assessments require payment (e.g., at the time of writing, the CliftonStrengths assessment costs $19.99 per student). That said, if your course is career-oriented and/or this activity is used as part of a work-related lecture, the CliftonStrengths assessment may be a better choice since it provides a several-page career advice–relevant report. Like the VIA assessment, the CliftonStrengths assessment is well-researched and has been used in several strengths-based interventions (e.g., Asplund et al., 2007). Do note that the videos you choose and the slide listing strengths that you show will need to be matched with your chosen strengths assessment approach. In addition, you may want to inform your students that most strengths websites collect data for validation and research purposes.

job they could prioritize that utilize/capitalize on their strengths. This step may be completed in class or at home (i.e., as a reflection essay or as a message board post).

DISCUSSION

In my experience, students really enjoy this activity, and research shows that the simple act of identifying strengths and thinking about how to use them in new ways is tied to well-being benefits (Seligman et al., 2005). It allows them to learn about themselves in a new and interesting way and to think about concrete steps they could take to improve their own well-being (by capitalizing on their strengths). Obviously, the results of this activity will vary from student to student, as they will all have different combinations of strengths—but generally, students should conclude this activity with a deeper understanding of the concept of signature strengths, including how they are measured, and with some knowledge of how they can apply this concept to their own lives.

Toward the beginning of the discussion (i.e., at the start of Step 5 and/or 6), it is useful for the instructor to give students an example or two from their own life/strengths list to "get the ball rolling." For example, at the start of Step 6, I typically share with my students that one of my strengths is "zest" and that this strength especially comes through when I am teaching a large course because of my high levels of enthusiasm. This is a useful strength for capturing the attention of hundreds of students in a lecture hall. However, the strengths required to teach a small course are a bit different; a naturally talented graduate seminar leader, for example, would likely be strong in "love of learning," "perspective," and/or "social intelligence" (none of which are my top strengths). As a result, I am very good at teaching large courses but less good at teaching graduate seminars. Using strengths-based reasoning, I was able to trade my small classes for large classes, and this switch was very successful, with benefits for both myself and my students. This is also a good time to direct students toward the additional reading list, which includes two articles that examine the application of signature strengths in the workplace.

In a class discussion of signature strengths, it is very common for some students to mention or perseverate on their "least strong" strengths (i.e., the strengths that get ranked last), mistakenly thinking that their primary goal should be to work on improving their lowest ranked strengths instead of focusing/capitalizing on the strengths they already possess. Indeed, we are naturally predisposed to focus on our shortcomings, but doing so leaves us with a significant cost: the cost of failing to pay attention to, identify, and build on what works (Linley, 2008). In these cases, I try to help students understand the error in their thinking by giving the following examples: (a) Think for a moment about Simone Biles—she is an extremely accomplished Olympic gymnast, having won seven Olympic medals (including four gold medals). Although, of course, she had to train extremely hard to be as successful as she is, she also has a natural talent for this sport and a body that is well-suited to it (4 feet,

8 inches tall and 104 pounds). Imagine if, after winning lots of gymnastics competitions in high school, she were to say, "Hey, I'm obviously great at gymnastics, so I don't really need to work on getting better at that. Instead, I should focus on the sport I am the worst at: basketball!" And then imagine that she spent all her time and energy training to be a basketball player. Would she have ever made it to the Olympic basketball team? Not a chance! But instead, she identified her strength, and she put all her energy into that, making her one of the best in the world; and (b) Imagine that you are a pretty good piano player and a pretty terrible painter. Now imagine that you have the time and money to invest in 1 year of individualized lessons from an expert, and you can either take piano lessons or painting lessons. If you choose the piano lessons, you will go from pretty good to really good—and you will be able to make beautiful music for you, your family, your friends, and maybe even people on the internet to enjoy, bringing joy to a lot of people. However, if you choose the painting lessons, you will go from being a pretty terrible painter to a mediocre painter—and the paintings that you produce will not really give anyone any joy (because, ultimately, they will be "only okay"). Furthermore, you will probably get more pleasure out of making music than you will making paintings, seeing as research shows that using our strengths is tied to our well-being (e.g., Ghielen et al., 2018). Which option makes the most sense—the piano lessons or the painting lessons?

Finally, for students who still insist on working on their lesser strengths (i.e., relative weaknesses), it may be worthwhile to point out there is some evidence that working on your signature strengths and your lesser strengths can be beneficial (e.g., Chérif et al., 2021; Rust et al., 2009). Therefore, it can be okay to work on improving their lesser strengths if they wish, as long as doing so does not prevent them from capitalizing on (and further building on) their top signature strengths as well.

So, how exactly does one go about working on their signature strengths? The first study to test the effectiveness of working/focusing on one's signature strengths (Seligman et al., 2005) gave participants relatively straightforward instructions, telling them to "use one of their top strengths in a new and different way every day for one week." However, subsequent studies have added additional components that students may find helpful. For example, students who enjoy journaling may wish to write reflective essays on a daily or weekly basis based on prompts provided by Rust et al. (2009):

> Describe an event or occurrence in the past when you used this strength successfully, or describe hearing about or seeing someone else use this strength successfully (friend, relative, movie, book, etc.). Describe a plan or situation for the upcoming day or week in which you will apply this strength. (p. 470)

And/or the writing prompts provided by Duan et al. (2014):

> By what means are you using this (these) strength(s)? After using your strength(s), how did you feel? If you are used to performing similar behaviors or activities in the same manner but you were not formally aware of it (them) as your strengths until this study, how do you feel now? (p. 1352)

If students are having trouble coming up with ideas of how to apply their strengths, they may benefit from choosing from an activity from a prewritten list, such as resources from Tayyab Rashid and Jon Haidt's websites, which can be found in the Online Materials section of this chapter. Furthermore, if this activity is being performed by students in an internship course, they may benefit from the approach used by Forest et al. (2012), in which employees are first asked to describe in detail how they are working and how they are feeling *before* using their signature strengths at work and to describe in detail how they *would be* working and feeling after using signature strengths. Then, after spending some time using their signature strengths in new ways within their current job or internship environment, they should reflect on the positive consequences of using their strengths at their workplace.

Finally, although many students find this activity beneficial, there are some limitations of strengths-based assessments/approaches that should be noted. First, although several studies have demonstrated the effectiveness of signature strengths interventions (e.g., Mitchell et al., 2009; Seligman et al., 2005), the actual number of studies examining this type of intervention is still quite small. For example, a meta-analysis by Schutte and Malouff (2019) identified only 14 studies examining signature strengths interventions—compare this, for example, with meta-analyses on mindfulness (e.g., Goyal et al., 2014, with 47 studies), exercise (e.g., Brito et al., 2022, with 49 studies), or expressive writing (e.g., Frattaroli, 2006, with 146 studies). Furthermore, several of the 14 strengths intervention studies did not use random assignment (e.g., Duan et al., 2014; Proctor et al., 2011), and still others did not include active control groups (e.g., Forest et al., 2012; Waters & Sun, 2016). As such, strong evidence regarding this intervention is still developing. In addition, with 240 questions in the VIA measure, these assessments are quite time consuming, which runs the risk of students getting bored, losing focus, or not completing the assessment properly. Finally, because many of these strengths assessments are proprietary, it can be difficult to learn information on how they are scored. For example, when you complete the VIA measure online, the website provides you with your scored results—but how were those results calculated? To find out, you would need to jump through some hoops, including creating a researcher account on the VIA website and agreeing only to use the items and scoring key for the purposes of your research project (read more at https://www.viacharacter.org/faq). It is worthwhile to make students aware of these limitations.

ASSIGNMENT

This activity can easily be turned into a journal entry, small homework assignment, or message board topic—see the worksheet in Appendix 15.2 for instructions and question prompts.

For an optional follow-up assignment to the in-class activity, have students spend 1 week in which they intentionally engage in an activity that utilizes/capitalizes on at least one of their top strengths every day, keep a daily log of these activities (and how they felt afterward), and then write a brief reflection on the entire experience at the end of the week. Students should complete pretest and posttest assessments of their well-being at the start and end of this mini-project to measure its effects; the Authentic Happiness Inventory (Peterson, 2005), the 21-item Depression Anxiety Stress Scale (Lovibond & Lovibond, 1995), and/or the Satisfaction With Life Scale (Diener et al., 1985) are good choices here, given that these measures have been shown to improve in response to strengths interventions (e.g., Chérif et al., 2021; Duan & Bu, 2019; Rust et al., 2009). This would be especially impactful if you collected the pre-/posttest data from students and then shared the findings with the class (which should demonstrate that, on average, students show increases in happiness and satisfaction with life—and decreases in negative affect—from before to after the activity/intervention).

ONLINE MATERIALS

For use during the activity:

- Signature strengths PowerPoint: https://tinyurl.com/MATPPch15-1

- Brief video clip describing how we can use our signature strengths to enhance our lives: https://tinyurl.com/MATPPch15-2

- VIA Signature Strengths website: https://www.viacharacter.org/survey/surveys/takesurvey

- Haidt Different Ways to Use Strengths (see appendix): https://people.stern.nyu.edu/jhaidt/strengths_analysis.doc

- Rashid Different Ways to Use Strengths: https://tayyabrashid.com/pdf/via_strengths.pdf

Optional viewing for more information on signature strengths:

- TEDx talk by Dr. Ryan Niemiec entitled, "A Universal Language That Describes What's Best in Us": https://tinyurl.com/MATPPch15-3

- TEDx talk by Dr. Shane Lopez entitled, "Focusing on Your Strengths": https://tinyurl.com/MATPPch15-4

APPENDIX 15.1: An Overview of How Signature Strengths Can Enhance Your Life

Your signature strengths are the qualities that make you unique and help you thrive. They are the things you are naturally good at and enjoy doing. When you use your signature strengths, you feel energized and fulfilled. You are also more likely to be successful in your personal and professional life.

There are many ways to use your signature strengths to enhance your life. One way is to identify your top five strengths and then find ways to use them every day. You can do this by

- Reflecting on your past experiences. Think about the times when you felt most alive, engaged, and successful. What were you doing during those times? What were your strengths?

- Talking to friends and family. Ask them to describe your strengths and how you use them.

- Taking a strengths assessment. There are many free online assessments that can help you identify your strengths.

Once you know your strengths, you can start using them in new and creative ways. Here are a few ideas:

- Volunteer your time to a cause you care about. This is a great way to use your strengths to help others.

- Take on a new challenge at work or school. This will help you grow and develop your strengths.

- Start a new hobby or project. This is a fun way to explore your strengths and find new ways to use them.

- Spend time with people who appreciate your strengths. This will help you feel good about yourself and your abilities.

Using your signature strengths is a great way to live a happy and fulfilling life. So, take some time to identify your strengths and then find ways to use them every day. You'll be glad you did!

A printable version of this appendix can be downloaded from the APA website at https://www.apa.org/pubs/books/more-activities-teaching-positive-psychology.

APPENDIX 15.2: Signature Strengths Handout

Instructions: As we discussed in class, character strengths (or signature strengths) are personal characteristics that contribute to a person's happiness without diminishing the happiness of others. For this activity, you should find out what your own top five signature strengths are by completing the VIA Signature Strengths questionnaire on the VIA website (https://www.viacharacter.org/survey/surveys/takesurvey). Please note that you will need to create a (free) account on this website in order to complete the questionnaire. The VIA Character Strengths website collects data for validation and research purposes, but you will not receive any unwanted emails. The questionnaire takes about 15 to 20 minutes to complete, so please plan accordingly. After completing the VIA Signature Strengths questionnaire and reading over your results, please briefly answer each of the following questions (and then be prepared to discuss your answers in class):

1. What are your top five strengths?

2. What top signature strengths resonated with you the most and why?

3. Were you surprised by any of your top strengths, and if yes, why?

4. Describe an example of a recent time in your life when you utilized one of your top five strengths—Which strength did you use, and how did you use it? How did you feel during this experience? What effect (if any) do you think this experience had on you and/or on people around you?

5. Research indicates that there are well-being benefits to using your strengths regularly. What activities (at work, at school, with your friends or family, or in your spare time) do you think you could do to practice using your strengths?

6. What careers do you think match your strengths?

A printable version of this appendix can be downloaded from the APA website at https://www.apa.org/pubs/books/more-activities-teaching-positive-psychology.

REFERENCES

Asplund, J., Lopez, S. J., Hodges, T., & Harter, J. (2007). *The Clifton StrengthsFinder 2.0 technical report: Development and validation*. The Gallup Organization.

Brito, H. S., Carraça, E. V., Palmeira, A. L., Ferreira, J. P., Vleck, V., & Araújo, D. (2022). Benefits to performance and well-being of nature-based exercise: A critical systematic review and meta-analysis. *Environmental Science & Technology, 56*(1), 62–77. https://doi.org/10.1021/acs.est.1c05151

Chérif, L., Wood, V. M., & Watier, C. (2021). Testing the effectiveness of a strengths-based intervention targeting all 24 strengths: Results from a randomized controlled trial. *Psychological Reports, 124*(3), 1174–1183. https://doi.org/10.1177/0033294120937441

Diener, E., Emmons, R. A., Larsen, R. J., & Griffin, S. (1985). The Satisfaction With Life Scale. *Journal of Personality Assessment, 49*(1), 71–75. https://doi.org/10.1207/s15327752jpa4901_13

Duan, W., & Bu, H. (2019). Randomized trial investigating a single-session character-strength-based cognitive intervention on freshman's adaptability. *Research on Social Work Practice, 29*(1), 82–92. https://doi.org/10.1177/1049731517699525

Duan, W., Ho, S. M., Tang, X., Li, T., & Zhang, Y. (2014). Character strength-based intervention to promote satisfaction with life in the Chinese university context. *Journal of Happiness Studies, 15*(6), 1347–1361. https://doi.org/10.1007/s10902-013-9479-y

Emmons, R. A. (2023). Positive psychology. In R. Biswas-Diener & E. Diener (Eds.), *Noba textbook series: Psychology*. DEF Publishers. http://noba.to/9z4jf5xe

Forest, J., Mageau, G. A., Crevier-Braud, L., Bergeron, É., Dubreuil, P., & Lavigne, G. L. (2012). Harmonious passion as an explanation of the relation between signature strengths' use and well-being at work: Test of an intervention program. *Human Relations, 65*(9), 1233–1252. https://doi.org/10.1177/0018726711433134

Frattaroli, J. (2006). Experimental disclosure and its moderators: A meta-analysis. *Psychological Bulletin, 132*(6), 823–865. https://doi.org/10.1037/0033-2909.132.6.823

Ghielen, S. T. S., van Woerkom, M., & Meyers, M. C. (2018). Promoting positive outcomes through strengths interventions: A literature review. *The Journal of Positive Psychology, 13*(6), 573–585. https://doi.org/10.1080/17439760.2017.1365164

Goyal, M., Singh, S., Sibinga, E. M., Gould, N. F., Rowland-Seymour, A., Sharma, R., Berger, Z., Sleicher, D., Maron, D. D., Shihab, H. M., Ranasinghe, P. D., Linn, S.,

Saha, S., Bass, E. B., & Haythornthwaite, J. A. (2014). Meditation programs for psychological stress and well-being: A systematic review and meta-analysis. *JAMA Internal Medicine, 174*(3), 357–368. https://doi.org/10.1001/jamainternmed.2013.13018

Hodges, T. D., & Clifton, D. O. (2004). Strengths-based development in practice. In P. A. Linley & S. Joseph (Eds.), *Positive psychology in practice* (pp. 256–268). Wiley. https://doi.org/10.1002/9780470939338.ch16

Linley, P. A. (2008). *Average to A+: Realising strengths in yourself and others.* CAPP Press.

Linley, P. A., Nielsen, K. M., Gillett, R., & Biswas-Diener, R. (2010). Using signature strengths in pursuit of goals: Effects on goal progress, need satisfaction, and well-being, and implications for coaching psychologists. *International Coaching Psychology Review, 5*(1), 6–15. https://doi.org/10.53841/bpsicpr.2010.5.1.6

Lopez, S. J., Pedrotti, J. T., & Snyder, C. R. (2018). *Positive psychology: The scientific and practical explorations of human strengths.* Sage Publications.

Lovibond, P. F., & Lovibond, S. H. (1995). The structure of negative emotional states: Comparison of the Depression Anxiety Stress Scales (DASS) with the Beck Depression and Anxiety Inventories. *Behaviour Research and Therapy, 33*(3), 335–343. https://doi.org/10.1016/0005-7967(94)00075-U

Merritt, S., Huber, K., & Bartkoski, T. (2019). Application of signature strengths at work: A dual-level analysis. *The Journal of Positive Psychology, 14*(1), 113–124. https://doi.org/10.1080/17439760.2018.1519589

Mitchell, J., Stanimirovic, R., Klein, B., & Vella-Brodrick, D. (2009). A randomised controlled trial of a self-guided internet intervention promoting well-being. *Computers in Human Behavior, 25*(3), 749–760. https://doi.org/10.1016/j.chb.2009.02.003

Peterson, C. (2005). *Authentic Happiness Inventory* [Measurement instrument]. APA PsycTests. https://www.authentichappiness.sas.upenn.edu/questionnaires/authentic-happiness-inventory

Peterson, C., & Seligman, M. E. (2004). *Character strengths and virtues: A handbook and classification* (Vol. 1). Oxford University Press.

Proctor, C., Tsukayama, E., Wood, A. M., Maltby, J., Eades, J. F., & Linley, P. A. (2011). Strengths gym: The impact of a character strengths-based intervention on the life satisfaction and well-being of adolescents. *The Journal of Positive Psychology, 6*(5), 377–388. https://doi.org/10.1080/17439760.2011.594079

Rath, T. (2007). *StrengthsFinder 2.0.* Simon and Schuster.

Rust, T., Diessner, R., & Reade, L. (2009). Strengths only or strengths and relative weaknesses? A preliminary study. *The Journal of Psychology, 143*(5), 465–476. https://doi.org/10.3200/JRL.143.5.465-476

Schutte, N. S., & Malouff, J. M. (2019). The impact of signature character strengths interventions: A meta-analysis. *Journal of Happiness Studies, 20*(4), 1179–1196. https://doi.org/10.1007/s10902-018-9990-2

Schutte, N. S., & Malouff, J. M. (2021). Using signature strengths to increase happiness at work. In J. Marques (Ed.), *The Routledge companion to happiness at work* (pp. 13–22). Routledge; Taylor & Francis Group. https://doi.org/10.4324/9780429294426-2

Seligman, M. E. P. (2004). *Authentic happiness: Using the new positive psychology to realize your potential for lasting fulfilment.* Atria Books.

Seligman, M. E. P., Steen, T. A., Park, N., & Peterson, C. (2005). Positive psychology progress: Empirical validation of interventions. *American Psychologist, 60*(5), 410–421. https://doi.org/10.1037/0003-066X.60.5.410

Waters, L., & Sun, J. (2016). Can a brief strength-based parenting intervention boost self-efficacy and positive emotions in parents? *International Journal of Applied Positive Psychology, 1*(1–3), 41–56. https://doi.org/10.1007/s41042-017-0007-x

III

POSITIVE COGNITIONS: EVALUATIONS, EXPECTANCIES, AND EXPERIENCES

INTRODUCTION: POSITIVE COGNITIONS: EVALUATIONS, EXPECTANCIES, AND EXPERIENCES

In this section, you will find many classic topics in positive psychology, including meaning, flow, passion, and hope, which all represent different types of positive thinking. Positive thinking topics are great early on in a positive psychology course, or for a positive psychology section of introductory psychology, because most students entering the course will be expecting these themes, given how mainstream many of them are. Students may have even signed up for your course specifically to learn about these areas, meaning that student engagement will likely be high. Further, many students expect that they already know about these topics, having had some personal experience with them—providing an excellent opportunity for instructors to show what the field has to offer their understanding of a topic above and beyond their lived experience.

First, students explore the topic of whose life is meaningful and remove the incorrect assumption that having a meaningful life is difficult and extraordinary, pointing out that a sense of meaning is readily available in everyday life. Next, we invite students to investigate how to live a life of passion and critically discover that there are different types of passion with different outcomes. We then delve into the popular topic of flow and not only help students find their own sources of flow but also teach them to understand the construct at a deeper level. Finally, and great for student populations with big goals, we have a hope-promoting activity that invites students to use hope to come up with concrete short- and long-term plans that will help them achieve all of their goals. This is a great activity to run early in your course, as it allows students to develop agentic goals for what they want to learn while working with you.

In this section, we provide instructors with wonderful class activities that will help students learn how to better understand these sometimes misunderstood topics and apply and promote these positive thoughts through various activities. Further, students will be able to take advantage of using self-assessments to increase their understanding of themselves as well as the constructs they are studying, and they will have an opportunity to glean what they can do to change their current levels of these measures.

16

Whose Life Is Meaningful?

Samantha J. Heintzelman

This activity examines distinctions between beliefs about meaningful lives and lived experiences of meaningfulness to illuminate the common nature and everyday sources of meaning in life.

CONCEPT

We often think about meaning in life as an extraordinary achievement and position this experience atop a moral hierarchy. However, the science has demonstrated that experiencing meaning in life is a common human phenomenon linked to everyday—and some seemingly mundane—sources, including interpersonal relationships, positive moods, and even engagement in routine actions. The following activity will illuminate students' beliefs about meaning in life and how these beliefs may diverge from lived experiences. Namely, this activity will demonstrate that while we tend to think of meaningful lives as exceptional and extraordinary, most people find their lives to be quite meaningful and find this sense of meaning from sources that are readily available in everyday life. This activity will fit into lectures focused on meaning in life, broadened conceptualizations of psychological well-being beyond subjective well-being, lay beliefs about experiences, or self-report survey data.

https://doi.org/10.1037/0000417-016
More Activities for Teaching Positive Psychology: A Guide for Instructors, S. D. Pressman and A. C. Parks (Editors)

MATERIALS NEEDED

To complete this activity, students will need to access survey materials. Ideally, instructors will create online surveys using survey software, such as Qualtrics, that students will access and complete using an internet-connected device. Instructors will need basic data analysis software (e.g., R, SPSS, Excel) to conduct simple data analyses with the responses provided by students.

ACTIVITY SETTING

This activity will begin with an online survey, which students will complete prior to the class activity session. The remainder of the task can be completed in an in-person or virtual classroom setting. This activity can be run in conjunction with lectures on life meaning or related eudaimonic well-being topics.

ACTIVITY DURATION

Students will complete a 5-minute survey prior to the class activity session. The in-class discussion will require approximately 15 to 30 minutes.

SUGGESTED READINGS

- Pre- or postactivity reading:
  - King et al. (2016)
- Supplemental readings:
  - Heintzelman and King (2014)
  - Lambert et al. (2010)
  - Martela and Steger (2016)
  - King and Hicks (2021)

BACKGROUND AND INSTRUCTIONS

Meaning in life is a subjective experience that arises from a combination of (a) felt significance, or value, worth, and mattering; (b) purpose, or engagement in goal-directed pursuits; and (c) coherence, or the ability to make sense of the world and our experiences (George & Park, 2017; Martela & Steger, 2016). Meaning in life is often seen as a lofty endpoint achieved only by a select few exemplars who have reached the pinnacle of life through acts of extraordinary accomplishment. However, the science of meaning in life has demonstrated that feeling that one's life is meaningful is a common human experience—a vast majority of people report that their lives are quite meaningful (Heintzelman & King, 2014). While adults at later life stages tend to report higher meaning in life compared with younger adults (Steger et al., 2009), meaning in life is commonly experienced throughout the lifespan. Furthermore, experiences of meaning in life emerge from readily available sources that are part of everyday living (King et al., 2016). When university student participants are asked to identify the top sources of meaning in their lives, they identify family, friends, and happiness as the top three aspects of life that provide them with a sense of meaning (Lambert et al., 2010). This pattern has been replicated in broader samples across eight countries on four continents (Heintzelman et al., 2020). Additional correlational, longitudinal, experience sampling, and experimental research has demonstrated that meaning in life follows from these and other widely accessible sources, including social relationships (Lambert et al., 2013), social inclusion (Zadro et al., 2004), positive social events (Machell et al., 2015), positive affect (King et al., 2006; Ward & King, 2016), and even engagement in mundane routine behaviors (Heintzelman & King, 2019; Mohideen & Heintzelman, 2023). Meaningful lives need not be exceptional lives; instead, we experience meaning readily in everyday life.

This class activity is designed to illuminate distinctions and overlaps between common thinking about meaning in life and lived experiences of meaning in life. Students will examine their assumptions about meaning in life by identifying meaningful exemplars in small group discussions. The class will then compare these ideas about meaning to reports of their own trait levels of meaning in life and their reported sources of meaning. To build in data collection and analysis experience and increase sample size numbers for class demonstration data, instructors may assign students to collect trait meaning in life and sources of meaning reports from additional subjects prior to class and direct small groups of students through basic data processing and analytic steps in class.

INSTRUCTOR PREPARATION: SURVEY CREATION

- Create a survey that includes (a) a trait measure of meaning in life and (b) ratings of sources of meaning.

- Code for a template Qualtrics survey with a measure of meaning in life and sources of meaning is provided at https://osf.io/xvnzf/. Instructors can import this code into their own Qualtrics account and can modify the survey template for their own specifications.

- Instructors can alternately use another online survey tool, or if preferred, this could be formatted as a paper survey.

- Full scales for two different trait measures of meaning in life—from which instructors can select one measure to include in the survey—are provided in Appendix 16.1. These scales differ in length and construct specificity. The first scale, the Meaning in Life Questionnaire (Steger et al., 2006), is a short five-item scale assessing meaning in life, generally, and should be selected if time is a concern. The Multidimensional Meaning in Life Scale (Costin & Vignoles, 2020) is a longer 16-item scale assessing general meaning in life that also includes items designed to measure significance, purpose, and coherence independently to form facet subscales. This scale should be chosen if the instructor wishes to engage in more discussion about the facets of meaning in life separately. The Multidimensional Meaning in Life Scale is provided in the template Qualtrics survey.

- An assessment of sources of meaning is provided in Appendix 16.2 and is provided in the template Qualtrics survey.

DATA GATHERING

- Distribute and assign the survey for students to complete prior to the class activity session using your preferred strategy from the options provided next. All ratings should be completed far enough in advance of the class activity session to ensure adequate time for the instructor to process and analyze the data prior to class.
  - Send students a link to the online survey to complete on their own time with a deadline for completion prior to the class activity session.
  - Share a QR code linked to the survey on class slides in a class session prior to this class activity session to have students complete the survey using a phone or laptop during this class time. If you program the survey in Qualtrics, you can select "QR code" from the distribution options to generate a QR code directly on the platform. Alternately, you can use a search engine to identify one of many QR code generator websites where you will simply enter the URL of the survey to generate a unique QR code to send your students to the appropriate survey link.
  - Before the activity date, distribute paper surveys for students to complete in or out of class. Collect the surveys and enter the data manually prior to the activity.
  - Embed survey items into a classroom polling system and collect student responses using iClickers or similar classroom hardware in a class session prior to the class activity session or, if the data automatically generate averages and frequency distribution visualizations, these data can be collected during the class activity session.
- Optional data collection extension: This activity can be extended to give students experience collecting data from additional participants and processing these data to produce basic descriptive statistics. To involve students as data collectors, instructors may assign students to distribute the trait meaning in life and sources of meaning survey to a set number of additional respondents—I recommend three to five additional people each. Instructors can ask students to collect these data from people they know or to recruit unknown participants from public spaces around campus. As with the student responses, these surveys can be distributed in several different ways:

- Paper surveys: Provide students with the assigned number of surveys.

- Survey link or QR code link: Provide students with the appropriate link to direct participants to the survey on their phones or computers.

- To track student completion of the data collection assignment, the participants can include the student's name in the survey while themselves remaining anonymous.

- If the instructor wishes to include these additional participants with the rest of the class data, collect and enter responses from the paper surveys prior to the class activity session and enter the data along with the surveys from the students themselves or use the same survey link the students used and an appropriate deadline for inclusion in presession data analyses.

- If the instructor elects to use these additional surveys, they can assign students to bring their paper surveys to the class activity session or divide students into small groups prior to the data collection assignment and give each small group a unique survey link so the responses collected by their small group are separate from those collected by the rest of the class. Alternatively, all students can share the same online survey and all groups will work with the full data set in the optional class data processing portion of the activity.

INSTRUCTOR PREPARATION: DATA PROCESSING

- Export students' data from the online survey software platform into a format compatible with your preferred data analysis software, or enter data manually if electing the paper survey format.

- Compute composite meaning in life scores following scale instructions provided in Appendix 16.1. Next, generate mean scores of meaning in life for the class data. Create a histogram to display the frequency distribution of class responses to the meaning in life measure.

- Compute the mean ratings for each of the sources of meaning listed in Appendix 16.2. Create a bar chart showing the mean ratings for each item and list the top three sources of meaning identified by the class.

IN-CLASS GROUP DISCUSSION INSTRUCTIONS

- Exemplars with meaningful lives
  - Divide students into small groups of four to six for around 5 minutes. Ask each group to identify two people who have meaningful lives and list the reasons they selected these individuals. You can leave the instructions for this open. For instance, students may ask whether their selections need to be living or people they know personally. Confirm that the selection can be anyone at all, including living or dead, personally known or not.

  - Additionally, ask each group to think about the meaningfulness of their average classmate's life and to generate an estimate of how meaningful this average student's life is on a scale from 1 (*not at all meaningful*) to 7 (*very meaningful*).

  - Return to the large group and ask each small group to elect a representative to tell the class about their meaningful exemplar and their qualifications for this category. Record these responses on the board to refer to later in the activity. Then, gather and display their predictions for the meaning in life rating of their average classmate.

- Average meaning in life ratings

  - Optional data processing activity: If you have assigned students to collect data from additional participants, break students back into their small groups of four to six to compile their results across their team of student researchers, compute a composite meaning in life variable, generate the mean meaning in life rating across participants, and create a frequency distribution histogram of these means for the data collected by their group members. If all the data were recorded in the same online survey, provide each group with the full data file in which to examine these means.

  - Present the data analyses you performed on the class data, whether these data were the students' responses only or their responses together with the additional participants from whom the students gathered data. Compare the average meaning in life rating to students' earlier predictions about the meaning in life of their average classmate.

- Sources of meaning in life

  - Present the mean ratings for each source of meaning item and the bar chart showing the ratings for all potential meaning sources. Compare the highest rated sources of meaning to the reasons meaningful exemplars were selected by students earlier in class.

DISCUSSION

Expected activity results

- Exemplars with meaningful lives

  - When generating exemplar individuals with high levels of meaning in life, students typically produce examples of people who have achieved extraordinary accomplishments or those who have made or are making major impacts on the world, for example, Harriet Tubman, "conductor" of the Underground Railroad or climate activist Greta Thunberg. They rarely raise *regular* people like their classmates or known others as examples of people living meaningful lives. Furthermore, they often list big achievements or extraordinary contributions as the reasons these individuals are living (or lived) a meaningful life.

- Average meaning in life ratings
  - Despite calling to mind extraordinary achievements as a precursor for meaningful lives, research shows that most people report that their lives are quite meaningful.
  - Heintzelman and King (2014) reviewed large, representative data sets including measures of meaning in life and found consistently high ratings of meaning in life across samples. They also examined mean ratings on the Meaning in Life Questionnaire from 122 samples and found that the mean rating across studies, 4.56 (*SD* = 0.59), was significantly higher than the neutral scale midpoint (Figure 16.1).
  - Examinations of student responses and any additional data they collected as researchers should show this consistently replicated pattern, with mean ratings of meaning in life higher than the neutral scale midpoint. Furthermore, these ratings tend to be higher than the estimates students make for the average classmate earlier in their group discussions.

- Sources of meaning in life
  - The top three sources of meaning identified by university student participants in Lambert et al. (2010) were (a) family, (b) happiness, and (c) friends. Social relationships and happiness consistently emerged as the two highest rated sources of meaning in life in samples from Angola, Germany, Japan, Korea, Portugal, Singapore, and the United States (Heintzelman et al., 2020). Student data typically follow this same pattern, with social relationships and happiness rated as stronger sources of meaning for students compared with loftier concepts like achievement, justice, or growth, though these latter categories are more frequently cited in justifications for the meaning in exemplar individuals' lives.

Additional discussion questions or prompts:

- Why do we think meaningful lives are exceptional while most people report that their own lives are meaningful?

- Why do we point to exceptional achievements or major societal impacts as the basis for meaningful lives when we find our own sense of meaningfulness in the more basic aspects of daily living, like our family, friends, and happiness?

- How might our ideas about meaning in life shape our experiences of meaning and well-being more broadly? In what ways could this be helpful or harmful?

- How do the data suggesting that meaning in life is a common human experience shape or change your perceptions of this construct or the way you pursue meaning in life?

- What cultural messages around us shape our ideas about meaningful lives?

- How could cultural messages about meaning in life be changed to better align with the science of meaning in life? What impact do you think those revised messages would have on individuals and society as a whole?

FIGURE 16.1. Average Meaning in Life Ratings From Large Data Sets and Published Studies

Study	MIL measure	Response
Health and Retirement Study (*N* = 1,062)	Did you feel that your life has meaning? (Yes/No)	95%: Yes
Gallup Global (*N* = 132,678)	Do you feel your life has an important purpose or meaning? (Yes/No)	91%: Yes
Baylor Religion Survey (*N* = 1,648)	Do you feel your life has an important purpose or meaning? (1 to 5)	83% agreed or strongly agreed
Americans Changing Lives (*N* = 1,660)	I have a sense of purpose in life; In the final analysis I'm not sure my life adds up to much. (R) (1 to 4)	3.5
Centers for Disease Control (*N* = 5,399)	3 items from the MLQ (1 to 5)	3.80

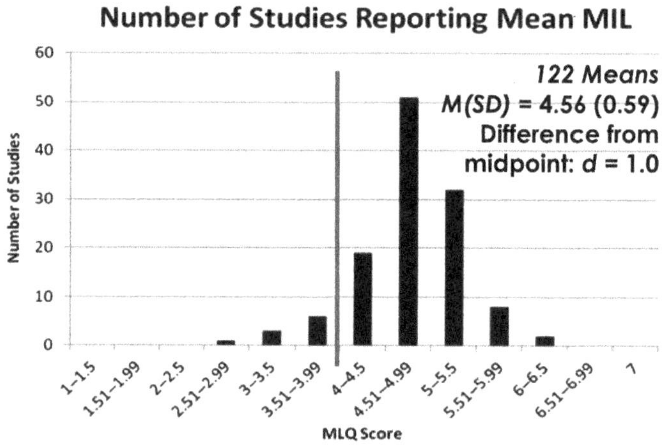
Number of Studies Reporting Mean MIL
122 Means
M(SD) = 4.56 (0.59)
Difference from midpoint: d = 1.0
Number of Studies
60
50
40
30
20
10
0
1–1.5
1.51–1.99
2–2.5
2.51–2.99
3–3.5
3.51–3.99
4–4.5
4.51–4.99
5–5.5
5.51–5.99
6–6.5
6.51–6.99
7
MLQ Score

Note. MIL = meaning in life; MLQ = Meaning in Life Questionnaire. Adapted from "Life Is Pretty Meaningful," by S. J. Heintzelman and L. A. King, 2014, *American Psychologist*, *69*(6), p. 566 (https://doi.org/10.1037/a0035049). Copyright 2014 by the American Psychological Association.

We often receive messages that our lives need to be exceptional and extraordinary to be meaningful. People can be left with the impression that feelings of meaning in life result from self-actualization or are hard-won through intensive and effortful construction of meaning in one's experiences. However, actual experiences of meaning in life are common and can be extracted from regular parts of our everyday lives, like spending time with close others and simply engaging in enjoyable activities. Acknowledging the ubiquity of meaning in life can help students to transform this experience from an abstract and seemingly unreachable end goal of attaining a meaningful life and can encourage students to notice and embrace the meaningfulness of everyday life.

APPENDIX 16.1: Trait Meaning in Life Measures

MEANING IN LIFE QUESTIONNAIRE: PRESENCE SUBSCALE

Please take a moment to think about what makes your life feel important to you. Please respond to the following statements as truthfully and accurately as you can, and also please remember that these are very subjective questions and that there are no right or wrong answers. Please answer according to the scale below:

1	2	3	4	5	6	7
Absolutely untrue	Mostly untrue	Somewhat untrue	Can't say true or false	Somewhat true	Mostly true	Absolutely true

1. I understand my life's meaning.
2. My life has a clear sense of purpose.
3. I have a good sense of what makes my life meaningful.
4. I have discovered a satisfying life purpose.
5. My life has no clear purpose.*

Scoring instructions:

- Reverse score Item 5.*
- Compute mean of Items 1–5.

Note. Adapted from "The Meaning in Life Questionnaire: Assessing the Presence of and Search for Meaning in Life," by M. F. Steger, P. Frazier, S. Oishi, and M. Kaler, 2006, *Journal of Counseling Psychology*, *53*(1), p. 93. (https://doi.org/10.1037/0022-0167.53.1.80). Copyright 2006 by M. F. Steger. Adapted with permission. For more information on the Meaning in Life Questionnaire, see https://www.michaelfsteger.com/

MULTIDIMENSIONAL MEANING IN LIFE SCALE

Using the scale, please indicate your current feelings by selecting how much you agree or disagree with the following statements:

1	2	3	4	5	6	7
Strongly disagree	Disagree	Somewhat disagree	Neither agree nor disagree	Somewhat agree	Agree	Strongly agree

1. My life as a whole has meaning.
2. My entire existence is full of meaning.
3. My life is meaningless.*
4. My existence is empty of meaning.*
5. I can make sense of the things that happen in my life.
6. Looking at my life as a whole, things seem clear to me.
7. I can't make sense of events in my life.*
8. My life feels like a sequence of unconnected events.

9. I have a good sense of what I am trying to accomplish in life.
10. I have certain life goals that compel me to keep going.
11. I don't know what I am trying to accomplish in life.*
12. I don't have compelling life goals that keep me going.*
13. Whether my life ever existed matters even in the grand scheme of the universe.
14. Even considering how big the universe is, I can say that my life matters.
15. My existence is not significant in the grand scheme of things.*
16. Given the vastness of the universe, my life does not matter.*

Scoring instructions:

- Reverse score Items 3, 4, 7, 11, 12, 15, 16.*
- Meaning in life judgments: Compute mean of Items 1, 2, 3, 4.
- Coherence: Compute mean of Items 5, 6, 7, 8.
- Purpose: Compute mean of Items 9, 10, 11, 12.
- Mattering/significance: Compute mean of Items 13, 14, 15, 16.

A printable version of this appendix can be downloaded from the APA website at https://www.apa.org/pubs/books/more-activities-teaching-positive-psychology.

Note. Adapted from "Meaning Is About Mattering: Evaluating Coherence, Purpose, and Existential Mattering as Precursors of Meaning in Life Judgments," by V. Costin and V. L. Vignoles, 2020, *Journal of Personality and Social Psychology, 118*(4), p. 884 (https://doi.org/ 10.1037/pspp0000225). Copyright 2020 by the American Psychological Association.

APPENDIX 16.2: Sources of Meaning Measure

Below, you will see a list of things other people have mentioned that provide their lives with meaning. We would like you to think about whether these things influence your experience of meaning in life too.

After thinking about what gives your life meaning, please indicate the extent to which each of the items below influences your experience of meaning in life.

1	2	3	4	5	6	7
Not at all						Very much so

Achievements
Family
Friends
Happiness
Helping others
Intimacy
Justice/fairness
Personal goals
Personal growth
Religious faith
Self-acceptance
Self-worth

Note. You may present these items in a random order; they are presented here alphabetically.

A printable version of this appendix can be downloaded from the APA website at https://www.apa.org/pubs/books/more-activities-teaching-positive-psychology.

REFERENCES

Costin, V., & Vignoles, V. L. (2020). Meaning is about mattering: Evaluating coherence, purpose, and existential mattering as precursors of meaning in life judgments. *Journal of Personality and Social Psychology, 118*(4), 864–884. https://doi.org/10.1037/pspp0000225

George, L. S., & Park, C. L. (2017). The Multidimensional Existential Meaning Scale: A tripartite approach to measuring meaning in life. *The Journal of Positive Psychology, 12*(6), 613–627. https://doi.org/10.1080/17439760.2016.1209546

Heintzelman, S. J., & King, L. A. (2014). Life is pretty meaningful. *American Psychologist, 69*(6), 561–574. https://doi.org/10.1037/a0035049

Heintzelman, S. J., & King, L. A. (2019). Routines and meaning in life. *Personality and Social Psychology Bulletin, 45*(5), 688–699. https://doi.org/10.1177/0146167218795133

Heintzelman, S. J., Mohideen, F., Oishi, S., & King, L. A. (2020). Lay beliefs about meaning in life: Examinations across targets, time, and countries. *Journal of Research in Personality, 88*, Article 104003. https://doi.org/10.1016/j.jrp.2020.104003

King, L. A., Heintzelman, S. J., & Ward, S. J. (2016). Beyond the search for meaning: A contemporary science of the experience of meaning in life. *Current Directions in Psychological Science, 25*(4), 211–216. https://doi.org/10.1177/0963721416656354

King, L. A., & Hicks, J. A. (2021). The science of meaning in life. *Annual Review of Psychology, 72*(1), 561–584. https://doi.org/10.1146/annurev-psych-072420-122921

King, L. A., Hicks, J. A., Krull, J. L., & Del Gaiso, A. K. (2006). Positive affect and the experience of meaning in life. *Journal of Personality and Social Psychology, 90*(1), 179–196. https://doi.org/10.1037/0022-3514.90.1.179

Lambert, N. M., Stillman, T. F., Baumeister, R. F., Fincham, F. D., Hicks, J. A., & Graham, S. M. (2010). Family as a salient source of meaning in young adulthood. *The Journal of Positive Psychology, 5*(5), 367–376. https://doi.org/10.1080/17439760.2010.516616

Lambert, N. M., Stillman, T. F., Hicks, J. A., Kamble, S., Baumeister, R. F., & Fincham, F. D. (2013). To belong is to matter: Sense of belonging enhances meaning in life. *Personality and Social Psychology Bulletin, 39*(11), 1418–1427. https://doi.org/10.1177/0146167213499186

Machell, K. A., Kashdan, T. B., Short, J. L., & Nezlek, J. B. (2015). Relationships between meaning in life, social and achievement events, and positive and negative affect in daily life. *Journal of Personality, 83*(3), 287–298. https://doi.org/10.1111/jopy.12103

Martela, F., & Steger, M. F. (2016). The three meanings of meaning in life: Distinguishing coherence, purpose, and significance. *The Journal of Positive Psychology, 11*(5), 531–545. https://doi.org/10.1080/17439760.2015.1137623

Mohideen, F., & Heintzelman, S. J. (2023). Routines and meaning in life: Does activity content or context matter? *Personality and Social Psychology Bulletin, 49*(7), 987–999. https://doi.org/10.1177/01461672221085797

Steger, M. F., Frazier, P., Oishi, S., & Kaler, M. (2006). The Meaning in Life Questionnaire: Assessing the presence of and search for meaning in life. *Journal of Counseling Psychology, 53*(1), 80–93. https://doi.org/10.1037/0022-0167.53.1.80

Steger, M. F., Oishi, S., & Kashdan, T. B. (2009). Meaning in life across the life span: Levels and correlates of meaning in life from emerging adulthood to older adulthood. *The Journal of Positive Psychology, 4*(1), 43–52. https://doi.org/10.1080/17439760802303127

Ward, S. J., & King, L. A. (2016). Poor but happy? Income, happiness, and experienced and expected meaning in life. *Social Psychological & Personality Science, 7*(5), 463–470. https://doi.org/10.1177/1948550615627865

Zadro, L., Williams, K. D., & Richardson, R. (2004). How low can you go? Ostracism by a computer is sufficient to lower self-reported levels of belonging, control, self-esteem, and meaningful existence. *Journal of Experimental Social Psychology, 40*(4), 560–567. https://doi.org/10.1016/j.jesp.2003.11.006

17

Engaging in an Activity With Passion

How the Situation Affects Our Mindset

Jany St-Cyr, Virginie Paquette, and Robert J. Vallerand

This activity allows students to become aware of the mindset that they use when engaging in an activity that they are passionate about.

CONCEPT

We hear a lot about passion through the media and even advertisements, where it is portrayed as the key to happiness. We hear things like, "Make a living out of your passion and be happy ever after" or "I overcame hardships and succeeded because this is what I am passionate about." But what exactly is passion, and does it always lead to positive outcomes? This activity will introduce students to the dualistic model of passion (Vallerand, 2015) and help them explore the differences between harmonious versus obsessive passions by drawing on their own personal activity interests. By the end of the activity, students will be able to (a) differentiate between harmonious and obsessive passions and the different outcomes they entail, (b) identify the types of passion with which they generally engage with their favorite activity, and (c) identify the situations more conducive to each type of passion.

https://doi.org/10.1037/0000417-017
More Activities for Teaching Positive Psychology: A Guide for Instructors, S. D. Pressman and A. C. Parks (Editors)

MATERIALS NEEDED

The materials needed will vary depending on personal preferences and whether the activity is done in person or online. Students will need something to write and record their answers with; for example, paper and pencil, a laptop, or an online survey. A device for keeping time will also be needed.

ACTIVITY SETTING

It is preferable that students complete this activity individually. It can be done prior to or during class. This activity can be done in person or online. In past research, the experimental induction of passion has been conducted in both settings.

ACTIVITY DURATION

The activity of writing two short essays takes about 10 minutes (5 minutes per essay). Following the mindset induction, we recommend a classroom discussion in order to unpack the writing exercise more fully. The entire session can take anywhere between 20 and 45 minutes, depending on the length of the discussion and whether the writing component is done prior to versus in class.

SUGGESTED READINGS

- Recommended readings for before the activity:
    - Vallerand et al. (2003)[1]
    - Curran et al. (2015)
    - Schellenberg et al. (2019)

- Optional readings for after the activity:
    - Bélanger et al. (2013)[2]
    - Lafrenière et al. (2013)
    - Schellenberg et al. (2016)

BACKGROUND AND INSTRUCTIONS

In positive psychology, much importance is given to the experience of outcomes such as flow, positive emotions, mindfulness, and psychological well-being. According to the dualistic model of passion (Vallerand, 2015; Vallerand et al., 2003, 2020), passion (especially harmonious passion) is one psychological

---

[1] Note: If you wish to select only one of these recommended readings before the activity, we suggest reading Vallerand et al. (2003).

[2] Note: If you wish to select only one of these optional readings for after the activity, we suggest reading Bélanger et al. (2013, Studies 3 and 4).

process leading to these positive experiences. As such, *passion* is defined as a strong inclination toward an activity that one likes (or even loves), finds important, in which one invests time and energy, and is part of one's identity. For example, if I play piano and am passionate about it, I can define myself as a pianist, or if I am passionate about playing basketball, I am a basketball player. Furthermore, the dualistic model of passion posits that there are two types of passion: harmonious passion and obsessive passion. *Harmonious passion* (HP) is the result of an autonomous internalization of the activity into one's identity. It mainly leads to adaptive processes and outcomes, as one can maintain a balance with other activities and aspects of one's life while fully engaging in one's passion. Moreover, research has shown that HP promotes coping, positive emotions, well-being, and physical and mental health (Schellenberg et al., 2019; St-Cyr et al., 2021; St-Louis et al., 2016; Vallerand, 2015). *Obsessive passion* (OP), on the other hand, is the result of a more controlled internalization of the activity that one loves into one's identity (Vallerand, 2015; Vallerand & Houlfort, 2019). It is typically associated with less adaptive and, at times, more harmful consequences, such as negative emotions and the adoption of rigid and risky behaviors (St-Louis et al., 2016; Vallerand, 2015).

Let's take an example. Imagine the following situation: It's Thursday night, you're studying for next week's exam, and your friends invite you to an impromptu party. If you have a predominant OP for your studies, you might decline your friends' invitation to the party and continue studying. While studying, you may at times have difficulties concentrating on your studies, as you may think about the lost opportunity for fun with your friends. On the other hand, if you accept and go to the party, you may experience negative emotions of guilt and anxiety and ruminate about the fact that you are not studying. Conversely, if your predominant passion is HP for your studies, you should be able to put aside studying and attend your friends' party. Before going to the party, however, you should take notes of where you are in your studying and what remains to be done. Such a mental download would allow you to fully focus on the party, experience positive emotions, and have fun with your friends. As you can see in this example, the engagement is more rigid with OP than with HP. People with a predominant OP display a rigid persistence toward their favorite activity and may experience negative emotions and rumination when prevented from engaging in their favorite activity. On the other hand, people with a predominant HP display flexibility and can temporarily disengage from their favorite activity. As a consequence, they can experience positive emotions inside and outside of their favorite activity. Furthermore, HP and OP are not dichotomous. Indeed, both types of passion coexist within someone who is passionate about an activity. Thus, even if one has a predominant passion for a specific activity, the type of passion at play may vary depending on the situation and context at a given time (Vallerand, 2015). So, maybe you are usually harmoniously passionate about your studies, but you display OP toward the end of the semester when you have several exams and assignments due. Therefore, when people have a passion for a given activity, it is possible to trigger HP or OP because both types of passion have been internalized in their identity to different degrees.

This activity can be used to introduce the dualistic model of passion and put the theory into practice. It is up to you, the instructor, to choose whether you want to present the dualistic model of passion before or after the activity. The activity is done individually. So, if you are in an in-person setting, the students can all stay in the same room as long as they are not talking to each other, or the students can be provided with the writing instructions ahead of time to do the homework before class. Handouts for students to complete the writing task and posttask passion evaluation are available in the appendices.

- The first step in this activity is to ask students to identify an activity they are passionate about by using the following statement, which refers to the definition of passion (Vallerand et al., 2003):
    - "Determine an activity that you like (or love), that is important to you, and in which you invest a significant amount of time on a regular basis."

If students are having trouble identifying a passionate activity, you can ask them the following questions to guide them:

- "What do you do in your spare time?"
- "What do you like to do?"
- "If you have to introduce yourself to someone, is there an activity that you mention that you do often?"

- Second, give students at least 5 minutes (preferably more) to write about the following statement, which is used to induce OP:
    - OP: "Write about a time when you had difficulties controlling your urge to do your favorite activity and you felt that this activity was the only thing that gave you excitement. Recall this event vividly and include as much detail in your writing as you can to relive the experience."

If needed, as they are writing, here are some additional follow-up questions you can provide to help students detail their experience:

- "How did you feel specifically?"
- "What were you thinking at the time?"
- "What did you do exactly?"
- "What decision did you make?"

- Third, when the 5 minutes are over, ask every student to read their answers and to respond to the manipulation check questions below on a Likert scale from 1 (*do not agree at all*) to 7 (*very strongly agree*).
    - Check question for OP: "I have the impression that my activity controls me."
    - Check question for HP: "My activity is in harmony with other activities in my life."

Another option is to have students complete the full Passion Scale, which is used in research to assess the two types of passion and will provide more complete scores on OP and HP (see the Online Materials section) instead of the previously mentioned manipulation check questions.

- Fourth, as an optional step, students could complete a positive and negative emotions scale to help them identify how they feel following the manipulation (see Appendix 17.3).

- Fifth, take a break for about 10 minutes and then discuss with students their first impressions and observations. Some possible questions to raise include:
  - "How did you feel?"

  For this question, you might refer to the emotions scale mentioned in Step 4.
  - "What was the context of the event you recalled? Was it a performance context?"
  - "Did this event have an impact on your life outside of your passionate activity?"

- Sixth, repeat Steps 2 to 5, but, this time, ask students to write about the following statement, which is used to induce HP:
  - HP: "We're going to have you do this activity again, but this time, please write about a time when your favorite activity was in harmony with other things that are part of you and you felt that your favorite activity allowed you to live a variety of experiences. Recall this event vividly and include as much detail as you can to relive the experience."

  If students have a hard time coming up with an example, you could help them by referring to the definition of HP (compared with OP). For example, students should elaborate on a time when they were in control of their engagement in their favorite activity. In other words, they enjoyed their involvement in the activity but did not experience it as an uncontrollable urge.

- After writing the two essays, you could use the items of the Passion Scale to stimulate a conversation about the typical ways in which HP and OP unfold. Furthermore, if the students have completed the full Passion Scale, you could inform them that having a mean score of 4 or above on the subscales (HP and/ or OP) indicates that they display a moderate to high level of this type of passion. You should also inform them of the outcomes associated with each type of passion. Please see below for certain elements that will help foster an excellent postactivity discussion.

DISCUSSION

Briefly, we have seen that passion is a strong inclination toward an activity that people like (or even love), find important, invest time and energy in, and which is part of their identity (Vallerand, 2015; Vallerand et al., 2003). There are two types of passion, HP and OP, associated with different processes and outcomes. HP facilitates positive psychological experiences such as flow, positive emotions, and psychological well-being, whereas OP is generally negatively related or unrelated to these consequences (Vallerand, 2015). When you are passionate about an activity, you may have a predominant type of passion for a specific activity. However, both types of passion may be at play at different times depending on the situation and context.

Inspired by experimental research methods, this activity was designed to trigger HP or OP. Thus, students were able to experience a momentary shift in their mindset while thinking about the activity for which they are passionate and then reflect on it. Initially based on Avnet and Higgins's (2003) study, past research on passion has used similar manipulations to experimentally induce one or the other types of passion and assess the outcomes that they trigger (for some examples, see Bélanger et al., 2013; Lafrenière et al., 2013; Schellenberg et al., 2016). First used in Bélanger et al. (2013) and then replicated in several other studies, the results of the situational induction of passion showed that the different types of passion can cause the experience of different emotions, cognition, and behavior (see Vallerand, 2015, for a review). Thus, passion is a dynamic construct that refers to both a general disposition toward a specific activity as well as a situational inclination toward the activity at a specific point in time in reaction to some environmental cues. Previous research has also supported the construct validity of this manipulation by showing that participants in the HP condition report higher levels of this type of passion than OP and that the opposite is observed for participants in the OP condition (see Vallerand, 2015). Construct validity was also supported by the fact that the situational induction of passion had the same effects on outcomes as the correlations between the HP and OP subscales of the Passion Scale and cognitive, affective, and behavioral outcomes (Vallerand, 2015). In short, this activity allows students to experience a targeted type of passion and to better understand what passion is and how the two types of passion are related to outcomes.

To illustrate how HP and OP are related to outcomes, you can initiate discussion with students by asking them how they felt during the activity. Were the emotions they experienced during the OP and HP situational inductions similar or different? Were these emotions more positive or negative? Were they similar to the emotions they usually experience in their lives? Research has shown that passion is important not only in regard to the situational affect experienced during the passionate activity but also in regard to the general affect that is transferred in other areas of life outside the activity (Curran et al., 2015; Vallerand, 2015). Indeed, HP leads to positive emotions during engagement in the activity, and this positive affect seems to generalize to life in general. On the other hand, OP facilitates the experience of negative emotions both during and after engagement in the activity. It is also strongly related to negative affect when one cannot engage in the passionate activity. Furthermore, positive affect experienced when fully engaging in an activity out of HP promotes adaptive outcomes such as physical, psychological, and relational well-being (e.g., St-Cyr et al., 2021;

St-Louis et al., 2016; Vallerand, 2012, 2013). With OP, such results should not be observed as it leads to fewer positive experiences and even some negative ones.

To deepen the discussion, you may also ask students to talk about the importance placed on performance in the event they recalled during the activity. Were they trying to perform up to their (or someone else's) expectations? Were they satisfied with their performance? Research has shown that passion is related to performance through two roads: the harmonious and the obsessive roads. The first road to performance originates from HP. On this road, one engages in a passionate activity with the specific goal of improving one's skills using deliberate practice, and it ultimately leads to high levels of performance (e.g., Bonneville-Roussy et al., 2013; Vallerand et al., 2007; Verner-Filion et al., 2017). In addition to performance, such a mastery-oriented goal (Elliot, 1999; Elliot & Church, 1997) typically leads to other adaptive outcomes such as well-being and high-quality relationships. The second, obsessive, road to performance originates from OP and is less adaptive. Indeed, although it may lead to some performance increases through a mastery orientation, this second road also leads people to try to be better than others and to avoid performing worse than other performers. Whereas trying to be better than others is generally positively associated with performance, trying to avoid failing generally undermines performance (Van Yperen et al., 2015) and psychological well-being. The in-class discussion could lead students to reflect on the two roads to performance when under the influence of HP or OP. Can they tell the difference when on the harmonious or the obsessive road?

The situational induction of passion allows us to better understand its effects. However, these effects are only momentary. Maybe you and the students are wondering, "How can we change our passion mindset in the long run? How can we engage in our passion in a more harmonious way?" These represent good questions to explore with students, but more research is needed to provide definitive answers. For now, research on the determinants of passion can guide us toward some preliminary answers. A first step to guide us toward changing our mindset in the long term would be to ask ourselves why we are passionate about this activity and identify what it brings us intrinsically. In addition, attempting to find connections between the activity and one's identity helps facilitate passion. Then, possible solutions would be, for example, to engage autonomously in the activity that we are passionate about without seeking recognition (esteem, approval). Selecting environments to engage in the passionate activity where autonomy support from others is provided is likely to promote HP (Vallerand, 2015). Such environments give us choices on how to engage in the activity, give us positive feedback, and acknowledge our feelings and viewpoints. A second step in changing our mindset is to use our signature strengths (i.e., characteristics that energize and motivate us, e.g., creativity, curiosity, leadership; Peterson & Seligman, 2003) as they provide the feeling of using one's full potential, promote HP and, in turn, well-being (Forest et al., 2012). Finally, we can foster HP by seeking a balance between our passion and the other areas of our life or by finding other passionate activities (see Vallerand, 2015). We can reflect and wonder if we are neglecting some areas of our life. If so, is it possible to remedy the situation? Finding a balance between the activity we are passionate about and the other areas of our life can have positive consequences for our well-being, not only in our activity but also in general. Sometimes, adding a new and fun activity that we engage in with close ones may be sufficient to diminish the obsessiveness associated with one activity.

ASSIGNMENT

Put It Into Practice

The following are some suggested assignments that students can complete after the activity:

- A day or a few days after the activity, students can complete the Passion Scale by reflecting on the activity they are passionate about. Do they see a difference between their response to the scale and the one experienced during the activity?

- Students can use media (newspaper articles, audio clips, videos, etc.) to try to identify the passions of other people when they are doing an activity they are passionate about. Sports, music, and work are examples of areas where it may be easier to detect passion in others. Once they have identified a real-life situation, they can describe the type of passion they think is predominant in that person. Does it seem to be more harmonious or obsessive? And why?

Open Writing Reflections

Here are some reflections that students can make following this activity:

- Do you think it is important to have a passion? Why or why not?

- How would you characterize your passion?

- When you think about the activity you are passionate about, can you identify situations or times when your passion was more obsessive or harmonious?
  - What distinguishes these situations or moments?
  - If you experience OP in a given situation, using the HP mindset induction, how can you try to change your passion type during such situations?

ONLINE MATERIALS

- A website with more information about passion, which also provides access to the Passion Scale (listed under "scales"): https://www.lrcs.uqam.ca/en/home/.
- A detailed video presentation of the dualistic model of passion by Robert J. Vallerand: https://vimeo.com/30755287.
- A video on making a difference in people's lives by Robert J. Vallerand: https://tinyurl.com/MATPPch16.

APPENDIX 17.1: Instructions for the Situational Induction of the Obsessive and Harmonious Passions

Determine an activity that you like (or love), that is important to you, and in which you invest a significant amount of time on a regular basis.

Write about a time when you had difficulties controlling your urge to do your favorite activity and you felt that this activity was the only thing that gave you excitement. Recall this event vividly and include as much detail in your writing as you can to relive the experience.

Write about a time when your favorite activity was in harmony with other things that are part of you and you felt that your favorite activity allowed you to live a variety of experiences. Recall this event vividly and include as much detail as you can to relive the experience.

A printable version of this appendix can be downloaded from the APA website at https://www.apa.org/pubs/books/more-activities-teaching-positive-psychology.

APPENDIX 17.2: Manipulation Check Questions for Harmonious Passion and Obsessive Passion Respectively

My activity is in harmony with other activities in my life.

Do not agree at all	Very slightly agree	Slightly agree	Moderately agree	Mostly agree	Strongly agree	Very strongly agree
1	2	3	4	5	6	7

I have the impression that my activity controls me.

Do not agree at all	Very slightly agree	Slightly agree	Moderately agree	Mostly agree	Strongly agree	Very strongly agree
1	2	3	4	5	6	7

A printable version of this appendix can be downloaded from the APA website at https://www.apa.org/pubs/books/more-activities-teaching-positive-psychology.

APPENDIX 17.3: Positive and Negative Emotions Scale

This scale consists of a list of words that describe different feelings and emotions. Read each item carefully and indicate how much you felt this way in the situation you have just recalled.

Not at all	A little	Moderately	Quite a bit	Completely
1	2	3	4	5

In this situation, I felt . . .

1. tense, nervous, anxious
2. upset, irritated, unpleased, angry with myself
3. determined, alert, active, interested
4. happy, satisfied, optimistic
5. discouraged, depressed, disappointed
6. enthusiastic, excited, energized

Once you have completed this scale, please calculate your mean score on both positive and negative emotions using the items below.

Positive emotion items: 3, 4, 6.
Negative emotion items: 1, 2, 5.

A printable version of this appendix can be downloaded from the APA website at https://www.apa.org/pubs/books/more-activities-teaching-positive-psychology.

REFERENCES

Avnet, T., & Higgins, E. T. (2003). Locomotion, assessment, and regulatory fit: Value transfer from "how" to "what". *Journal of Experimental Social Psychology, 39*(5), 525–530. https://doi.org/10.1016/S0022-1031(03)00027-1

Bélanger, J. J., Lafrenière, M.-A. K., Vallerand, R. J., & Kruglanski, A. W. (2013). When passion makes the heart grow colder: The role of passion in alternative goal suppression. *Journal of Personality and Social Psychology, 104*(1), 126–147. https://doi.org/10.1037/a0029679

Bonneville-Roussy, A., Vallerand, R. J., & Bouffard, T. (2013). The roles of autonomy support and harmonious and obsessive passions in educational persistence. *Learning and Individual Differences, 24*, 22–31. https://doi.org/10.1016/j.lindif.2012.12.015

Curran, T., Hill, A. P., Appleton, P. R., Vallerand, R. J., & Standage, M. (2015). The psychology of passion: A meta-analytical review of a decade of research on intra-personal outcomes. *Motivation and Emotion, 39*(5), 631–655. https://doi.org/10.1007/s11031-015-9503-0

Elliot, A. J. (1999). Approach and avoidance motivation and achievement goals. *Educational Psychologist, 34*(3), 169–189. https://doi.org/10.1207/s15326985ep3403_3

Elliot, A. J., & Church, M. A. (1997). A hierarchical model of approach and avoidance achievement motivation. *Journal of Personality and Social Psychology, 72*(1), 218–232. https://doi.org/10.1037/0022-3514.72.1.218

Forest, J., Mageau, G. A., Crevier-Braud, L., Bergeron, É., Dubreuil, P., & Lavigne, G. L. (2012). Harmonious passion as an explanation of the relation between signature strengths' use and well-being at work: Test of an intervention program. *Human Relations, 65*(9), 1233–1252. https://doi.org/10.1177/0018726711433134

Lafrenière, M.-A. K., Vallerand, R. J., & Sedikides, C. (2013). On the relation between self-enhancement and life satisfaction: The moderating role of passion. *Self and Identity, 12*(6), 597–609. https://doi.org/10.1080/15298868.2012.713558

Peterson, C., & Seligman, M. E. (2003). Character strengths before and after September 11. *Psychological Science, 14*(4), 381–384. https://doi.org/10.1111/1467-9280.24482

Schellenberg, B. J. I., Bailis, D. S., & Mosewich, A. D. (2016). You have passion, but do you have self-compassion? Harmonious passion, obsessive passion, and responses to passion-related failure. *Personality and Individual Differences, 99*, 278–285. https://doi.org/10.1016/j.paid.2016.05.003

Schellenberg, B. J. I., Verner-Filion, J., Gaudreau, P., Bailis, D. S., Lafrenière, M. K., & Vallerand, R. J. (2019). Testing the dualistic model of passion using a novel quadri-partite approach: A look at physical and psychological well-being. *Journal of Personality, 87*(2), 163–180. https://doi.org/10.1111/jopy.12378

St-Cyr, J., Vallerand, R. J., & Chénard-Poirier, L. A. (2021). The role of passion and achievement goals in optimal functioning in sports. *International Journal of Environmental Research and Public Health, 18*(17), Article 9023. https://doi.org/10.3390/ijerph18179023

St-Louis, A. C., Carbonneau, N., & Vallerand, R. J. (2016). Passion for a cause: How it affects health and subjective well-being. *Journal of Personality, 84*(3), 263–276. https://doi.org/10.1111/jopy.12157

Vallerand, R. J. (2012). The role of passion in sustainable psychological well-being. *Psychology of Well-Being: Theory, Research and Practice, 2*(1), Article 1. https://doi.org/10.1186/2211-1522-2-1

Vallerand, R. J. (2013). Passion and optimal functioning in society: A eudaimonic perspective. In A. S. Waterman (Ed.), *The best within us: Positive psychology perspectives on eudaimonic functioning* (pp. 183–206). American Psychological Association. https://doi.org/10.1037/14092-010

Vallerand, R. J. (2015). *The psychology of passion: A dualistic model.* Oxford University Press. https://doi.org/10.1093/acprof:oso/9780199777600.001.0001

Vallerand, R. J., Blanchard, C., Mageau, G. A., Koestner, R., Ratelle, C., Léonard, M., Gagné, M., & Marsolais, J. (2003). Les passions de l'âme: On obsessive and harmonious passion. *Journal of Personality and Social Psychology, 85*(4), 756–767. https://doi.org/10.1037/0022-3514.85.4.756

Vallerand, R. J., Chichekian, T., & Paquette, V. (2020). Passion in education: Theory, research, and applications. In G. A. D. Liem & D. M. McInerney (Eds.), *Promoting motivation and learning in contexts: Sociocultural perspectives on educational interventions* (pp. 115–141). Information Age Publishing.

Vallerand, R. J., & Houlfort, N. (Eds.). (2019). *Passion for work: Theory, research, and applications.* Oxford University Press. https://doi.org/10.1093/oso/9780190648626.001.0001

Vallerand, R. J., Salvy, S.-J., Mageau, G. A., Elliot, A. J., Denis, P. L., Grouzet, F. M. E., & Blanchard, C. (2007). On the role of passion in performance. *Journal of Personality, 75*(3), 505–533. https://doi.org/10.1111/j.1467-6494.2007.00447.x

Van Yperen, N. W., Blaga, M., & Postmes, T. (2015). A meta-analysis of the impact of situationally induced achievement goals on task performance. *Human Performance, 28*(2), 165–182. https://doi.org/10.1080/08959285.2015.1006772

Verner-Filion, J., Vallerand, R. J., Amiot, C. E., & Mocanu, I. (2017). The two roads from passion to sport performance and psychological well-being: The mediating role of need satisfaction, deliberate practice, and achievement goals. *Psychology of Sport and Exercise, 30*, 19–29. https://doi.org/10.1016/j.psychsport.2017.01.009

18

Flow in Daily Life

Ajit Singh Mann, Patrick Robinson, and Jeanne Nakamura

This activity helps students identify the pursuit in which they most frequently find flow. Additionally, it allows them to evaluate, understand, and consider how to increase their experience of flow while sharpening their understanding of the flow model of optimal experience.

CONCEPT

The goals of the activity described in this chapter are to (a) provide a structured reflection on activities in which one already experiences flow, potentially without having had a label for these absorbing experiences; (b) encourage identification of ways to find increased flow in daily life; and (c) contribute to students' understanding of the concept of flow. Flow may best be taught alongside topics such as attention and motivation, given that the experience of flow is characterized by focused, effortless concentration and intrinsic motivation. Flow can also be taught in conjunction with engagement, one of several pathways to live a good life (Csikszentmihalyi, 1990; Huta & Waterman, 2014).

MATERIALS NEEDED

Appendix 18.1 clarifies common misconceptions about flow experience. The instructor can review this conceptual resource and then share it with the students alongside a brief instructor-led introduction to flow in class. The Conceptual Resource can be accessed via the publisher's website and shared digitally with

https://doi.org/10.1037/0000417-018
More Activities for Teaching Positive Psychology: A Guide for Instructors, S. D. Pressman and A. C. Parks (Editors)

students and/or can be printed out if the instructor chooses to share physical copies.

The Activity Worksheet (Appendix 18.2) will need to be printed out for students if paper-based delivery is adopted. A digital version of the worksheet can be downloaded from the publisher's website if web-based delivery is preferred in the physical classroom or over videoconferencing platforms. A calculator may be needed to compute an average score for one of the questions in the Activity Worksheet. An optional assignment prompt (Appendix 18.3) can be administered to students, digitally or physically, after the in-class activity is complete.

ACTIVITY SETTING

This activity can be conducted in both physical and online classrooms. This chapter describes how to conduct the activity synchronously during a classroom session; however, instructors are encouraged to adapt the activity as they see fit for asynchronous classes.

The inspiration for this activity is an exercise that students have completed for a number of years in a positive psychology overview course designed and taught by Mihaly Csikszentmihalyi and Jeanne Nakamura, which includes both synchronous and asynchronous components. In that activity, students first familiarize themselves with the concept of flow via suggested readings (please see the recommended reading for before the activity) and then select and reflect on one activity in their daily lives. Next, students spend a few days outside the classroom engaging with and modifying their chosen activity with the goal of experiencing more flow in the activity. This hands-on process is followed by a written reflection about their experience of modifying their chosen activity based on flow theory and previous empirical research. Finally, in order to promote collaborative learning, students discuss, in small groups, their successful and unsuccessful strategies for making their chosen activity more flow conducive. The outside-of-class activity (experiential exercise and written reflection) is included as an optional assignment in Appendix 18.3 in case instructors would like to use it.

Although the interaction between theory and lived experience, and the potentially deepening relationship between students and their chosen activity over the course of the week, are strengths of this approach, it is not feasible to conduct it within one classroom session. Accordingly, we describe a shorter variation of this activity here with the same intention of helping students identify and reflect on existing flow activities.

ACTIVITY DURATION

The full activity requires approximately 50 to 60 minutes. About 10 minutes will be needed for a brief instructor-led introduction to the concept of flow (see Appendix 18.1), followed by 10 to 15 minutes for students to fill out the worksheet (refer to Appendix 18.2). The remaining time can be divided into a 15- to 20-minute group discussion about students' results generated by the worksheet and a 15-minute instructor-led report-out and debrief. Instructors are also recommended to provide students with 4 to 5 days of experiential engagement with the task described in the optional assignment (please see Appendix 18.3) if the instructor chooses to follow up the in-class activity by requesting a written reflection from students.

SUGGESTED READINGS

- Recommended reading for before the activity:
  - Nakamura and Csikszentmihalyi (2021)

- Optional readings for after the activity:
  - Abuhamdeh (2021)
  - Csikszentmihalyi (1975b)
  - Csikszentmihalyi (1990)

- Optional video:
  - Csikszentmihalyi (2004)

BACKGROUND AND INSTRUCTIONS

Although there are several ways to live a good life, rich and deep engagement is often described as one such way; Csikszentmihalyi called this experience of full involvement flow (Csikszentmihalyi, 1990; Huta & Waterman, 2014; Nakamura & Csikszentmihalyi, 2021). Research indicates that flow experiences are characterized by nine dimensions: a balance between perceived challenge and skill levels, clear and emergent goals, immediate feedback, focused concentration, a sense of control, merging of action and awareness, distortion of time, loss of self-consciousness, and a sense that the experience is rewarding in itself (also see Appendix 18.1). Finding flow in an activity can enhance the quality of subjective experience in daily life. Furthermore, the quality of experience while engaging in an activity is associated with motivation to continue the activity in the long term (Csikszentmihalyi et al., 1997; Nakamura et al., 2022).

The subjective experience of flow has been reported across a wide range of cultures (Delle Fave et al., 2011), ages (Tse et al., 2022), and activities (Csikszentmihalyi, 1997; Csikszentmihalyi & Csikszentmihalyi, 1988; Ullén et al., 2012). This class activity is designed in such a way that it does not make assumptions about students' previous experiences, current sources of flow, or prior familiarity with the flow state. Rather, it focuses on describing a certain type of experience and letting students reflect on their lives to inform the course of their participation in this classroom activity.

Overall, this activity is intended to facilitate the recognition and cultivation of pursuits that are intrinsically rewarding—that is, the things people enjoy doing for their own sake. While many flow activities may begin with external motivations (e.g., practicing for an upcoming performance, writing a paper for an assignment) or lead to desirable results (e.g., improved performance, completion of a satisfying paper), these are commonly reported as merely positive by-products of the flow experience, which is rewarding in itself (Nakamura & Csikszentmihalyi, 2021).

Instructors leading this activity are encouraged to familiarize themselves with the concept of flow beforehand, especially by reviewing the recommended reading (please refer to the Suggested Readings section). In addition, the Conceptual Resource (Appendix 18.1) can further help clarify common misconceptions about the nine dimensions of flow and can be a resource for instructors and students both before and during the in-class activity.

Activity Steps

1. Assign students the recommended reading (i.e., Nakamura & Csikszentmihalyi, 2021) with a reasonable timeline to complete before the class session.

2. Drawing from the suggested readings and the Conceptual Resource (Appendix 18.1), begin class with a short lecture introducing the concept of flow (approximately 10 minutes).

3. In class, provide students with the Activity Worksheet (Appendix 18.2), which asks them to identify a flow activity and reflect upon how they typically feel when participating in their chosen activity (approximately 10–15 minutes).

4. Divide students into small groups (on average, groups of four to six students) to discuss their responses to the worksheet (approximately 15–20 minutes). Some discussion questions are listed next. Please note that these questions are mainly guiding points, and discussion is encouraged to flow freely.

   • What activity did you identify as your main flow activity? How many different activities did you identify?

   • Was it easy or difficult to identify flow activities for yourself?

   • If you identified more than one flow activity, did you notice any similarities among these various activities after being introduced to flow theory?

   • Are the activities identified among members of your group similar or different? Why do you think this may be?

   • Are most of your flow activities pursued with others or alone? Is the experience affected by the presence or absence of others? If so, why?

   • Does the intensity or depth of your flow experiences vary based on the type of activity you find flow in?

   • Were there any activities you identified that didn't seem to fit the description of flow from the recommended reading? Why or why not?

   • Based on your ratings of the nine flow dimensions, were some dimensions less present than the others? If so, why?

- Were any of the nine dimensions of the flow state most decisive for you when identifying the activities you experience flow in?

- What could you do to experience flow more often in the activities you identified?

- How can flow theory be applied to enhance enjoyment and reduce boredom or anxiety in less engaging activities?

5. Following the small-group discussions, lead a full class discussion (approximately 15 minutes). This may include either inviting representatives from each group to report out from their small-group discussions or moving directly to a debrief and discussion with the full class. Any guiding questions listed in the previous step that are not covered during the small-group discussion may help structure the full class debrief at the end of the activity. This is also an ideal time to address students' questions and clarify common misconceptions by sharing information from the Conceptual Resource (Appendix 18.1).

6. If desired, conclude the activity by sharing the optional written assignment for students to complete after class (please see the Assignment section and Appendix 18.3).

DISCUSSION

The Activity Worksheet (Appendix 18.2) presents students with quotations from the Flow Questionnaire (Csikszentmihalyi, 1982), a mixed-methods tool that has been used in extensive cross-cultural research (Delle Fave et al., 2011). Csikszentmihalyi drew the quotes from his original interviews about people's experience of activities such as basketball, chess, and rock climbing. In completing the Activity Worksheet, students also rate their main flow activity on the nine flow dimensions. The items comprise the Flow Short Scale (Martin & Jackson, 2008), one of several scales that have been used to measure flow.

Students might wonder how frequently people experience flow. In a U.S. sample of working adults who read the quotes describing the flow state, 30% reported experiencing the state daily, while 13% said they did not know the experience (Csikszentmihalyi, 1982). Another question that may arise after completing this exercise concerns the kinds of pursuits in which people commonly experience flow. Sports and games are mentioned often, as are arts and crafts of all kinds as well as physical practices such as yoga—it is as if they were built for flow. These may be the clearest examples of cultural practices that persisted and evolved because they provide experiences of flow (Csikszentmihalyi & Massimini, 1985). However, Csikszentmihalyi contended that virtually any activity holds opportunities for flow. Other common sources of intrinsically rewarding absorption in the stretching of one's capacities are cooking, talking with friends, gardening, reading, and, perhaps surprisingly, working (Csikszentmihalyi, 1990; Delle Fave et al., 2011; Engeser & Baumann, 2016; Nakamura & Csikszentmihalyi, 2021).

Across cultures, the subjective experience of flow is largely equivalent, whereas the activities in which people find flow tend to differ (Csikszentmihalyi & Asakawa, 2016). For example, students from Western cultures (e.g., Italy, U.S.) have been found to experience flow more often in leisure activities, whereas students belonging to non-Western cultures (e.g., Nepal, Uganda) have been found to experience flow in learning activities (Delle Fave et al., 2011). Furthermore, individual differences in sociodemographic factors may also have an effect on flow (Nakamura & Tse, 2020). For example, Shernoff and Schmidt (2008) found that U.S. students from low socioeconomic status communities reported greater levels of flow in the classroom compared to students from high socioeconomic status communities.

Students may want to contextualize and discuss their score on the flow scale included in the Activity Worksheet (i.e., Question 6, the Flow Short Scale; Martin & Jackson, 2008). Higher scores on the scale denote a greater tendency to experience flow in students' self-identified flow activity (in Question 5). To facilitate discussion, Figure 18.1 presents average flow scores in various types of activities based on previous research. Please note that these findings are largely based on samples consisting of adults.

Because one person's flow activity—solving statistics problems, for example—may be dreadful for another person due to boredom or anxiety, a question for researchers is whether it is possible to reliably trigger flow in the laboratory. Several researchers have employed a classic video game called Tetris (e.g., Keller & Bless, 2008; Moller et al., 2010; Rankin et al., 2019), the goal of which is to position steadily falling blocks of seven different shapes so that they form a solid wall at the bottom of the screen and fall away. It is worth considering why it is effective from the standpoint of the flow model. Some likely features include the simplicity of the game, low initial level of challenge, moment-by-moment goal-setting, continuous feedback about progress, open-ended design (it is not possible

FIGURE 18.1. Tendency to Experience Flow in Various Activities

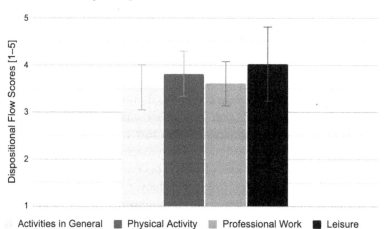

Note. Activities in general (Ovington et al., 2018), physical activity (Jackson et al., 2008), professional work (Tobert & Moneta, 2013), and leisure (Chang, 2020). Error bars represent ±1 *SD*.

to end the game by winning), and, of course, the function of the screen as a "limited stimulus field" (Csikszentmihalyi, 1975a, p. 40).

Research on flow began with questions about play, enjoyment, and creativity (Csikszentmihalyi, 1975a, 2014). What eventually emerged from this research were the nine dimensions of flow, or the commonly reported conditions and characteristics of activities that people tend to enjoy and engage in for the sheer sake of doing them (Csikszentmihalyi, 2014). However, correlations between flow and performance as well as productivity (Jackson et al., 2001; Jackson & Roberts, 1992; Peifer & Wolters, 2021) have led to flow often being discussed as a means to improving performance and productivity. Such interpretations tend to underemphasize the autotelic nature of flow and may even misrepresent the theory as a tool for performance enhancement rather than a description of optimal experience. Although the enticement of optimizing human performance is understandably alluring, the goal of flow theory has been to illuminate how to improve the quality of one's experience and, in turn, the quality of one's life.

ASSIGNMENT

If the instructor chooses, students can be assigned a written reflection after they fill out the Activity Worksheet. The prompt for the assignment is included in Appendix 18.3. As described there, this written assignment will benefit from 4 to 5 days of experiential learning before students can meaningfully draft a written response to it. If possible, instructors may want to allow students at least 1 week for this written assignment.

While the assignment encourages students to draw from the assigned readings on their own to explore enhancing their experience or likelihood of experiencing flow, students may request more direct guidance for how to do so. As previously mentioned, games tend to be reliable flow activities because they inherently provide clearly defined objectives and opportunities for feedback, such as scoring systems, and they reduce the relevant stimuli—or what is worth paying attention to—to the field, court, board, or screen for the duration of the game (Csikszentmihalyi, 1975a, 1990, 1997; Jackson & Csikszentmihalyi, 1999). Along these lines, one suggestion is manipulating the relationship between challenge and skill in order to create an optimally engaging activity that is neither frustratingly difficult nor uninspiringly boring (Csikszentmihalyi, 1997). Similarly, focusing on clear, emergent goals in the activity can make experiencing flow more likely, as can devising ways of identifying and using feedback about how well one is doing to correct the course of action from moment to moment (Csikszentmihalyi, 2014). Deliberately removing distractions—for example, wearing headphones while studying, which both eliminate ambient sound and discourage casual interruptions by others (Dubin, 2018)—can help to narrow the stimulus field and focus attention (Csikszentmihalyi, 1975a).

APPENDIX 18.1: Conceptual Resource—Clarifying Common Misconceptions About Flow

This resource provides brief descriptions of the nine dimensions of flow experience and clarifies common misconceptions often associated with them to aid in your small-group discussion. The nine dimensions of flow experiences are categorized below as conditions and characteristics. Whereas the conditions are necessary, but not sufficient, in order for a flow experience to occur and continue, the characteristics describe the subjective state during the ongoing flow experience. In general, it may be more fruitful to target and modify the conditions to make an activity more conducive to flow rather than attempting to modify or control the experiential characteristics of flow experiences themselves.

DIMENSIONS OF FLOW

Conditions

Challenge–Skill Balance

The balance between levels of perceived challenge and perceived skills is a central condition of a flow experience (Nakamura & Csikszentmihalyi, 2021). When the perceived level of challenge is below a person's skill level, they are likely to feel bored and disengaged. When the perceived level of challenge is well above a person's level of skill, they are likely to feel anxious. The balance between the two, with challenges very slightly stretching a person's perceived skills, is most conducive to experiencing flow. Note that levels of challenge and skill, and their balance, are not determined by objective criteria associated with an activity. Rather, both levels of challenge and skill are those perceived by the individual themself.

Clear and Emergent Goals

The experience of flow occurs within a system of dynamic and open motivation. Clear goals in the context of flow experience refer to goals that emerge in a person's awareness as their subjective experience unfolds, and do not create ambiguity about what to do next (Nakamura & Csikszentmihalyi, 2021). The immediate and momentary nature of emergent goals is in contrast to broader, more general goals that a person may have in mind while engaging in daily tasks. For example, a student may set a goal to finish a written assignment in a given amount of time. However, such goals do not represent clear and emergent goals in the case of flow. Rather, goals that emerge once a student begins writing their assignment, such as selecting an idea to start their draft with, brainstorming about their response, drafting an outline, elaborating on specific points they wish to highlight in their response, reviewing their draft for logical consistency, even just completing one sentence and assessing whether it links logically with the next, are more representative of a flow experience. In other words, clear goals during flow emerge in the moment within a person's subjective awareness as opposed to being set before the activity even begins.

Immediate Feedback

Immediate and continuous feedback about how well one is doing helps sustain flow and can be thought of as an ongoing condition of a flow experience operating alongside clear and emergent goals (Nakamura & Csikszentmihalyi, 2021). Similar to the balance between challenge and skill levels as well as clear emergent goals, feedback, as immediately received in the present moment, is subjectively perceived and assessed by the person themself. This is in contrast to external feedback that a person may receive later about their performance in an activity, such as that received from another person (e.g., a letter grade or score assigned to a student's assignment).

Characteristics

Focused Concentration

Completely focused concentration representative of deep absorption in the task at hand is a key characteristic of flow experience (Csikszentmihalyi, 1990; Nakamura & Csikszentmihalyi, 2021). However, unlike deliberate regulation of attention to concentrate on a particular stimulus, focused concentration in the case of flow experience emerges as a function of the flow conditions being satisfied. Focused attention within flow experience is often reported as feeling effortless, in contrast to effortful focus that may characterize other experiences of focused attention (Csikszentmihalyi & Nakamura, 2010). In other words, flow states are unlikely to occur simply because one has chosen to intentionally and effortfully concentrate. Instead, complete concentration is more often the product of a situation in which the perceived levels of challenge and skill are balanced and emergent goals and feedback are clear.

Merging of Action and Awareness

The merging of action and awareness within flow experience represents the subjective perception of feeling at one with the activity. During flow, the distinction between the individual and the activity is not at the forefront of awareness. Many accounts of the flow state describe an experience in which one action flows into the next without pausing for conscious evaluation (Csikszentmihalyi, 1975a, 1990). In other words, many people report that during flow, one action seamlessly follows the next because the action and the awareness of that action tend to merge into one unified experience.

Sense of Control

People often report feeling in control of their actions when experiencing flow. For example, a rock climber may report feeling in control of where to place their hand next as they climb up the face of a mountain. Although a flow experience is often accompanied by a sense of control, it is contextualized against the backdrop of feeling that control may be lost at any given moment (Csikszentmihalyi, 1990). In this sense, perceptions of control that emerge during flow experiences can be distinguished from feelings of complete control that may be more characteristic of relaxation or actions that have become automatic.

The sense of control that accompanies flow experiences exhibits a paradoxical nature (Csikszentmihalyi, 1990; Logan, 1988); many people report feeling completely in control, yet a true feeling of complete control is at odds with one's skills being stretched by an attainable challenge. To be completely in control would imply that one is not actually being challenged or that one might not fall out of control at any given moment if concentration is not maintained. The allure of flow, however, is in the satisfaction of exercising control in normally difficult-to-control situations or experiencing the possibility, rather than the actuality, of control (Csikszentmihalyi, 1990). Importantly, like the balance of challenge and skills, the sense of control during flow is an individual's subjective perception of control rather than an objective assessment.

Time Distortion

As attention is fully focused on the task or activity at hand during flow, spare attentional resources are not available to keep track of the passage of time. As a result, people often report completely losing track of time during flow. Once the flow experience ends, the passage of time tends to feel different than normal, and the perception of time having passed by very quickly or rather slowly during the flow experience is a common occurrence (Csikszentmihalyi, 1990).

Loss of Self-Consciousness

Attention is fully focused on the present moment during flow. Similar to losing track of time passing, spare attention is not available during flow experiences to consciously view oneself as a social actor engaged in a task or activity. Rather, a person simply acts without thinking self-consciously about themself or how others will perceive their actions. In other words, during flow, attention is fully focused on what one is doing rather than being invested in consciously monitoring the self.

Note that the loss of self-consciousness does not mean the loss of consciousness altogether, as in the case of fainting, for instance. In addition, the loss of self-consciousness does not represent a complete lack of control and regulation of one's behavior. In fact, a person is fully conscious of their actions during flow, as in the case of rock climbing, but simply not conscious of themselves as a separate participant in their subjective experience.

Autotelic Experience

Flow experience is autotelic in that it is pursued for its own sake. The term autotelic is derived from the Greek words *auto* (i.e., self) and *telos* (i.e., goal). In other words, experiences of flow are ends in themselves rather than simply serving as a means to another end. Although flow is associated with beneficial outcomes such as positive mood and higher performance, such outcomes are not generally why people want to replicate flow once they experience it in a particular activity. Such benefits may best be seen as by-products of flow rather than the primary reason to pursue such an experience.

Furthermore, while one could begin a potential flow activity with an external goal in mind (e.g., rehearsing for a future performance or competition, completing an assignment), the experience during flow makes the activity a worthwhile end in itself, regardless of the final outcome. With that said, skill development is often associated with flow since the enjoyable nature of flow itself motivates people to seek a similar quality of experience in the future. With each subsequent flow experience, skills tend to gradually improve, leading one to seek out greater challenges in order to maintain an optimal balance of challenge and skills (Csikszentmihalyi, 1990; Nakamura & Csikszentmihalyi, 2021).

A printable version of this appendix can be downloaded from the APA website at https://www.apa.org/pubs/books/more-activities-teaching-positive-psychology.

APPENDIX 18.2: Activity Worksheet

1. Please read the following quotes:[1]

   "My mind isn't wandering. I am totally involved in what I am doing and I am not thinking of anything else. My body feels good . . . the world seems to be cut off from me . . . I am less aware of myself and my problems."

   "My concentration is like breathing . . . I never think of it . . . When I start, I really do shut out the world."

   "I am so involved in what I am doing . . . I don't see myself as separate from what I am doing."

2. Have you ever had similar experiences as described in the above quotes?

   • Yes
   • No

3. If yes, what activities were you engaged in when you had such experiences?

   _____
   _____
   _____
   _____
   _____

4. How often do you carry out the activities identified above?
   Please indicate the frequency of each activity (daily, weekly, monthly, yearly, rare events).

   _____
   _____
   _____
   _____
   _____

---

[1] *Note.* Quotations are adapted from the Flow Questionnaire originally developed by Mihaly Csikszentmihalyi and published in "Toward a Psychology of Optimal Experience," by M. Csikszentmihalyi, in L. Wheeler (Ed.), *Review of Personality and Social Psychology* (Vol. 3, p. 23), 1982, Sage Publications. Copyright 1982 by Sage Publications. Adapted with permission.

5. Of the activities you identified, now please think about which one best represents the experience described in the three quotations (from Step 1)—in other words, the activity where you feel this experience with the highest intensity.

Then, please record the activity you have chosen here:

_____

6. Next, please answer the following questions in relation to your experience while you are participating in your chosen activity. Think about how often you experience each of these during your activity, then select the number that best matches your experience. You may experience these thoughts and feelings some of the time, all of the time, or none of the time. There are no right or wrong answers.

In general, when I take part in _____ (your main activity)[2]:

• I feel I am competent enough to meet the demands of the situation.

Never		Frequently		Always
1	2	3	4	5

• I do things spontaneously and automatically without having to think.

Never		Frequently		Always
1	2	3	4	5

• I have a strong sense of what I want to do.

Never		Frequently		Always
1	2	3	4	5

• I have a good idea about how well I am doing while I am involved in the task/activity.

Never		Frequently		Always
1	2	3	4	5

• I am completely focused on the task at hand.

Never		Frequently		Always
1	2	3	4	5

• I have a feeling of total control over what I am doing.

Never		Frequently		Always
1	2	3	4	5

• I am not worried about what others may be thinking of me.

Never		Frequently		Always
1	2	3	4	5

---

[2] *Note.* Flow Short Scale: Adapted from "Brief Approaches to Assessing Task Absorption and Enhanced Subjective Experience: Examining 'Short' and 'Core' Flow in Diverse Performance Domains," by A. J. Martin and S. A. Jackson, 2008, *Motivation and Emotion,* 32(3), p. 155 (https://doi.org/10.1007/s11031-008-9094-0). Copyright 2008 by Springer. Adapted with permission.

- The way time passes seems to be different from normal.

Never		Frequently		Always
1	2	3	4	5

- The experience is extremely rewarding.

Never		Frequently		Always
1	2	3	4	5

7. Now, please calculate your total and average score for Question 6. Your total score will be in the range of 9 to 45. Your average score will range between 1 and 5. You are welcome to use a calculator for this step of the activity.

    Total score (sum of scores on Questions 6a–6i): _____

    Average score (total score divided by 9): _____

8. What could you do to experience flow more often in this activity (your main activity)?

    _____

    _____

    _____

    _____

    _____

A printable version of this appendix can be downloaded from the APA website at https://www.apa.org/pubs/books/more-activities-teaching-positive-psychology.

APPENDIX 18.3: Prompt for Optional Assignment

DO

Spend a couple of days noticing some activities you must regularly do but dislike doing. Choose one of these activities to focus on for this exercise. Spend the rest of the week tweaking the activity so that you are more likely to experience flow while doing it.

WRITE

In one to two pages:

Describe the activity you focused on: what you did to make it more like a flow activity, and why this made sense based on the implications of theory from the readings. In what ways did your intervention work? In what ways did it not work? If you subsequently made adjustments to your initial intervention, why did you do so (referencing theory) and what effect did it have? What are the implications of this for other unengaging activities that you undertake on a regular basis?

Note. If it is not feasible for the assignment to include an experiential component, students may be asked to write what they would or could do (based on flow theory) to make flow more likely in an unengaging activity.

A printable version of this appendix can be downloaded from the APA website at https://www.apa.org/pubs/books/more-activities-teaching-positive-psychology.

REFERENCES

Abuhamdeh, S. (2021). On the relationship between flow and enjoyment. In C. Peifer & S. Engeser (Eds.), *Advances in flow research* (2nd ed., pp. 155–169). Springer. https://doi.org/10.1007/978-3-030-53468-4_6

Chang, L. C. (2020). Relationship between flow experience and subjective vitality among older adults attending senior centres. *Leisure Studies, 39*(3), 433–443. https://doi.org/10.1080/02614367.2020.1763441

Csikszentmihalyi, M. (1975a). *Beyond boredom and anxiety.* Jossey-Bass.

Csikszentmihalyi, M. (1975b). Play and intrinsic rewards. *Journal of Humanistic Psychology, 15*(3), 41–63. https://doi.org/10.1177/002216787501500306

Csikszentmihalyi, M. (1982). Toward a psychology of optimal experience. In L. Wheeler (Ed.), *Review of personality and social psychology* (Vol. 3, pp. 13–36). Sage Publications.

Csikszentmihalyi, M. (1990). *Flow: The psychology of optimal experience.* Harper Perennial.

Csikszentmihalyi, M. (1997). *Finding flow.* Basic Books.

Csikszentmihalyi, M. (2004, February). *Flow, the secret to happiness* [Video]. TED Conferences. https://www.ted.com/talks/mihaly_csikszentmihalyi_flow_the_secret_to_happiness?language=en

Csikszentmihalyi, M. (2014). *The collected works of Mihaly Csikszentmihalyi.* Springer.

Csikszentmihalyi, M., & Asakawa, K. (2016). Universal and cultural dimensions of optimal experiences. *Japanese Psychological Research, 58*(1), 4–13. https://doi.org/10.1111/jpr.12104

Csikszentmihalyi, M., & Csikszentmihalyi, I. S. (1988). *Optimal experience: Psychological studies of flow in consciousness.* Cambridge University Press. https://doi.org/10.1017/CBO9780511621956

Csikszentmihalyi, M., & Massimini, F. (1985). On the psychological selection of bio-cultural information. *New Ideas in Psychology, 3*(2), 115–138. https://doi.org/10.1016/0732-118X(85)90002-9

Csikszentmihalyi, M., & Nakamura, J. (2010). Effortless attention in everyday life: A systematic phenomenology. In B. Bruya (Ed.), *Effortless attention* (pp. 179–190). MIT Press. https://doi.org/10.7551/mitpress/8602.003.0009

Csikszentmihalyi, M., Rathunde, K., & Whalen, S. (1997). *Talented teenagers: The roots of success and failure.* Cambridge University Press.

Delle Fave, A., Massimini, F., & Bassi, M. (2011). *Psychological selection and optimal experience across cultures: Social empowerment through personal growth.* Springer. https://doi.org/10.1007/978-90-481-9876-4

Dubin, M. (2018). *Experiencing flow at work as a digital native in an accelerated knowledge economy* (Publication No. 13418706) [Doctoral dissertation, Claremont Graduate University]. ProQuest Dissertations and Theses Global. http://ccl.idm.oclc.org/login?url=https://www.proquest.com/dissertations-theses/experiencing-flow-at-work-as-digital-native/docview/2163300535/se-2?accountid=10141

Engeser, S., & Baumann, N. (2016). Fluctuation of flow and affect in everyday life: A second look at the paradox of work. *Journal of Happiness Studies, 17*(1), 105–124. https://doi.org/10.1007/s10902-014-9586-4

Huta, V., & Waterman, A. S. (2014). Eudaimonia and its distinction from hedonia: Developing a classification and terminology for understanding conceptual and operational definitions. *Journal of Happiness Studies, 15*(6), 1425–1456. https://doi.org/10.1007/s10902-013-9485-0

Jackson, S. A., & Csikszentmihalyi, M. (1999). *Flow in sports: The keys to optimal experiences and performances.* Human Kinetics Books.

Jackson, S. A., Martin, A. J., & Eklund, R. C. (2008). Long and short measures of flow: The construct validity of the FSS-2, DFS-2, and new brief counterparts. *Journal of Sport & Exercise Psychology, 30*(5), 561–587. https://doi.org/10.1123/jsep.30.5.561

Jackson, S. A., & Roberts, G. C. (1992). Positive performance states of athletes: Toward a conceptual understanding of peak performance. *The Sport Psychologist, 6*(2), 156–171. https://doi.org/10.1123/tsp.6.2.156

Jackson, S. A., Thomas, P. R., Marsh, H. W., & Smethurst, C. J. (2001). Relationships between flow, self-concept, psychological skills, and performance. *Journal of Applied Sport Psychology, 13*(2), 129–153. https://doi.org/10.1080/104132001753149865

Keller, J., & Bless, H. (2008). Flow and regulatory compatibility: An experimental approach to the flow model of intrinsic motivation. *Personality and Social Psychology Bulletin, 34*(2), 196–209. https://doi.org/10.1177/0146167207310026

Logan, R. D. (1988). Flow in solitary ordeals. In M. Csikszentmihalyi & I. S. Csikszentmihalyi (Eds.), *Optimal experience: Psychological studies of flow in consciousness* (pp. 172–180). Cambridge University Press. https://doi.org/10.1017/CBO9780511621956.010

Martin, A. J., & Jackson, S. A. (2008). Brief approaches to assessing task absorption and enhanced subjective experience: Examining 'short' and 'core' flow in diverse performance domains. *Motivation and Emotion, 32*(3), 141–157. https://doi.org/10.1007/s11031-008-9094-0

Moller, A. C., Meier, B. P., & Wall, R. D. (2010). Developing an experimental induction of flow: Effortless action in the lab. In B. Bruya (Ed.), *Effortless attention* (pp. 191–204). MIT Press. https://doi.org/10.7551/mitpress/9780262013840.003.0010

Nakamura, J., & Csikszentmihalyi, M. (2021). The experience of flow: Theory and research. In S. J. Lopez, L. M. Edwards, & S. C. Marques (Eds.), *Oxford handbook of positive psychology* (3rd ed., pp. 279–296). Oxford University Press. https://doi.org/10.1093/oxfordhb/9780199396511.013.16

Nakamura, J., & Tse, D. C. K. (2020). Flow: Expression and applications. In B. J. Carducci, C. S. Nave, J. S. Mio, & R. E. Riggio (Eds.), *The Wiley encyclopedia of personality and individual differences: Clinical, applied, and cross-cultural research* (pp. 551–556). Wiley. https://doi.org/10.1002/9781118970843.ch356

Nakamura, J., Tse, D. C. K., & Mann, A. S. (2022). Quality of experience in prosocial activity and intent to continue: An experience sampling study. *Psychology and Aging, 37*(2), 190–196. https://doi.org/10.1037/pag0000658

Ovington, L. A., Saliba, A. J., & Goldring, J. (2018). Dispositions toward flow and mindfulness predict dispositional insight. *Mindfulness, 9*(2), 585–596. https://doi.org/10.1007/s12671-017-0800-4

Peifer, C., & Wolters, G. (2021). Flow in the context of work. In C. Peifer & S. Engeser (Eds.), *Advances in flow research* (2nd ed., pp. 287–321). Springer. https://doi.org/10.1007/978-3-030-53468-4_11

Rankin, K., Walsh, L. C., & Sweeny, K. (2019). A better distraction: Exploring the benefits of flow during uncertain waiting periods. *Emotion, 19*(5), 818–828. https://doi.org/10.1037/emo0000479

Shernoff, D. J., & Schmidt, J. A. (2008). Further evidence of an engagement–achievement paradox among U.S. high school students. *Journal of Youth and Adolescence, 37*(5), 564–580. https://doi.org/10.1007/s10964-007-9241-z

Tobert, S., & Moneta, G. B. (2013). Flow as a function of affect and coping in the workplace. *Individual Differences Research, 11*(3), 102–113. https://psycnet.apa.org/record/2013-36101-002

Tse, D. C. K., Nakamura, J., & Csikszentmihalyi, M. (2022). Flow experiences across adulthood: Preliminary findings on the continuity hypothesis. *Journal of Happiness Studies, 23*(6), 1–24. https://doi.org/10.1007/s10902-022-00514-5

Ullén, F., de Manzano, Ö., Almeida, R., Magnusson, P. K., Pedersen, N. L., Nakamura, J., Csikszentmihalyi, M., & Madison, G. (2012). Proneness for psychological flow in everyday life: Associations with personality and intelligence. *Personality and Individual Differences, 52*(2), 167–172. https://doi.org/10.1016/j.paid.2011.10.003

19

Promoting Hope Through Goal Setting

Matthew W. Gallagher

Promoting hopeful thinking by generating goals and reflecting on pathways and agency thoughts linked to those goals.

CONCEPT

Students will be asked to specify goals for the future as well as strategies/obstacles/resources for pursuing their goals as a means of demonstrating the benefits of hopeful thinking about the future. The activity is a simple way to help students reflect on and better understand the importance of hope by identifying goals, pathways, and agency thinking.

MATERIALS NEEDED

All that is needed for this activity is paper and a pen or any electronic device that students can type with. A specialized worksheet could be used to provide structure or length parameters to the content but is not necessary.

https://doi.org/10.1037/0000417-019
More Activities for Teaching Positive Psychology: A Guide for Instructors, S. D. Pressman and A. C. Parks (Editors)

ACTIVITY SETTING

This activity could be done fully in the classroom but is best done as homework followed by a class period designated for discussion of experiences. The discussion could be done in an in-person class or an online class via a video platform. This activity is more impactful when done earlier in the semester so that students can then reflect back upon and discuss any revisions to their goals and strategies at the end of the semester. It also works well to introduce this activity when covering related positive expectancy constructs such as optimism and self-efficacy so students understand how the different theories of positive thinking are all distinct and uniquely impactful. This may also help students to understand how this theory of hope is different from lay conceptions of hope that are defined as more of a passive desire for the future.

ACTIVITY DURATION

It typically takes students 30 to 60 minutes to complete the independent activity, followed by a discussion in class of up to an hour, depending on class size and course time available. You can adjust the duration of the discussion by using more or less of the discussion prompts provided. Students often take 2 to 3 minutes to summarize their experience of completing the goal activity, so depending on class size, you could have each student present or just have five to ten students summarize their experiences before moving to the broader discussion.

SUGGESTED READINGS

- Recommended reading for before the activity:
  - Rand and Rogers (2022)

- Optional enrichment readings for after the activity:
  - Snyder (2002)
  - Gallagher and Lopez (2018)
  - Lopez (2013)

BACKGROUND AND INSTRUCTIONS

Hope has been a topic of interest for philosophers and psychologists for centuries. However, it was not until the early 1990s that scientific research has shown that hope is not a harmful delusion, as Freud once argued, but rather an important source of resilience that predicts positive outcomes in many areas of life (Snyder, 1994). The key turning point in this field was C. R. Snyder's development of his theory and measures of hope, which provide the theoretical foundation for more than 3 decades of empirical research demonstrating the beneficial effects of hope (Gallagher & Lopez, 2018; Snyder, 2000).

Snyder's theory defines hope as a cognitive trait that drives human behavior primarily by the pursuit of goals and identifies hope as an important factor in how we identify and pursue our goals. Specifically, Snyder's model defines *hope* as the reciprocal interaction of (a) pathways thinking, or the perceived capacity to identify strategies to effectively pursue one's goals; and (b) agency thinking, or the motivation to use the identified pathways and persevere in the face of obstacles. Hope is, therefore, not primarily an emotional construct in Snyder's model, and emotions are instead conceptualized largely to be signals that reflect the perceived progress toward or completion of one's goals. Snyder also developed trait measures of hope that can be used in adults and children, as well as a state measure of hope that is appropriate when the focus is on changes in hope within individuals. Alternative models that focus on hope as more of an emotional or spiritual construct (e.g., Scioli, 2023) have been proposed. Snyder's model remains the most widely studied model of hope within psychology. It has now been studied in hundreds of empirical studies across the world and is conceptually and empirically distinct from related positive psychology constructs such as optimism and self-efficacy (Rand, 2018).

Hope is an important predictor of improved outcomes across many life domains (Gallagher & Lopez, 2018). A consistent finding is that individuals higher in hope are more likely to use more effective coping strategies in the pursuit of their goals, which has benefits both in reducing mental illness and promoting well-being but also in promoting positive outcomes and achievement in many diverse settings. Meta-analytic reviews have demonstrated that higher levels of hope are associated with improved outcomes in work settings (Reichard et al., 2013), academic settings (Marques et al., 2017), and various indicators of psychological and physical well-being (Alarcon et al., 2013). Consistent with Snyder's theory, hope is, therefore, an important source of resilience and promotes well-being and positive functioning in many areas of life.

Hope is a trait that is generally quite stable in the absence of an intervention (Marques & Gallagher, 2017), but there is clear evidence that multiple effective interventions exist that can be used to increase levels of hope. Hope has been found to play an important role in promoting recovery during empirically supported treatments of many of the most common forms of mental illness (Gallagher et al., 2020). A specific form of hope therapy has also been developed and found to have promising effects in terms of reducing symptoms of depression and anxiety and increasing levels of well-being (Cheavens et al., 2006). Brief interventions have also been shown to be promising, with evidence that a single 90-minute session can be effectively used to promote hope in college students (Feldman & Dreher, 2012). The promotion of hope is therefore possible and important, and making hope happen in the classroom has many benefits for the academic achievement and well-being of students (Lopez, 2013). Ongoing directions in the scientific study of hope include further development of hope interventions that can be effective in different settings and with different populations and conducting additional research to understand how the promotion and benefits of hope may differ for individuals of different backgrounds. The activity described in this chapter is a simple way to help students reflect on and better understand the importance of hope by identifying goals, pathways, and agency thinking.

After reviewing Snyder's theory of hope and the empirical research highlighting the benefits of hope across different contexts, students are asked to engage in a goal-setting activity (instructions found in Appendix 19.1) in which they will concretely identify the three components of hope: goals, pathways thinking, and agency thinking. Specifically, students are asked to identify two to three goals they have for three distinct timeframes of varying lengths. For example, in a classroom of predominantly advanced undergraduates, the timeframes for the goals could be (a) this semester; (b) the remaining time you have in college (if this is your last semester, focus on the first year after graduating); and (c) the first 5 years after you graduate. The time anchors are flexible, however, and could be adjusted as appropriate depending on the setting in which the activity is used. The goal is simply to have a range of time horizons so that students specify goals over the short, medium, and long term.

After identifying their goals, students are asked to think through the pathways and agency components of hope. Specifically, students should brainstorm how they think they can pursue their goals and try to identify concrete and specific ideas for pathways or strategies that might be effective means of pursuing their goals. They should also reflect on what potential obstacles or challenges they might expect to encounter and what strategies may be useful for managing such challenges. Students are encouraged to thoroughly think this through for each goal to foster pathways thinking but, for the purpose of the requirement, are only asked to write about one to two pathways and obstacles for each goal to minimize burden. To promote agency thinking, students are asked to reflect on internal and external resources, activities, and sources of support that will be useful for maintaining motivation while pursuing their goals. As with the pathways thinking, students are encouraged to identify as many potential agency thoughts that could be helpful, but for the purpose of the homework writing assignment (Appendix 19.1), they are only asked to write down the most important or representative ideas.

After generating goals and reflecting on pathways and agency thinking in relation to those goals, students are then asked to write a brief reaction paper that summarizes what they learned from spending time more intentionally thinking about all of the different components of hope. Students are asked to write roughly half a page, single-spaced, about insights gained in terms of whether (a) they better understand their goals, (b) their understanding of the relative importance of different goals has changed, (c) they recognize a disconnect between how their short-term goals may support the pursuit of their long-term goals, (d) their understanding of potential pathways and resources to maintain agency thinking has changed, and (e) they are more confident in achieving their goals after completing the activity. This reaction paper can then be used as a starting point during the class discussion. An optional component is to have students complete the State Hope Scale (Appendix 19.2; Snyder et al., 1996) before the homework assignment is done and then again after the discussion to help quantify how their hope may have been impacted by the activity.

DISCUSSION

You might start the discussion by asking students to describe one or two of their goals, the corresponding pathways and agency resources they have identified, and their overall reactions to the activity. Once you have gotten a few examples and discussed them with students, you can move on to this broader set of discussion questions:

• Did thinking about hope as an active, motivating trait rather than a passive process change how you viewed your levels of hope and your goals for the future?

• Were you surprised by how easy/difficult it was to generate goals or surprised by what you identified as your goals when you spent time reflecting on them?

• When you reflect on your goals across different timeframes, are they compatible? Do they build upon each other, or do they seem disconnected?

• Did you notice any common themes when identifying potential strategies or obstacles for pursuing your goals?

• Did your motivation or confidence in pursuing your goals differ based on the timeframe or focus of the goals?

• Did writing about your existing goals highlight whether any have become more or less important than they were previously?

• Do you think it would be helpful to review your goals and strategies/motivation once or twice per year to reflect upon and revise your plans?

• If you struggled with some parts of the activity but not others, does that reveal anything about your goals for the future that you hadn't realized? For example, was it easier to generate goals/pathways/agency for the short term versus long term?

• Are you more confident that you can achieve your goals after completing this exercise?

• Do you notice more positive emotions and fewer negative emotions when thinking about your goals now that you've completed the exercise?

This activity can help students understand how reflecting on their goals can help them to promote and maintain hope, particularly when facing setbacks. The science of hope remains a vibrant topic within the field of positive psychology (Gallagher et al., 2018), and there is increasing evidence that promoting hope can improve academic and mental health outcomes. The activity in this chapter can hopefully provide an accessible opportunity for students to better understand the role of hope in their lives and is something they could continue to practice outside of the classroom.

APPENDIX 19.1: Promoting Hope Assignment (Student Handout)

Welcome to the Promoting Hope Assignment, an opportunity to explore and enhance your understanding of the concept of hope in positive psychology. In this activity, you will embark on a journey of self-discovery, setting meaningful goals, and planning your path to success. Here are some instructions to help you get started:

STEP 1: SETTING YOUR GOALS

Identify two goals that you have for each of the following timeframes (six total goals):

1. This semester.
2. The remaining time you have in college (if this is your last semester, focus on the first year after graduating).
3. The first 5 years after you graduate.

STEP 2: STRATEGIES AND PATHWAYS

For each of your selected goals, think about two pathways or strategies that may lead you to success. There are the actionable steps or methods you'll use to make progress.

STEP 3: IDENTIFYING AND OVERCOMING OBSTACLES

Anticipate potential challenges or obstacles that might stand in your way as you pursue these goals. For each goal, come up with one or two solutions or approaches to overcome these obstacles.

STEP 4: STAYING MOTIVATED

Consider what resources, people, activities, or support systems can inspire and energize you along the way. These will be your sources of motivation and encouragement.

SUBMISSION

You will be asked to share your insights in class during a group discussion. Prior to the discussion, organize your findings and be prepared to present the following:

1. A list of your chosen goals, strategies, obstacles, and motivating resources for each goal. Keep each component concise, with just one to two sentences per item.

2. Additionally, write a brief (half-page) reaction paper describing what you've learned during this goal-setting exercise. Share the impact it had on your outlook and mindset.

These two components can be used as a starting point for the discussion of what you have learned from identifying and reflecting on your goals. This activity is a unique opportunity for self-reflection and personal growth. By setting your sights on the future and devising a plan, you're fostering hope. Enjoy the journey!

A printable version of this appendix can be downloaded from the APA website at https://www.apa.org/pubs/books/more-activities-teaching-positive-psychology.

APPENDIX 19.2: Adult State Hope Scale

Read each item carefully. Using the scale shown below, please select the number that best describes how you think about yourself right now and put that number in the blank before each sentence. Please take a few moments to focus on yourself and what is going on in your life at this moment. Once you have this "here and now" set, go ahead and answer each item according to the following scale:

Definitely false	Mostly false	Somewhat false	Slightly false	Slightly true	Somewhat true	Mostly true	Definitely true
1	2	3	4	5	6	7	8

1. If I should find myself in a jam, I could think of many ways to get out of it.
2. At the present time, I am energetically pursuing my goals.
3. There are lots of ways around any problem that I am facing now.
4. Right now, I see myself as being pretty successful.
5. I can think of many ways to reach my current goals.
6. At this time, I am meeting the goals that I have set for myself.

Scoring instructions:

- Pathways subscale score: Add Items 1, 3, and 5. Scores on this subscale can range from 3 to 24, with higher scores indicating higher levels of pathways thinking.

- Agency subscale score: Add Items 2, 4, and 6. Scores on this subscale can range from 3 to 24, with higher scores indicating higher levels of agency thinking.

- Total hope score: Add the pathways and agency subscales together. Scores can range from 6 to 48, with higher scores representing higher hope levels.

Note. The scale is adapted from "Development and Validation of the State Hope Scale," by C. R. Snyder, S. C. Sympson, F. C. Ybasco, T. F. Borders, M. A. Babyak, and R. L. Higgins, 1996, *Journal of Personality and Social Psychology, 70*(2), p. 335 (https://doi.org/10.1037/0022-3514.70.2.321). Copyright 1996 by the American Psychological Association.

A printable version of this appendix can be downloaded from the APA website at https://www.apa.org/pubs/books/more-activities-teaching-positive-psychology.

REFERENCES

Alarcon, G. M., Bowling, N. A., & Khazon, S. (2013). Great expectations: A meta-analytic examination of optimism and hope. *Personality and Individual Differences*, *54*(7), 821–827. https://doi.org/10.1016/j.paid.2012.12.004

Cheavens, J. S., Feldman, D. B., Gum, A., Michael, S. T., & Snyder, C. R. (2006). Hope therapy in a community sample: A pilot investigation. *Social Indicators Research*, *77*(1), 61–78. https://doi.org/10.1007/s11205-005-5553-0

Feldman, D. B., & Dreher, D. E. (2012). Can hope be changed in 90 minutes? Testing the efficacy of a single-session goal-pursuit intervention for college students. *Journal of Happiness Studies*, *13*(4), 745–759. https://doi.org/10.1007/s10902-011-9292-4

Gallagher, M. W., Cheavens, J. S., Edwards, L. M., Feldman, D. B., Gum, A. M., Marques, S. C., Rand, K. L., Ritschel, L., Teramoto Pedrotti, J., & Shorey, H. S. (2018). Future directions in the science of hope. In M. W. Gallagher & S. J. Lopez (Eds.), *Handbook of hope* (pp. 353–362). Oxford University Press.

Gallagher, M. W., Long, L. J., Richardson, A., D'Souza, J., Boswell, J. F., Farchione, T. J., & Barlow, D. H. (2020). Examining hope as a transdiagnostic mechanism of change across anxiety disorders and CBT treatment protocols. *Behavior Therapy*, *51*(1), 190–202. https://doi.org/10.1016/j.beth.2019.06.001

Gallagher, M. W., & Lopez, S. J. (Eds.). (2018). *The Oxford handbook of hope*. Oxford University Press.

Lopez, S. J. (2013). *Making hope happen: Create the future you want for yourself and others*. Simon and Schuster.

Marques, S. C., & Gallagher, M. W. (2017). Age differences and short-term stability in hope: Results from a sample aged 15 to 80. *Journal of Applied Developmental Psychology*, *53*, 120–126. https://doi.org/10.1016/j.appdev.2017.10.002

Marques, S. C., Gallagher, M. W., & Lopez, S. J. (2017). Hope- and academic-related outcomes: A meta-analysis. *School Mental Health*, *9*(3), 250–262. https://doi.org/10.1007/s12310-017-9212-9

Rand, K. L. (2018). Hope, self-efficacy, and optimism: Conceptual and empirical differences. In M. W. Gallagher & S. J. Lopez (Eds.), *The Oxford handbook of hope* (pp. 45–58). Oxford University Press.

Rand, K. L., & Rogers, S. K. (2022). Cognitive models of hope. *Current Opinion in Psychology*, *49*, Article 101510. https://doi.org/10.1016/j.copsyc.2022.101510

Reichard, R. J., Avey, J. B., Lopez, S., & Dollwet, M. (2013). Having the will and finding the way: A review and meta-analysis of hope at work. *The Journal of Positive Psychology*, *8*(4), 292–304. https://doi.org/10.1080/17439760.2013.800903

Scioli, A. (2023). Emotional and spiritual hope: Back to the future. *Current Opinion in Psychology*, *49*, Article 101493. https://doi.org/10.1016/j.copsyc.2022.101493

Snyder, C. R. (1994). *The psychology of hope: You can get there from here*. Simon and Schuster.

Snyder, C. R. (Ed.). (2000). *Handbook of hope: Theory, measures, and applications*. Academic Press.

Snyder, C. R. (2002). Hope theory: Rainbows in the mind. *Psychological Inquiry*, *13*(4), 249–275. https://doi.org/10.1207/S15327965PLI1304_01

Snyder, C. R., Sympson, S. C., Ybasco, F. C., Borders, T. F., Babyak, M. A., & Higgins, R. L. (1996). Development and validation of the State Hope Scale. *Journal of Personality and Social Psychology*, *70*(2), 321–335. https://doi.org/10.1037/0022-3514.70.2.321

IV

SOCIAL CONNECTIONS

INTRODUCTION: SOCIAL CONNECTIONS

In this section, we focus on one of the most important correlates of well-being: social relationships. This includes the social behaviors, cognitions, and characteristics connected to our social feelings and experiences. As Dr. Chris Peterson put it, "other people matter," and these activities make this statement abundantly clear. This may be particularly salient to your student population, who are often experiencing numerous social transitions and stressors, such as the struggle to form new relationships in a new environment or thinking about how relationships may look different in adulthood. The chaos of the student's social environment can be clarified through exploration of relevant research related to social relationships and characteristics.

We start by focusing on one of the most important relationships—the one we have with ourselves—in a beautiful exercise on the construct of self-compassion. As a point of contrast, the "Acts of Kindness" chapter shows us that while being good to ourselves is good, being kind to others is even more impactful for our well-being in a kindness-intervention activity. These activities are followed by a section focused on understanding how culture influences the extent to which our happiness comes from our social relationships, a contextual topic that is explored further in Section V of this book. We end with two creative activities focused on improving the classroom environment via better relationships. The first is a fun activity that will help your students quickly form higher quality relationships with one another, and the second lets students evaluate their social network in the class to try to understand who the positive and energizing leaders in the group are. This final activity might be of special interest to individuals in business schools, those teaching industrial/organizational psychology topics, and those who want to wrap up their course with interesting ways to apply positive psychology to different contexts.

Self-Compassion

Ashley L. Kuchar and Kristin D. Neff

Students reflect on how they treat themselves when they are struggling as well as how they treat others in similar situations.

CONCEPT

We all make mistakes, face adversity, and experience life's difficulties. Learning to cope with challenging situations in productive ways is vital for maintaining healthy relationships and well-being (Allen & Leary, 2010). This activity introduces the concept of self-compassion and provides practical ways to apply a self-compassionate approach to setbacks. This concept may be taught alongside emotional states and processes (e.g., emotion-focused coping), cognitive states and processes (e.g., mindfulness), or prosocial behavior (e.g., positive relationship behaviors).

MATERIALS NEEDED

Paper and pen.

ACTIVITY SETTING

This activity can be done in a classroom setting (online or in person). It can also be conducted in an asynchronous or synchronous format. Suggestions for each method are provided in the instructions that follow.

https://doi.org/10.1037/0000417-020
More Activities for Teaching Positive Psychology: A Guide for Instructors, S. D. Pressman and A. C. Parks (Editors)

ACTIVITY DURATION

This activity requires 20 to 30 minutes, depending on the amount of class discussion. Approximately, 5 minutes are needed for students to take the Self-Compassion Scale (optional), 5 to 7 minutes for the writing activity, 5 to 7 minutes for a small group discussion, and 7 to 10 minutes for a large group discussion.

SUGGESTED READINGS

- Recommended reading for after the activity:
  - K. D. Neff (2003b)

- Optional reading for after the activity:
  - K. Neff (2011)
  - Ferrari et al. (2019)

BACKGROUND AND INSTRUCTIONS

Self-compassion involves treating oneself with kindness and understanding in times of struggle with the goal of alleviating suffering (K. D. Neff, 2003b). Self-compassion consists of three core components: mindfulness, common humanity, and self-kindness (K .D. Neff, 2003b). *Mindfulness* is a nonjudgmental present-moment awareness (Kabat-Zinn, 1990). *Common humanity* is understanding that, as humans, we all make mistakes and experience setbacks. *Self-kindness* means treating ourselves with warmth and understanding, much like we might treat a close friend. Self-compassion can be tender and comforting (e.g., soothing oneself, accepting one's imperfections) or fierce and action-oriented (e.g., setting boundaries, constructive criticism; Germer & Neff, 2019). Self-compassion is linked to improved well-being, such as less depression, stress, and anxiety, as well as increased happiness and life satisfaction (MacBeth & Gumley, 2012).

The following activity introduces the concept of self-compassion and prepares students to discuss how they might benefit from taking a self-compassionate approach in various life situations. Each step is outlined in detail next.

- Prior to the writing exercise (optional): Invite students to take the 26-item Self-Compassion Scale (SCS; K. D. Neff, 2003a). This may be completed together in class or on their own before class. Set aside approximately 5 to 7 minutes for students to complete the SCS and to report their scores (if desired). You do not need to provide any context before asking students to take this measure.
  - You may invite students to take the SCS using the scale and scoring information in Appendix 20.1 or online at https://self-compassion.org/ (see the Online Materials section). Please note that the online version includes automatic scoring, which will save time.

    – You may also ask students to report their self-compassion scores in an anonymous format so that you can discuss your class averages after the writing activity. Using online tools such as Google Sheets is an effective way for students to report their scores anonymously. If using Google Sheets, change the sharing settings to "anyone on the internet with this link can edit." This will allow all of your students to access the document without any issues and will keep all student responses anonymous. Please refer to the Online Materials section for a Google Sheet that you can download and use for your class. Once students have taken the SCS, provide the link to your class's Google Sheet and invite students to report their scores in the column titled "SCS Total." The class average, standard deviation, and graph of class scores will automatically update as new scores are added.

- Writing preparation: Invite students to take out a sheet of paper and something to write with. Inform students that they will be doing a writing exercise where they reflect on their responses to challenging events. Since the purpose of the exercise is to introduce the concept of self-compassion through reflection, you do not need to provide any additional context. These instructions remain the same for asynchronous classes.

- Writing exercise: Ask students to answer the following questions thoroughly as you read the prompts out loud. Make sure to pause after each question and give ample time for writing. In our experience, students need approximately 1 to 2 minutes per question. You may also wish to print these writing prompts as a worksheet for in-person classes or provide the Word document for asynchronous online classes (see Appendix 20.2).

Writing Prompts

Please read the following: "Please answer the following writing prompts individually. Afterward, you will discuss your experience with this exercise in small groups. You will not have to share the details of what you write, so please be open and respond honestly."

1. Think about times when a close friend feels really bad about themselves or is really struggling in some way. How do you typically respond to your friend in these situations (especially when you're at your best)? Write down what you typically do or say and note the tone in which you talk to your close friends.

2. Now think about times when you feel bad about yourself or are struggling in some way. How do you typically respond to yourself in these situations? Please write down what you typically do or say and note the tone in which you talk to yourself.

3. Did you notice any differences? If so, write down potential reasons why.

4. Finally, how do you think things might change if you responded to yourself in the same way that you typically respond to your friends?

• Small group discussion: After the writing exercise, break students into small groups of two or three to discuss their experience for 5 to 7 minutes. Encourage students to talk about any differences they noticed between how they treat themselves compared with others they are close to. What would change if they treated themselves the same way they treat others? Alternatively, what would happen if they treated others the same way they treat themselves? Note that the students do not need to share the details of what they wrote down but rather can discuss their overall experience with the reflection exercise.

  – *Note.* For online classes, it can be helpful to use a shared Google Doc during the breakout-room discussions. Please see the Online Materials section for access to a Google Doc that you can copy and use in your class. The Google Doc for this activity has the discussion prompts at the top as well as a space for each group to write their responses. You might assign a scribe in each group (e.g., the person with the next birthday) or allow students to volunteer.

    There are several advantages to using a shared Google Doc during breakout rooms. First, it can help students keep track of the discussion prompts and stay on task. Second, it can help the instructor observe what each group is discussing without having to be present in each breakout room. Instructors can use what students write in the shared Google Doc as a springboard for the large group discussion.

    Before sharing the link to the Google Doc and sending students into their breakout rooms, please change the sharing settings on the Google Doc to "anyone on the internet with this link can edit." This will allow for easier access to the document and will keep student responses anonymous.

  – Another option for online classes that are held asynchronously or synchronously is to use a virtual and participatory whiteboard. This is an interactive way to collect student responses to the discussion questions and to gain an overall sense of what the class learned from the exercise.

    Please see the Online Materials section for a virtual whiteboard that you can copy and use in your own class. The first frame has instructions for using the sticky notes function to respond to the discussion questions. The second frame reminds students of the prompts from the writing activity. The final three frames have the discussion questions listed at the top (e.g., "What differences, if any, did you notice with how you treat yourself compared with your friends?" "When you are struggling, would anything change if you treated yourself the same way you treat your friends?" "When your friends are struggling, what would happen if you treated them the same way you treat yourself?").

    Before sharing the link to the class virtual whiteboard materials with your students, change the sharing settings of your chosen system so that anyone can edit (note that different systems will have different options to do this that may or may not keep student responses anonymous). If you would like to grant credit based on their participation, you may invite students to write their names at the end of their comments.

- Large group discussion: Following the small group meeting, lead a discussion with the whole class to build on what they learned (7–10 minutes). If you used a shared online document (e.g., Google Docs) where students wrote their insights from the small group discussions, you might use those responses to start the large group conversation. Additional discussion questions and teaching points are described below.

DISCUSSION

Ask the class what surprised them the most from their small group discussions. Most students will report that they are much kinder to their friends when they are struggling than they are to themselves. Many students will be surprised that many of their classmates also use harsh self-criticism when they make a mistake or are struggling in some way. Students often say they would be more motivated, happy, and productive if they treated themselves more positively. Some students may also bring up a common worry that being overly kind will decrease performance. Each of these points can lead to a discussion of the advantages of using a self-compassionate approach compared with a harshly self-critical one. A few key teaching points are described next:

- Self-criticism: According to evolutionary psychology, it is natural for perceived threats to activate a threat–defense response. This is an adaptive approach for threats to our physical selves; however, it is much less adaptive for more internal threats (e.g., threats to our self-concept). For threats to our self-concept, this fight, flight, or freeze response may manifest as self-criticism, avoidance, and rumination, which can lead to anxiety and depression over time (Gilbert, 2009). Self-compassion offers a more productive approach to managing these internal threats.

- Tender and fierce self-compassion: Self-compassion can be accepting and reassuring (i.e., tender) as well as motivating and active (i.e., fierce; Germer & Neff, 2019). Each situation is unique and may require a different approach. For example, students who tend to procrastinate on their work due to high fear of failure might need to take a more tender approach to help get them started (e.g., words of encouragement and a reminder that their self-worth is not dependent on achievement). On the other hand, students who tend to procrastinate because they lack appropriate time management skills may need to take a fiercer approach (e.g., draw boundaries for activities that encroach on study time). Mindfulness helps students acknowledge the difficulty caused by procrastination (e.g., "It makes things harder") with clarity and nonjudgment. Mindfulness also helps students identify what type of support they need at that moment. Common humanity helps students recognize that procrastination is a common problem (e.g., "I'm not alone") and that it is something they can overcome. Kindness emphasizes acceptance and encouragement (e.g., "It's okay to make mistakes, but I want the best for myself"). Understanding the nuances of self-compassion can help students see how it is strong, supportive, and motivating. Finally, when applying self-compassion, remind students to consider their short-term and long-term goals. Self-compassion is about more than momentary relief or pleasure.

- Common misperceptions: There are four main myths of self-compassion. It is weak, selfish, self-indulgent, and will undermine your motivation. Research disproves all these myths. Self-compassion is not weak but gives people the strength to cope with life challenges, such as natural disasters, combat, illness, and family pressures. It is also not selfish, because the more compassion flows inward, the more there is available to flow outward. Research shows self-compassionate individuals are more giving in relationships, more compassionate to others, and more able to care for others without burning out. Although some people confuse self-compassion with self-indulgence, the latter means choosing short-term pleasure at the expense of long-term health. Self-compassionate people are more likely to eat right, exercise, go to the doctor, and generally prioritize long-term well-being. Finally, the number one block to self-compassion is the belief it undermines motivation. To the contrary, the desire for the self's well-being encourages learning and growth and improves performance. No drawbacks to self-compassion have been identified in research as long as the desire to alleviate one's suffering is authentic. However, people low in conscientiousness may think they're being self-compassionate when they're really being self-indulgent. For instance, self-compassion—by definition—promotes well-being; if it is harmful, it is not self-compassion (see Ferrari et al., 2019; Röthlin et al., 2019, for review).

- Interventions: Self-compassion is a learnable skill. The Mindful Self-Compassion program (MSC; K. D. Neff & Germer, 2013) is an empirically based intervention used to teach self-compassion. The MSC course is an 8-week program, with each session lasting approximately 2.5 hours. MSC uses discussions, writing exercises, and meditations to teach various positive psychology principles, including mindfulness, savoring, gratitude, kindness (toward self and others), and values. MSC helps individuals cultivate the emotional strength and flexibility they need to support themselves mentally, emotionally, and physically (Germer & Neff, 2019). Self-compassion interventions have also been developed for specific populations, including health care workers (K. D. Neff et al., 2020), athletes (Kuchar et al., 2023), teens (Bluth et al., 2016), and more. See Ferrari et al. (2019) for review or visit https://CenterforMSC.org.

- Self-Compassion Scale (optional): The SCS (K. D. Neff, 2003b) measures three aspects of positive self-responding (mindfulness, common humanity, self-kindness) as well as three aspects of negative self-responding (overidentification, isolation, self-judgment). These six subscales form a holistic measure of one's self-compassion level. Although there are no clinical norms for the SCS, many researchers use a median split to determine high and low levels of self-compassion. Additionally, you can use the following rubric as a general guide: low = 1.0–2.49, moderate = 2.5–3.5, high = 3.51–5.0. The SCS has been correlated with numerous aspects of positive psychological functioning including, but not limited to, hope, life satisfaction, gratitude, happiness, optimism, wisdom, grit, forgiveness, empathy, and personal growth (K. D. Neff et al., 2018). See Appendix 20.1 for more details on the SCS items and scoring information.

- Applied self-compassion examples for students:
  - Situation: poor grade on an exam
    - Self-compassionate approach
      - Mindfulness: "I didn't get the grade I wanted. This hurts."
      - Common humanity: "It's only human to fail sometimes. It happens."
      - Self-kindness: "This grade doesn't define me or my abilities. I can learn from this experience and try a new approach to studying next time."
    - Self-critical approach
      - Overidentification: "This is a catastrophe!"
      - Isolation: "I probably got the worst grade in the class."
      - Self-judgment: "I'm an idiot. I don't know why I even try."
  - Situation: burnout
    - Self-compassionate approach
      - Mindfulness: "I am feeling overwhelmed. This is a really challenging week."
      - Common humanity: "I am not alone. Other students struggle with these types of feelings too."
      - Self-kindness: "I need to take better care of myself and get more rest. I need to take it day by day and focus on one task at a time."
    - Self-critical approach
      - Overidentification: "I clearly can't hack it."
      - Isolation: "I'm not capable like everyone else is."
      - Self-judgment: "It's all my fault. If only I could pull it together."

ASSIGNMENT

Please refer to Appendix 20.1 for the SCS (optional), Appendix 20.2 for the assignment writing prompts, and the Online Materials section for various tools that can be used to enable small and large group discussions.

ONLINE MATERIALS

- SCS (includes automatic scoring): https://self-compassion.org/self-compassion-test/
- Google Drive folder: https://tinyurl.com/SCmaterials
    - Reporting self-compassion scores (Class Google Sheet)
    - Small group discussion tools (Class Google Doc and online whiteboard app)

APPENDIX 20.1: Self-Compassion Scale

HOW I TYPICALLY ACT TOWARD MYSELF IN DIFFICULT TIMES

Please read each statement carefully before answering. For each item, indicate how often you behave in the stated manner using the following 1–5 scale. Please answer according to what really reflects your experience rather than what you think your experience should be.

Almost never				Almost always
1	2	3	4	5

1. I'm disapproving and judgmental about my own flaws and inadequacies.
2. When I'm feeling down, I tend to obsess and fixate on everything that's wrong.
3. When things are going badly for me, I see the difficulties as part of life that everyone goes through.
4. When I think about my inadequacies, it tends to make me feel more separate and cut off from the rest of the world.
5. I try to be loving toward myself when I'm feeling emotional pain.
6. When I fail at something important to me, I become consumed by feelings of inadequacy.
7. When I'm down, I remind myself that there are lots of other people in the world feeling like I am.
8. When times are really difficult, I tend to be tough on myself.
9. When something upsets me, I try to keep my emotions in balance.
10. When I feel inadequate in some way, I try to remind myself that feelings of inadequacy are shared by most people.
11. I'm intolerant and impatient toward those aspects of my personality I don't like.
12. When I'm going through a very hard time, I give myself the caring and tenderness I need.
13. When I'm feeling down, I tend to feel like most other people are probably happier than I am.
14. When something painful happens, I try to take a balanced view of the situation.

15. I try to see my failings as part of the human condition.
16. When I see aspects of myself that I don't like, I get down on myself.
17. When I fail at something important to me, I try to keep things in perspective.
18. When I'm really struggling, I tend to feel like other people must be having an easier time of it.
19. I'm kind to myself when I'm experiencing suffering.
20. When something upsets me, I get carried away with my feelings.
21. I can be a bit cold-hearted toward myself when I'm experiencing suffering.
22. When I'm feeling down, I try to approach my feelings with curiosity and openness.
23. I'm tolerant of my own flaws and inadequacies.
24. When something painful happens, I tend to blow the incident out of proportion.
25. When I fail at something that's important to me, I tend to feel alone in my failure.
26. I try to be understanding and patient toward those aspects of my personality I don't like.

Scoring Key

- Self-kindness items: 5, 12, 19, 23, 26
- Self-judgment items (reverse scored): 1, 8, 11, 16, 21
- Common humanity items: 3, 7, 10, 15
- Isolation items (reverse scored): 4, 13, 18, 25
- Mindfulness items: 9, 14, 17, 22
- Overidentification items (reverse scored): 2, 6, 20, 24

To compute a total self-compassion score, first reverse score ($1 = 5, 2 = 4, 3 = 3, 4 = 2, 5 = 1$) the negative subscale items—self-judgment, isolation, and overidentification. Then, take the mean of each subscale and compute a total mean (the average of the six subscale means).

When examining subscale scores, higher scores on the self-judgment, isolation, and overidentification scale indicate less self-compassion before reverse coding and more self-compassion after reverse coding.

Note. Self-Compassion Scale is adapted from "Development and Validation of a Scale to Measure Self-Compassion," by K. D. Neff, 2003, *Self and Identity*, *2*(3), pp. 231–232 (https://doi.org/10.1080/15298860309027). Copyright 2003 by Kristin Neff. Adapted with permission.

Please visit https://self-compassion.org/self-compassion-scales-for-researchers/ for more information regarding additional versions of the Self-Compassion Scale (SCS; e.g., SCS short form, SCS for youths). Dr. Kristin Neff grants permission to use the SCS (K. D. Neff, 2003b) for any purpose, including research, clinical work, teaching, etc. Please cite the reference listed above.

A printable version of this appendix can be downloaded from the APA website at https://www.apa.org/pubs/books/more-activities-teaching-positive-psychology.

APPENDIX 20.2: Written Exercise Worksheet

Please answer the following writing prompts. Afterward, you will discuss your experience with this exercise in small groups. You will not have to share the details of what you write, so please be open and respond honestly.

1. Think about times when you feel bad about yourself or are struggling in some way. How do you typically respond to yourself in these situations? Please write down what you typically do or say and note the tone in which you talk to yourself.

2. Now think about times when a close friend feels really bad about themselves or is really struggling in some way. How do you typically respond to your friend in these situations (especially when you're at your best)? Again, write down what you typically do or say, and note the tone in which you talk to your close friends.

3. Did you notice any differences? If so, write down potential reasons why.

4. Finally, how do you think things might change if you responded to yourself in the same way that you typically respond to your friends?

A printable version of this appendix can be downloaded from the APA website at https://www.apa.org/pubs/books/more-activities-teaching-positive-psychology.

REFERENCES

Allen, A. B., & Leary, M. R. (2010). Self-compassion, stress, and coping. *Social and Personality Psychology Compass, 4*(2), 107–118. https://doi.org/10.1111/j.1751-9004.2009.00246.x

Bluth, K., Gaylord, S. A., Campo, R. A., Mullarkey, M. C., & Hobbs, L. (2016). Making friends with yourself: A mixed methods pilot study of a Mindful Self-Compassion program for adolescents. *Mindfulness, 7*(2), 479–492. https://doi.org/10.1007/s12671-015-0476-6

Ferrari, M., Hunt, C., Harrysunker, A., Abbott, M. J., Beath, A. P., & Einstein, D. A. (2019). Self-compassion interventions and psychosocial outcomes: A meta-analysis of RCTs. *Mindfulness, 10*(8), 1455–1473. https://doi.org/10.1007/s12671-019-01134-6

Germer, C., & Neff, K. (2019). *Teaching the Mindful Self-Compassion program: A guide for professionals.* Guilford Press.

Gilbert, P. (2009). *The compassionate mind: A new approach to life's challenges.* New Harbinger.

Kabat-Zinn, J. (1990). *Full catastrophe living: Using the wisdom of your body and mind to face stress, pain, and illness.* Dell.

Kuchar, A. L., Neff, K. D., & Mosewich, A. D. (2023). Resilience and Enhancement in Sport, Exercise, & Training (RESET): A brief self-compassion intervention with NCAA student-athletes. *Psychology of Sport and Exercise, 67*, Article 102426. https://doi.org/10.1016/j.psychsport.2023.102426

MacBeth, A., & Gumley, A. (2012). Exploring compassion: A meta-analysis of the association between self-compassion and psychopathology. *Clinical Psychology Review, 32*(6), 545–552. https://doi.org/10.1016/j.cpr.2012.06.003

Neff, K. D. (2003a). The development and validation of a scale to measure self-compassion. *Self and Identity, 2*(3), 223–250. https://doi.org/10.1080/15298860309027

Neff, K. D. (2003b). Self-compassion: An alternative conceptualization of a healthy attitude toward oneself. *Self and Identity, 2*(2), 85–101. https://doi.org/10.1080/15298860309032

Neff, K. (2011). *Self-compassion: The proven power of being kind to yourself.* William Morrow Paperbacks.

Neff, K. D., & Germer, C. K. (2013). A pilot study and randomized controlled trial of the Mindful Self-Compassion program. *Journal of Clinical Psychology, 69*(1), 28–44. https://doi.org/10.1002/jclp.21923

Neff, K. D., Knox, M. C., Long, P., & Gregory, K. (2020). Caring for others without losing yourself: An adaptation of the Mindful Self-Compassion Program for Healthcare Communities. *Journal of Clinical Psychology, 76*(9), 1543–1562. https://doi.org/10.1002/jclp.23007

Neff, K. D., Long, P., Knox, M. C., Davidson, O., Kuchar, A., Costigan, A., Williamson, Z., Rohleder, N., Tóth-Király, I., & Breines, J. G. (2018). The forest and the trees: Examining the association of self-compassion and its positive and negative components with psychological functioning. *Self and Identity, 17*(6), 627–645. https://doi.org/10.1080/15298868.2018.1436587

Röthlin, P., Horvath, S., & Birrer, D. (2019). Go soft or go home? A scoping review of empirical studies on the role of self-compassion in the competitive sport setting. *Current Issues in Sport Science, 4*, 1–14. https://doi.org/10.15203/CISS_2019.013

21

Acts of Kindness

The Well-Being Benefits of Prosocial Versus Self-Focused Behaviors

John K. Coffey and S. Katherine Nelson-Coffey

On two separate days, students will plan then complete three acts of kindness for themselves and then for others before an optional reflection and class discussion.

CONCEPT

Prosocial behavior (i.e., acts of kindness for others) remains one of the best ways to enhance well-being (e.g., Curry et al., 2018; Oarga et al., 2015). Yet popular culture encourages focusing on oneself to improve one's mood (e.g., a focus in the media on "treating yourself"; e.g., Spencer, 2020). In this activity, students compare these competing perspectives by performing acts of kindness for themselves and for others. These two activities are drawn from experimental research on the benefits of kindness for psychological flourishing and physical health (e.g., Nelson et al., 2016; Nelson-Coffey et al., 2017). First, students plan to do three acts of kindness for themselves (i.e., "treat yourself" activity) all within 1 day. Next, they plan and do three acts of kindness for others all within 1 day. After doing both activities, students reflect on how they felt and which activity they thought was more closely related to happiness.

https://doi.org/10.1037/0000417-021
More Activities for Teaching Positive Psychology: A Guide for Instructors, S. D. Pressman and A. C. Parks (Editors)

MATERIALS NEEDED

- Pen and paper.

- Optional: Measures for students to complete to track emotions (e.g., self-report, daily diaries, Experience Sampling Method app). Appendix 21.1 offers a brief handout option that includes space to record their acts and feelings for the day.

- Activity instructions are provided here and in Appendix 21.2.

ACTIVITY SETTING

This activity consists of two flexible phases completed over 3 (nonconsecutive) days (spread apart how you like). The first phase involves planning and completing acts of kindness for self and for others, respectively. Initial instructions for both kindness days can be given outside of class (e.g., worksheet, email, online course management system like Blackboard), in an in-person class, or in a virtual class. Students will need at least 1 day for each set of kindness acts and it is probably better not to have them on back to back days. The second phase includes instruction, reflection, and discussion.

This activity relates to a variety of positive psychological concepts, such as positive psychology activities, prosocial behavior, positive emotions, and affective forecasting. Thus, this activity could be conducted around lectures focused on affect, social relationships/prosocial activities, or interventions more broadly. We recommend assigning this activity early in the term to generate enthusiasm for positive psychology activities among students and to be referenced later in the semester as appropriate.

ACTIVITY DURATION

This activity involves two phases. Phase 1, assigning self-kindness and other-kindness to be completed outside of class, can be implemented either during or outside of class. If implemented during class, you can assign each kindness activity in 3 to 5 minutes. Plan for an additional 5 minutes if you want them to start planning out activities during class. Students will need at least 1 day to complete each kindness task and (optional) daily emotions measure. After students have completed their kindness tasks, the instruction phase typically includes an in-class discussion (approximately 15–30 minutes) with an optional lecture, assigned readings, or reflection.

SUGGESTED READINGS

- Optional readings that directly examine self- and other-kindness. We recommend assigning these after students complete the activity to avoid spoiling the results:

- – Nelson et al. (2016)
- – Nelson-Coffey et al. (2017)
- – Nelson-Coffey et al. (2021)

- Related enrichment readings on positive psychology interventions and pro-social behavior:
  - – Aknin et al. (2020)
  - – Curry et al. (2018)

BACKGROUND AND INSTRUCTIONS

Psychologists have been investigating the motivations for and consequences of prosocial actions since at least the 1970s (Coke et al., 1978). Positive psychologists have incorporated acts of kindness into positive psychological interventions to investigate the well-being benefits of being kind to others (e.g., Curry et al., 2018; Nelson et al., 2016). Despite this empirical evidence indicating that being kind to others is an important predictor of well-being, many Western cultures emphasize a focus on oneself (e.g., treat yourself) to improve well-being. The current activity provides students the opportunity to complete two conditions from studies (Nelson et al., 2016; Nelson-Coffey et al., 2017) that compare and contrast the effects of performing acts of kindness for others or themselves. As detailed later in this chapter, this activity introduces several relevant concepts, such as the importance of making evidence-based recommendations and highlighting how kindness for others is generally more beneficial for personal well-being than self-focused kindness activities.

Preparation

- This activity takes place in two phases over at least two class periods—one class period for getting started (unless instructions for kindness days are given online) and one class period for follow-up discussion and lecture. In the first phase, the instructor will assign students to perform acts of kindness for themselves (i.e., self-kindness) and then for others (i.e., other-kindness), respectively. Phase 2 includes reflection and connection to course concepts.

- Keeping students blind to relevant research on self- and other-kindness can enhance the effectiveness of the activities, so we recommend assigning readings related to this intervention after students complete both activities.

- We also prefer to keep students blind to the other-kindness activity until after they complete their acts of self-kindness, but this is optional.

- Possible timelines for Phase 1 (assigning activities):
  - – One class period: Before a weekend, assign students to complete self-kindness acts on Saturday and other-kindness acts on Sunday. If you want to keep

students blind to the other-kindness activity, you can send digital instructions later (e.g., via email, Blackboard).

- Two back-to-back class periods: Assign self-kindness acts on the first class of the week (e.g., Tuesday), then assign other-kindness acts on the second class of the week (e.g., Thursday). This option can improve students' adherence to each activity.

- Two class periods (1 week apart):[1] Assign self-kindness acts on the last class of the week (e.g., Monday) to be completed on 1 day over the weekend. Assign other-kindness acts on the last day of the following week (e.g., the next Monday). This is closer to the original research study design (Nelson et al., 2016) that this activity is based on, allows for scheduling consistency, and increases time for introspection about differences in the acts.

• Optional step: To have students learn about emotion measurement and more concretely compare their emotions, instructors can assign students to measure their emotions after they complete each acts-of-kindness activity. Including these emotion measures could facilitate conversation about experimental design and emotion measurement and provide students with data they could use to reflect on which activity (kindness for self or kindness for others) was most beneficial for their well-being.

- One option would be to use an end-of-day diary (see Appendix 21.1). If using a written form, you could have students submit information (e.g., Qualtrics, Google Forms) before class discussion day so you can compare activity averages.

- An alternative option would include having students install an experience sampling app on their phone (see the Online Materials section) so they can track their emotions daily over an extended period of time (e.g., 1–2 weeks). Using this approach, emotions can be reported before (e.g., baseline measurement) and after both kindness days are completed.

Activity Phases

• Phase 1: Acts of kindness for self

- Instructors can provide written instructions, or they may wish to spend some time discussing the activities with students. Instructions are included in this section and provided in Appendix 21.2. To minimize student expectations about which activity they think will make them feel happier, we recommend *not* telling them about the other-kindness day until after they have done their self-kindness day.

- Assign the self-kindness day instructions below. Provide instructions in class or via written format (Appendix 21.2) and have students plan their acts. Then, give students at least 1 day to complete all three acts of self-kindness.

---

[1] Our recommendation if time permits.

- Instructions:
  - "On ____[insert timeline/specific day], you are to do three intentional acts of kindness *for yourself* all in one day. These nice things don't need to be big, costly, or timely unless you want them to be—those details are up to you. The acts do need to be intentional (planned in advance—not retroactively decided after you do something nice for yourself) and out of the ordinary. Use your common sense—avoid anything that would be illegal or dangerous to yourself or others."
  - Optional examples: "Examples include having your favorite meal, treating yourself to a massage, or spending time on your favorite hobby. These nice things you do for yourself do not need to be the same as the examples listed above, and although they may involve other people, they should be things that you do explicitly for yourself, not others."
  - Another optional prompt is "Adjustments to your original plans are okay. If one of your original plans does not work out, you can adjust and determine another intentional act of kindness for yourself to do during that day."
- Note: Having students record their completed acts (see Appendix 21.1) can help them recall their experiences for reflection writing and in-class discussion.
- Add a reminder if you plan to have students complete an emotion measurement.
- Phase 1: Acts of kindness for others
  - After students have completed their acts of kindness for themselves, they will complete acts of kindness for others.
    - Instructions:
      - "On ____[insert timeline/specific day], you are to do three intentional acts of kindness *for others* all in one day. These acts do not need to be for the same person. These nice things don't need to be big, costly, or timely unless you want them to be—those details are up to you. The acts do need to be intentional or planned in advance and out of the ordinary. In other words, they should not be retroactively decided after you do something nice for someone else (e.g., randomly compliment your friend and then decide it was one of your acts). Use your common sense—avoid anything that would be illegal or dangerous to yourself or others."
      - Optional examples: "Examples include making cookies for a friend, doing a chore for a family member, helping someone out, paying for someone's coffee in line behind you, video calling with a relative, or writing a thank you letter."
      - Another optional prompt is "Adjustments to your original plans are okay. If one of your original plans does not work out, you can adjust

and determine another intentional act of kindness toward someone else during that day."

- Provide a reminder if you plan to have students complete an emotion measurement.

- Phase 2: Instruction
  - You may want to begin by informing students that not all positive psychology activities will work for everyone and that the scientific results often indicate group-level findings (be sure to explain this concept). Further, encourage honest reflections where students can indicate they did or did not think an activity worked for them. Regardless, they should still try to explain their conclusion through connection to class concepts. We will go over person–activity fit later in the course.
  - After students have completed each of these activities, the instruction component may include reflection essays, in-class discussion (see prompts in the Discussion section) about the activity and other positive activity interventions, and lectures.
  - When we use this activity in our own classes, we typically assign a reflection essay to prepare students for an in-class discussion. When students have completed a reflection beforehand, they are more likely to express a broader range of ideas in a discussion and to conclude other-kindness acts worked better.
  - Instructors can ask students to submit some or all of their emotion data to make a basic comparison of self- versus other-kindness group-level means for certain questions (e.g., happy, meaning, connected). If students submit their emotion reports for each activity, a bar graph demonstrating their reported happiness, meaning, and connection for each activity could be displayed to help students visualize the efficacy of the activities. As discussed later in this chapter, kindness for others is more commonly linked to connection, meaning, and positive emotions.
  - To begin the in-class discussion, ask students to discuss their experiences in pairs and then as a class (e.g., think–pair–share) so they can hear their classmates' ideas and connections.
  - Following the in-class discussion, we typically give a short lecture connecting this activity to material on positive psychology activities or prosocial behavior. To facilitate these activities in your classes, this chapter provides details about the studies comparing self- and other-kindness, prompts for a reflection essay, and discussion questions.
  - There are different options for grading. For example, you can evaluate the content of the reflections and/or simply verify that students planned and attempted the acts of kindness or surveys and grade for completion of the components assigned.

DISCUSSION

The instructions for this activity are drawn directly from research on the benefits of prosocial behavior for happiness, flourishing, and health. Specifically, longitudinal experiments using this paradigm indicate that practicing acts of kindness for others leads to greater well-being than practicing acts of kindness for oneself or a neutral control activity (Nelson et al., 2016; Nelson-Coffey et al., 2021). Many see the findings as counterintuitive. In these studies, participants are typically randomly assigned to one condition where they do acts of kindness for others, acts of kindness for themselves, or a neutral control activity (e.g., keep track of daily activities). Participants do three kindness acts per their condition once a week for 4 weeks. Results of this research indicate that participants who do acts of kindness for others, but not themselves, show greater improvements in positive emotions, mental health flourishing, and reductions in anxiety and depressive symptoms relative to the neutral control condition (Nelson et al., 2016; Nelson-Coffey et al., 2021). Similarly, research suggests that spending money on other people (i.e., prosocial spending) results in greater well-being improvements than spending money on oneself (i.e., personal spending; Aknin et al., 2020).

Additional research using the paradigm for this activity indicates physical benefits of kindness as well. In one study, practicing other-focused kindness for 4 weeks led to greater improvements in immune-related gene expression relative to self-kindness or a neutral control (Nelson-Coffey et al., 2017), suggesting that acts of kindness for others are not only beneficial for psychological health but potentially for physical health as well. Another set of studies found that spending money on others resulted in healthier blood pressure levels than those who spent money on themselves (Whillans et al., 2016).

At the start of this activity, students are likely to be more excited about self-kindness and think it is going to make them happier. After students complete this activity, the majority of the class typically concludes that doing other-kindness was more effective than self-kindness, which aligns with the experimental findings described previously. Notably, some students may think self-kindness worked better or be unsure. All of these perspectives can be used to facilitate a broader discussion of the differences between the kindness activities and potential moderating variables. The questions later in this section address each of these options.

In discussing the activity with students, we recommend prompting them to generate hypotheses about why performing acts of kindness is beneficial (see prompts), which can provide valuable opportunities to connect to relevant course material. For example, students might note that other-kindness is rewarding because they see others enjoy or benefit from their actions. Some note that self-kindness did not last or even led to negative emotions (e.g., guilt, stress from taking time off). Others note that self-kindness is something that they can and probably do more often than intentional other-kindness. Additionally, they may note that their intention to help themselves or others may not have worked out the way they planned, which can also be useful to discuss with regard to their experience. For example, a student might indicate they complimented someone but that the person did not appreciate it.

Although the majority of students are likely to report that other-kindness worked best, students' responses may vary—especially since this activity design lacks the randomized nature of the studies or formal reporting of emotions (if measurement is not included). We welcome and encourage these differences to be shared. Some students might not feel either activity was better because neither helped or both helped. Others might feel self-kindness was more effective. These observations can provide an opportunity to examine the limitations of this activity or person–activity fit (Layous & Lyubomirsky, 2014).

Students might also note that certain types of kindness were better for their well-being than others. When looking for a pattern, they might observe that acts of kindness (for self or for others) that were social in nature were better (a great point to connect to the value of relationships). Others might note that it felt forced or unnatural because of the assignment, which can lead to a nice discussion on the benefits of extrinsic versus intrinsic motivation. Often, students will recognize that other-kindness still works even when compelled, which aligns with prosocial behavior literature (Curry et al., 2018; Helliwell et al., 2017). Almost always, some students will admit they were surprised by the findings, which can be an avenue to explore affective forecasting (see Chapter 8, this volume). The following assignments and discussion questions may help to bring out some of these ideas.

Another topic of discussion might focus on how types of kindness benefit the community even if the individual does not see or feel a direct benefit. Similarly, many people help others in ways that they may not enjoy. For example, they do jobs that are not enjoyable and are tough but give them a sense of purpose, help them to grow their own competency, or support their families (all forms of eudaimonic well-being).

Prompts for Discussion May Include

- Which type of kindness (self or other) seemed to be better for your happiness? Were you surprised by this outcome? Why or why not?
  - This could be a good question to explore links to affective forecasting (discussed in Chapters 8 and 11, this volume) or why so many people may do things they think will bring them happiness but do not (similar to the points made in Chapter 13, this volume).

- What was different about acts of kindness for others? Did you anticipate these differences?

- Were there specific types of self-kindness activities that worked better or worse?
  - Acts of self-kindness that may be beneficial for well-being: self-kindness involving others, fitness, and nature.
  - Acts of self-kindness that may not benefit well-being: time-consuming (e.g., binging TV) and mindless or even aggravating (e.g., social media).

- These responses could generate a discussion about the difference between self-care and self-indulgence (emotions like guilt), as well as how self-compassion differs from the types of kind acts students did for themselves.

- What circumstances might lead self-kindness to be relatively more beneficial?
  - Stressed-out students or those who are typically putting others' needs above their own might appreciate a self-kindness activity. People high in selflessness may not take time to be kind to themselves, so it could be helpful in that regard.

- How many of your acts of kindness for others involved spending money? Did other-kindness benefit you when there was no financial cost, or does other-kindness only work if you spend money on others?
  - This can be a good time to discuss differences in spending money on the self versus others. Research suggests that it is better to spend money on others than on the self as a way to boost personal happiness (Aknin et al., 2020).

- In what ways was the recipient of other-kindness important? For other-kindness, do you think it works better or worse to pick recipients who are close to you? Why?
  - Some work suggests closer ties might be better (e.g., Rowland & Curry, 2019), yet other research finds that acts for the world (e.g., Nelson et al., 2016) and for dogs can boost happiness (White et al., 2022).

- Do you think other-kindness (or world-kindness) and self-kindness have different impacts or implications at a community level?

- When thinking about eudaimonic well-being, how are self-kindness and other-kindness different? How are they the same?

- During a self-compassion unit, students can consider how self-compassion is similar to and different from acts of self-kindness.

- During a motivation unit, students could consider how being assigned activities differs from intrinsic activities.
  - Research suggests that more autonomously motivated acts of kindness result in relatively greater well-being benefits (Nelson et al., 2015; Weinstein & Ryan, 2010).

Additional Optional Post Activity Lecture Materials

After an in-depth discussion, instructors can include a short lecture based on some of the findings discussed in this activity or they can assign any of the suggested readings. One method might be to provide a brief overview of the core findings (summarized earlier in this chapter) from the studies that have used this design (e.g., Nelson et al., 2016; Nelson-Coffey et al., 2017), and then have students follow up with a reading that is more generally about one of the key ideas (e.g., kindness).

- Follow-up questions about positive psychology activity dosage or hedonic adaptation can be used here. For example:
  - Do you think the results would have been the same if they were to do one act of kindness every day instead of three in 1 day?
    - See work by Layous and Lyubomirsky (2014) on dosage.
  - Can you do too much kindness for others?
    - Raise issues of the harms of unmitigated communion (e.g., Helgeson & Fritz, 1998) and more general public quotes on being unable to pour from an empty cup.
  - Why did researchers have them do three acts of kindness on 1 day rather than just doing one act every day?
    - Research tends to suggest that doing multiple acts in 1 day can be better than spreading them out across a week (Layous & Lyubomirsky, 2014).
  - Do you think people would continue to experience the same emotional benefits from continuing to perform acts of kindness for a month? Six months? Why or why not?
    - Acts of kindness/volunteering are one of the best, longest lasting interventions (e.g., Curry et al., 2018) that can produce connection and meaning that might reduce adaptation.

ASSIGNMENT

As an optional additional assignment, this activity could be paired with a reflection essay prompting students to consider their experiences completing acts of kindness for themselves and others to prepare them for class discussion. If time permits, a quick read of students' reflections prior to class discussion may also allow the instructor to connect the class discussion to ideas presented in students' reflections. Note that themes from year to year are typically similar, so after you have done the activity one time, you will know what to expect. Reflection prompts can be tailored according to the specific structure of the course and content being covered. Two possible reflection prompts are provided in this section. The first is a broad reflection prompt that asks students to connect their experiences during this activity to positive psychology theories or concepts by defining and explaining the connections. The second is a more specific reflection that asks students about their personal experience with the activity (either asked by the professor as part of a discussion or provided as a handout for students to complete in writing) using a range of specific questions.

1. Now that you have completed a day of three acts of kindness for yourself and a day of three acts of kindness for others, you will write a reflection. In this reflection, think about the two different kindness activities and how they related to your happiness and well-being. Support your thinking by using concepts or theories from the class. Be sure to define concepts and theories and use them to explain how and why you think one was more or less effective than the other.

2. Now that you have completed a day of three acts of kindness for yourself and a day of three acts of kindness for others, you will write a reflection. In this reflection, think about the two different kindness activities and how they related to your happiness and well-being. Use the questions below to guide your thinking about this activity:

   • Which type of kindness seemed to be better for your happiness? Why?
   • What surprised you about your experiences?
   • Were there self-kindness activities that worked better or worse?
   • Are there times or people that self-kindness might help more than others?
   • Why does helping others seem like an effective way to help ourselves?
   • Additional questions and ideas can be adapted from the discussion questions.

ONLINE MATERIALS

Apps for logging emotions using smartphones: These are easy-to-use apps designed by emotion researchers that allow students to record their emotions. You may wish to test them out before using them. Both are free apps that start with a few questions about you. They then send random emotion checks throughout the day, and these are used to generate a personalized happiness report.

• Track Your Happiness app: https://go.trackyourhappiness.org/ (Note: This may only work for iPhones).
• How We Feel app: https://howwefeel.org/

APPENDIX 21.1: Daily Diary Document

The document can be modified. Students can use it to track emotions at the end of the day.

Acts completed:

1.
2.
3.

On this day, how much are you feeling each of these:

1 = not at all   *4 = some*   *7 = completely*

	1	2	3	4	5	6	7
	1	2	3	4	5	6	7
Happy	1	2	3	4	5	6	7
Sad	1	2	3	4	5	6	7
Calm	1	2	3	4	5	6	7
Loved	1	2	3	4	5	6	7
Angry	1	2	3	4	5	6	7
Sad	1	2	3	4	5	6	7
Guilty	1	2	3	4	5	6	7
Pride	1	2	3	4	5	6	7
Connected	1	2	3	4	5	6	7

Overall, today my day felt meaningful:

1 = not at all   *4 = some*   *7 = completely*
1   2   3   4   5   6   7

Other thoughts:

- Which acts (self or other) do you think were better for your overall happiness? Why?
- Does your happiness score reflect that?

A printable version of this appendix can be downloaded from the APA website at https://www.apa.org/pubs/books/more-activities-teaching-positive-psychology.

APPENDIX 21.2: Instructions for Self-Kindness Day and Other-Kindness Day

SELF-KINDNESS DAY: TREAT YOURSELF

You are to do three intentional acts of kindness for yourself all in 1 day. These nice things don't need to be big, costly, or timely unless you want them to be—those details are up to you. The acts do need to be intentional (planned in advance—not retroactively decided after you do something nice for yourself) and out of the ordinary. Use your common sense—avoid anything that would be illegal or dangerous to yourself or others.

Optional Examples

Examples include having your favorite meal, treating yourself to a massage, or spending time on your favorite hobby. These nice things you do for yourself do not need to be the same as the examples listed above, and although they may involve other people, they should be things that you do explicitly for yourself, not others.

Adjustments to your original plans are okay. If one of your original plans does not work out, you can adjust and determine another intentional act of kindness for yourself to do during that day.

Adjust Based on How/If You Would Like Students to Track Their Emotions

Remember at the end of the day to write down your three acts and complete your emotion report using _____.

OTHER-KINDNESS DAY: PAY IT FORWARD

You are to do three intentional acts of kindness for others all in 1 day. These acts do not need to be for the same person. These nice things don't need to be big, costly, or timely unless you want them to be—those details are up to you. The acts do need to be intentional or planned in advance and out of the ordinary. In other words, they should not be retroactively decided after you do something nice for someone else (e.g., randomly compliment your friend and then decide it was one of your acts). Use your common sense—avoid anything that would be illegal or dangerous to yourself or others.

Optional Examples

Examples include making cookies for a friend, doing a chore for a family member, helping someone out, paying for someone's coffee in line behind you, video calling with a relative, or writing a thank you letter.

Adjustments to your original plans are okay. If one of your original plans does not work out, you can adjust and determine another intentional act of kindness toward someone else during that day.

Adjust Based on How/If You Would Like Students to Track Their Emotions

Remember at the end of the day to write down your three acts and complete your emotion report using _____.

A printable version of this appendix can be downloaded from the APA website at https://www.apa.org/pubs/books/more-activities-teaching-positive-psychology.

REFERENCES

Aknin, L. B., Dunn, E. W., Proulx, J., Lok, I., & Norton, M. I. (2020). Does spending money on others promote happiness?: A registered replication report. *Journal of Personality and Social Psychology, 119*(2), e15–e26. https://doi.org/10.1037/pspa0000191

Coke, J. S., Batson, C. D., & McDavis, K. (1978). Empathic mediation of helping: A two-stage model. *Journal of Personality and Social Psychology, 36*(7), 752–766. https://doi.org/10.1037/0022-3514.36.7.752

Curry, O. S., Rowland, L., Van Lissa, C., Zlotowitz, S., McAlaney, J., & Whitehouse, H. (2018). Happy to help? A systematic review and meta-analysis of the effects of performing acts of kindness on the well-being of the actor. *Journal of Experimental Social Psychology, 76*, 320–329. https://doi.org/10.1016/j.jesp.2018.02.014

Helgeson, V. S., & Fritz, H. L. (1998). A theory of unmitigated communion. *Personality and Social Psychology Review, 2*(3), 173–183. https://doi.org/10.1207/s15327957pspr0203_2

Helliwell, J. F., Aknin, L. B., Shiplett, H., Huang, H., & Wang, S. (2017). Social capital and prosocial behavior as sources of well-being. In E. Diener, S. Oishi, & L. Tay (Eds.), *Handbook of well-being*. DEF Publishers.

Layous, K., & Lyubomirsky, S. (2014). The how, why, what, when, and who of happiness. In J. Gruber & J. T. Moskowitz (Eds.), *Positive emotion: Integrating the light sides and dark sides* (pp. 473–495). Oxford University Press. https://doi.org/10.1093/acprof:oso/9780199926725.003.0025

Nelson, S. K., Della Porta, M. D., Jacobs Bao, K., Lee, H. C., Choi, I., & Lyubomirsky, S. (2015). "It's up to you": Experimentally manipulated autonomy support for prosocial behavior improves well-being in two cultures over six weeks. *The Journal of Positive Psychology, 10*(5), 463–476. https://doi.org/10.1080/17439760.2014.983959

Nelson, S. K., Layous, K., Cole, S. W., & Lyubomirsky, S. (2016). Do unto others or treat yourself? The effects of prosocial and self-focused behavior on psychological flourishing. *Emotion, 16*(6), 850–861. https://doi.org/10.1037/emo0000178

Nelson-Coffey, S. K., Bohlmeijer, E. T., & Schotanus-Dijkstra, M. (2021). Practicing other-focused kindness and self-kindness among those at risk for mental disorders: Results of a randomized controlled trial. *Frontiers in Psychology, 12*, Article 741546. https://doi.org/10.3389/fpsyg.2021.741546

Nelson-Coffey, S. K., Fritz, M. M., Lyubomirsky, S., & Cole, S. W. (2017). Kindness in the blood: A randomized controlled trial of the gene regulatory impact of prosocial behavior. *Psychoneuroendocrinology, 81*, 8–13. https://doi.org/10.1016/j.psyneuen.2017.03.025

Oarga, C., Stavrova, O., & Fetchenhauer, D. (2015). When and why is helping others good for well-being? The role of belief in reciprocity and conformity to society's expectations. *European Journal of Social Psychology, 45*(2), 242–254. https://doi.org/10.1002/ejsp.2092

Rowland, L., & Curry, O. S. (2019). A range of kindness activities boost happiness. *The Journal of Social Psychology, 159*(3), 340–343. https://doi.org/10.1080/00224545.2018.1469461

Spencer, S. (2020, October 13). Treat Yo' Self Day: Why 'Parks and Recreation' fans celebrate October 13. *Newsweek*. https://www.newsweek.com/parks-recreation-treat-yo-self-day-october-13-1538534

Weinstein, N., & Ryan, R. M. (2010). When helping helps: Autonomous motivation for prosocial behavior and its influence on well-being for the helper and recipient. *Journal of Personality and Social Psychology, 98*(2), 222–244. https://doi.org/10.1037/a0016984

Whillans, A. V., Dunn, E. W., Sandstrom, G. M., Dickerson, S. S., & Madden, K. M. (2016). Is spending money on others good for your heart? *Health Psychology, 35*(6), 574–583. https://doi.org/10.1037/hea0000332

White, M. W., Khan, N., Deren, J. S., Sim, J. J., & Majka, E. A. (2022). Give a dog a bone: Spending money on pets promotes happiness. *The Journal of Positive Psychology, 17*(4), 589–595. https://doi.org/10.1080/17439760.2021.1897871

22

Increasing Your Interdependent Happiness

Hidefumi Hitokoto and Yukiko Uchida

Students will learn about the concept of interdependent happiness from a cross-cultural lens and how to assess it. They will then participate in an activity that will change feelings of interdependent happiness.

CONCEPT

In this cross-culturally focused activity, students will be instructed to rate themselves on a scale of interdependent happiness, followed by a recollection task where they recollect their social resources (e.g., social support, belongingness, social capital). Next, they will rate themselves again on their interdependent happiness to examine any changes from the task. This will be followed up by a discussion on cultural differences in what it means to be "happy" and "well" as well as different sources of day-to-day interdependent happiness.

MATERIALS NEEDED

Instructors will need to provide students with copies of the baseline and follow-up (Table 22.1) as a paper handout or in digital format for students to complete on their electronic devices. Students will also need a blank piece of paper or an open blank document on their computer to complete the recollection task. The instructor will need copies of the instructions and discussion points. Should you

https://doi.org/10.1037/0000417-022
More Activities for Teaching Positive Psychology: A Guide for Instructors, S. D. Pressman and A. C. Parks (Editors)

249

TABLE 22.1. Interdependent Happiness Scale

Item	Strongly disagree	Disagree	Neither agree nor disagree	Agree	Strongly agree
1. I believe that I and those around me are happy.	1	2	3	4	5
2. I feel that I am being positively evaluated by others around me.	1	2	3	4	5
3. I make significant others happy.	1	2	3	4	5
4. Although it is quite average, I live a stable life.	1	2	3	4	5
5. I do not have any major concerns or anxieties.	1	2	3	4	5
6. I can do what I want without causing problems for other people.	1	2	3	4	5
7. I believe that my life is just as happy as that of others around me.	1	2	3	4	5
8. I believe I have a similar standard of living as those around me.	1	2	3	4	5
9. I generally believe that things are going well for me in a way that is similar to others around me.	1	2	3	4	5

Note. Instruction: Please indicate the degree to which these statements accurately describe you.

have a large class and want to explore the effects of demographic differences in your class (see the Discussion section) on interdependent happiness and/or the results of the activity, you may want to consider using an online survey where you collect and show the data to the class, perhaps with an illustration of how some moderators change the results.

ACTIVITY SETTING

This activity is designed to be done in a live lecture format, but it could easily be done online synchronously. Some parts could be done in advance asynchronously (i.e., the surveys and manipulation), but the discussion is best done live to allow for class participation. It is well-suited for inclusion in lectures focused on social connections or cultural differences in well-being.

ACTIVITY DURATION

This activity will take approximately 25 minutes for the surveys/activities and another 5 to 10 minutes for discussion. It could be altered for online synchronous learning.

RECOMMENDED READINGS

- Students may supplementally read the following articles after the task:
  - Hitokoto and Uchida (2015)
  - Hitokoto and Takahashi (2021)
  - Hitokoto and Adeclas (2022)

BACKGROUND AND INSTRUCTIONS

Happiness as Interdependent

Interdependent happiness is a global, subjective assessment of whether one is interpersonally harmonizing with other people, being quiescent, and seeking an ordinary and well-balanced life (Hitokoto & Uchida, 2015). Its measurement has been operationalized as individual ratings on the Interdependent Happiness Scale (IHS), which consists of three subconcepts: relational harmony, quiescence, and ordinariness. *Relational harmony* is the feeling of mutual positivity shared with close friends and family. *Quiescence* is the feeling of calmness that comes from the absence of negative emotions. *Ordinariness* is the feeling that one's level of achievement is on par with that of others. One's criteria for being well or happy depends on the shared meaning of these terms in a society that prescribes how to be well or how to understand the self. Cultural construals of the self as independent or interdependent have long provided insight into the impact of culture on human cognition, emotion, and motivation, all of which are anchored to agency, which is plastic and, thus, shaped by participation in cultural mandates.

Most psychological scales of happiness or well-being are created based on the assumption that the target of assessment is the personal self: whether *I* am happy or not. This approach is limited when the self is understood as being well when considered in the context of others, such as when one is obliged to someone (e.g., obliged to one's family or kin), must abide by a norm (e.g., behave in accord with societal expectation as a student), or must willingly respond to others' expectations (e.g., try not to let your partner down). In these situations, one may weigh oneself in terms of whether one is responsible enough, has done what one has to do, or is able to enhance one's close others' feelings adequately. When one is interdependent, the target of one's own assessment may shift to more relational aspects of one's actions and their outcomes. Interdependent happiness is about whether the rater and those around the rater are feeling happy, making the target of the assessment the harmony or the wellness secured in the connection between the self and close others. In interdependent happiness, the emotional tendencies that are more likely to be valued tend toward calmness and peacefulness. Also, harmony implies preserving an ordinary life and avoiding the risks entailed by being conspicuously unique and sticking out from the normative ways followed by others, which potentiates disharmony via inviting others' negative evaluation.

At first glance, this conceptualization of happiness may seem relevant only to members of collectivist cultures. However, we argue that it is relevant to all human beings, as our basic ways of being are founded on fundamental sociality (Delle Fave et al., 2016). Additionally, considering that the modern West may have evolved from, rather than independently of, the various forms of interdependence in the Eurasian continent (Kitayama et al., 2022) and that the internally attributed conception of happiness may be an invention of post-1920s North America (Oishi, Graham, et al., 2013), interdependent happiness could be a predecessor, rather than a mere cultural alternative, to the assessment of the personal self that is taken as a premise of well-being measurement.

Validity

Interdependent happiness is positively explained by the interdependent self across cultures, irrespective of the independent self (Hitokoto & Adeclas, 2022; Hitokoto & Uchida, 2015). It is positively correlated with other well-being concepts such as *hedonic well-being* (i.e., whether one is feeling satisfied with one's life and feeling more positive than negative), *eudaimonic well-being* or *flourishing* (i.e., whether one finds meaning and has a purpose in life), and *minimalist well-being* comprising gratitude (Datu et al., 2016; Hitokoto & Uchida, 2015). It is positively correlated with physical and behavioral health, such as the quality of sleep, and a healthy student lifestyle represented by school attendance (Kitazawa et al., 2019). It was also negatively (i.e., suppressively) correlated with infectious symptoms (i.e., fever) during the pandemic (Hitokoto & Adeclas, 2022). Finally, the feeling of interdependent happiness is stronger among older individuals in collectivist countries (Hitokoto & Takahashi, 2021; Hitokoto & Uchida, 2017), suggesting lifelong development of this type of happiness depending on what society affords across their lifespan (Kitayama et al., 2006).

Intervention

These findings suggest that the interdependent context may require individuals to relate to the collective via interdependent means, such as being concerned about one's social standing and/or connections. When this mindset is acquired and sustained, one's close others take care of the self, creating an interdependent or social resource that can be used to secure the self. Expanding on this, when one's social connections are positive, or even remind one to be positive by realizing that the self is embedded in a positive network of interpersonal relationships, this may temporarily boost interdependent happiness. The exercise described in this chapter draws on this point of view, temporarily boosting the students' interdependent happiness by making them realize how they are positively embedded in their close relationships.

A Japanese indigenous therapy known as *Naikan* involves reminding people of how an individual owes something to their parents, thus making clear how parents offer a social resource in the form of an obligation to intervene in juvenile delinquency (Murase, 2007). Temporal enhancement of one's social resources, such as feeling that you are understood by someone, has a profound impact on boosting resilience (Oishi, Schiller, & Gross, 2013). Hitokoto (2020) found that those Japanese students who reported having a positive network of relationships were also the ones with higher levels of interdependent happiness 1 month later. According to Furman and Buhrmester (1985, 2009), the positive qualities of one's network of relationships can be captured by dimensions of companionship, intimate disclosure, instrumental aid, nurturance, reassurance of worth, reliable alliance, and affection. These positive features of interpersonal relationships might serve as a typical reminder of one's interdependent/social resources. In the current class exercise, reminding oneself of this is set as a task, and participants are asked to respond to the IHS before and after the task to see if their scores temporarily increase, thereby upping their interdependent happiness.

Step 1: Baseline Measurement (3 Minutes)

Start by measuring the participants' baseline interdependent happiness using the IHS (see Table 22.1). The IHS consists of nine items and is rated on a 5-point Likert scale from 1 (*strongly disagree*) to 5 (*strongly agree*). Since the three subconcepts described earlier correlate with each other, the nine items can be summed to form a summary/overall IHS scale score. A survey with the whole IHS printed on its first page can be prepared and handed out to students. If the exercise is conducted online, the first page should include the nine items on a single page. After the rating, instruct the participants to average all nine ratings to come up with their unique baseline score on the IHS and to keep the score to themselves.

Step 2: Recollection Task (15 Minutes)

Students will need a blank piece of paper or a blank document on their computer to write their ideas down freely. Instructors can use the following prompt: "Please choose the most important friend you have. You may select someone who is your most important friend now or was in the past. Do *not* include one of your family members." The instructors may give this instruction verbally or textually when the exercise is prepared as a survey to take asynchronously/as homework. Take a few moments to allow the participants to come up with who to imagine as their important friend. Consecutively, instruct participants to think about each of the seven questions listed in Table 22.2 for the friend they have just nominated ("Interdependent/social resources [Friend] condition" column). Give them approximately 15 minutes to recollect and write down anything that comes to mind on their sheet of paper or in a response space provided in the survey should you create something for them. Make sure that participants keep their responses to themselves; they are not to be disclosed publicly to the class because some responses may be personal and sensitive.

Step 3: Postmeasurement (5 Minutes)

Participants will be requested to calculate their second round of IHS ratings as a postmanipulation measurement. Some demographics can be measured here for discussion. Again, when the rating is done, instruct them to calculate the average

TABLE 22.2. Recollection of Interdependent/Social or Independent/Personal Resources

Interdependent/social resource (friend) condition		Independent/personal resource (self) condition	
Content	Type	Content	Type
1. Think about a time when you went to places and did enjoyable things with this person. For example, where did you go, and how did you feel or think?	Companionship	1. Think about a time when you went to places and did enjoyable things alone. For example, where did you go, and how did you feel or think?	Personal enjoyment
2. Think about a time when you told this person everything that you were going through. For example, what did you talk about, and how did you feel or think?	Intimate disclosure	2. Think about a time when you became the sole presenter in a class and talked. For example, what did you talk about, and how did you feel or think?	Presentation
3. Think about a time when this person helped you figure out or fix things. For example, how did this person help you, and how did you feel or think about it?	Instrumental aid	3. Think about a time when you figured out or fixed things. For example, what did you do, and how did you feel or think about it?	Problem solving
4. Think about a time when you took care of this person. For example, how did you treat him/her, and how did you feel or think?	Nurturance	4. Think about a time when you engaged in your personal hobbies (i.e., what you personally like). For example, what did you do, and how did you feel or think?	Pleasure activity
5. Think about a time when this person treated you like you were admired and respected. For example, how were you treated, and how did you feel or think about it?	Reassurance of worth	5. Think about a time when you felt proud of yourself. For example, what happened, and how did you feel or think about it?	Reassurance of own worth
6. Think about how sure you are that this relationship will last no matter what. For example, even under what adverse circumstances do you think this relationship will last?	Reliable alliance	6. Think about how sure you are that your self-confidence will last no matter what. For example, even under what adverse circumstances do you think you can keep yourself confident?	Self-confidence
7. Think about a time when this person really cared about you. For example, how did he/she treat you, and how did you feel or think?	Affection	7. Think about a time when you really cared about yourself. For example, what did you care about, and how did you feel or think?	Self-care

of the nine ratings to come up with their postscore on the IHS. What is expected here is that the average increases from pre- to postrecollection. Instructors may ask the participants to raise their hands if their postscore became higher than their baseline score to see the overall impact in the class or use some type of online polling service (e.g., Zoom surveys, Poll Everywhere) to look at change scores for the class from before to after recollection.

In order to make the activity more convincing, instructors may also want to include an independent/personal resource condition in which half the class, instead of all the students, are instructed to engage in the "independent/ personal resource (self) condition" task listed in Table 22.2. These students should then compare their score increase to that of the "interdependent/ social resource (friend) condition." Based on the results in Figure 22.1, one can expect that the former would not show an increase in the IHS, while the latter would.

Example Results

Forty-six East Asian students (40 female, six male, mean age 20.04; 41 Japanese, five were of either Korean or Chinese origin) participated in the same recollection task described earlier in this chapter. Twenty-one recalled an interdependent/social resource they had with an important friend, while the remaining 25 recalled a self-based counterpart—recalling an independent/personal resource (Japanese version was created based on the translation by Yoshitake et al., 2014). The IHS was measured within participants before and after the task. As shown in Figure 22.1, while the "independent/personal resource (self)" recollection did not increase the IHS, the "interdependent/social resources (friend)" recollection did. This effect was independent of gender, and the effect size was medium, $F(1, 43) = 4.66$, $p = .04$, $\eta^2 = .10$. Interestingly, a 1-week follow-up found no change in the increased scores, suggesting that this intervention will last beyond the duration of your class.

DISCUSSION

The size of the change in score may depend on several sociocultural or background variables, one of which is the affiliated cultural identity, favoring independent or interdependent orientations. Various studies have shown that this basic variability in selfhood coincides with the extent to which an individual subscribes to more individualist or collectivist societal ideas (Markus & Kitayama, 1991) that in the real world may correspond to having an East Asian or European identity (Kim & Markus, 1999). A South American cultural context may also upregulate the impact of this intervention (Hitokoto & Takahashi, 2021). Within-country demographic differences are reported, such as whether the participants are from the middle class or working class (Stephens et al., 2012), are male or female (Kashima et al., 1995), and so on (Markus & Conner, 2013).

FIGURE 22.1. Effect of the Recollection Task on the Interdependent Happiness Scale

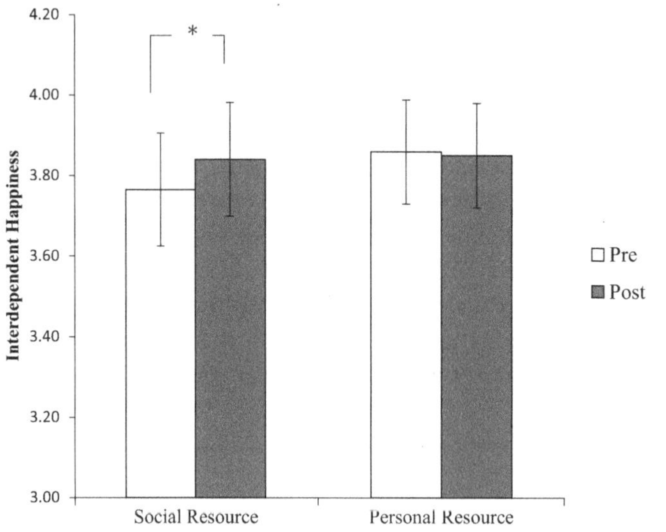

*p < .05.

Studies on social ecology add that a good deal of this variability may be rooted in the property of relationships as mobile or stable (Oishi & Graham, 2010), which can translate to whether participants have residentially moved a lot or not a lot in their life (after becoming 5 years old). Also, those with more frequent contact with close others (i.e., frequent communications, both online and offline) may show larger score changes, for these individuals may have real-world opportunities to enrich their social resources, making the task more effective. In contrast, if they currently have little contact with the imagined friend, their score increase may be marginal.

Asking these cultural or demographic background questions and allowing participants to share this information with the class could enrich their understanding of the nature of the score as cultural. For example, those with collectivist cultural experiences or backgrounds may show larger score changes than those with individualist cultural experiences or backgrounds. As far as participants are willing to share their cultural experiences with the class, instructors may compare the size of the change across two or more subgroups in the class (i.e., compare the number of participants who exceeded the class-average score change across two or more demographic groups within the class). Alternatively, participants can discuss what exactly made them feel more harmonized, as measured in the IHS, by elaborating their self-view during the recollection task compared with the baseline. Note: if your class is large and highly diverse, you could consider collecting the IHS data alongside demographic and cultural data (e.g., using Qualtrics or Google Forms), which would allow you to examine some of these questions using class data.

The new approach to measuring interdependent happiness is a promising line of research, but there are still some frontiers to explore. First, it is important to determine whether the IHS is comparable across cultures. We have recently been studying this question (Hitokoto & Adeclas, 2022; Hitokoto & Takahashi, 2021). Overall, the scale shows comparability across nations in terms of correlations with other measures. However, simple average score comparisons across nations may be contaminated by systematic errors such as response style. More research is needed to determine whether the IHS can be used to compare happiness across cultures in a reliable way. Second, the IHS is based on the notion of self as a cultural product. This means that the score may be impacted by social ecology, or the way that people interact with their environment (Hitokoto & Uchida, 2015). More research is needed to determine how social ecology affects the IHS score in different ecological contexts within a nation. Third, the IHS may be implicated in physical health across nations (Hitokoto & Adeclas, 2022). However, the specific process by which this occurs is not yet known. More research is needed to understand how the IHS affects physical health. These points suggest future directions for the study of the IHS. Further work is needed to validate the scale and to understand its cultural functions.

Overall, the current activity designed for students is a miniaturization of the possible psychological mechanisms involved in the link between interdependent culture and social resource enrichment, such as an accumulation of social capital. Replication is needed both in and out of East Asian cultures to fully appreciate the true impact of interdependent/social resource interventions on the upping of interdependent happiness. We recommend that you conclude the class discussion by highlighting the reasons that it is important to study and understand interdependent happiness in the context of positive psychology as a whole and how this concept could be used to foster a better understanding of well-being and/or more culturally informed interventions. For this, instructors may additionally bring up how students felt during their recollection, such as recalling how one is accepted, trusted, or needed by their friend; how one is important to them; what emotions they felt (e.g., gratitude, indebtedness); and finally to have students recall how they might have temporarily forgotten about their existing bond to this person. Such reminders could buffer feelings of loneliness that are known to be detrimental to human health. In terms of the impact of culture, students may further discuss what social factors might have contributed to losing connections in the first place, what kind of institutional set-ups can be secured in a community to prevent social unhappiness, and what specific situations were nominated among students of different origins. Finally, you could wrap up with a discussion of the essential psychological differences between social versus personal resources concerning happiness. Since the effects of positive psychology interventions are under debate (e.g., White et al., 2019), the medium impact we presented previously, and those shown in your classes, could directly contribute to supporting how positive psychology interventions can be effective in the social domain of well-being. Further, how these effects are intertwined with culture is an important future direction for research. Instructors can end the discussion with the key point that happiness, a seemingly personally defined concept, can actually be very much interdependent.

REFERENCES

Datu, J. A. D., King, R. B., & Valdez, J. P. M. (2016). The benefits of socially-oriented happiness: Validation of the Interdependent Happiness Scale in the Philippines. *Child Indicators Research, 9*(3), 631–649. https://doi.org/10.1007/s12187-015-9333-3

Delle Fave, A., Brdar, I., Wissing, M. P., Araujo, U., Castro Solano, A., Freire, T., Hernández-Pozo, M. R., Jose, P., Martos, T., Nafstad, H. E., Nakamura, J., Singh, K., & Soosai-Nathan, L. (2016). Lay definitions of happiness across nations: The primacy of inner harmony and relational connectedness. *Frontiers in Psychology, 7,* Article 30. https://doi.org/10.3389/fpsyg.2016.00030

Furman, W., & Buhrmester, D. (1985). Children's perceptions of the personal relationships in their social networks. *Developmental Psychology, 21*(6), 1016–1024. https://doi.org/10.1037/0012-1649.21.6.1016

Furman, W., & Buhrmester, D. (2009). The Network of Relationships Inventory: Behavioral systems version. *International Journal of Behavioral Development, 33*(5), 470–478. https://doi.org/10.1177/0165025409342634

Hitokoto, H. (2020). *Quality of the network of relationships as a factor of interdependent happiness* [Conference session]. 61st Annual Conference of the Japanese Society of Social Psychology, Online Conference.

Hitokoto, H., & Adeclas, J. (2022). Harmony and aversion in the face of a pandemic. *Japanese Psychological Research, 64*(2), 222–243. https://doi.org/10.1111/jpr.12416

Hitokoto, H., & Takahashi, Y. (2021). Interdependent happiness across age in Costa Rica, Japan, and the Netherlands. *Asian Journal of Social Psychology, 24*(4), 445–462. https://doi.org/10.1111/ajsp.12437

Hitokoto, H., & Uchida, Y. (2015). Interdependent happiness: Theoretical importance and measurement validity. *Journal of Happiness Studies, 16*(1), 211–239. https://doi.org/10.1007/s10902-014-9505-8

Hitokoto, H., & Uchida, Y. (2017). Interdependent happiness: Progress and implications. In M. Demir & N. Sümer (Eds.), *Close relationships and happiness across cultures* (pp. 19–39). Springer.

Kashima, Y., Yamaguchi, S., Kim, U., Choi, S. C., Gelfand, M. J., & Yuki, M. (1995). Culture, gender, and self: A perspective from individualism–collectivism research. *Journal of Personality and Social Psychology, 69*(5), 925–937. https://doi.org/10.1037/0022-3514.69.5.925

Kim, H., & Markus, H. R. (1999). Deviance or uniqueness, harmony or conformity? A cultural analysis. *Journal of Personality and Social Psychology, 77*(4), 785–800. https://doi.org/10.1037/0022-3514.77.4.785

Kitayama, S., Mesquita, B., & Karasawa, M. (2006). Cultural affordances and emotional experience: Socially engaging and disengaging emotions in Japan and the United States. *Journal of Personality and Social Psychology, 91*(5), 890–903. https://doi.org/10.1037/0022-3514.91.5.890

Kitayama, S., Salvador, C. E., Nanakdewa, K., Rossmaier, A., San Martin, A., & Savani, K. (2022). Varieties of interdependence and the emergence of the Modern West: Toward the globalizing of psychology. *American Psychologist, 77*(9), 991–1006. https://doi.org/10.1037/amp0001073

Kitazawa, M., Yoshimura, M., Hitokoto, H., Sato-Fujimoto, Y., Murata, M., Negishi, K., Mimura, M., Tsubota, K., & Kishimoto, T. (2019). Survey of the effects of internet usage on the happiness of Japanese university students. *Health and Quality of Life Outcomes, 17*(1), Article 151. https://doi.org/10.1186/s12955-019-1227-5

Markus, H. R., & Conner, A. (2013). *Clash!: 8 cultural conflicts that make us who we are.* Hudson Street Press.

Markus, H. R., & Kitayama, S. (1991). Culture and the self: Implications for cognition, emotion, and motivation. *Psychological Review, 98*(2), 224–253. https://doi.org/10.1037/0033-295X.98.2.224

Murase, T. (2007). *Naikan: Riron to bunkateki kanrensei* [NaiKan: Theory and its relation to culture]. Seishin-Shobo

Oishi, S., & Graham, J. (2010). Social ecology: Lost and found in psychological science. *Perspectives on Psychological Science, 5*(4), 356–377. https://doi.org/10.1177/1745691610374588

Oishi, S., Graham, J., Kesebir, S., & Galinha, I. C. (2013). Concepts of happiness across time and cultures. *Personality and Social Psychology Bulletin, 39*(5), 559–577. https://doi.org/10.1177/0146167213480042

Oishi, S., Schiller, J., & Gross, E. B. (2013). Felt understanding and misunderstanding affect the perception of pain, slant, and distance. *Social Psychological & Personality Science, 4*(3), 259–266. https://doi.org/10.1177/1948550612453469

Stephens, N. M., Fryberg, S. A., & Markus, H. R. (2012). It's your choice: How the middle-class model of independence disadvantages working-class Americans. In S. T. Fiske & H. R. Markus (Eds.), *Facing social class: How societal rank influences interaction* (pp. 87–106). Russell Sage Foundation.

White, C. A., Uttl, B., & Holder, M. D. (2019). Meta-analyses of positive psychology interventions: The effects are much smaller than previously reported. *PLOS ONE, 14*(5), Article e0216588. https://doi.org/10.1371/journal.pone.0216588

Yoshitake, N., Utsumi, S., & Sugawara, M. (2014). *Investigating the social network qualities in adulthood: Application of the Japanese version of Network Relationships Inventory* [Conference session]. The 78th Annual Convention of the Japanese Psychological Association, Kyoto, Japan.

23

Building High-Quality Connections

Jane Dutton, Arne Carlsen, and Sally Maitlis

This activity engages people in the challenge of quickly building a high-quality connection with another person, either in person or virtually.

CONCEPT

Every year, more and more evidence shows that social relationships are critical to human health and well-being. We also know that the quality of these relationships and the interactions that compose them are not all equal. Some interactions and relationships are literally life-giving, while others can drain the life out of us.

This activity focuses on the power of brief (40 seconds is sufficient; Trzeciak & Mazzarelli, 2019) positive interactions with others that leave both people better off. These brief interactions can be thought of as the micro bits of more enduring positive relationships, which have typically been the focus of positive psychologists (e.g., Roffey, 2013). While historically psychology has focused more on romantic, friendship, or family relationships that tend to be more lasting, our approach has emerged from studying short interactions that often take place outside of these contexts. As positive organizational scholars, we tend to study these connections in work contexts.

High-quality connections are short-term interactions with another person that leave both people better off psychologically, physiologically, and socially (Dutton, 2003; Dutton & Heaphy, 2003; Heaphy & Dutton, 2008; Stephens et al., 2011). There are several behavioral moves or actions that are helpful in building these

https://doi.org/10.1037/0000417-023
More Activities for Teaching Positive Psychology: A Guide for Instructors, S. D. Pressman and A. C. Parks (Editors)

beneficial connections. This activity demonstrates the variety of behavioral moves that individuals can make that create a high-quality connection with another person. The activity is well-suited for teaching about building positive connections with other people, positive relationships, interpersonal communication, and networking.

MATERIALS NEEDED

No materials are needed except a device for keeping time, a physical or virtual space, and a means for two people to communicate with each other, either face-to-face or via video (e.g., in a virtual breakout room separated from a larger group). If this activity is done in a classroom setting, we also recommend using a bell, gong, or other device that makes a sound clearly audible over the buzz of many people talking. It can get noisy!

ACTIVITY SETTING

This activity can be done in a classroom or on an online video platform. It does need to be done with another person. We have used this activity in teaching settings (online or in person), in many workshops, and also as a warm-up to build connections before retreats, lectures, and other gatherings.

ACTIVITY DURATION

The activity itself takes about 10 to 15 minutes. The live debrief (discussion) can take anywhere between 10 and 30 minutes, depending on what concepts/ideas the instructor is most interested in conveying. In addition, if the instructor wishes to give homework outside of class or reflections "on your own," this time of live debrief might be shortened. We give time estimates for homework and reflections in the Writing Reflections section.

SUGGESTED READINGS

- Recommended reading for before the activity:
  - Dutton (2014)

- Optional readings:
  - Stephens et al. (2011)
  - Dutton and Heaphy (2003)
  - Blog Post No. 1: https://tinyurl.com/MATPPch23-blog1
  - Blog Post No. 2: https://tinyurl.com/MATPPch23-blog2

BACKGROUND AND INSTRUCTIONS

High-quality connections are the interactions with others that leave us more energized, affirmed, and healthier in the moment. Over time, these micro bits or connections can build more enduring relationships. However, these types of connections do not have to be enduring to be valuable. Even a 40-second high-quality connection can contribute positively to both people involved in an exchange. Each of us can learn and grow in our effectiveness at creating these salutary forms of interaction, which is the rationale for this exercise.

• This exercise can be used either to introduce the idea of high-quality connections or to elaborate on the idea of high-quality connections after the concept has been introduced.

• If used to introduce and motivate understanding of high-quality connections, provide a quick rationale for the exercise without explaining the concept of high-quality connections in detail. First, briefly identify high-quality connections as a burgeoning field of research consisting of micro bits of interrelating that are available to most people in the every day and can be energizing or depleting. Second, underline the value of learning by doing and keeping an open mind during the exercise.

• If used to elaborate on the idea of high-quality connections for students who have already been exposed to the concept, this exercise can be introduced as a way to better understand how to build high-quality connections and some of their impacts.

• The exercise:
  – First, ask everyone to stand next to the person they know the least in the room or someone they don't really know. If doing the exercise virtually, put people into random pairs. If a student is paired with a person they know well, no problem—it offers the opportunity to compare high-quality building strategies used by people in the well-known and less well-known pairs.

  – Explicitly ask them not to try to connect until you give them the "begin" signal. (Note: On virtual platforms, you can typically deliver messages to breakout groups, letting them know when to start interacting.)

  – Tell them that each person will have a chance to lead in connection building and to decide who will lead first.

  – Give each person 60 seconds to lead in building a high-quality connection with the other person (here is where the clearly audible bell or other instrument allows you to easily signal when 60 seconds is up.)

  – Encourage each person to use what actions they think will work well in building a high-quality connection with others.

- Instructors should observe how people are standing, how they listen, and their body language (orientation toward the other, gestures, mirroring, eye contact, smiling, "tuning in" moves, etc.). Note the change in energy in the room as people engage in the exercise, as the change in energy will be a valuable discussion point.

- When you stop after 2 minutes and both people have had a chance to lead the activity, ask each person to give at least one piece of feedback to the other person about what they did that they experienced as effective in building a high-quality connection.

- If doing this in person, keep people standing for the following debrief so they can remain connected and can demonstrate the behaviors they used to build the connection. It is advisable to stand in the middle of the pairings as you debrief.

- If a student is socially anxious and/or expresses real misgivings about participating in this exercise, invite them to play the role of observer and watch what people in the pairing are doing that seems effective in building a higher quality connection. Be sure to solicit their input during the exercise debrief.

DISCUSSION

The exercise is designed to teach four areas of knowledge about high-quality connections: (a) What are they? (b) What is the embodied experience of having a high-quality connection? (c) Why do they matter? And, most importantly, (d) what actions can you take to build them? Usually, the debrief starts with the fourth area of learning—strategies for building high-quality connections.

We begin the activity debrief with the question, "What worked in building a high-quality connection?" Participants can respond to this question based on their experience of trying to build a high-quality connection with their partner and also from the feedback they received about their connection-building strategies.

You can solicit input from participants in an open discussion format, or you can use tools like https://www.mentimeter.com, https://www.polleverywhere.com, or a word cloud (in person or virtually) so students can immediately see what other students have shared. Instructors can ask students to observe the range of strategies used, which ones are mentioned most frequently, and which are rare. Alternatively, the same question might be approached by having students write down the utilized strategies on sticky notes and physically place the connecting moves in clusters on a whiteboard. This latter strategy invites students to see how their moves were similar or different from others and is visually compelling in seeing the range and distribution of connecting strategies.

We explore participants' observations about the variety of behavioral moves that foster high-quality connecting (Dutton, 2003), making sure to reveal multiple avenues that people can use to foster high-quality connecting. This may include but not be limited to

1. greeting with respect (e.g., the combination of bodily gestures and utterances conveying openness and positive expectations)
2. conveying interest and/or care (e.g., by asking meaningful questions that display genuine curiosity and/or concern about the other person)
3. listening well (e.g., by conveying through body language or follow-up questions that you have heard what the other person is saying)
4. showing kindness or appreciation (e.g., by communicating gratitude to the other person)
5. demonstrating responsiveness (e.g., communicating that you have heard the other person's need or concern and offering a helpful reaction of some kind)
6. identifying commonalities and/or shared interests (e.g., noticing common ground, inquiring or building on similarities you share with the other person)
7. disclosing vulnerability (e.g., opening up with the other person and sharing some personal concern, worry, or struggle)
8. expressing affirmation (e.g., looking for and seizing opportunities to express confirmation of the other)
9. generating laughter (e.g., laughing at oddities, jokes, hints of banter at the situation and its time constraints)

Instructors can follow up this discussion of what worked with an exploration of what people found difficult in building a high-quality connection. Sometimes people will mention the artificial nature of being "forced" to build a high-quality connection, which undercuts a sense of genuineness or authenticity. This thread can be worth exploring further (depending on the context in which you are using the exercise). It is helpful to mention that research shows people underestimate how pleasant it will be to interact with people they don't know (e.g., Schroeder et al., 2022) and how much others appreciate it. In addition, many students may have been advised to network with others for jobs or other instrumental outcomes, which, for some people, may make forced interactions seem distasteful. Exploring this possibility may open up consideration that encouraging the building of high-quality connections provides a different logic for human connections than a networking logic, one that is more focused on the mutual enhancement of both people in the connection.

It is also possible to explore what differences were evident in the moves used between pairs of strangers versus people who know each other. For the pairs who know each other better, there is often a base level of trust and knowledge to build on, making the moves more targeted and deeper than if people are total strangers. In contrast, the pairs of strangers may spend more time on more open-ended questions and have interactions that are charged with two-way curiosity and less prone to limiting preconceptions.

A baseline for a high-quality connection is that it should feel natural rather than fake. However, we believe that all efforts to do something better may involve a modification of people's habits that can feel uncomfortable at first

(Ashford, 2021; Molinsky, 2017). Adopting a growth-mindset approach here means we trust that, with practice, people can get better at building high-quality connections.

After exposing the multiple moves people can use to build connections, we share observations. First, these actions are small, yet they are potent in building a sense of connectedness. Second, the first moves matter as we tend to form rapid impressions about another person's interest and care for us, which, if favorable, tends to engage reciprocity or further investment in the connection from the other person. Third, any one of us has a choice in which moves we make (first or otherwise), giving us some degree of efficacy or agency in building connections with others (Sundet & Carlsen, 2019). Fourth, the moves to build high-quality connections take relatively little time. In less than a minute, people can meaningfully affect the quality of their connection with another person.

The next set of questions used in the debrief explores the indicators that a high-quality connection is being built. At a basic level, this probe explores what a high-quality connection is. It can sometimes help to ask participants to compare differences in how they felt and thought about the other person before and after they engaged in the connecting activity. We might ask, "How did you know that what the other person was doing was working in connecting with you?" or "How did you sense that a high-quality connection was being built?" Here, we are probing to see if people sensed a higher level of vitality or energy, an enhanced desire to respond (mutuality), and/or an increase in positive regard (thinking more highly of the other person). These are three of the defining features of a high-quality connection (Dutton & Heaphy, 2003). It is important for people to be more aware of what they are doing that is helpful in building a high-quality connection, but this requires that we have some way to gauge whether or not a high-quality connection is being built. We need to get better at sensing when we are in a higher quality connection.

Because high-quality connections include a physiological component (Heaphy & Dutton, 2008), inquire what participants may have noticed in their bodies as they engaged with the other person or after as they reflect on the interaction. What was their bodily "felt sense" (Gendlin, 1962/1997) of the connection? Often, people will mention feeling a sense of ease or increased openness, a lightness within their body, or more zest. For some, this may be an overall sense; others may notice a shift in a specific part of their bodies, such as looser shoulders or deeper breathing.

The final element in the debrief invites consideration of the benefits of being in a high-quality connection (for both people) but also why high-quality connections might matter in a social group (team, club, organization). This part of the debrief is engaged by simply asking, "What difference do these kinds of connections make?" and "How did paying attention to or building a high-quality connection affect you? How do you think it affected the other person?" We want participants to identify benefits that have been supported by research, such as individual-level benefits and group-level benefits.

Individual-Level Benefits

- greater openness
- enhanced trust
- desirable physiological effects such as a decrease in felt stress
- greater sense of dignity and respect
- feeling more included and a sense of belonging
- greater individual creativity and learning
- greater sense of individual agency or enhanced sense of efficacy in relating to another person
- enhanced desire to help or assist others (more prosocial motivation)
- greater well-being over time

Group-Level Benefits

- greater psychological safety
- higher collaboration potential
- greater collective learning
- enhanced decision-making capabilities
- greater sense of collective agency
- stronger feelings of togetherness and shared identity
- enhanced collective resilience
- more supportive organizational climate

A Possible Exercise Variation

- The description of the exercise assumes instructors will do just one round of pairing up students to build a high-quality connection. However, if instructors have more time and want to give students more experience in connection building, they might try a two-round design. In the first pairing, an instructor asks the students to interact as they normally would, each taking the lead to connect and then sharing how it felt and what worked. However, in the second round, instructors would emphasize the goal of building a high-quality connection and follow the same instructions. Then, invite students to compare differences in what they did to build connection and how the connection felt between the two rounds. Assuming the students discover a bigger uplift in the motivated versus nonmotivated interaction, there could be an invitation to consider what people can do to activate intentions to connect in a high-quality manner.

ASSIGNMENT

Writing Reflections

Here are three possible reflection assignments:

1. Reflect on people with whom you consistently have high-quality connections. Based on what you know about what facilitates high-quality connection

building, how might you explain these persistent high-quality connections? Now, choose a person with whom you would like to build a high-quality connection but, thus far, have not done so. It could, for example, be someone who seems isolated and in need of strengthening, someone you would like to invite into collaboration, or simply a person you would like to get to know better. Identify three strategies you could use to build a high-quality connection with this person (15–20 minutes).

2. Reflect on an experience you have had of personal growth (perhaps after adversity or in other circumstances). Consider how significant others (e.g., a friend, a colleague, a partner, professionals) helped you in your growth, and identify two or three concrete episodes of interaction that you believe were important in this process. Reflect on what it was about these interactions that supported your personal growth (30–45 minutes).

3. Reflect on your experience of the high-quality connection exercise you did in class. How did your behavior compare to how you usually act when meeting someone for the first time? If you did anything different, consider what impact it may have had—on you or the other person. If you behaved exactly as you normally do, reflect on what you might try next time to increase the likelihood or strength of a high-quality connection (30 minutes).

Case Assignment

Case assignments based on scenes from movies, plays, and/or literature where rich interactions of high-quality connections are brought to life and analyzed also offer valuable learning. One example uses a scene from the movie *Invictus* (2009) where Nelson Mandela meets the captain of the Springboks, the national rugby team, in his office. The scene is about 4 to 5 minutes long, depending on how you choose to cut it. It vividly illustrates a range of microinteractions that can build high-quality connections.[1] This includes greetings, expressing interest, demonstrating presence, active listening, inviting questions, conveying vulnerability, communicating affirmation, expressing warmth, using humor, and signaling respect, as well as a rich display of accompanying touches, gestures, eye contact,

---

[1] The American–South African biographical sports drama film *Invictus* tells the story of how the new South African nation under the leadership of Nelson Mandela experienced a moment of national transformation when the national team, Springboks, won the 1995 Rugby World Cup. Based on John Carlin's book *Playing the Enemy: Nelson Mandela and the Game That Made a Nation*, it tells the story of how the Springboks team was not expected to perform well at the competition, having just returned to high-level international competition following the dismantling of apartheid. Springboks were perceived as a redneck team that to many Black people represented prejudice and apartheid. In the movie, there is a powerful scene of the first major meeting between Mandela and the captain of the Springboks, François Pienaar. The meeting has, at its core, a set of open-ended questions: "So tell me, François, what is your philosophy of leadership? How do you inspire your men to be better than they think they can be?" The meeting works as an invitation to join forces and make the Rugby World Cup a shared project, one that can build bridges, unite people, and inspire the nation.

and other forms of body language. We suggest you provide context, then show the scene and ask students to pay attention to the microinteractions: "What do you see that Mandela and Pienaar are doing in this situation that creates high-quality connections?" (30 minutes)

Action Experiment

Another way to help participants apply their knowledge of high-quality connections to their lives outside of class involves the use of action experiments. Action experiments entail students self-designing and applying strategies for building high-quality connections in a life situation. This works best after doing and debriefing from the high-quality connections exercise, including discussing a repertoire of moves for building high-quality connections. Here is an example of text you can use to introduce this assignment:

1. Start from the strategies for building high-quality connections that we have exemplified and discussed in this class/workshop, including those described in the readings and cases.

2. Select a small number of situations in which you want to experiment with different ways of building high-quality connections. Try to select in a way that enables comparison (e.g., the same strategy across different contexts, several strategies in one context).

3. Do the experiments in a way that feels natural to you, but do make an effort to experiment!

4. Take one to three pages of notes (what happened, how did the other person respond, how did you experience it). These will be submitted to the instructor. Please come prepared to share experiences during our next session/meeting (if across multiple sessions).

REFERENCES

Ashford, S. J. (2021). *The power of flexing: How to use small daily experiments to create big life-changing changes*. Harper Collins.

Dutton, J. (2003). *Energize your workplace: How to build and sustain high-quality connections at work*. Jossey-Bass Publishers.

Dutton, J. (2014). Build high-quality connections. In G. Spreitzer & J. Dutton (Eds.), *How to be a positive leader: Small actions, big impacts* (pp. 11–21). Berrett-Koehler. https://drive.google.com/file/d/114Y41NdhIvLWAQfTNz71TciupR7pAOiN/view

Dutton, J., & Heaphy, E. (2003). The power of high-quality connections. In K. Cameron, J. Dutton, & R. E. Quinn (Eds.), *Positive organizational scholarship* (pp. 263–278). Berrett-Koehler. https://drive.google.com/file/d/11SMyL_80eYTNov0f948zENbMt-n3nqSh/view

Gendlin, E. (1997). *Experiencing and the creation of meaning*. Northwestern University Press. (Original work published 1962)

Heaphy, E., & Dutton, J. (2008). Positive social interactions and the human body at work: Linking organizations and physiology. *Academy of Management Review*, *33*(1), 137–162. https://doi.org/10.5465/amr.2008.27749365

Molinsky, A. (2017). *Reach: A new strategy to help you step outside your comfort zone*. Penguin Books.

Roffey, S. (Ed.). (2013). *Positive relationships: Evidence based practice across the world.* Springer.

Schroeder, J., Lyons, D., & Epley, N. (2022). Hello, stranger? Pleasant conversations are preceded by concerns about starting one. *Journal of Experimental Psychology: General, 151*(5), 1141–1153. https://doi.org/10.1037/xge0001118

Stephens, J. P., Heaphy, E., & Dutton, J. (2011). High-quality connections. In K. S. Cameron & G. M. Spreitzer (Eds.), *Handbook of positive organizational scholarship* (pp. 385–399). Oxford University Press. https://drive.google.com/file/d/115aEW1Rdd7nqH34dqGgZObelbpYyuQv-/view

Sundet, J., & Carlsen, A. (2019). Cultivating relational agency through high-quality connecting. In R. Burke & A. Richardson (Eds.), *Creating psychologically healthy workplaces* (pp. 251–269). Edward Elgar.

Trzeciak, S., & Mazzarelli, A. (2019). *Compassionomics: The revolutionary scientific evidence that caring makes a difference.* Studer Group.

24

Identifying Positively Energizing Leaders

Kim Cameron

Positive energy is the capacity to help other people dream more, learn more, do more, and become more than they could otherwise. This activity explores how to identify, measure, and utilize positive energy and positive energizers in your team or organization.

CONCEPT

All human beings are inherently inclined toward positive energy. In nature, the sun is a source of life-giving, positive energy. For example, if a plant is in a window, over time, it will lean toward the light. This illustrates the *heliotropic effect*, or an inclination toward light or positive energy. All living systems, including all human beings, are inclined toward and flourish in the presence of life-giving, positive energy, and they avoid and languish in the presence of life-depleting, negative energy.

Abundant evidence confirms that the performance of human beings is significantly enhanced by exposure to positive energy or forces that are life-enhancing (Loeb & Northrop, 1917; Northrop & Loeb, 1923). This is especially true of leaders. Leaders' energy has been shown to be the single most important factor in accounting for variance in organizational performance. And, as it turns out, positive energy helps differentiate especially effective leaders from others, so successful leaders are almost always positive energizers (Owens et al., 2016, 2018). Similarly, positive energizers have an outsize impact on the success of groups they're a part of as well as on the well-being of group members.

https://doi.org/10.1037/0000417-024
More Activities for Teaching Positive Psychology: A Guide for Instructors, S. D. Pressman and A. C. Parks (Editors)

People are happier and flourish more in the presence of positive energizers than when energizers are absent (Baker, 2015).

Importantly, every person can be a positive energizer. Title, demographic characteristics, or hierarchical position do not determine who the energizers are. However, knowing who the positive energizers and de-energizers are in any team or organization provides a major advantage. Creating teams of positive energizers, for example, markedly impacts the success of change efforts. Positive energizers help others support change initiatives and diminish their resistance. Positive energizers can coach and mentor other members, and they can help individuals who are less positively energizing to become substantially more so (Baker et al., 2003; Cross et al., 2003). The activity in this chapter is designed to help you identify positive energizers and find ways to capitalize on their resources.

MATERIALS NEEDED

This activity involves gathering data from individuals in your team, class, or organization by having each individual address the following question in relation to each other: "When I interact with this person, what happens to my energy?" ("Am I uplifted, elevated, and energized, or am I depleted, exhausted, and diminished?"). Several alternatives exist for obtaining this information. One way is to gather it online, in which case you will need access to the internet and one of many free online programs for creating network maps. Other ways involve gathering information from individuals using paper and a pencil or through email. With each alternative, you will need a list of the names of the members of your team, group, or organization.

In large classes or organizations, I usually gather the data online via email or by using paper and pencil in the classroom. You can gather information from the entire classroom at once by asking each class member to respond to every other class member, or you can divide students into smaller groups, for example, by having students respond just to members of a subgroup. You also may want to create randomized groups of students ranging in size from 10 to 25 or so.

ACTIVITY SETTING

This activity can be completed in a synchronous online or in-person face-to-face setting, or it can be obtained in a virtual classroom setting. Critically, this activity needs to occur after individuals have been together for enough time that they have developed impressions of one another. In class, this can be as soon as the second or third day or after some get-to-know-you activities. It is often accomplished in existing teams or organizations where people know one another. Alternatively, for students who have jobs outside of the classroom or who belong to other groups (e.g., student organizations), this activity might be helpful in identifying energizers who can be especially effective leaders in those settings.

In addition, you could use this as a take-home exercise that students work on with groups they know well.

As far as when/where to teach this, this activity works well as an exercise for a workplace/applied-oriented lecture in a positive psychology course, in an industrial/organizational psychology lecture, or as part of a workplace consulting activity. It might also work well in a discussion of individual differences (e.g., personality), leadership, or personal strengths.

ACTIVITY DURATION

Depending on the number of individuals in a team or organization, the activity can be accomplished in as few as 2 or 3 minutes or in as many as 15 minutes. In one version of the exercise, each member of a team rates his or her interaction with every other team member. In another version of the exercise, individuals write down the names of two or three individuals they deem as the most positively energizing people in their group.

SUGGESTED READING

- Optional reading for before the exercise:
  - K. Cameron (2021b; Chapters 1 and 2)

BACKGROUND AND INSTRUCTIONS

Positive energy and positive energizers are important themes in the field of positive organizational psychology, and they encompass the effects of positivity on individual well-being, group dynamics, and organizational performance. As defined by K. Cameron (2021a), positive energizers are individuals who radiate positivity and uplift those around them, playing a pivotal role in elevating team performance and enhancing individual flourishing (K. S. Cameron & Winn, 2012). Numerous empirical studies and theoretical articles (e.g., Baker, 2019; Dutton, 2003; Heaphy & Dutton, 2008; Owens et al., 2016; Quinn et al., 2012) highlight their significance. In particular, research findings show that the more positive energy that resides in an organization among its members, the higher the performance of the organization (Owens et al., 2018), the more likely change efforts will be successful (Baker, 2015), and the more well-being and engagement is experienced by employees (Owens et al., 2016). The concept extends beyond professional settings, as research underscores the influence of positive energy on physical health (Pressman & Cohen, 2012), mental resilience (Fredrickson, 2009), and overall life satisfaction (Lyubormirsky et al., 2005).

The findings from research are very clear: Positive energizers are a tremendous resource because they help other people flourish, they affect the performance of teams and organizations in a major way, and they help foster organizational improvements and change. The activity in this chapter helps you utilize the power of positive energy and the key role of positive energizers in fostering more flourishing and thriving organizations and individuals.

Four different strategies exist for identifying positive energizers in your team or organization.

(1) Creating an Energy Network Map

The most sophisticated method for identifying positive energizers is to create a network map of all possible relationships in a team or organization. This is done by creating a list of every person in the organization. Each person responds to the following question regarding each other person on the list: "When I interact with this person, what happens to my energy? That is, to what extent am I enthused, elevated, and uplifted, or, on the other hand, diminished and exhausted, when I interact with this person?" Responses are graded on the following scale:

7 = *I am very positively energized when I interact with this person.*
6 = *I am moderately positively energized when I interact with this person.*
5 = *I am slightly positively energized when I interact with this person.*
4 = *I am neither energized nor de-energized when I interact with this person.*
3 = *I am slightly de-energized when I interact with this person.*
2 = *I am moderately de-energized when I interact with this person.*
1 = *I am very de-energized when I interact with this person.*

Having each person rate his or her energizing connection with every other person in the group produces a set of ratings associated with each person's name. These associated ratings are entered into a network mapping program (there are many available online free of charge, e.g., https://www.goodfirms.co/blog/best-free-and-open-source-network-mapping-software), which creates a network map based on relational energy—that is, the energy exchanged when two people interact (see Figure 24.1). Similar to a network map in the back of an airline magazine, you can identify which individuals have lots of connections (as with an airline hub city) and which have few connections (as with peripheral cities on an airline map). Those with lots of energizing connections—that is, a lot of other people rated them as a 6 or 7 on the Likert scale—are the most positively energizing people.

You can also create a de-energizing map in the same way. Individuals who have a lot of ratings of 1 or 2 are considered to be de-energizing members of the team or organization. These folks may benefit from coaching or mentoring to help them learn how to be more positively energizing. It is important, however, not to embarrass or diminish individuals by making sensitive data public. I often keep all names anonymous if I am just using the data to illustrate positive energizing, or I provide each individual only with his or her personal feedback along with an offer to discuss the results in private.

FIGURE 24.1. An Illustration of an Energy Network Map

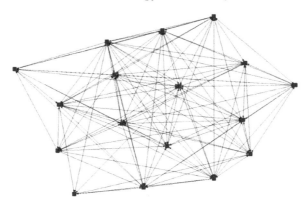

It is often useful to gather more information than just ratings of relational energy. For example, you may gather information regarding hierarchical position in an organization, locations, functions, or demographics. We have discovered in our research that people in senior positions in organizations are no more likely than people in junior positions to be positive energizers (see discussion in K. Cameron, 2021b). Demographic characteristics are also not related to energizing. That is because being a positive energizer is demonstrated by behaviors, not by positions, ranks, or physical characteristics.

These data can also provide information about the relative amount of energizing occurring in the entire organization. In Figure 24.1, it is relatively easy to see, for example, that person "E" is more of a positive energizer than is, for example, person "H." "E" received more ratings of 6 or 7 than did "H." In addition, note that 70% of all pairwise connections are rated as positively energizing, and this is a relatively high level of positive energy in the entire organization. The more dense the energy network (in this case 70% density), the higher the performance of the overall organization.

(2) Creating a Bubble Chart

Another way to identify the positive energizers in an organization or group in a short amount of time is to ask all members to confidentially write down the names of the two or three most positively energizing people in the group (more names can be requested in larger groups). Have each person submit the names to you on a slip of paper or in an email. Then, count the number of nominations that each person receives. Create a bubble chart showing different-sized bubbles, with the largest bubbles displaying those with the largest number of nominations and the smallest bubbles showing the smallest number of nominations (see Figure 24.2). The results are usually shown anonymously, with numbers rather than names in the bubbles. This avoids embarrassing or deflating individuals in the group, but it allows the leader to get a good sense of who the energizing people are, and it shows the variability of energy. I usually ask the group to recommend what they would do to help this organization improve their performance.

FIGURE 24.2. A Bubble Chart of Energy Ratings

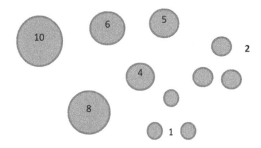

(3) A Pulse Survey

A pulse survey monitors the overall energy levels of group or organization members over time (see Figure 24.3). Individuals are asked on a weekly basis (or more frequently) the following question: "On a scale of 1 to 10, what is your positive energy today?" The energy of individuals in the organization is monitored on a regular basis using a one-question email to get a picture of the collective energy of the group or organization. Several CEOs use this quick survey to assess the energy of their various offices or locations.

   If energy scores are changing—either up or down—the pulse survey plot can help guide diagnoses regarding what is changing over time, what is going well, what factors are affecting scores, and what impact this has on bottom-line results. It is also possible to see which team or organization members are struggling or flourishing. This is less likely to be useful as a one-off class activity, but it could be done at the beginning, middle, and end of the class to assess class climate.

(4) Rating Positively Energizing Leaders

A quick and simple way to evaluate the positive energy of a single leader is to use this short, five-question assessment (Owens et al., 2016). Employees rate their leader on these five attributes, each of which characterizes their impressions of the leader. This can also be used to evaluate other individual team members . The question is: "To what extent is the leader of this organization a positive leader?" (The question could also be worded: "To what extent is my team a positively

FIGURE 24.3. A Pulse Graph of Energy

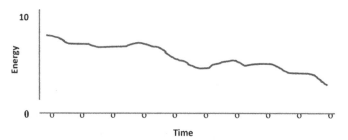

energizing team?") A 7-point Likert response scale can be used, ranging from 7 (*very typical of this leader*) to 1 (*very atypical of this leader*).

- I feel invigorated when I interact with this person.
- After interacting with this person, I feel more energy to do my work.
- I feel increased vitality when I interact with this person.
- I would go to this person when I need to be "pepped up."
- After an exchange with this person, I feel more stamina to do my work.

Aggregating the responses of employees in a particular business unit or team provides a mean score. This score does not identify the specific behaviors being displayed by the leader of a unit, but it does provide a quick way to determine the extent to which employees are being positively energized by their leader (or their team members).

One possible extension that could demonstrate this concept in a large undergraduate class would be to show brief videos of leaders and then have students rate the leaders on this scale. These data could then be collected via an in-class live survey method so that the results could be shared regarding which leaders are the most energizing, what attributes are most notable, and what impact energy has on the leaders' organizations.

These four alternatives are generally useful in different settings. The Network Map (Alternative 1) is the most sophisticated and produces the richest information on energizing connections and energy density. However, it requires that you gather the information in advance of the class in which you feed back the data and discuss its implications. This alternative is frequently used in organizations (e.g., top management teams) to identify energizers and their positions in the organization.

In a classroom setting, especially one with a large enrollment, I rely on the Bubble Chart (Alternative 2) to get a quick and straightforward idea of who the positive energizers are and discuss why this is relevant. The Pulse Survey (Alternative 3) is best used to monitor energy over time in a team or organization, and rating individuals (Alternative 4) gauges the positive energy of the leader(s) in a team or organization.

To avoid embarrassing individuals who may not be rated as positively energizing, I very rarely share the labeled results of the energy analysis with all the participants at once. In an organization—say, with a management team—the senior executive receives the results of the energy analysis with names attached, but individual participants only receive an unlabeled energy network as well as their own data individually. The same is true in a classroom. The instructor knows the entire analysis, including names, but individual students only receive their personal data along with an unlabeled energy profile of the classroom. In other words, the senior executive has a picture of who the positive energizing leaders are, but individuals are not embarrassed by having their scores shared. Each individual receives an offer for personal, one-on-one debriefing if desired.

The purpose of these assessments is to help participants understand the importance and impact of being a positive energizer as well as the influence of positive energizers on the entire system. Rather than discouraging individuals, the intent of having them receive their own data is to motivate them to continue to develop their positively energizing skills.

DISCUSSION

The heliotropic effect highlights a fundamental inclination of living organisms to orient themselves toward light and life-giving positive energy (Romanes, 1893). Numerous scientific studies, including the work of Doidge (2016, pp. 116–117), affirm that humans are naturally drawn to light and the energy it offers. Hamblin's (2017, 2018) research at Harvard Medical School further demonstrates light's potential to provide life-giving energy, combat cancer cells, aid in injury recovery, address traumatic brain injuries, treat dementia, and facilitate substantial wound healing. Physiological evidence underscores our innate dependency on and affinity for light and the resulting positive energy, which plays a crucial role in our well-being. The heliotropic effect elucidates why humans are profoundly influenced by positive energy (see K. Cameron, 2021a, for additional references).

Various forms of energy exist, each with distinct characteristics. Physical energy depletes as it is expended, necessitating recovery after activities like running or athletic contests. Similarly, the use of mental energy requires breaks, weekends, and downtime to recuperate from cognitive exertion. Emotional energy diminishes with use, and we require time to recover after intense interactions, such as debates, conflicts, or even enthusiastic cheering at events.

In contrast, relational energy, the energy exchanged between individuals during interactions, is different. Unlike other types of energy, relational energy typically increases or intensifies when expressed. Interactions with loved ones in supportive relationships rarely lead to exhaustion. Trusting, caring connections do not deplete us; instead, they serve as sources of renewal and revitalization. In essence, relational energy is self-enhancing and self-renewing, making it a unique and vital aspect of our interpersonal experiences.

Numerous studies underscore the life-extending benefits of experiencing positive relational energy, with a staggering two to fourfold increase in the likelihood of premature death for those lacking consistent exposure to it (K. Cameron, 2021a, Chapter 1; Holt-Lunstad et al., 2010; Pressman & Cohen, 2012; Pressman et al., 2019). Social integration, closely tied to positive relational energy, surpasses factors like smoking, excessive drinking, and obesity as a predictor of long-term health and mortality (Holt-Lunstad et al., 2010).

Relational energy significantly amplifies employee performance, fostering a propensity to seek and share information and resources among positive energizers (Tenny et al., 2016). Its impact is particularly striking when demonstrated by leaders, setting apart highly effective leaders from their counterparts. Within organizations, research in this area has yielded three fundamental conclusions. First, individuals who radiate positive energy outperform their peers across physical, emotional, and cognitive domains, resulting in above-average organizational output (Baker, 2000; Baker et al., 2003; Cross et al., 2003). Individuals' positions in the positive energy network proves more pivotal in predicting performance than their standing in the information or influence networks. Energy, rather than information or influence, takes precedence in explaining individual and unit performance.

This discovery holds particular significance due to the traditional emphasis on information and influence management by organizational leaders. Paradoxically, the management of positive energy often remains overlooked, and individuals who radiate positivity seldom receive the recognition, rewards, or promotions commensurate with their profound impact on performance. Empirical evidence firmly underscores the imperative of prioritizing energy management, given its fundamental influence on both individual and organizational performance, surpassing the customary focus on information and influence (Baker, 2000; Baker et al., 2003; K. Cameron, 2021a; Cross et al., 2003).

A second key finding emphasizes the influence of positive energizers on the performance of those with whom they interact. Positive energizers play a disproportionately significant role in performance, as individuals tend to thrive in their presence. This phenomenon is evident in professional sports, where teams acquire players known for their positive energy and clubhouse contributions, even if their peak performance years are behind them. Positive energizers in locker rooms have been shown to significantly impact team victories by boosting the performance of their teammates.

Empirical research also highlights a third crucial insight: Highly successful organizations boast a substantially higher number of positive energizers, often up to 3 times more, than typical organizations. Importantly, positive energizers can be found at any hierarchical level within an organization, and anyone can cultivate the attributes of a positive energizer. This is because positive energy is not equated with personality attributes such as extroversion nor temporary emotional states such as a good mood or depression. Rather, positively energizing people display particular behaviors.

Positively energizing leaders are not self-aggrandizing, dominant individuals who seek the limelight. They are not always in charge or up-front. Instead, they are individuals who produce growth, development, and improvement among others with whom they interact. They exude a certain kind of light that is uplifting and helps others become their best. In interviews with hundreds of positively energizing leaders (K. Cameron, 2021a, Chapter 3), 15 key behaviors emerged as characteristic of the most positively energizing leaders. This is not a comprehensive list, of course, because circumstances and culture may alter what is most effective in certain organizations. Other attributes may be effective in certain circumstances and in diverse cultures. However, this list is universal enough that it can guide efforts to develop more positively energizing leadership attributes. None of these 15 attributes was mentioned more often than others in the interviews, so none necessarily predominated above others.

Positively energizing leaders

- help other people flourish without expecting a payback
- express gratitude

- instill confidence and self-efficacy in others
- smile frequently
- forgive weaknesses in others
- focus on the person, not on demographic attributes
- are generous and share plum assignments
- listen actively and empathetically
- help solve problems
- mostly see opportunities rather than roadblocks
- inspire others by clarifying meaningfulness
- are trusting and trustworthy
- are genuine and authentic
- motivate others to exceed performance standards
- mobilize other positive energizers

Notice that none of these attributes is unusual, difficult to develop, or uncommon. When you think of people in your own life that are positively energizing to you, it is almost certain that many of these characteristics will describe them. Each attribute is characterized by behaviors that are easily displayed and quite obvious. For example, just expressing gratitude regularly and frequently is, surprisingly, not typical. In one study by the Greater Good Science Center, only 10% of employees indicated that they expressed gratitude to colleagues each day, and 60% stated that they never did! Assisting others in need, telling the truth, forgiving rather than holding grudges, encouraging others, expressing compassion, recognizing someone, and just having a pleasant look on your face all sound like grandmothers' advice. Yet, these are precisely the behaviors that lead to extraordinarily successful organizational performance, flourishing interpersonal relationships, and high levels of employee engagement and well-being. Anyone, or everyone, can become a positive energizer.

Despite this, it is not uncommon for some individuals to label positively energizing leadership as superficial, fluffy, substanceless, or commonsensical happiology—"Just think happy thoughts and everything will turn out alright," "I'm not in a good mood, so I can't positively energize others," or "Being positive all the time is disingenuous." Adopting these perspectives is a deflection from the power that resides in positively energizing leadership behaviors. Positive energizing is not merely a good mood, smiling, exuberance, or thinking cheerful thoughts. Rather, empirical research indicates that displaying specific behaviors produces especially desirable outcomes for organizations and individuals.

The reason we rely so much on empirical research in this discussion is because of the skepticism that exists and the dismissal of this topic as superficial. A sample of relevant findings, for example, has found that brain activity is significantly affected by exposure to positive energy and positive practices (Sharot et al., 2007). More mental acuity and mental activation occurs when experiencing a positive compared with a negative condition, so people perform better on memory, memorization, and problem-solving tasks. Heart rhythms are significantly affected by exposure to the positive (McCraty & Childre, 2004); the heart beats more rhythmically when experiencing a positive state compared with a negative state, thus extending longevity. Central nervous system functioning (i.e., vagus nerve health) operates most effectively when positive emotions are fostered (Kok et al., 2013), so internal organs are healthier. Bodily rhythm coherence (an alignment of brain and heart rhythms) is at its peak when experiencing positive energy (McCraty, 2016).

Aside from individual physiological benefits, positive energy and positive practices also affect organizations' performance. Bottom-line performance—meaning profitability, productivity, quality, innovation, customer satisfaction, and employee engagement—increases significantly when scores on positive practices improve (K. S. Cameron et al., 2004; K. Cameron et al., 2011; K. S. Cameron & Lavine, 2006). Even in organizations where it is probable that positive practices and positive energy might be interpreted as too soft, syrupy, and irrelevant—such as financial services, firms engaged in downsizing, the military, or health care organizations in the midst of a recession—performance on bottom-line indicators exceeded industry averages by a factor of 4–10 when they experienced high levels of positive energy and positive energizing leadership.

Research on positive practices and positive energy continues to emerge, and it is clear that oversimplification and superficiality are certainly not accurate descriptors of the impact of positive energy. The empirical case for positive energy is firmly grounded and strengthening. On the other hand, as is the case in any newly emerging field, a variety of issues and uncertainties still exist. For example, issues such as timing (How long does it take?), frequency (How much does it take?), and cultural differences (How does it manifest differently in Southeast Asia, the Middle East, or South America?) are just a fraction of the yet-to-be investigated questions. Hopefully, this exercise will help some students uncover insight into such questions.

ASSIGNMENT

Once you have identified who the positive energizers are (e.g., in your group, team, organization), you are left with the challenge of determining how to unleash their power, how to develop more of them, and how to use their influence to improve performance (see K. Cameron, 2021a, Chapters 3 and 4 for examples of ways to develop positive energizers). The exercise in this chapter is limited to assessing and identifying positive energizers, but the additional reading and references will help you address questions regarding how to develop positive energizers, how to utilize them, and how to help organizations capitalize on them to improve performance and make desired changes.

Here are some questions to contemplate once you have identified the positive energizers in your team or organization:

1. Who are the positive energizers in your organization or in your life? What behaviors and attributes do they display?

2. What are the most effective ways you have found to enhance positive relational energy in your team, your family, or your organization?

3. In trying times when people are stressed and overloaded, in what ways can developing positive energy help them flourish?

4. How can you take advantage of the heliotropic effect in your team or organization and in your own life?

5. In what ways is positive energy diminished or strengthened in your relationships?

6. How do you reconcile the seeming conflict between the idea that "bad is stronger than good" and the fact that an inherent tendency toward positive energy exists in all human beings?

7. What are the most effective ways you deal with issues related to diversity, equity, and inclusion in your organization, and how can capitalizing on positive energy help?

REFERENCES

Baker, W. (2000). *Achieving success through social capital: Tapping the hidden resources in your personal and business networks.* Jossey-Bass.

Baker, W. (2015, September 15). The more you energize your coworkers, the better everyone performs. *Harvard Business Review.* https://hbr.org/2016/09/the-energy-you-give-off-at-work-matters

Baker, W. (2019). Emotional energy, relational energy, and organizational energy: Toward a multilevel model. *Annual Review of Organizational Psychology and Organizational Behavior,* 6(1), 373–395. https://doi.org/10.1146/annurev-orgpsych-012218-015047

Baker, W., Cross, R., & Wooten, M. (2003). Positive network analysis and energizing relationships. In K. S. Cameron, J. E. Dutton, & R. E. Quinn (Eds.), *Positive organizational scholarship* (pp. 328–342). Berrett-Koehler.

Cameron, K. (2021a). Applications of positive organizational scholarship in institutions of higher education. In M. L. Kern & M. L. Wehmeyer (Eds.), *Palgrave handbook of positive education* (pp. 741–766). Palgrave Macmillan.

Cameron, K. (2021b). *Positively energizing leadership: Virtuous actions and relationships that create high performance.* Berrett-Koehler.

Cameron, K. S., Bright, D., & Caza, A. (2004). Exploring the relationships between organizational virtuousness and performance. *American Behavioral Scientist,* 47(6), 766–779. https://doi.org/10.1177/0002764203260209

Cameron, K., Mora, C., Leutscher, T., & Calarco, M. (2011). Effects of positive practices on organizational effectiveness. *Journal of Applied Behavioral Science,* 47(3), 266–308. https://doi.org/10.1177/0021886310395514

Cameron, K. S., & Lavine, M. (2006). *Making the impossible possible: Leading extraordinary performance—The Rocky Flats story.* Berrett Koehler.

Cameron, K. S., & Winn, B. (2012). *Virtuousness in organizations. The Oxford handbook of positive organizational scholarship.* Oxford University Press.

Cross, R., Baker, W. E., & Parker, A. (2003). What creates energy in organizations? *Sloan Management Review,* 44, 51–56.

Doidge, N. (2016). *The brain's way of healing.* Penguin Books.

Dutton, J. E. (2003). *Energize your workplace: How to create and sustain high-quality connections at work.* Jossey-Bass.

Fredrickson, B. L. (2009). *Positivity.* Crown Publishing.

Hamblin, M. R. (2017). Ultraviolet irradiation of blood: "The cure that time forgot"? *Advances in Experimental Medicine and Biology, 996,* 295–309. https://doi.org/10.1007/978-3-319-56017-5_25

Hamblin, M. R. (2018). Photobiomodulation for traumatic brain injury and stroke. *Journal of Neuroscience Research, 96*(4), 731–743. https://doi.org/10.1002/jnr.24190

Heaphy, E. D., & Dutton, J. E. (2008). Positive social interactions and the human body at work: Linking organizations and physiology. *Academy of Management Review, 33*(1), 137–162. https://doi.org/10.5465/amr.2008.27749365

Holt-Lunstad, J., Smith, T. B., & Layton, J. B. (2010). Social relationships and mortality risk: A meta-analytic review. *PLOS Medicine, 7*(7), Article e1000316. https://doi.org/10.1371/journal.pmed.1000316

Kok, B. E., Cohen, M. A., Catalino, L. I., Vacharlksemsuk, T., Algoe, S. B., Brantley, M., & Fredrickson, B. M. (2013). How positive emotions build physical health: Perceived positive social connections account for the upward spiral between emotions and vagal tone. *Psychological Science, 24*(7), 1123–1132. https://doi.org/10.1177/0956797612470827

Loeb, J., & Northrop, J. H. (1917). Heliotropic animals as photometers on the basis of the validity of the Bunsen–Roscoe law for heliotropic reactions. *Proceedings of the National Academy of Sciences of the United States of America, 3*(9), 539–544. https://doi.org/10.1073/pnas.3.9.539

Lyubormirsky, S., King, L., & Diener, E. (2005). The benefits of frequent positive affect: Does happiness lead to success? *Psychological Bulletin, 131*(6), 803–855. https://doi.org/10.1037/0033-2909.131.6.803

McCraty, R. (2016). *Science of the heart: Exploring the role of the heart in human performance: An overview of the research conducted by the HeartMath Institute* (Vol. 2). HeartMath Institute.

McCraty, R., & Childre, D. (2004). The grateful heart: The psychophysiology of appreciation. In R. A. Emmons & M. E. McCullough (Eds.), *The psychology of gratitude* (pp. 230–255). Oxford University Press.

Northrop, J. H., & Loeb, J. (1923). The photochemical basis of animal heliotropism. *The Journal of General Physiology, 5*(5), 581–595. https://doi.org/10.1085/jgp.5.5.581

Owens, B. P., Baker, W. E., Sumpter, D. M., & Cameron, K. S. (2016). Relational energy at work: Implications for job engagement and job performance. *Journal of Applied Psychology, 101*(1), 35–49. https://doi.org/10.1037/apl0000032

Owens, B. P., Sumpter, D. M., Cameron, K. S., & Baker, W. E. (2018, May 28). *Relational energy and well-being* [Conference session]. The Cesar Ritz Well-being Conference, Brigg, Switzerland.

Pressman, S. D., & Cohen, S. (2012). Positive emotion words and longevity in famous deceased psychologists. *Health Psychology, 31*(3), 297–305. https://doi.org/10.1037/a0025339

Pressman, S. D., Jenkins, B. N., & Moskowitz, J. T. (2019). Positive affect and health: What do we know and where next should we go? *Annual Review of Psychology, 70*(1), 627–650. https://doi.org/10.1146/annurev-psych-010418-102955

Quinn, R. W., Spreitzer, G. M., & Lam, C. F. (2012). Building a sustainable model of human energy in organizations: Exploring the critical role of resources. *The Academy of Management Annals, 6*(1), 337–396. https://doi.org/10.1080/19416520.2012.676762

Romanes, C.J. (1893). Experiments in heliotropism. *Proceedings of the Royal Society of London, 54,* 333–335. https://doi.org/10.1098/rspl.1893.0080

Sharot, T., Riccardi, A. M., Raio, C. M., & Phelps, E. A. (2007). Neural mechanisms mediating optimism bias. *Nature, 450*(7166), 102–106. https://doi.org/10.1038/nature06280

Tenny, E. R., Poole, J. M., & Diener, E. (2016). Does positivity enhance work performance?: Why, when, and what we don't know. *Research in Organizational Behavior, 36,* 27–46. https://doi.org/10.1016/j.riob.2016.11.002

V

IMPLEMENTING POSITIVE PSYCHOLOGY ACROSS CONTEXTS: CULTURE, STRESS, AND HEALTH

INTRODUCTION: IMPLEMENTING POSITIVE PSYCHOLOGY ACROSS CONTEXTS: CULTURE, STRESS, AND HEALTH

In this final section, we explore how different contexts interact with positive psychology, a key topic as we understand more and more how the benefits of different well-being interventions vary across groups, how well-being constructs mean different things to different people, and how contextual factors can influence our well-being on their own. Through these activities, students can be encouraged to broaden their worldview and think about how things that matter a lot to them may matter less to someone else—and vice versa. It may even be the first time they have been asked to think in this way! A student's own happiness is a rich lens through which to explore contextual differences, as their happiness will feel very real to them, maybe even absolute, and yet there will be many ways they can discover happiness's subjectivity.

The first two chapters (Chapters 25 and 26) in this section explore two growing subjects in the field of emotion and positive psychology: the interesting concept of ideal affect, or the idea that different people prefer to experience different affective states, and the related construct of fear of happiness, the important finding that not everyone around the world wants to be equally happy. These topics are relatively new and not well-represented in positive psychology textbooks; thus, we hope they will add some important diversity-focused discussions to your classrooms. Also relating to diversity is the next chapter (Chapter 27), which promotes strengths in diverse meso and macro settings. This fun grant competition activity has students struggle with the complexity of applying popular positive psychology interventions into complex and diverse contexts (at a community level), which we hope will provoke an enriching discussion on the typical individual focus of many activities in this book and the implications of that. Next, we take a more health and clinical psychology-focused approach to applying positive psychology by integrating it into the concepts of stress and resilience, critical topics for students in high-pressure education environments. In Chapter 28, you will have the opportunity to give your students a positive (i.e., self-affirmation) boost prior to a stressful examination, with the hopes of improving their confidence, well-being, and perhaps even their performance. In Chapter 29, you will be able to foster an interesting discussion on how different coping strategies can be helpful or harmful in the context of improving resilience to stress, a theme that is of central interest to many areas of psychology and one that can be easily connected to the real world and the day-to-day lives of college students. Finally, in the last chapter of the book (Chapter 30), students can learn about the old adage that "we are what we eat" by examining the impact of their diet on their personal happiness. The area of positive health (e.g., the study of connections between physical and psychological well-being) is a burgeoning one, and this activity would be a great entree into a discussion of the important ways happiness and other positive factors are connected to health.

25

How Ideal Affect Shapes Judgments of and Responses to Smiles

Elizabeth Blevins and Jeanne L. Tsai

In this activity, through their own data collection, students will learn about their ideal affect (i.e., the emotions they ideally want to feel) and how it shapes their perceptions of and behavior toward others.

CONCEPT

When we meet someone for the first time, we make snap judgments about how friendly and trustworthy (or mean and deceitful) that person is, which influences how we treat them. On what do we base these snap judgments? The following activity will illustrate that these judgments partly reflect the affective states we ideally want to feel, or our ideal affect. This activity will fit into lectures focused on cultural and individual differences in values, beliefs, and ideals regarding emotion, conceptions of happiness, and perceptions of positive emotion.

MATERIALS NEEDED

If the activity is done during class, you will need a way to show pictures (e.g., via a laptop and LCD projector) and students will need a way to record their answers (e.g., on a piece of paper, on a laptop, an anonymous virtual poll on Zoom). If the

https://doi.org/10.1037/0000417-025
More Activities for Teaching Positive Psychology: A Guide for Instructors, S. D. Pressman and A. C. Parks (Editors)

activity is done prior to class, you will need to create an online survey (e.g., on Qualtrics) and students will need internet access and a device (e.g., mobile phone, tablet, laptop) to complete the survey.

ACTIVITY SETTING

This activity can be done during class, either in person or online via a video platform (e.g., Zoom). Additionally, this activity can be done prior to class through an online survey (e.g., Qualtrics). In our studies, we have administered different versions of this social judgment task in person as well as online.

ACTIVITY DURATION

If the activity is done during class (see Appendix 25.1 for sample slides), it requires approximately 10 minutes, followed by at least 15 minutes of discussion. If the activity is administered as an online survey and includes an abridged measure of the Affect Valuation Index as well as other demographics (see Appendices 25.2 and 25.3), it will take students about 10 to 20 minutes to complete prior to class. Allow at least 15 minutes for discussion during class.

SUGGESTED READINGS

- Preactivity readings:
  - Tsai (2007)
  - Tsai et al. (2006)
- Postactivity readings:
  - Tsai (2021)
  - Tsai et al. (2019)
  - Park et al. (2020)

BACKGROUND AND INSTRUCTIONS

When we meet someone for the first time, we often make snap judgments about how friendly and trustworthy (or mean and deceitful) that person is (Abele & Bruckmüller, 2011; Todorov, 2008). How do we make these snap judgments? Growing evidence suggests that people use nonverbal facial cues, like emotional expressions, to make these judgments. For instance, in most cultures, people judge targets who smile (i.e., show happiness) as warmer and friendlier than targets who grimace or frown (i.e., show anger and sadness; Knutson, 1996; Montepare & Dobish, 2003). People also rate targets who express authentic, or *Duchenne*, smiles as more trustworthy than those who express inauthentic, non-Duchenne smiles (Gunnery & Ruben, 2016; Krumhuber et al., 2007). Our research suggests that people's ideal affect, or the affective states they value and ideally want to feel, also influences how they judge and respond to emotional targets.

Although most people want to feel good, the specific positive states that people ideally want to feel vary. While some people want to feel excited, enthusiastic, and other high arousal positive states, others want to feel calm, relaxed, and other low arousal positive states. Moreover, cultures differ in what specific positive states they implicitly or explicitly teach their members to value (Tsai, 2007; Tsai et al., 2006). These affective ideals are reflected in and reinforced by different forms of popular media (e.g., Tsai et al., 2007, 2016). For instance, U.S. contexts value high arousal positive states more than many East Asian contexts (Tsai et al., 2006), while many East Asian contexts value low arousal positive states more than the U.S. and other Western contexts (see findings from a mega-analysis of over 100 data sets suggesting that cultural differences in low arousal positive states may be less stable than cultural differences in high arousal positive states; e.g., Bencharit et al., 2019; Tsai et al., 2023). These differences are reflected in children's storybook illustrations, magazine advertisements, and leaders' official website photos (Tsai, 2007; Tsai et al., 2007, 2016).

Do these differences in ideal affect shape how we judge and respond to others? In a series of studies, European Americans judged targets with open-mouth, excited smiles as friendlier and more trustworthy than East Asians did (Park et al., 2017; Tsai et al., 2019). These differences were due to European Americans valuing high arousal positive states more than East Asians. Importantly, European Americans rated excited targets as friendlier and more trustworthy than East Asians did, regardless of the target's race (i.e., White, Asian) or sex (i.e., male, female). In other words, the target's emotional expressions mattered more than the target's race or sex for judgments of friendliness and trustworthiness. We have replicated the effects of ideal affect match, or rating targets who express people's own culturally valued emotions, on social judgments using both static, computer-generated faces as well as dynamic, realistic videos.

These differences in judgments of friendliness and trustworthiness based on ideal affect in turn influence how people treat others. For example, compared with East Asians, European Americans are more likely to give money to excited (vs. calm) targets (Park et al., 2017) and to hire excited (vs. calm) job applicants (Bencharit et al., 2019; Tsai et al., 2019) because they judge them to be friendlier and more trustworthy than East Asians do. And, as stated previously, these differences in judgments are related to how much European Americans value high arousal positive states compared with East Asians.

This teaching activity is designed to illustrate these findings. Although the findings are based on European American and East Asian participants, this activity can be conducted with students of all ethnicities and nationalities. In this activity, students will view pairs of targets that are the same race (White, Asian) and sex (male, female), but within each pair, one target will have an open-mouth, excited smile and the other target will have a closed-mouth, calm smile. Students will choose which target they want to share resources with, initiate a conversation with, and which they want as a leader of their organization. Next, students will choose whether they prefer to feel excited, enthusiastic, and passionate or calm, relaxed, and peaceful. Finally, students will choose which target is friendlier and more trustworthy.

- Before class, create five slides for each pair of excited and calm faces (see Appendix 25.1 for sample slides; you are free to choose your own faces). On each slide, add one of the following questions about the pair of faces: (a) "Which person would you rather give money to?" (b) "Which person would you rather start a conversation with?" (c) "Which person would you rather have as a leader of your organization?" (d) "Which person seems friendlier?" (e) "Which person seems more trustworthy?" One of the faces should be labeled "A" and the other should be labeled "B." Create one slide to measure students' ideal affect: "Which set of positive emotions would you rather feel more? Excited, enthusiastic, and passionate or calm, relaxed, and peaceful." One set of emotions should be labeled "A" and the other should be labeled "B."

- In class, tell students they will see different faces and will be asked to answer the questions on the top of the slide. Also tell students that you are interested in their immediate reactions and that they should make their choices as quickly as they can, writing their answer down on a piece of paper (or responding to the poll, etc.). To encourage students to make their choices quickly, show each slide for at most 4 seconds. First, show students the slides asking which person they would rather give money to, initiate a conversation with, and have as a leader. Then, show students the slide asking what positive emotions they would prefer to feel. Finally, show students the slides asking which person seems friendlier and more trustworthy.

- After students make their choices, go through each slide again and ask students to raise their hands if they chose "A" or "B" for each question. After they indicate their choices, ask students why they made them. Repeat this step for the first three slides. Then, ask students whether they chose the excitement states or the calm states (Slide 4) and ask if they think their responses to this question might be related to their responses to the earlier question. You can then tell students that among our study participants, those who preferred to be excited, enthusiastic, and passionate were more likely to share more money with, initiate a conversation with, and choose as a leader the excited target. Ask why ideal affect might be related to the first three responses. Finally, ask students how they responded to the questions about friendliness and trustworthiness and in what ways their judgments of friendliness and trustworthiness might also be related to their ideal affect. You can tell them that this is what our research shows: The more people value excitement states, the more likely they are to see the excited face as friendlier than the calm one and the more likely they are to share resources with them (Tsai et al., 2019).

There are different versions of the task. In one version, you could have students respond to an anonymous poll (e.g., Poll Everywhere) to provide more precise results as well as to decrease social desirability concerns that may occur when students see their peers' responses. In another version, you could have students complete the task prior to class via an online survey and simply go over the results together in class.

There are also different ways of presenting the faces. For the in-class activity, we suggest presenting the faces in pairs (Appendix 25.1), but in some of the actual studies, we presented each face separately and asked participants to indicate how much money they would give to each face on a scale from $0 to $10. You could also ask students to use a 5-point Likert scale (1 = *not at all* to 5 = *extremely*) to indicate how likely they would be to initiate a conversation with the target and to select the target as a leader of their organization. Similarly, in previous work, we had participants rate each face separately in terms of how friendly and trustworthy each face was on a 5-point Likert scale (1 = *not at all* to 5 = *extremely*). In the online survey, you could present the faces in this format (Appendix 25.2) and administer an abridged measure of ideal affect (Appendix 25.3) and a demographics questionnaire (e.g., sex, race, country of birth, parents' race, parents' country of birth). This would allow you to examine the links between ideal affect and social judgments and to see if there is cultural variation in the valuation of high and low arousal positive states, as in the actual study (Tsai et al., 2019). You could analyze the data prior to class, present the results in class, and discuss similarities and differences between class results and those reported in Tsai et al. (2019).

DISCUSSION

In our previous studies, we compared how European Americans and East Asians judge excited and calm smiling targets that vary in race (White, Asian) as well as sex (male, female), but obviously future research is needed to see if our results generalize to other cultural contexts as well as to targets of different ages and races. If your class has European American and East Asian students, you could see whether their responses are consistent with our previous results. More specifically, European American students should be more likely to share resources with, talk to, and choose as leaders excited faces rather than calm faces compared with East Asian students. Similarly, European Americans should be more likely to view the excited face as friendlier and more trustworthy than the calm face compared with East Asians. If you don't see this, you could talk about variation in ideal affect within cultural groupings.

If you use this activity in a classroom where students have different cultural backgrounds or use faces of different races, other patterns may emerge. You can still have students do the task but instead focus on individual differences. For instance, based on our findings, within a culture, students who value excited over calm states will share more money with excited (vs. calm) faces and will view excited (vs. calm) faces as friendlier and more trustworthy, in contrast with other students who value calm over excited states. To get an idea of students' ideal affect, you could administer an abridged measure of the Affect Valuation Index (Appendix 25.3) after the rating task. Alternatively, you could focus on the most common cultures in your classroom, see if there is any systematic variation, and discuss whether the patterns are similar to previously studied European Americans or East Asians.

In addition, during the discussion, you could

1. Ask students to identify why they made their choices and what cues they used to make their judgments ("Why did you decide to give more of your money to A vs. B?" "Why did you think A was friendlier than B?").

2. Ask students whether they would expect to see a similar pattern for traits other than friendliness and trustworthiness ("Do you think differences in the valuation of excitement and other high arousal positive states influence our judgments of other traits like assertiveness and competence?"). In previous work, we found that, across cultures, both European Americans and East Asians rated the excited face as more assertive than the calm face, whereas they rated the calm face as more competent than the excited face (Tsai et al., 2019). Students could brainstorm potential reasons they think the valuation of excitement might influence friendliness and trustworthiness more than other traits.

3. Tell students about relevant findings (i.e., European Americans were more likely to give money to the excited vs. calm targets than East Asians were regardless of the target's race and sex because European Americans value excitement and other high arousal positive states more). Ask students if they are surprised by this finding and, if so, why ("Did you expect choices to depend more on race and sex than they did in the research studies?").

4. Ask students to think about how people learn to value specific states ("Where do you think messages about ideal affect come from?"). Students could be encouraged to consider different forms of media (e.g., advertisements, official website photos) that teach people which states are ideal (e.g., Tsai et al., 2007, 2016).

5. Ask students to brainstorm other situations in which ideal affect might influence choices (e.g., health care, employment, education). For example, cultural and individual differences in ideal affect and social judgments are related to whom people choose as their physician (Sims et al., 2014) as well as whom people hire (Bencharit et al., 2019). Students could be encouraged to consider how their ideal affect might influence their judgments of their dormmates, classmates, and professors.

6. Ask students to think about potential problems of ideal affect match and possible solutions. For instance, if people judge others as friendly because their emotional expressions match people's ideal affect, they may inaccurately judge others' friendliness, especially if their ideal affect differs from their targets' ideal affect. Why is this problematic? Is there a way to curb these ideal affect biases?

These discussions could be conducted with the entire class, or students could be encouraged to discuss these questions in a smaller group or with a partner before sharing with the rest of the class.

ASSIGNMENT

You might want to assign a postactivity reflection assignment. Any of the questions in the Discussion section could be used for this assignment, as well as the following:

1. Think about your cultural background. What emotions have you been taught to value? Individuals differ in how they respond to their culture's ideals. Do you think you are more or less aligned with your culture's ideals, and in what ways?

2. How do your culture's affective ideals influence how you judge others?

3. Tsai's affect valuation theory distinguishes between *ideal affect* (how people ideally want to feel) and *actual affect* (how people actually feel). In the studies already described, ideal affect predicted social judgments but actual affect did not. Why might ideal affect matter more than actual affect in these cases?

4. When judges and targets are from the same culture or share the same affective ideals, ideal affect match is more likely to lead to accurate social judgments. When might this be helpful? When judges and targets are from different cultures or hold different affective ideals, social judgment errors are more likely to occur. When might this be harmful?

5. If students completed the Affect Valuation Index, you could ask the following questions: How did your actual affect differ from your ideal affect? Which states do you ideally want to feel more than you actually feel? What are some things you can do to bring your actual affect more in line with your ideal affect?

APPENDIX 25.1: Sample Slides for In-Class Activity

Below are sample images for the in-class activity. You can use different excited and calm targets for each question using the photos of your choice.

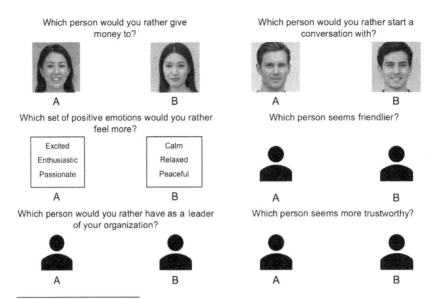

Note. Photos in the example slides and surveys were drawn with permission from the Academic Dataset by Generated Photos. These photos were not the faces used in the research described in this chapter.

A printable version of this appendix can be downloaded from the APA website at https://www.apa.org/pubs/books/more-activities-teaching-positive-psychology.

APPENDIX 25.2: Sample Online Survey

Below is a sample online survey variation of the activity. If using this format, you will have to create questions for each excited and calm target.

If you had $10, how much money would you give to this person?

$0	$1	$2	$3	$4	$5	$6	$7	$8	$9	$10
○	○	○	○	○	○	○	○	○	○	○

To what extent is this person...

	Not at all 1	2	Moderately 3	4	Extremely 5
friendly?	○	○	○	○	○
trustworthy?	○	○	○	○	○

Note. Photos in the example slides and surveys were drawn with permission from the Academic Dataset by Generated Photos. These photos were not the faces used in the research described in this chapter.

A printable version of this appendix can be downloaded from the APA website at https://www.apa.org/pubs/books/more-activities-teaching-positive-psychology.

APPENDIX 25.3: Affect Valuation Index (Abridged for Teaching Purposes)

Listed below are a number of words that describe feelings. Some of the feelings are very similar to each other, whereas others are very different from each other. Read each word and then rate how often you ACTUALLY have that feeling over the course of a typical week, using the following scale:

1	2	3	4	5
Never	A small amount of the time	Half the time	Most of the time	All the time

Over the course of a typical week, I ACTUALLY feel ...

enthusiastic _____	happy _____	inactive _____
lonely _____	sad _____	nervous _____
satisfied _____	calm _____	relaxed _____
sleepy _____	fearful _____	aroused _____
excited _____	sluggish _____	angry _____

Note. "Aroused" means activated or energized, physically and mentally. If it's helpful, you can provide a definition in the measure.

Now, please read each word again and rate how often you would IDEALLY like to have that feeling over the course of a typical week, using the following scale:

1	2	3	4	5
Never	A small amount of the time	Half the time	Most of the time	All the time

Over the course of a typical week, I would IDEALLY like to feel ...

enthusiastic _____	happy _____	inactive _____
lonely _____	sad _____	nervous _____
satisfied _____	calm _____	relaxed _____
sleepy _____	fearful _____	aroused _____
excited _____	sluggish _____	angry _____

Scoring:

- To calculate actual high arousal positive scores, average how much students reported actually feeling "enthusiastic" and "excited." To calculate ideal high arousal positive scores, average how much students reported ideally wanting to feel "enthusiastic" and "excited."

- To calculate actual low arousal positive scores, average how much students reported actually feeling "calm" and "relaxed." To calculate ideal low arousal positive scores, average how much students reported ideally wanting to feel "calm" and "relaxed."

- To calculate actual positive scores, average how much students reported actually feeling "satisfied" and "content." To calculate ideal positive scores, average how much students reported ideally wanting to feel "satisfied" and "content."

- To calculate actual negative scores, average how much students reported actually feeling "lonely" and "sad." To calculate ideal negative scores, average how much students reported ideally wanting to feel "lonely" and "sad."

- To calculate actual high arousal negative scores, average how much students reported actually feeling "fearful," "nervous," and "angry." To calculate ideal high arousal negative scores, average how much students reported ideally wanting to feel "fearful," "nervous," and "angry."

- To calculate actual low arousal negative scores, average how much students reported actually feeling "sleepy" and "sluggish." To calculate ideal low arousal negative scores, average how much students reported ideally wanting to feel "sleepy" and "sluggish."

- To calculate actual high arousal scores, take the rating for how much students reported actually feeling "aroused." To calculate ideal high arousal scores, use the rating for how much students reported ideally wanting to feel "aroused."

- To calculate actual low arousal scores, take the rating for how much students reported actually feeling "inactive." To calculate ideal low arousal scores, use the rating for how much students reported ideally wanting to feel "inactive."

In addition to calculating raw scores, you could also calculate ipsatized scores to control for individual and cultural differences in response styles. To calculate ipsatized scores, for each student, first calculate the mean and standard deviation across all 15 actual emotion ratings. Next, for each individual actual emotion item, subtract the mean and divide by the standard deviation. Repeat these steps for ideal emotions: First, calculate the mean and standard deviation across all 15 ideal emotion ratings, and then for each individual ideal affect item, subtract the mean and divide by the standard deviation. After ipsatizing scores, you can calculate the aggregates as described.

A printable version of this appendix can be downloaded from the APA website at https://www.apa.org/pubs/books/more-activities-teaching-positive-psychology.

REFERENCES

Abele, A. E., & Bruckmüller, S. (2011). The bigger one of the "Big Two"? Preferential processing of communal information. *Journal of Experimental Social Psychology*, 47(5), 935–948. https://doi.org/10.1016/j.jesp.2011.03.028

Bencharit, L. Z., Ho, Y. W., Fung, H. H., Yeung, D. Y., Stephens, N. M., Romero-Canyas, R., & Tsai, J. L. (2019). Should job applicants be excited or calm? The role of culture and ideal affect in employment settings. *Emotion*, 19(3), 377–401. https://doi.org/10.1037/emo0000444

Gunnery, S. D., & Ruben, M. A. (2016). Perceptions of Duchenne and non-Duchenne smiles: A meta-analysis. *Cognition and Emotion*, 30(3), 501–515. https://doi.org/10.1080/02699931.2015.1018817

Knutson, B. (1996). Facial expressions of emotion influence interpersonal trait inferences. *Journal of Nonverbal Behavior*, 20(3), 165–182. https://doi.org/10.1007/BF02281954

Krumhuber, E., Manstead, A. S., & Kappas, A. (2007). Temporal aspects of facial displays in person and expression perception: The effects of smile dynamics, head-tilt, and gender. *Journal of Nonverbal Behavior*, 31(1), 39–56. https://doi.org/10.1007/s10919-006-0019-x

Montepare, J. M., & Dobish, H. (2003). The contribution of emotion perceptions and their overgeneralizations to trait impressions. *Journal of Nonverbal Behavior*, 27(4), 237–254. https://doi.org/10.1023/A:1027332800296

Park, B., Blevins, E., Knutson, B., & Tsai, J. L. (2017). Neurocultural evidence that ideal affect match promotes giving. *Social Cognitive and Affective Neuroscience*, 12(7), 1083–1096. https://doi.org/10.1093/scan/nsx047

Park, B., Genevsky, A., Knutson, B., & Tsai, J. (2020). Culturally valued facial expressions enhance loan request success. *Emotion*, 20(7), 1137–1153. https://doi.org/10.1037/emo0000642

Sims, T., Tsai, J. L., Koopmann-Holm, B., Thomas, E. A. C., & Goldstein, M. K. (2014). Choosing a physician depends on how you want to feel: The role of ideal affect in health-related decision making. *Emotion*, 14(1), 187–192. https://doi.org/10.1037/a0034372

Todorov, A. (2008). Evaluating faces on trustworthiness: An extension of systems for recognition of emotions signaling approach/avoidance behaviors. *Annals of the New York Academy of Sciences*, 1124(1), 208–224. https://doi.org/10.1196/annals.1440.012

Tsai, J. L. (2007). Ideal affect: Cultural causes and behavioral consequences. *Perspectives on Psychological Science*, 2(3), 242–259. https://doi.org/10.1111/j.1745-6916.2007.00043.x

Tsai, J. L. (2021). Why does passion matter more in individualistic cultures? *Proceedings of the National Academy of Sciences of the United States of America*, 118(14), Article e2102055118. https://doi.org/10.1073/pnas.2102055118

Tsai, J. L., Ang, J. Y., Blevins, E., Goernandt, J., Fung, H. H., Jiang, D., Elliott, J., Kölzer, A., Uchida, Y., Lee, Y. C., Lin, Y., Zhang, X., Govindama, Y., & Haddouk, L. (2016). Leaders' smiles reflect cultural differences in ideal affect. *Emotion*, 16(2), 183–195. https://doi.org/10.1037/emo0000133

Tsai, J. L., Blevins, E., Bencharit, L. Z., Chim, L., Fung, H. H., & Yeung, D. Y. (2019). Cultural variation in social judgments of smiles: The role of ideal affect. *Journal of Personality and Social Psychology*, 116(6), 966–988. https://doi.org/10.1037/pspp0000192

Tsai, J. L., Chen, D., Yang, A., Cachia, J., et al. (2023). Two decades of ideal affect: Enduring and emerging patterns [Manuscript under review].

Tsai, J. L., Knutson, B., & Fung, H. H. (2006). Cultural variation in affect valuation. *Journal of Personality and Social Psychology, 90*(2), 288–307. https://doi.org/10.1037/0022-3514.90.2.288

Tsai, J. L., Louie, J. Y., Chen, E. E., & Uchida, Y. (2007). Learning what feelings to desire: Socialization of ideal affect through children's storybooks. *Personality and Social Psychology Bulletin, 33*(1), 17–30. https://doi.org/10.1177/0146167206292749

26

Fear of Happiness

Liudmila Titova

This activity can be used to introduce or lead further discussion of the concept of fear of happiness and also explore cultural aspects of definitions of happiness.

CONCEPT

This activity uses a combination of reflection, self-report scale assessment, and discussion to explore different understandings of happiness for students themselves and across cultures. Specifically, it introduces the concept of fear of happiness—a common phenomenon in some non-Western cultures. This activity could be integrated with a discussion of topics on culture and happiness, emotions, and well-being.

MATERIALS NEEDED

Students will need either a piece of paper or a laptop to record their reflections. They will also need a copy of the Fear of Happiness scale (Appendix 26.1) and the table of the scores by country (Appendix 26.2).

ACTIVITY SETTING

This activity can be done in an in-person or online classroom. Because there are multiple steps involved in the activity, it is best to do it in a synchronous format (either in-person or via video call), but it can also be adapted to asynchronous learning environments.

https://doi.org/10.1037/0000417-026
More Activities for Teaching Positive Psychology: A Guide for Instructors, S. D. Pressman and A. C. Parks (Editors)

ACTIVITY DURATION

All steps of this activity will take about 30 minutes.

SUGGESTED READINGS

- Optional readings for after the activity:
  - Oishi et al. (2013)
  - Joshanloo et al. (2014)

BACKGROUND AND INSTRUCTIONS

It is common for Westerners to see happiness as a universally desirable goal and define happiness in a very positive way. Moreover, happiness has been identified as an important policy goal by some nations, such as the U.K., France, and Bhutan, among others (Oishi et al., 2013). However, viewing happiness as one of the most important goals in life is not a worldwide vision, which may be due to many cultural traditions employing very different views of happiness. For instance, people in some cultures are likely to experience a *fear of happiness*, that is, a belief that happiness has a "dark side" and is accompanied by negativity (Joshanloo, 2013; Joshanloo et al., 2014). The understanding of happiness in many non-Western cultures is ambivalent and not as straightforwardly positive as in the Western understanding (Lu & Gilmour, 2004). For example, some of the traditional beliefs suggest that experiencing happiness and joy is always followed by negative events or misfortune (Joshanloo et al., 2014). In other traditions, expressing happiness is believed to be connected to the *evil eye*, the idea that the envy of others can cultivate hardship or bad luck (Sheldon et al., 2017). Additionally, while in many Western cultures people who express their happiness to others through smiling are perceived positively, in other cultures, smiling people are seen as less intelligent and more dishonest (Krys et al., 2016). Another cultural difference is connected to the permanency of happiness. Specifically, in the United States, the pursuit of happiness is seen as a fundamental human right and something that can be permanently acquired, whereas many non-Westerners tend to define happiness as temporary and connected to luck or fortune and, therefore, not worth pursuing (Oishi et al., 2013). These views and beliefs can lead to hesitation or even fear of happiness in these cultures.

This activity can take place before or after students learn about the concept of fear of happiness. This concept is a good fit with discussions about culture and happiness, emotions, and religion. If students haven't yet been introduced to the concept, depending on students' cultural background, the concept might seem surprising to them. On the other hand, if students have already learned about fear of happiness, they might see the connection between some of the questions asked in the activity and the concept and perhaps will be able to engage in a more in-depth discussion. Either way, this activity will provide students with an opportunity to engage in active learning and further their understanding of the material. Before the activity, the instructor will need copies of the questionnaire (Appendix 26.1)[1] and the table of the scores by country (Appendix 26.2).

1. Ask students the following question: "What is your personal definition of happiness?" Students should jot down their thoughts. After they have a few minutes to think about this question, ask students to discuss their definitions in small groups. Then, ask students to share the main points from their group discussions with the rest of the class and the instructor.

2. Next, ask students to return to their small groups and discuss the following questions: "What were the defining features of happiness in your definitions? What aspects of your definitions were similar to your classmates, and what aspects were different? Did you define happiness as something permanent or fleeting? As something connected to inner emotional states or outside circumstances? In the personal definitions of happiness that you discussed, was there an element of negativity? Meaning was your definition strictly positive, or did it have other emotions mixed in? If yes, please elaborate. If not, please consider the role that negative emotions play in our understanding of happiness. How would you revise your definition to include negative emotions or feelings?" Again, after students have some time to discuss these questions in groups, ask them to share their thoughts with the rest of the class and the instructor.

3. Ask students to complete the Fear of Happiness scale (Appendix 26.1) and calculate their average score.

4. After calculating students' scores, show them the table of scores from different countries (Appendix 26.2) and have them compare their Fear of Happiness score to the averages presented. The table doesn't include results from many of the Western countries your students might be coming from, which makes it even more interesting to compare. If you are teaching in a country that is not represented in the table, you can ask students to propose where the national average from your country would fall in this table if it were to be added.

5. Finally, ask students to go back to their small groups and discuss the following questions: "What are your thoughts after completing the scale? What do you think of the items of the scale and the concept of fear of happiness? What factors might contribute to the cultural differences in the levels of fear of happiness? Why do you think it is important to discuss this

---

[1] When I conducted this activity, I created an online version of the scale using Qualtrics that showed the mean score on the scale to students upon completion. This might be something to consider doing with your class, and if students are from many countries, you could even present data in real time as part of the class exercise on how the scores from class varied by country of origin in the class and other demographic variables (e.g., sex).

concept when learning about happiness and positive psychology? What practical implications does it have for living in an increasingly multicultural world?"[2] Again, after students have enough time to discuss these questions, ask them to share their thoughts with the rest of the class and the instructor.

6. This in-class activity can also be continued as an out-of-class assignment. Specifically, students can be asked to write a short paper or prepare a presentation examining cultural differences in definitions of happiness, experiences of emotions, and cultural traditions that lead to fear of happiness.

DISCUSSION

For Westerners, happiness is often seen as an ultimate goal or at least something that is highly desired. If your students are predominantly from a Western culture, you will probably see this when asking students about their definition of happiness. However, viewing happiness as strictly positive and desirable is not a worldwide phenomenon, as the concept of fear of happiness demonstrates. At first glance, it might appear like a foreign phenomenon for a Westerner, but when you ask students to specifically consider if their definition of happiness includes something negative or some mixed emotions, you will hear students saying they might endorse this belief at least to some extent. If your students come from cultures where this view of happiness (i.e. happiness not being seen as a strictly positive concept) is more common, that might be seen in their personal definitions from the beginning and might become even more pronounced with further questions that ask them to consider the role of negative emotions in their understanding of happiness. The discussion of fear of happiness is connected to varying definitions of happiness across cultures and among individuals, and that is why this activity starts with students thinking about their personal definitions.

If you are teaching in the United States, you can also connect this discussion to changes in the definition of happiness throughout time in the United States. Oishi et al. (2013) extensively reviewed the definitions of happiness and their changes throughout history. They found that the understanding of happiness in the United States used to be quite similar to a lot of other cultures today—that it has an accidental characteristic, as being connected to luck or fate. However, this view was seen only before the 1920s in the United States. Since then, the more modern American view of happiness being a personal pursuit connected to an array of positive emotions has been prevalent (Oishi et al., 2013; Titova & Sheldon, 2019). Moreover, this definition of happiness in the United States that concentrates on positive inner feelings is not widely shared across the globe;

---

[2] Depending on when this activity is introduced, the depth of discussion might vary. If students have not heard about the concept yet, their discussion would be more preliminary, but if they were already introduced to the concept in prior lectures or coursework, they might be able to get into deeper discussion on this topic.

instead, happiness is often understood through favorable external circumstances that can be fleeting (Lu & Gilmour, 2004; Oishi et al., 2013).

If you are teaching in areas where fear of happiness is endorsed, you can spend time discussing what cultural and religious beliefs help explain the likelihood of such endorsement. Additionally, you can discuss what beliefs and views that Westerners share make fear of happiness less common (for instance, the mention of the pursuit of happiness in the Declaration of Independence in the United States).

It is important to explore cultural differences in viewing and pursuing happiness while learning about positive psychology. It is often assumed that everyone wants to be happy and do things to achieve happiness; however, as fear of happiness demonstrates, it is not always the case. This also has a very important practical implication of using activities designed to promote happiness, as they should not be applied to all without a better understanding of the cultural context in which they might be occurring. Research has shown that cultural differences in experiencing emotions and the understanding of happiness lead to varied results when the same activities are performed by different cultural groups (Layous et al., 2013; Parks & Titova, 2016; Titova et al., 2017).

This activity demonstrates that people's definitions of happiness can vary, and this variation is especially pronounced when comparing across cultures. Moreover, this activity introduces the phenomenon of fear of happiness and explores it further in a cultural context.

APPENDIX 26.1: Fear of Happiness Scale

The link to the online version of this (in Qualtrics) can be found at https://osf.io/5qjfs/

STEP 1

Please rate the extent to which you agree with each statement, using this scale from 1 to 7:

1	2	3	4	5	6	7
Strongly disagree						Strongly agree

1. I prefer not to be too joyful because usually joy is followed by sadness.

2. I believe the more cheerful and happy I am, the more I should expect bad things to occur in my life.

3. Disasters often follow good fortune.

4. Having lots of joy and fun causes bad things to happen.

5. Excessive joy has some bad consequences.

Note. Adapted from "The Influence of Fear of Happiness Beliefs on Responses to the Satisfaction With Life Scale," by M. Joshanloo, 2013, *Personality and Individual Differences*, *54*(5), p. 648 (https://doi.org/10.1016/j.paid.2012.11.011). Copyright 2013 by Elsevier. Adapted with permission.

STEP 2

To calculate your score on the scale, add your responses to the five statements above, then divide them by five. This will give you your average score (or a mean score) on the scale. If calculated correctly, this number should be somewhere between one and seven.

A printable version of this appendix can be downloaded from the APA website at https://www.apa.org/pubs/books/more-activities-teaching-positive-psychology.

APPENDIX 26.2: National Levels of Fear of Happiness Scores

Country	Average score
Brazil	1.98
New Zealand	2.39
Iran	2.47
Korea	2.65
Russia	2.84
Japan	3.17
Malaysia	3.32
Singapore	3.39
Kuwait	3.55
Kenya	3.56
Hong Kong	3.74
Taiwan	3.76
Pakistan	3.80
India	3.88

Note. Adapted from "Cross-Cultural Validation of Fear of Happiness Scale Across 14 National Groups," by M. Joshanloo, Z. Lepshokova, T. Panyusheva, A. Natalia, W. Poon, V. Yeung, S. Sundaram, M. Achoui, R. Asano, T. Igarashi, S. Tsukamoto, M. Rizwan, I. A. Khilji, M. C. Ferreira, J. S. Pang, L. S. Ho, G. Han, J. Bae, and D. Jiang, 2014, *Journal of Cross-Cultural Psychology*, *45*(2), p. 250 (https://doi.org/10.1177/002202211350 5357). Copyright 2014 by SAGE Publications. Adapted with permission.

A printable version of this appendix can be downloaded from the APA website at https://www.apa.org/pubs/books/more-activities-teaching-positive-psychology.

REFERENCES

Joshanloo, M. (2013). The influence of fear of happiness beliefs on responses to the Satisfaction With Life Scale. *Personality and Individual Differences, 54*(5), 647–651. https://doi.org/10.1016/j.paid.2012.11.011

Joshanloo, M., Lepshokova, Z., Panyusheva, T., Natalia, A., Poon, W., Yeung, V., Sundaram, S., Achoui, M., Asano, R., Igarashi, T., Tsukamoto, S., Rizwan, M., Khilji, I. A., Ferreira, M. C., Pang, J. S., Ho, L. S., Han, G., Bae, J., & Jiang, D. (2014). Cross-cultural validation of Fear of Happiness scale across 14 national groups. *Journal of Cross-Cultural Psychology, 45*(2), 246–264. https://doi.org/10.1177/0022022113505357

Krys, K., Vauclair, C.-M., Capaldi, C. A., Lun, V. M. C., Bond, M. H., Domínguez-Espinosa, A., Torres, C., Lipp, O. V., Manickam, L. S., Xing, C., Antalíková, R., Pavlopoulos, V., Teyssier, J., Hur, T., Hansen, K., Szarota, P., Ahmed, R. A., Burtceva, E., Chkhaidze, A., . . . Yu, A. A. (2016). Be careful where you smile: Culture shapes judgments of intelligence and honesty of smiling individuals. *Journal of Nonverbal Behavior, 40*(2), 101–116. https://doi.org/10.1007/s10919-015-0226-4

Layous, K., Lee, H., Choi, I., & Lyubomirsky, S. (2013). Culture matters when designing a successful happiness-increasing activity: A comparison of the United States and South Korea. *Journal of Cross-Cultural Psychology, 44*(8), 1294–1303. https://doi.org/10.1177/0022022113487591

Lu, L., & Gilmour, R. (2004). Culture and conceptions of happiness: Individual oriented and social oriented SWB. *Journal of Happiness Studies, 5*(3), 269–291. https://doi.org/10.1007/s10902-004-8789-5

Oishi, S., Graham, J., Kesebir, S., & Galinha, I. C. (2013). Concepts of happiness across time and cultures. *Personality and Social Psychology Bulletin, 39*(5), 559–577. https://doi.org/10.1177/0146167213480042

Parks, A. C., & Titova, L. (2016). Positive psychology interventions: An overview. In A. M. Wood & J. Johnson (Eds.), *The Wiley handbook of positive clinical psychology: An integrative approach to studying and improving well-being* (pp. 307–320). Wiley-Blackwell.

Sheldon, K. M., Titova, L., Gordeeva, T. O., Osin, E. N., Lyubomirsky, S., & Bogomaz, S. (2017). Russians inhibit the expression of happiness to strangers: Testing a display rule model. *Journal of Cross-Cultural Psychology, 48*(5), 718–733. https://doi.org/10.1177/0022022117699883

Titova, L., & Sheldon, K. M. (2019). Why do I feel this way? Attributional assessment of happiness and unhappiness. *The Journal of Positive Psychology, 14*(5), 549–562. https://doi.org/10.1080/17439760.2018.1519081

Titova, L., Wagstaff, A. E., & Parks, A. C. (2017). Disentangling the effects of gratitude and optimism: A cross-cultural investigation. *Journal of Cross-Cultural Psychology, 48*(5), 754–770. https://doi.org/10.1177/0022022117699278

27

Promoting Positive Psychological Character Strengths in Diverse Meso- and Macrosettings

Laura P. Kohn-Wood, Guerdiana Thelomar, and Brittney R. Denson (Davis)

Students will break into small groups to conceptualize a community organization–focused, strength-based, positive psychology intervention and compete for a hypothetical $100,000 grant. The activity will highlight the complexity of applying positive psychology interventions at the meso- or macroscale and in multicultural groups rather than the typical individual focus of most activities.

CONCEPT

Positive psychology researchers have sought not just to define and categorize character strengths (e.g., C. Peterson & Seligman, 2004) but to understand whether strengths can be individually and collectively expressed; whether character traits are innate, learned, developed, or influenced by a variety of factors; and how strengths are linked to flourishing or, conversely, related to languishing and civic disengagement. Psychological strengths research, however, has been critiqued as ignoring oppressed communities and people of color (Henrich et al., 2010; L. P. Kohn-Wood & Thomas, 2016) for whom the development and expression of strengths like resilience, perseverance, and transcendence have been utilized as cultural tools to survive and thrive despite denigration. Further,

https://doi.org/10.1037/0000417-027
More Activities for Teaching Positive Psychology: A Guide for Instructors, S. D. Pressman and A. C. Parks (Editors)

positive psychology constructs such as strengths and virtues have been described as "deeply rooted in Western ideologies" (van Zyl et al., 2024, p. 221) that focus on the independence of the self and ignore Eastern concepts of interdependence (Hendriks et al., 2019; Kristjánsson, 2013; van Zyl et al., 2024). Researchers therefore assert that cultural biases are facilitated in the assessment and development of positive characteristics (Christopher, 2014; Kristjánsson, 2013; van Zyl et al., 2024). Others have suggested that positive psychology ignores societal structural contexts and is therefore systematically biased with regard to ethnicity, culture, and socioeconomic status (Englar-Carlson & Smart, 2014; Fernández-Ríos & Novo, 2012). Thus, it is crucial for students to understand human behavior within multidimensional meso- and macrosystems while also learning to interrogate how specific character strengths may or may not apply to diverse populations or may reflect existing culturally based characteristics related to the endurance and survival of minoritized communities.

The following activity provides an opportunity for students to review positive psychology character strengths while attempting to expand, complicate, and apply the concepts to large, diverse units of analysis. Students will also be able to critique the translation and promotion of character strengths in real-world settings. Finally, this quasi-gamified activity should stimulate a high level of student engagement given the faux competitive conditions. Instructors can amp up the level of competitiveness by providing tangible prizes for the winning group(s) that could include snacks or small gifts, among others.

MATERIALS NEEDED

As a classroom-based activity, providing either a handout or projected (e.g., PowerPoint slide) image of the Values in Action six virtues and 24 character strengths can be helpful. An example list of virtues and strengths with brief definitions and links can be found on the Positivity Project website at https://posproject.org/character-strengths/. Not providing the definitions may force students to research the concepts in service of completing the task and thereby reinforce learning, but it may take more time. Giving students a general overview of the terms, however, may be more equitable for students with different learning/access needs, and students will still have to do the work to develop and defend proposals or create the funders' rubric. Also, providing easily accessible instructions to both the project groups and the funder group will allow the activity to move more quickly.

ACTIVITY SETTING

This activity fits into class topics of positive psychology character strengths[1] and virtues, the applicability and translational potential of positive psychology, and diversity as it relates to positive psychology concepts. Ancillary topics of this

---

[1] This activity will be easier for students if completed after learning about character strengths and/or doing a strengths-oriented learning activity such as Chapter 15 in this book.

activity are related to community-based work, funding for community interventions, and collaborative processes to promote change. This classroom activity can be completed in person, in a synchronous remote class, or, with additional planning, in an asynchronous remote classroom where students can meet virtually to discuss, plan, and present.

For in-person facilitation, groups can meet in locations outside and around the classroom, depending upon available facilities to minimize noise and distractions. If that is not possible, students would need to be able to cluster in small groups within the classroom. While the intervention groups are meeting, the funder group should review the character strengths, discuss how they can or cannot be applied in diverse macro- and mesosettings, and develop criteria and a rubric for rating and ranking the intervention presentations they will hear. After all the presentations are delivered, the funder group will need some time for private deliberation. During this time, the intervention groups can either take a break or the instructor can facilitate a larger class discussion about the process of the project, challenges the groups faced, why the groups chose the strength and intervention they presented, and whether they learned something new about positive psychology character strengths from trying to incorporate them in a community-based activity.

If the class is being taught synchronously and virtually, links to a list of the strengths and the instructions for the activity can be provided remotely. Students can be divided into groups and put in breakout rooms on the remote platform to discuss and develop their intervention. After working in small groups, the whole class can come back together to present the intervention. The funder group can go into a breakout room to deliberate while the intervention groups continue with the aforementioned discussion in the main classroom setting.

If the class is being taught asynchronously, instructions for the activity and the list of strengths can be provided on the teaching platform discussion board. The small groups can be predetermined and listed along with additional information about how the groups can work together remotely on a predetermined schedule using a common platform. Students would need access to instructions on how groups can record and upload their presentations and/or submit a written document describing the intervention. They will also need a platform (e.g., discussion board) on which to work together. The funder group can similarly work together at a predetermined time to create their rubric for assessing the interventions, share their rankings, notify the final winner(s) via email or other online communication tool, and record and upload a video presenting the winner(s) and the criteria applied to determine success.

ACTIVITY DURATION

This activity takes a considerable amount of time, so it is ideal if the entire class time can be devoted to the activity, assuming a 50-, 60-, or 75-minute class period. The activity can be completed in a minimum of 45 minutes, but given previous experience, allotting a shorter amount of time decreases the quality and detail of the intervention projects. If the activity is to be done in 30 to 45 minutes, consider removing one or two of the components of the intervention, such as not requiring a budget or addressing assessment or effectiveness. The bulk of the time—at least 30 minutes—should be devoted to developing the intervention (or the criteria and evaluation rubric for the group judging the interventions). The rest of the time should be devoted to small group presentations of their interventions with a strict time limit of 3 to 7 minutes (Shark Tank–style), depending on class size. The remaining 5 to 8 minutes would be devoted to the funder group's deliberations and presentation of the criteria and winner(s).

Alternatively, the activity could be split into two shorter class periods. For example, the instructor could introduce the activity and facilitate grouping for 10 minutes at the end of one class period and have groups prepare the intervention presentation or criteria and evaluation rubric as a homework assignment. Groups could then present and have their intervention presentations judged in the next class period, which would only require an additional 30 minutes of in-class time.

As a synchronous class activity, similar timings would be necessary, or perhaps a little less time would be needed since there would be no need for students to move around a physical classroom. Obviously, an asynchronous activity will not take up class time per se, but 20 to 30 minutes should be set aside for groups to meet, discuss, and record the presentation, plus additional time for students to watch the video presentations.

SUGGESTED READINGS

- Preactivity readings:
  - C. Peterson and Park (2006)
  - Park and Peterson (2009)
- Postactivity readings:
  - Kelly (1971)
  - Schutte and Malouff (2019)
  - L. P. Kohn-Wood and Thomas (2016)

BACKGROUND AND INSTRUCTIONS

The fields of community psychology and multicultural psychology critically emerged in the late nineties as a contradiction to traditional psychology's persistent focus on individual medicalized distress and the comparative nature of psychological research that consistently portrayed people of color with a deficit lens. For example, traditional psychology focuses on individual functioning without including cultural and contextual realities. Community psychology, for instance, challenges the individualistic approach by emphasizing the influence of systemic factors like social inequality, while multicultural psychology underscores the importance of culturally sensitive interventions, critiquing the one-size-fits-all methods in traditional psychology. These critiques reflect the growing recognition that understanding human well-being requires a broader, more inclusive, and contextually relevant perspective.

Community psychology is a field with roots in the community mental health and social change movements in the late sixties and early seventies. The field explicitly identifies an ecological or contextual, rather than individual, focus in research and practice (Kelly, 1971). Community psychology also utilizes an epistemological model that centers on nested and interdependent micro (individual/family), meso (organizations/communities), and macro (cultures/societies) factors in systems that are seen as determinants of human behavior (Bronfenbrenner, 1977). This ecological framework counters traditional psychology's focus on understanding isolated individual and independent variables as uniquely determining outcomes. Community psychology emphasizes the importance of culture and context (Kelly, 1971, 1986; O'Donnell, 2006; Trickett, 2009) and centers research and action on preventing negative conditions and promoting positive characteristics versus exclusively focusing on reactive interventions. Further, the field holds an explicit orientation toward individual (Rappaport, 1987; Zimmerman, 1995) and organizational empowerment (N. A. Peterson & Zimmerman, 2004), individual and community assets and strengths (Maton et al., 2004; Perkins et al., 2002), and the potential for positive social change (Heller & Monahan, 1977; Maton, 2008; Seidman, 1988). While the field has never gained the same traction that positive psychology has, community psychologists have been examining positive traits of individuals and communities for at least 3 decades prior to the emergence of positive psychology, characterized as a science for the "new century [that] will allow psychologists to understand and build those factors that allow individuals, communities, and societies to flourish" (Seligman & Csikszentmihalyi, 2000, p. 13).

Similarly, a growing number of diverse psychology researchers in the field began to openly question the Eurocentric nature of the field in the late sixties and early seventies, noting that most psychology studies included nondiverse participants and rendered findings that were assumed to be universal. When people of color were included in psychological research, differences in cognition, learning, behavior, and other outcomes were assumed to be problematic, abnormal, and reflective of a deficit in functioning. Research that focused solely on people of color was routinely rejected by psychology journals for not including an adequate comparison group, which was usually defined as White, with the assumption that psychologists would not be able to conclude anything from monoracial samples unless they were compared with a sample derived from a White majority group. Despite these challenges, researchers persisted in developing and growing a research literature that evolved from cross-cultural psychology and other comparative approaches, including Black psychology, Latino/a psychology, and Asian psychology bodies of work with concomitant peer-reviewed journal outlets and divisions of the American Psychological Association. This emergent literature was sometimes collectively identified as the field of multicultural psychology.

It is within these traditions of scholarship that emerging knowledge began to build regarding race-based and cultural perceptions, including, among others, effective methods of coping with denigration among minoritized groups (Brondolo et al., 2009; Clark & Harrell, 1982; L. P. Kohn-Wood et al., 2012; Plummer & Slane, 1996; Sanders Thompson, 2006; Utsey et al., 2000), the positive direct and indirect effects of racial identity (Banks & Kohn-Wood, 2007; Sellers et al., 2006; Sellers & Shelton, 2003), and the epidemiological evidence for protective factors related to relatively high levels of flourishing (Eshun & Packer, 2016; Keyes, 2009) and lower risk for psychiatric disorder (Breslau et al., 2006; L. Kohn-Wood et al., 2016; Williams et al., 2007).

Given these oft-ignored psychological foundations that predate positive psychology, it is critically important that students understand the overlapping conceptual bases for the constructs they encounter when learning about positive psychologists' work, particularly the identification and study of positive character strengths (C. Peterson & Seligman, 2004). Acknowledging the foundational work of community psychologists in terms of the promotion of positive social and behavioral functioning and the importance of understanding human behavior within systems across multiple levels provides a blueprint for the application of positive psychological principles. Awareness of the impetus for and presence of multicultural psychology traditions will provide students the intellectual space to interrogate the specific character strengths identified by positive psychology and consider how they may or may not apply to diverse populations or may reflect existing culturally based characteristics that are related to the endurance and survival of communities of color over centuries. In fact, psychological science has built a knowledge base almost entirely on what is described as WEIRD populations—Western, educated, industrialized, rich, and democratic people (Henrich et al., 2010). Despite this recognition, a 2017 study showed that in 2008, approximately 92% of published research in one area of psychology was composed of WEIRD participants, with no meaningful change over the next 7 years (Nielsen et al., 2017). As the authors point out, "lack of attention to cultural variation and its psychological consequences risks yielding incomplete, and potentially inaccurate, conclusions" (see Nielsen et al., 2017, p. 32, citing multiple studies).

This problem is equally present in positive psychology research, which is most frequently done with WEIRD samples (e.g., Hendriks et al., 2019), raising questions about the universality of interventions. Furthermore, there is a distinct weakness in character strengths research as it primarily relies on values rooted in Western individualism. Given that most of the world is communally oriented, particularly for some marginalized populations, character strengths theory may not adequately capture the values and strengths that matter most to these communities. Little work has been done on strengths at the community level, which could be especially relevant for such populations. Additionally, the character strengths list, as outlined by Peterson and Seligman in their 2004 handbook, was never intended to be definitive (e.g., Elizardi, 2012), and it is plausible that there are missing strengths that hold significant importance for certain populations, such as familism, ethnic identity, and spirituality (Jeglic et al., 2016). This underscores the need for a more culturally informed and inclusive approach to character strengths theory and research. While character strengths have been studied globally, including in some of the most remote areas of the planet (Biswas-Diener, 2006), and have shown remarkable similarity across numerous countries (Park et al., 2006), the potential limitations stemming from cultural and contextual variations cannot be ignored.

At best, the positive psychology character strengths risk ignoring how strengths and capacities long exemplified by diverse populations are manifested. At worst, the identified character strengths may be used as a neodeficit model framework for explaining away contextual and systemic factors that have prevented marginalized individuals and communities from flourishing. In fact, a robust review of "critiques and criticisms" of positive psychology describes positive psychology, including strengths and virtues, as a "decontextualized neo-liberalist ideology [that] facilitates cultural and gender biases and causes harm" (van Zyl et al., 2024, p. 220). Introducing constructs like character strengths in a class activity that both acknowledges the precursors in community and multicultural psychology and asks students to apply concepts in meso- or macrodiverse settings provides the opportunity to critique and grapple with the translational utility of positive psychology.

Instructions

Before class, create a handout that lists the six virtues and 24 character strengths (e.g., see online resources or a textbook chapter on virtues and strengths). In addition, create a slide and handout with instructions for the class activity (see Appendix 27.1). Alternatively, if there is a longer class period available, the first task for each small group should be to research the character strengths identified by positive psychology and provide the accompanying references.

In class, tell the students that they will compete in small groups by submitting a proposal for a hypothetical $100,000 grant from a positive psychology–focused foundation/funder group that seeks to promote character strengths within a community, organization, or large group. Ask students to count off to create groups of three to six students each, though the composition and size of the class will determine the best method for creating small groups (see the Activity Setting section for virtual classroom variations). This activity can be done in large lecture classes; however, if more than eight to 10 small groups are necessary, the facilitator should create an equivalent number of funder groups (at a ratio of one funder group per 8–10 small groups) so that pods of small groups can present their intervention ideas and receive evaluations from the pod's funder group simultaneously. One of the groups will represent the funder or foundation group and will develop a rubric to rate each proposal while the other small groups are developing their intervention proposal plans. The small groups will briefly present their intervention proposals to the entire class (at this point, it is important to provide the time limit for presentations), and the funder group will determine the ultimate winner.

The purpose of asking students to pitch their proposal ideas to a small funder group of their peers is to reflect the reality that resources for community-based interventions are limited and nonprofit community-based organizations often must compete for funding to promote initiatives that benefit constituents. The purpose of having one of the small groups serve as the funder group, which develops a rubric for evaluating and deciding who will receive the grant to implement an intervention, is to reinforce the process by which resources are often allocated and to develop critical thinking skills for assessing the value and impact of multiple intervention approaches.

The proposal groups must decide on one of the 24 positive psychology strengths they would like to promote and determine a community or organization (e.g., geographic neighborhood, school or campus, community-based organization) that will benefit from a programmatic intervention to enhance the positive psychology strength selected. They must acknowledge that

1. all communities possess existing strengths, and the task is to promote, empower, and amplify existing areas of positivity;

2. the expertise on any given community or organization lies within the community/group members themselves and not from an outsider; and

3. inculcating positive psychology strengths in a meso- or macrosetting is much more complex than working at the individual or microlevel.

The deliverable is a proposal for an intervention program that amplifies a positive psychology strength in the setting they have chosen that includes the following five components:

1. a definition of the selected positive psychology strength and why that strength was chosen

2. a description of the intervention activity/activities that will be implemented to promote the character strength

3. a description of the participants and what participants will do that leverages community strength and expertise

4. a description of the budget

5. a description of how they expect the participants will be affected at the macro- and mesolevels and an analysis plan for program effectiveness

While the small groups are discussing and creating their proposals, the funder group will gather to do the following:

1. review the 24 positive psychology character strengths

2. discuss, develop, and finalize criteria for judging the program proposals that the other small groups are developing

3. create a rubric for determining which of the proposals deserve to be funded from the $100,000 foundation funds they have to distribute with an emphasis on

   - how well the groups define the positive psychology strength,
   - how well the proposed intervention activities align with positive psychology and the promotion of strengths,
   - how well the groups provide evidence of how the intervention has been conceptualized at the macro- and mesolevels, and
   - how realistic and feasible the intervention will be.

After the proposal groups have completed their presentations and the funder group has completed the rating rubric, each group will choose how to present their program in a manner that integrates the participation of each group member. The presentations will be made to the funder group and will be rated based on the rubric developed. At this stage of the activity, it is helpful to remind students of a time limit for the presentations as well as an additional criterium on which the groups will be rated by the funder group (e.g., how persuasively and cohesively proposals can be presented in elevator- or Shark Tank–style presentations). Time can also be allotted for a brief question-and-answer portion after each presentation. Finally, the foundation funder groups will gather to compare ratings, briefly deliberate, and determine and announce the winning proposal(s) with justifications based on their rubric.

DISCUSSION

This exercise is designed to reinforce learning of the character strengths identified by the field of positive psychology while also acknowledging the critiques of the field as having ignored previous contributions of community and multicultural psychology research. The activity allows students to apply the concept of character strengths in a (perceived) real-world setting while incorporating important principles of community and multicultural psychology. Debriefing questions that the instructor can ask include the following:

- Why did your group choose the specific character strength selected?

- What was the most difficult aspect of designing the intervention?

- How can the promotion of character strengths be successfully implemented at the meso- or macrolevel?

- What would be the easiest and most challenging aspects of doing the intervention in reality?

- In what ways are positive psychology's identified character strengths culturally and individually bound (e.g., reflect WEIRD population bias, omit minoritized groups' individual or communal strengths)?

- What made for a particularly strong proposal?

- How do you think the identification and promotion of character strengths addresses the primary goal of positive psychology to help psychologists "learn how to build the qualities that help individuals and communities, not just ... endure and survive, but also to flourish" (Seligman & Csikszentmihalyi, 2000, p. 13)?

- What real-life examples of character strengths in action have you personally and recently witnessed?

When wrapping up this discussion, instructors can generally emphasize the importance of community psychology for understanding the concepts and principles of positive psychology, particularly when applying theoretical constructs in the field or attempting to promote positive behavior. There is, however, a need for more work in this area, given the traditional social science focus on individuals as the primary unit of analysis. Limitations in the field of community psychology include the need for (a) better tools to assess and analyze organizational, ecological, and macrolevel constructs; (b) increased delineation and measurement of cultural and contextual factors; and (c) improved utilization of community-based participatory action research to address inequity and the specific needs of marginalized populations (Rodriguez Espinosa & Verney, 2021). Additionally, a critical future challenge for community psychologists is to use the field's perspective to promote social change and transformation, particularly in an era of advanced technology and societal division. As this activity demonstrates, analysis, application, and intervention at micro-, meso-, and macrolevels is infinitely more complex than working with individuals or individual-level data.

Questions related to the proposed activity may arise, including the possibility of cultural or contextual issues associated to character strengths. Specifically, students may wonder if the list of character strengths is culturally bound or limited for understanding behavior in different settings, for example, various cultural communities or environments where basic needs are unmet and, therefore, different strengths that are more focused on surviving adversity may be primary. Other comments may focus on the peril or problem of ignoring individual behavior or individual differences in a group or system. When students perceive community psychology as blindly focusing on groups over individuals, it can be helpful to remind them that the field does not privilege one ecological level over another but rather posits that understanding individual behavior is greatly influenced by interactions across settings, and it is the bidirectional activity that often determines outcomes. Further, given the overwhelmingly primary focus on individuals in psychology in general, community psychology seeks to redress the balance by calling attention to other levels of the ecological framework.

ASSIGNMENT

The questions listed in the Discussion section could be used for a postactivity reflection paper assignment that allows each student to consider the discussion questions separately. In addition, the assignment could ask students to write about the following questions:

- In what ways do you think positive psychology is culturally bound (i.e., has been primarily focused on Western, educated, industrialized, or democratic societal ideals about what it means to flourish or to manifest a life of purpose, well-being, and happiness)?

- Why is it easier to conceptualize psychological constructs and to intervene at the individual level versus the organizational, community, or societal level?

APPENDIX 27.1: Instructions for Intervention Proposal Groups

You will compete in small groups for a $100,000 grant from a positive psychology–focused foundation that seeks to promote character strengths within a community, organization, or large group. One group of students will represent the foundation and develop a rubric to rate each proposal. You will present your proposal to the foundation (the small group representing the funders, that is, the group of individuals/judges at the foundation who decide which grants get awarded money) and the entire class, and the funders will rate your proposal based on a rubric they develop. You may choose to decide the best way to present your plan (Shark Tank–style), but bear in mind that each group will have only {INSERT TIME} minutes for this presentation. The presentation may be done by one, multiple, or all members of the small group, but be sure to integrate the contributions of each member.

First, your group must decide on one of the 24 positive psychology strengths you would like to promote, and you must determine a community or organization (e.g., geographic neighborhood, school or campus, community-based organization) that will benefit from a programmatic intervention to enhance the positive psychology strength selected.

In developing your plan, you must discuss

1. the fact that all communities possess existing strengths; therefore, your task is to promote, empower, and amplify existing areas of positivity;

2. how you will rely on the expertise of the community or organization rather than assume you know the best approach as an outsider; and

3. how inculcating positive psychology strengths in a meso- or macrosetting is much more complex than working at the individual or microlevel.

Your group's deliverable is a proposal for an intervention program that amplifies a positive psychology strength in the setting you have chosen that includes the following five components:

1. a definition of the selected positive psychology strength and why that strength was chosen

2. a description of the intervention activity/activities that will be implemented to promote the character strength

3. a description of the participants and what participants will do that leverages community strength and expertise

4. a description of the budget

5. a description of how you expect the participants to be affected at the macro- and mesolevels and an analysis plan for program effectiveness

After creating your plan, your group will present your proposal to the funder group (and the entire class) to be rated to determine which group will receive foundation funding.

INSTRUCTIONS FOR FOUNDATION FUNDERS GROUP

While the small groups are discussing and creating their proposals, you—the funder group (i.e., the group of judges that will decide who is awarded the foundation grant[s]) will gather to do the following:

1. review the 24 positive psychology character strengths

2. discuss, develop, and finalize criteria for judging the program proposals that are being developed by the other small groups

3. create a rubric for determining which of the proposals deserve to be funded from the $100,000 foundation funds they must distribute with an emphasis on

   • how well the groups define the positive psychology strength

   • how well the proposed intervention activities align with positive psychology and the promotion of strengths

   • how well the groups provide evidence of how the intervention has been conceptualized at the macro- and mesolevels

   • how realistic and feasible the intervention will be at the macro- and mesolevels

After the proposal groups have completed their presentations and you have completed the rating rubric, each group will choose how to present their program in a manner that integrates the participation of each group member. The presentations will be made to the funder group and will be rated based on the rubric developed. There will be a strict time limit for the presentations. As a foundation group of funders, you may add additional criteria on which the groups will be rated (e.g., how persuasively and cohesively can proposals be presented in elevator- or Shark Tank–style, time-limited presentations). After all the presentations, you will gather your group to compare ratings, briefly deliberate, and determine and announce the winning proposal(s) with justifications based on your rubric.

A printable version of this appendix can be downloaded from the APA website at https://www.apa.org/pubs/books/more-activities-teaching-positive-psychology.

REFERENCES

Barrks, K. H., & Kohn-Wood, L. P. (2007). The influence of racial identity profiles on the relationship between racial discrimination and depressive symptoms. *The Journal of Black Psychology, 33*(3), 331–354. https://doi.org/10.1177/0095798407302540

Biswas-Diener, R. (2006). From the equator to the North Pole: A study of character strengths. *Journal of Happiness Studies, 7*(3), 293–310. https://doi.org/10.1007/s10902-005-3646-8

Breslau, J., Aguilar-Gaxiola, S., Kendler, K. S., Su, M., Williams, D., & Kessler, R. C. (2006). Specifying race–ethnic differences in risk for psychiatric disorder in a USA national sample. *Psychological Medicine, 36*(1), 57–68. https://doi.org/10.1017/S0033291705006161

Brondolo, E., Brady ver Halen, N., Pencille, M., Beatty, D., & Contrada, R. J. (2009). Coping with racism: A selective review of the literature and a theoretical and methodological critique. *Journal of Behavioral Medicine, 32*(1), 64–88. https://doi.org/10.1007/s10865-008-9193-0

Bronfenbrenner, U. (1977). Toward an experimental ecology of human development. *American Psychologist, 32*(7), 513–531. https://doi.org/10.1037/0003-066X.32.7.513

Christopher, J. C. (2014). Putting "positive" and "psychology" in perspective: The role of Indian psychology. *Psychological Studies, 59*(2), 110–112. https://doi.org/10.1007/s12646-014-0256-8

Clark, V. R., & Harrell, J. P. (1982). The relationship among Type A behavior, styles used in coping with racism, and blood pressure. *The Journal of Black Psychology, 8*(2), 89–99. https://doi.org/10.1177/009579848200800203

Elizardi, E. (2012). Chris Peterson: The 25th character strength. *Psychology Today: Parent Pulse.* https://www.psychologytoday.com/us/blog/parent-pulse/201210/chris-peterson-the-25th-character-strength

Englar-Carlson, M., & Smart, R. (2014). Positive psychology and gender. In J. T. Pedrotti & L. M. Edwards (Eds.), *Perspectives on the intersection of multiculturalism and positive psychology* (pp. 125–141). Springer. https://doi.org/10.1007/978-94-017-8654-6_9

Eshun, S., & Packer, E. M. (2016). Positive psychology practice with African Americans: Mental health challenges and treatment. In E. C. Chang, C. A. Downey, J. K. Hirsch, & N. J. Lin (Eds.), *Positive psychology in racial and ethnic groups: Theory, research, and practice* (pp. 259–279). American Psychological Association. https://doi.org/10.1037/14799-013

Fernández-Ríos, L., & Novo, M. (2012). Positive psychology: Zeitgeist (or spirit of the times) or ignorance (or disinformation) of history? *International Journal of Clinical and Health Psychology, 12*(2), 333–344. https://www.redalyc.org/pdf/337/33723643010.pdf

Heller, K., & Monahan, J. (1977). *Psychology and community change.* Dorsey

Hendriks, T., Warren, M. A., Schotanus-Dijkstra, M., Hassankhan, A., Graafsma, T., Bohlmeijer, E., & de Jong, J. (2019). How WEIRD are positive psychology interventions? A bibliometric analysis of randomized controlled trials on the science of well-being. *The Journal of Positive Psychology, 14*(4), 489–501. https://doi.org/10.1080/17439760.2018.1484941

Henrich, J., Heine, S. J., & Norenzayan, A. (2010). Most people are not WEIRD. *Nature, 466*(7302), Article 29. https://doi.org/10.1038/466029a

Jeglic, E. L., Miranda, R., & Polanco-Roman, L. (2016). Positive psychology in the context of race and ethnicity. In E. C. Chang, C. A. Downey, J. K. Hirsch, & N. J. Lin (Eds.), *Positive psychology in racial and ethnic groups: Theory, research, and practice* (pp. 13–33). American Psychological Association. https://doi.org/10.1037/14799-002

Kelly, J. G. (1971). Qualities for the community psychologist. *American Psychologist, 26*(10), 897–903. https://doi.org/10.1037/h0032231

Kelly, J. G. (1986). Context and process: An ecological view of the interdependence of practice and research. *American Journal of Community Psychology, 14*(6), 581–589. https://doi.org/10.1007/BF00931335

Keyes, C. L. (2009). The Black–White paradox in health: Flourishing in the face of social inequality and discrimination. *Journal of Personality, 77*(6), 1677–1706. https://doi.org/10.1111/j.1467-6494.2009.00597.x

Kohn-Wood, L., Pollard, S., Becker Herbst, R., & Birichi, D. K. (2016). Ethnic minority mental health strengths in the United States. In H. S. Friedman (Ed.), *Encyclopedia of mental health* (2nd ed., Vol. 2, pp. 149–160). Academic Press. https://doi.org/10.1016/B978-0-12-397045-9.00155-5

Kohn-Wood, L. P., Powell, W. H., Haynes, T., Ferguson, K. K., & Jackson, B. A. (2012). Coping styles, depressive symptoms and race during the transition to adulthood. *Mental Health, Religion & Culture, 15*(4), 363–372. https://doi.org/10.1080/13674676.2011.577059

Kohn-Wood, L. P., & Thomas, A. (2016). Positive psychology assessment in African Americans. In E. C. Chang, C. A. Downey, J. K. Hirsch, & N. J. Lin (Eds.), *Positive psychology in racial and ethnic groups: Theory, research, and practice* (pp. 171–194). American Psychological Association. https://doi.org/10.1037/14799-009

Kristjánsson, K. (2013). *Virtues and vices in positive psychology: A philosophical critique.* Cambridge University Press. https://doi.org/10.1017/CBO9781139177818

Maton, K. I. (2008). Empowering community settings: Agents of individual development, community betterment, and positive social change. *American Journal of Community Psychology, 41*(1–2), 4–21. https://doi.org/10.1007/s10464-007-9148-6

Maton, K. I., Dogden, D. W., Leadbeater, B. J., Sandler, I. N., Schellenbach, C. J., & Solarz, A. L. (2004). Strengths-based research and policy: An introduction. In K. I. Maton, C. J. Schellenbach, B. J. Leadbeater, & A. L. Solarz (Eds.), *Investing in children, youth, families, and communities: Strengths-based research and policy* (pp. 3–12). American Psychological Association. https://doi.org/10.1037/10660-001

Nielsen, M., Haun, D., Kärtner, J., & Legare, C. H. (2017). The persistent sampling bias in developmental psychology: A call to action. *Journal of Experimental Child Psychology, 162,* 31–38. https://doi.org/10.1016/j.jecp.2017.04.017

O'Donnell, C. R. (2006). Beyond diversity: Toward a cultural community psychology. *American Journal of Community Psychology, 37*(1–2), 95–109. https://doi.org/10.1007/s10464-005-9010-7

Park, N., & Peterson, C. (2009). Character strengths: Research and practice. *Journal of College and Character, 10*(4), 1–10. https://doi.org/10.2202/1940-1639.1042

Park, N., Peterson, C., & Seligman, M. E. P. (2006). Character strengths in fifty-four nations and the fifty US states. *The Journal of Positive Psychology, 1*(3), 118–129. https://doi.org/10.1080/17439760600619567

Perkins, D. D., Hughey, J., & Speer, P. W. (2002). Community psychology perspectives on social capital theory and community development practice. *Community Development, 33*(1), 33–52. https://doi.org/10.1080/15575330209490141

Peterson, C., & Park, N. (2006). Character strengths in organizations. *Journal of Organizational Behavior, 27*(8), 1149–1154. https://doi.org/10.1002/job.398

Peterson, C., & Seligman, M. E. (2004). *Character strengths and virtues: A handbook and classification* (Vol. 1). Oxford University Press

Peterson, N. A., & Zimmerman, M. A. (2004). Beyond the individual: Toward a nomo-logical network of organizational empowerment. *American Journal of Community Psychology, 34*(1–2), 129–145. https://doi.org/10.1023/B:AJCP.0000040151.77047.58

Plummer, D. L., & Slane, S. (1996). Patterns of coping in racially stressful situations. *Journal of Black Psychology, 22*(3), 302–315. https://doi.org/10.1177/00957984960223002

Rappaport, J. (1987). Terms of empowerment/exemplars of prevention: Toward a theory for community psychology. *American Journal of Community Psychology, 15*(2), 121–148. https://doi.org/10.1007/BF00919275

Rodriguez Espinosa, P., & Verney, S. P. (2021). The underutilization of community-based participatory research in psychology: A systematic review. *American Journal of Community Psychology, 67*(3–4), 312–326. https://doi.org/10.1002/ajcp.12469

Sanders Thompson, V. L. (2006). Coping responses and the experience of discrimination. *Journal of Applied Social Psychology, 36*(5), 1198–1214. https://doi.org/10.1111/j.0021-9029.2006.00038.x

Schutte, N. S., & Malouff, J. M. (2019). The impact of signature character strengths interventions: A meta-analysis. *Journal of Happiness Studies, 20*(4), 1179–1196. https://doi.org/10.1007/s10902-018-9990-2

Seidman, E. (1988). Back to the future, community psychology: Unfolding a theory of social intervention. *American Journal of Community Psychology, 16*(1), 3–24. https://doi.org/10.1007/BF00906069

Seligman, M. E., & Csikszentmihalyi, M. (2000). Positive psychology: An introduction. *American Psychologist, 55*(1), 5–14. https://doi.org/10.1037/0003-066X.55.1.5

Sellers, R. M., Copeland-Linder, N., Martin, P. P., & Lewis, R. L. H. (2006). Racial identity matters: The relationship between racial discrimination and psychological functioning in African American adolescents. *Journal of Research on Adolescence, 16*(2), 187–216. https://doi.org/10.1111/j.1532-7795.2006.00128.x

Sellers, R. M., & Shelton, J. N. (2003). The role of racial identity in perceived racial discrimination. *Journal of Personality and Social Psychology, 84*(5), 1079–1092. https://doi.org/10.1037/0022-3514.84.5.1079

Trickett, E. J. (2009). Community psychology: Individuals and interventions in com-munity context. *Annual Review of Psychology, 60*(1), 395–419. https://doi.org/10.1146/annurev.psych.60.110707.163517

Utsey, S. O., Ponterotto, J. G., Reynolds, A. L., & Cancelli, A. A. (2000). Racial discrimination, coping, life satisfaction, and self-esteem among African Americans. *Journal of Counseling and Development, 78*(1), 72–80. https://doi.org/10.1002/j.1556-6676.2000.tb02562.x

van Zyl, L. E., Gaffaney, J., van der Vaart, L., Dik, B. J., & Donaldson, S. I. (2024). The critiques and criticisms of positive psychology: A systematic review. *The Journal of Positive Psychology, 19*(2), 206–235. https://doi.org/10.1080/17439760.2023.2178956

Williams, D. R., González, H. M., Neighbors, H., Nesse, R., Abelson, J. M., Sweetman, J., & Jackson, J. S. (2007). Prevalence and distribution of major depressive disorder in African Americans, Caribbean Blacks, and non-Hispanic Whites: Results from the National Survey of American Life. *Archives of General Psychiatry, 64*(3), 305–315. https://doi.org/10.1001/archpsyc.64.3.305

Zimmerman, M. A. (1995). Psychological empowerment: Issues and illustrations. *American Journal of Community Psychology, 23*(5), 581–599. https://doi.org/10.1007/BF02506983

28

Self-Affirmation for Stress Protection

Kennedy M. Blevins, Sarah D. Pressman, and David K. Sherman

Students will affirm one of their personal values prior to a midterm examination. This is followed by a postexam follow-up discussion on how and why affirmation can help reduce the harms of threat and how to use it in the future to uncouple stressful experiences from negative outcomes.

CONCEPT

In psychology, *self-affirmation* is described as any behavior that demonstrates a person's adequacy by reinforcing positive characteristics, skills, abilities, or identities (e.g., through thoughts, writing). Self-affirmation theory relies on the idea that individuals are motivated to maintain their self-worth or the sense that they are a good, moral person overall versus a specific aspect of the self (e.g., parent, student). Research has shown that self-affirmation is especially beneficial in the context of a threat to specific aspects of one's self. For this activity, potential stress arises from an upcoming academic examination. This intervention activity will show students that affirming personal values that are distinct from the student role prior to a test can be helpful in many ways. Discussion activities will also outline how to use this valuable tool to cope with future points of threat (e.g., identity and stereotype threats, stressful life experiences, health behavior change).

https://doi.org/10.1037/0000417-028
More Activities for Teaching Positive Psychology: A Guide for Instructors, S. D. Pressman and A. C. Parks (Editors)

MATERIALS NEEDED

- Students will need pen and paper or a computer to write the self-affirmation intervention.

- The instructor will need a way to collect baseline and follow-up data on various threat-related variables. We will provide survey links that instructors can use (and tailor to their needs) to examine changes before and after the stressful event (i.e., an exam or before a behavioral change or key transitional life period). This survey can also be edited and printed, and results/change scores can be calculated by hand for smaller classes. Please see the Online Materials section for a link to the survey templates.

ACTIVITY SETTING

This activity is best done live in class but could also be done online via virtual instruction. Students can easily do the first part of the affirmation (the 10-minute written values intervention) on their own with prerecorded or prewritten instructions as long as it is clear they must do this prior to their exam. The follow-up discussion is best done live (in person or virtually) so that students can break into groups and discuss situations when affirming might be helpful, different types of values they might affirm, and so forth.

ACTIVITY DURATION

This activity will take approximately 15 minutes for Part 1 (baseline survey, instructions for the self-affirmation intervention, time for students to write), 3 minutes for the follow-up surveys, and 15 minutes for the follow-up discussion.

SUGGESTED READINGS

- We do not recommend any readings prior to the activity to prevent any preconceived notions about the effects of affirmation. Following the affirmation activity and before the class discussion, we recommend:
  - Cohen and Sherman (2014)

- Additional optional reading:
  - Sherman et al. (2021)

- Optional video on self-affirmation:
  - https://tinyurl.com/MATPPch28-video

BACKGROUND AND INSTRUCTIONS

There are many different situations in life that threaten our sense of perceived self-adequacy. For example, our self-adequacy might be threatened when our favorite sports team loses, when we do badly on an evaluation (e.g., a work assessment), or when we are confronted with negative health information. Defensiveness or poor performance may result from these threats to self, among other negative outcomes such as greater reactivity to stress or lower self-esteem. One way to confront these poor outcomes is to use self-affirmation, which helps maintain self-worth by supporting individuals in drawing on a variety of identities to buffer against harm to any specific identity. For example, if one's academic identity is threatened (e.g., by performing badly on an exam), then perhaps by remembering and focusing on other identities, such as being a child or parent or a member of a religion, the threat and any resulting harm can be reduced. Self-affirmation may then ongoingly reinforce interactions between affirmed individuals and their environment. For example, if self-affirmation improves an individual's performance on an exam (e.g., because of enhanced confidence), this improved performance reaffirms an individual's sense of adequacy, potentially leading to enhanced performance in the future as well. Even in the context of poor performance, self-affirmation broadens one's perspective on the threat so that it has less impact on well-being.

There are a host of activities that can affirm the self, but the intervention that has been studied the most is what we will use for this activity: a values affirmation. In this activity, individuals write about an important value they hold (e.g., creativity, religion), for a few minutes. A key aspect of this exercise is that it is completed prior to stress or psychological threat. This allows people to broaden their self-concept beyond the specific identity under threat rather than being consumed by the threat. Essentially, it is a useful reminder of the self-resources that we all have to confront difficulties in our lives at a time when we may be narrowly focused on a particular stressor.

For this activity, students will highlight a value of theirs that is not related to their academic role or academic identity prior to a stressful examination period. This should help protect their esteem and sense of belonging (and perhaps reduce stress). Instructors will need to carefully plan the timing of this activity. Instructors could have students do Part 1 prior to any major midterm period (e.g., if the school has all exams the same week) and then Part 2 the week after. Alternatively, to have more control, instructors could have students complete this a few days or a week prior to an exam in class and then complete Part 2 in the next class after the examination.

Part 1: Baseline (Preexam)

- Prior to starting this activity, have students complete a very brief set of surveys on how they are feeling. This will assess feelings of stress, belonging, exam threat, and self-efficacy. You can view the set of questionnaires (with the

purpose of the activity and assessment hidden) at https://tinyurl.com/
Ch28part1. To use the questionnaires for your class, make a copy using the
following link at https://tinyurl.com/Ch28part1copy and edit it for your
class purposes.[1] Be sure to include some kind of identifier (e.g., student ID)
in order to link responses from the baseline and follow-up surveys so you
can assess class trends. There is a separate survey link for the second part of
the activity, to be completed postexam (see Part 2). Appendix 28.1 contains
instructions for either scoring the questionnaires yourself or providing a
handout so that students can complete scoring themselves.

- Provide students with a list of values (see Appendix 28.2 for an example) that
they can write about for the assignment. Ensure that you remove any values
related to the identity under threat (e.g., music if the exam is on music, a
value connected to academic achievement). Affirming the value under threat
may have the opposite of the intended effect by making the threatened value
more important to an individual's identity, thus increasing the potential for
negative outcomes.

- One small note before you start the writing instructions: Research has shown
that when individuals feel forced to do this activity, it is not as effective
(Silverman et al., 2013). While you should not note this specifically to your
students, you can prevent this issue by spending some time in this lecture and
others highlighting the academic value of these types of in-class activities and
how they are designed to help students do their best.

- Instructions to read to students:
  - "Please read the following values and consider which ones are most
    important to you (please see Appendix 28.2 for the whole list of values).
    Circle the values that resonate the most with you, and of these, rank your
    top three, focusing especially on which value is most important to you. If
    you don't see your most important value listed, please feel free to add a
    new one, but we request that you do not pick one related to academic
    performance today."
    - Note: You may want to provide students with a list to look at on a slide
      or as a handout (Appendix 28.2) so they can circle their top values.
  - "Now that you have completed your rankings, take about 10 minutes to
    write about your *most important value*, that is, the value you ranked as #1.
    When writing, you should focus on past times when this value has been
    relevant to you as well as why this value is meaningful and important to
    you. I won't be grading this writing, so feel free to express whatever you
    like, and don't worry too much about grammar or spelling. Rather, focus
    more on the thoughts and feelings you experience when you think about
    why this value or personal characteristic is important to you."

---

[1] The assessments in the survey include the feelings of self-worth, postthreat perspective
(Critcher & Dunning, 2015), and feelings of belonging on campus/in major (adapted
from Walton et al., 2015).

Part 2: Follow-Up (Postexam)

We recommend that prior to coming back to class for the follow-up discussion, students complete the follow-up survey (Appendix 28.1). This will include the surveys from baseline about values and an additional survey assessing students' perspectives on their values following the exam. You can find the set of questionnaires at https://tinyurl.com/Ch28part2. To use for your class, make a copy using the following link at https://tinyurl.com/Ch28part2copy. You will then have the opportunity to look at class trends. Using the scoring information provided in Appendix 28.1, you can calculate overall class change scores, means, and so forth to illustrate how the class scored on these assessments pre- to postintervention. Remember, you will need the same identifier (e.g., student ID) from the Part 1 surveys to link them to the Part 2 survey responses. Based on past research (e.g., Critcher & Dunning, 2015), you may observe differences such as a broadened perspective on both the threatened identity and identification of other nonthreatened identities. Specifically, looking at the positive self-worth scale (see Appendix 28.1), you may see a lower correlation between positive self-worth and perceptions of threat scales at follow-up compared with the baseline surveys. This reflects a broader perspective on the threat, which will also be reflected by a greater correlation between the positive self-worth and the perspective scales. It should be noted that this pattern of relationships is often moderated by the degree of threat the target group is under, the social environment surrounding the threat, or the size or level of threat to be mitigated. Based on this, you may not see overall group effects. For instance, students from marginalized ethnic backgrounds or from gender identities underrepresented in their field are typically at the greatest risk for a decreased sense of belonging when facing academic threat (Sherman, 2013). For these students, the activity may be especially helpful, but potential structural barriers must still be acknowledged. If you are interested in exploring this trend (e.g., if you have a class with high sex or race diversity), you might consider adding demographics to the Google Forms survey so you can discuss and explore this with your class and relate it to past research findings. This is an important point to raise with the students when talking about the potential benefits of the activity. If the expected trends are not seen, rather than using student data, you might instead draw on examples from the readings and raise the importance of a variety of key moderators in self-affirmation research. Figure 28.1, based on Binning et al. (2021), may help explain the effects of self-affirmation for class discussion. The figure demonstrates that increased threat over time may either send students' performance on an upward trajectory (Student 1) or a downward trajectory (Student 3) depending on how a student responds to the threat. However, for a student with a strong sense of self or who feels they are able to cope with the threat (Student 2), the threat is unlinked from performance. This is the typical effect of affirmation, which broadens one's sense of self, thus uncoupling the threat from performance.

FIGURE 28.1. Hypothetical Student Trajectories Showing the Link Between Threat and Average Academic Performance

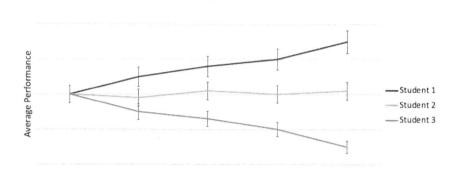

Note. Student 1 shows an upward trajectory, depicted by a positive link between threat and performance. Student 3 shows a downward trajectory, depicted by a negative link between threat and performance. For Student 2, threat and performance are not linked. Adapted from "Securing Self-Integrity Over Time: Self-Affirmation Disrupts a Negative Cycle Between Psychological Threat and Academic Performance," by C. Binning, J. E. Cook, V. P. Greenaway, J. Garcia, N. Apfel, D. K. Sherman, and G. L. Cohen, 2021, *Journal of Social Issues, 77*(3), p. 803 (https://doi.org/10.1111/josi.12461). Adapted with permission.

DISCUSSION

Self-affirmations are most effective when a key aspect of an individual's identity is under threat. These are moments when a person's trajectory could take one path or another (e.g., exams, transitions from high school to college). Rather than simply boosting positive constructs (i.e., targeting one's sense of belonging or acceptance) or decreasing negative constructs (i.e., targeting the threat or defensiveness toward the threat), self-affirmation—by having people write and reflect on the values and resources that are most important to them—can change the story that people tell themselves about threatening experiences. Instead of fixating on the threatening situation, self-affirmation allows people to focus on the bigger picture and how this small event fits into their larger view of themselves or their lives. This helps unlink the threatening stimuli from one's sense of well-being. Thus, affirming one's values gives a broader perspective on the threat, reducing the negative impact, which could, in turn, result in long-term benefits. Specifically, self-affirmation helps individuals accept threatening information (e.g., poor test performance) and reduces stress from upcoming threatening situations (e.g., pretest anxiety; Sherman et al., 2021). Affirming has also been shown to increase test performance, leading people to feel a greater sense of accomplishment and efficacy going forward. This positive cycle propagates, and with other supportive elements (e.g., positive feedback from teachers), can lead to an overall upward trajectory (Sherman et al., 2021).

Affirmation is especially helpful for groups of individuals whose identities are under greater threat. For instance, individuals from marginalized racial groups may experience the greatest benefit of self-affirmation. Therefore, students who perceived the exam as more threatening may show the greatest benefits from the self-affirmation exercise. However, as highlighted earlier, this is not because the threatened identity is seen as less important but by broadening the awareness of other identities that make up the self (Critcher & Dunning, 2015). Based on this, the class results will likely show students having a greater awareness of nonacademic identities following the exam and follow-up assessments. This activity is especially beneficial to students experiencing a high degree of threat; therefore, you may look at differences between different demographic groups in your class or students who scored higher versus lower on the perception of threat scale to assess differences in perspective postthreat. Students with higher perceptions of threat will likely show higher scores on the perspective scale postthreat (see Appendix 28.1 for all scales). Students may also show a greater sense of positive feelings of self-worth (see self-worth scale listed in Appendix 28.1) from pre- to postassessment, but not necessarily a change in negative self-worth.

People vary in the degree to which they spontaneously self-affirm or tend to respond to threats with self-affirming thoughts on their own (Harris et al., 2019). Awareness can decrease the benefits of self-affirmation. However, when individuals are allowed to choose to engage in self-affirmation, they still experience the benefits of affirming (Silverman et al., 2013). Importantly, self-affirmation may have negative effects when there is no psychological threat present. Briñol et al. (2007) found that self-affirmation led to overconfidence in nonthreatening situations, such that when individuals were self-affirmed, they were less able to differentiate between strong versus weak persuasive messages. Instructors may remind students that there are individual differences in self-affirmation. Those who self-affirm spontaneously may have seen more benefits, whereas others may not have seen benefits, for instance, if they were aware of the purpose of the exercise or if the affirmation backfired, creating greater awareness of the threatened identity rather than broadening one's perspective. These circumstances under which self-affirmation is more or less effective are targeted as key discussion points in this activity.

Values affirmations work best when supported by the environments in which they are situated. To address structural barriers for marginalized individuals, instructors may highlight other resources on their campus that may bolster a sense of belonging or improve academic performance. Further, instructors should highlight that self-affirmation does not eliminate structural barriers but rather decouples one's identity from threat so that an individual's sense of adequacy is placed in a larger context (Cohen & Sherman, 2014).

Here are some questions you can raise with your students as part of a class discussion with the main points from the readings for *instructors* listed below each question. Alternatively, you could reserve some of these questions for a take-home assignment (Appendix 28.3).

1. What aspects of an intervention are necessary to make self-affirmations effective?

   • Self-affirmation interventions should be well-timed to occur prior to key life transitions (e.g., transitioning from one grade level to the next) or threat (e.g., taking an exam, receiving negative health information).

   • There must be sufficient threat to one's sense of self.

   • Individuals must be engaged in the activity by thoughtfully contemplating their most important value and how it has helped them. If the activity is not taken seriously, it is less likely to be effective.

2. What are other situations in which you might apply self-affirmation?

   • Before going to the next grade level or entering college.

   • Before providing negative health information.

   • Political conflict negotiations.

   • To lessen defensiveness during relationship disagreements.

   • When adhering to medication use.

     – Importantly, this list is not exhaustive; self-affirmation may be useful for a variety of stressful experiences that may call into question a person's sense of self-worth.

3. Under what circumstances might self-affirmations be less effective? Why?

   • When individuals feel forced to affirm or are aware of the outcome of the intervention (e.g., improve one's sense of self-worth in response to threat).

   • If the intervention is not well-timed (e.g., after a threat has occurred, too soon before a key threat to self would occur) since the positive effects of self-affirmation build on one another.

   • When the target is not experiencing psychological threat.

     – Note: This is one reason that marginalized groups and those with a lower sense of belonging tend to benefit more from self-affirmation.

   • Structural and institutional barriers do not support ongoing positive reinforcement of the affirmation.

   • Some individuals already affirm spontaneously, on their own, and, thus, do not experience as much benefit from intervention.

4. What can you glean from the class survey results? Was there any observable benefit to our class from doing this exercise? If not, why do you think this is?

   • You may observe a lower correlation between positive self-worth or feelings of belonging and threat after the exam. This is because self-affirmation changes the self-narrative and puts the threat into context so that the threat (e.g., exam) has less impact on one's sense of self.

- You may not see these results if you are at a school that is particularly affluent, as self-affirmation is most effective for those with a greater threat of decreased belonging. Additionally, if students are experienced in academia, they may have already taken many college exams at this point, whereas less-experienced students' academic identities may be at greater threat, as they are just starting out.

To wrap up, please summarize the main points of the discussion. In particular, you may want to clarify the following points:

1. This activity highlights the effectiveness of self-affirmation in minimizing the negative effects of threats to one's self.
2. When well-timed before the threat, the benefits of affirmation can produce positive outcomes.
3. Students should understand that there are a variety of situations in which self-affirmation may be applied (including for themselves!).
4. There are certain contexts when focusing on personal values may be helpful or harmful, and this should be considered carefully.

ASSIGNMENT

Instructions: Be sure to read the required reading before answering these questions on your own or with a group. Think about the self-affirmation intervention and what you have learned about self-affirmation, then take some time to answer the following questions:

1. What aspects of an intervention are necessary to make self-affirmations effective?
2. What are other situations in which you might apply self-affirmation?
3. Under what circumstances might self-affirmations be less effective? Why?
4. What can you glean from the class survey results? Was there any observable benefit to our class from doing this exercise? If not, why do you think this is?

ONLINE MATERIALS

- Part 1 Questionnaires (to view): https://tinyurl.com/MATPPch28-Qview1
- Part 1 Questionnaires (to copy): https://tinyurl.com/MATPPch28-Qcopy1
- Part 2 Questionnaires (to view): https://tinyurl.com/MATPPch28-Qview2
- Part 2 Questionnaires (to copy): https://tinyurl.com/MATPPch28-Qcopy2
- Video on self-affirmation: https://tinyurl.com/MATPPch28-video

APPENDIX 28.1: Baseline and Follow-Up Questionnaires

Instructions for instructors: Below are the questions that we included in the Google Form listed in the activity. Should you choose to print your own handouts for the class, the below may be useful for this purpose. Note that depending on your teaching strategy, you may want to delete the scoring instructions and/or change the names of the scales so there is no reactance or expectation effects.

1. Positive Feelings of Self-Worth

Instructions: Complete the following based on how well each statement characterizes how you feel right now.

1. I currently feel proud.

   1   2   3   4   5   6   7   8   9
   not at all   completely

2. I currently feel confident.

   1   2   3   4   5   6   7   8   9
   not at all   completely

3. Overall, I feel positively toward myself right now.

   1   2   3   4   5   6   7   8   9
   not at all   completely

4. I feel like a successful individual.

   1   2   3   4   5   6   7   8   9
   not at all   completely

5. I currently feel pleased with myself.

   1   2   3   4   5   6   7   8   9
   not at all   completely

6. I feel good about myself right now.

   1   2   3   4   5   6   7   8   9
   not at all   completely

7. I feel very much like a person of worth.

   1   2   3   4   5   6   7   8   9
   not at all   completely

8. I do not feel very confident in myself right now.

   1   2   3   4   5   6   7   8   9
   not at all   completely

Scoring instructions: Add the values for numbers 1–7 and subtract the value of number 8 to get your total score. Divide your total score by 8.

2. Negative Feelings of Self-Worth

Instructions: Complete the following based on how well each statement characterizes how you feel right now.

1. I currently feel uneasy.

   1   2   3   4   5   6   7   8   9

   not at all   completely

2. I currently feel humiliated.

   1   2   3   4   5   6   7   8   9

   not at all   completely

3. I currently feel ashamed.

   1   2   3   4   5   6   7   8   9

   not at all   completely

4. I currently feel bothered.

   1   2   3   4   5   6   7   8   9

   not at all   completely

5. I feel inferior at this moment.

   1   2   3   4   5   6   7   8   9

   not at all   completely

6. I am frustrated or rattled.

   1   2   3   4   5   6   7   8   9

   not at all   completely

Scoring instructions: Add the values for numbers 1–6 and divide the total score by 6.

3. Feelings of Belonging

Instructions: Please complete the following questions based on how you feel right now.

1. I feel like I belong at my university.

   1   2   3   4   5   6   7

   strongly   strongly

   disagree   agree

2. I feel like I belong in my major department.

   1   2   3   4   5   6   7

   strongly   strongly

   disagree   agree

3. I feel confident that other people think I belong in my major department.

1	2	3	4	5	6	7
strongly disagree						strongly agree

Scoring instructions: Add the value of numbers 1–3 and divide by 3.

4. Perception of Threat

Instructions: Please answer the following statements based on how you feel generally.

1. I often worry about my performance on exams.

1	2	3	4	5	6	7
strongly disagree						strongly agree

2. It is important for me to do well on tests in school.

1	2	3	4	5	6	7
strongly disagree						strongly agree

3. If I do not do well on an exam, I feel like a bad student.

1	2	3	4	5	6	7
strongly disagree						strongly agree

Scoring instructions: Add the values of your responses to numbers 1–3 and divide by 3.

Follow-Up–Only Questionnaire

For instructors: The below questions are for the follow-up assessment only, but the baseline questionnaires (e.g., Positive Feelings of Self-Worth, Negative Feelings of Self-Worth, Feeling of Belonging, and Perception of Threat) should also be assessed at follow-up so that you can examine change from pre- to postaffirmation.

5. Perspective

Instructions: To what extent did the exercise prompt perspective on the threatened identity (e.g., made me think of one or more aspects of myself beyond my academic self)?

Report on what the exercise prompted you to think about or do, regardless of whether the instructions explicitly instructed you to or you did so spontaneously.

1. Writing about my values made me think of other aspects of myself beyond my academic self.

1	2	3	4	5	6	7
strongly disagree						strongly agree

2. Writing about my values led me to identify one or more of my nonacademic identities.

1	2	3	4	5	6	7
strongly disagree						strongly agree

3. Writing about my values led me to appreciate that I have multiple parts of who I am.

1	2	3	4	5	6	7
strongly disagree						strongly agree

Scoring instructions: Add the values of your responses to numbers 1–3 and divide by 3.

A printable version of this appendix can be downloaded from the APA website at https://www.apa.org/pubs/books/more-activities-teaching-positive-psychology.

APPENDIX 28.2: Example List of Values

Instructions: The following pages will not be graded. You will have approximately 15 minutes to complete this activity. First, please take a few minutes to circle the values that are MOST important to you. Write numbers 1, 2, and 3 next to the ones that are most important, with 1 meaning the MOST important:

- Art/music/theater
- Creativity
- Community/relationships with family and friends
- Political views
- Independence
- Learning and gaining knowledge
- Money, wealth, or status
- Your social/cultural/racial identity
- Honesty or integrity
- Helping society
- Achievement in athletics
- Connection with nature/the environment
- Career success
- Athleticism, fitness
- Morality, spirituality, or religion
- Sense of humor/having fun
- Other? _____

Now take 10 minutes to write about your most important value (the value you ranked as No. 1), focusing on times when this value was important to you and why this value is important to you. Focus on your thoughts and feelings—don't worry about spelling, grammar, or how well-written it is.

_____

_____

_____

_____

_____

_____

_____

_____

_____

_____

_____

_____

_____

_____

_____

_____

_____

_____

_____

_____

_____

A printable version of this appendix can be downloaded from the APA website at https://www.apa.org/pubs/books/more-activities-teaching-positive-psychology.

APPENDIX 28.3: In-Class or Take-Home Assignment Questions

1. What aspects of an intervention are necessary to make self-affirmations effective?

_____

_____

_____

_____

_____

_____

_____

_____

_____

_____

_____

_____

2. What are other situations in which you might apply self-affirmation?

_____
_____
_____
_____
_____
_____
_____
_____
_____
_____
_____
_____

3. Under what circumstances might self-affirmations be less effective? Why?

_____
_____
_____
_____
_____
_____
_____
_____
_____
_____
_____

4. What can you glean from the class survey results? Was there any observable benefit to the class from doing this exercise? If not, why do you think this is?

_____
_____
_____
_____
_____
_____
_____
_____
_____
_____
_____
_____

A printable version of this appendix can be downloaded from the APA website at https://www.apa.org/pubs/books/more-activities-teaching-positive-psychology.

REFERENCES

Binning, C., Cook, J. E., Greenaway, V. P., Garcia, J., Apfel, N., Sherman, D. K., & Cohen, G. L. (2021). Securing self-integrity over time: Self-affirmation disrupts a negative cycle between psychological threat and academic performance. *Journal of Social Issues, 77*(3), 801–823. https://doi.org/10.1111/josi.12461

Briñol, P., Petty, R. E., Gallardo, I., & DeMarree, K. G. (2007). The effect of self-affirmation in nonthreatening persuasion domains: Timing affects the process. *Personality and Social Psychology Bulletin, 33*(11), 1533–1546. https://doi.org/10.1177/0146167207306282

Cohen, G. L., & Sherman, D. K. (2014). The psychology of change: Self-affirmation and social psychological intervention. *Annual Review of Psychology, 65*(1), 333–371. https://doi.org/10.1146/annurev-psych-010213-115137

Critcher, C. R., & Dunning, D. (2015). Self-affirmations provide a broader perspective on self-threat. *Personality and Social Psychology Bulletin, 41*(1), 3–18. https://doi.org/10.1177/0146167214554956

Harris, P. R., Griffin, D. W., Napper, L. E., Bond, R., Schüz, B., Stride, C., & Brearley, I. (2019). Individual differences in self-affirmation: Distinguishing self-affirmation from positive self-regard. *Self and Identity, 18*(6), 589–630. https://doi.org/10.1080/15298868.2018.1504819

Sherman, D. K. (2013). Self-affirmation: Understanding the effects. *Social and Personality Psychology Compass, 7*(11), 834–845. https://doi.org/10.1111/spc3.12072

Sherman, D. K., Lokhande, M., Müller, T., & Cohen, G. L. (2021). Self-affirmation interventions. In G. M. Walton & A. J. Crum (Eds.), *Handbook of wise interventions: How social psychology can help people change* (pp. 63–99). Guilford Press

Silverman, A., Logel, C., & Cohen, G. L. (2013). Self-affirmation as a deliberate coping strategy: The moderating role of choice. *Journal of Experimental Social Psychology, 49*(1), 93–98. https://doi.org/10.1016/j.jesp.2012.08.005

Walton, G. M., Logel, C., Peach, J. M., Spencer, S. J., & Zanna, M. P. (2015). Two brief interventions to mitigate a "chilly climate" transform women's experience, relationships, and achievement in engineering. *Journal of Educational Psychology, 107*(2), 468–485. https://doi.org/10.1037/a0037461

Using Positive Coping Strategies to Boost Resilience

Emma L. Grisham and Marie P. Cross

This activity provides students with the opportunity to reflect on specific coping strategies that they use in their own lives and learn about strategies that have been empirically linked to resilience.

CONCEPT

We all engage in coping strategies in an attempt to deal with stress, but some strategies are more effective at preserving well-being and boosting resilience than others (e.g., Folkman & Moskowitz, 2004; Luthar et al., 2015). This activity prompts students to explore strategies that have and have not been effective in their own lives and highlights forms of coping that promote resilience and psychological well-being. This activity fits best within course content centered around resilience, coping with and overcoming stress, the function of positive emotions, or positive psychology applications in therapeutic contexts.

MATERIALS NEEDED

Worksheets (either physical handouts or electronic copies) and polling technology (e.g., iClicker, Poll Everywhere, Zoom) for larger classes and/or instructors wishing to poll students electronically.

https://doi.org/10.1037/0000417-029
More Activities for Teaching Positive Psychology: A Guide for Instructors, S. D. Pressman and A. C. Parks (Editors)

ACTIVITY SETTING

We describe this activity in a face-to-face class setting, but it is also possible to incorporate it into both synchronous and asynchronous online classes.

- Synchronous online classroom: Students can be paired in breakout rooms to complete the activity, and then the class can come back together for discussion.

- Asynchronous online classroom: Although there are a number of options for how to incorporate this activity, we recommend integrating it as a discussion board. In this scenario, all students would complete the worksheets and write a discussion post about what they learned about their own coping strategies. Then, they would be required to respond to the posts of one or more of their classmates, comparing and contrasting their own coping strategies with those of their classmates to further understand how different coping strategies might be beneficial for different people and in different scenarios.

ACTIVITY DURATION

This activity requires approximately 30 minutes, with roughly 10 minutes for students to work independently on the worksheets, 10 minutes for paired discussions, and 10 to 15 minutes for class discussion and debrief.

SUGGESTED READINGS

- Recommended preactivity reading:
  - Bonanno (2004)

- Optional postactivity readings:
  - Tugade and Fredrickson (2004)
  - Waters et al. (2022)

BACKGROUND AND INSTRUCTIONS

As humans navigate a complex and dynamic world, they are bound to encounter challenging circumstances. Adversity can assume many different forms, including daily hassles (e.g., arguments with a friend; Charles et al., 2013) and major life events (e.g., loss of a loved one; Lucas, 2007). Although experiencing adversity may be inevitable, suffering because of it is not; research has found that people commonly manage to maintain relatively stable levels of subjective well-being in the face of hardship (Bonanno, 2004; Luhmann et al., 2012). This ability to effectively adapt to difficult situations is known as resilience (Fletcher & Sarkar, 2013).

Despite considerable empirical attention, resilience remains a complex concept that has been difficult to define. For example, *resilience* has been defined variously as a stable, dispositional capacity to withstand life's challenges regardless of form and as a dynamic process of leveraging resources to meet the demands of a situation within a specific sociocultural context (Fletcher & Sarkar, 2013; Southwick et al., 2014). Although a single unified conceptualization of resilience remains elusive, researchers have identified a number of biological, psychological, social, and cultural determinants of resilience that interact to determine how we respond to stressful experiences in our lives (e.g., Southwick et al., 2014). Although many determinants of resilience are unalterable, such as its heritability (Feder et al., 2019), the way that people respond to and cope with stressful situations is changeable and, thus, provides an opportunity for intervention to strengthen our ability to adapt to adversity (e.g., Luthar et al., 2015).

Coping encompasses the diverse array of cognitive and behavioral efforts that people use to manage stress (Folkman et al., 1986). These different forms of coping, known as *coping strategies*, all aim to mitigate the harmful psychological and physiological effects of stress on well-being by either neutralizing the perceived threat or reducing the distress associated with it, but with varying degrees of effectiveness (Folkman & Moskowitz, 2004). Although stress may be an inevitable part of life, the use of appropriate coping strategies can boost resilience and, in turn, protect against the adverse consequences of stress and promote greater well-being.

From the resilience literature, several coping strategies have emerged that have been consistently associated with greater well-being and better mental health outcomes following adversity. Positive reappraisal (cognitively reframing an event as more positive), problem solving, meaning making, and social support have all been consistently linked to better psychological adjustment to stressful situations (e.g., Kalisch et al., 2015; Park, 2010; Ryff, 2014; Taylor & Stanton, 2007). Cultivating humor and positive emotions such as gratitude have also been demonstrated to be effective strategies for maintaining well-being despite experiencing stress (e.g., Fredrickson et al., 2003; Tugade & Fredrickson, 2004, 2007). Similarly, self-compassion, acceptance, and mindfulness can reduce stress and promote wellness, even during a major crisis like a pandemic (e.g., Naragon-Gainey et al., 2017; Waters et al., 2022).

Because coping is intricately tied to resilience, the goal of this activity is to encourage students to reflect on the coping strategies they have used in their own lives, independently and through discussion with their classmates, and how they might leverage coping strategies to foster greater resilience. In preparation for administering this activity, we recommend either printing physical copies of the provided worksheets (see Appendices 29.1 and 29.2) or uploading electronic copies to a shared course space before the class session. Instructors wishing to electronically poll their students after the paired discussions are also advised to program their poll question using their chosen software or platform (e.g., Zoom, iClicker, Poll Everywhere, Google Forms, Kahoot).

1. After introducing and defining the concept of resilience, provide students with the Resilience and Coping Worksheet (Appendix 29.1), a double-sided worksheet that includes a reflection prompt on each side.

2. Instruct students to first write about a specific recent experience in their lives in which they felt moderately stressed and were resilient (Appendix 29.1, Side A). Ask students to describe the stressful situation, how they coped with it, how they felt emotionally and physically while coping, and what factors contributed to their ability to be resilient in that situation. We suggest advising students to select an experience they would feel comfortable sharing with a classmate. In our experience, students often choose to discuss stressors such as exams or major assignments, roommate disagreements, arguments with friends or romantic partners, work stress, and difficulties balancing school and work. It may be helpful to provide these stressors as examples to help students get started if they are having trouble generating their own experiences.

3. Next, instruct students to write about a recent time in which they were moderately stressed and not resilient, meaning they succumbed to the stressor, were unable to manage their stress, and experienced negative emotions and/or diminished well-being for some time after experiencing the stressor (Appendix 29.1, Side B). Remind students that all people experience moments of nonresilience but that these moments offer opportunities to learn more effective ways to manage our responses to difficult situations. Advise students to again describe the stressful situation, how they coped with it, how they felt emotionally and physically while coping, and what factors contributed to their lack of resilience in that situation. Again, we suggest reminding students to choose an experience they would feel comfortable sharing with a classmate.

4. After students complete both self-reflection exercises, instruct students to pair up and discuss their reflections with their partners. If students seem unwilling or uncomfortable to share their own experiences, encourage them to talk about a time when they observed someone else (e.g., a family member, friend, roommate, classmate) experiencing a stressful situation and either responding with resilience or not. Instructors can also offer an example from their own life, of a situation either they personally experienced or observed a loved one experiencing, to initiate discussion. Advise students to compare and contrast the coping strategies they used in both situations, identify the strategies that seemed to be effective, and discuss the factors they believe promoted or thwarted their resilience.

5. Following paired discussions, ask the pairs to report which coping strategies they thought were most effective for managing stress and conferring resilience. After several pairs have shared their insights, ask students to share any other coping strategies they think might relate to resilience and why. Instructors may wish to poll students about these coping strategies to gauge class consensus on which ones are most commonly believed to be tied to

resilience. Polls can be conducted either by a simple show of hands or electronically (e.g., iClicker, Poll Everywhere, Zoom), depending on the mode of instruction (e.g., in-person, online, asynchronous), size of the class, technology available, and preference for identifiable or anonymous responses.

6. After this brief class discussion, provide students with the Resilience-Boosting Coping Strategies Handout (Appendix 29.2) and describe each of the 10 listed coping strategies that have been empirically linked to resilience. Ask students to indicate all of the coping strategies they have personally used in their lives. Instructors can then take a poll to assess which of the listed coping strategies are most commonly used by students in the class, either through a show of hands or via an electronic poll. Finish the activity with a class discussion about factors that might influence the effectiveness of these strategies (e.g., specific situations, cultural factors, socioeconomic status, personality differences). Additional information and guidance for facilitating class discussion is provided in the Discussion section.

DISCUSSION

People engage in coping on a daily basis but often without knowing which strategies actually help them manage their stress and preserve their well-being. Despite representing diverging theoretical perspectives, research on positive psychology interventions and coping strategies both seek to identify methods by which people maintain and improve their psychological well-being (Bolier et al., 2013; Taylor & Stanton, 2007). One area of psychological well-being that has been of particular interest within both positive psychology interventions and coping strategies is decreasing stress, a topic with which most college students are all too familiar. Thus, our activity aims to integrate insights from across these literatures to teach students about different types and forms of coping and encouraging them to reflect on which strategies help them successfully cope with stressful situations and build resilience in their own lives. Through independent reflection and paired discussion, students will identify the coping strategies that can be effective for managing stress and maintaining well-being, with the hope that they can apply those insights and develop a deeper understanding of how to leverage coping strategies to build resilience.

To debrief this activity with students, we recommend initiating a class discussion using real-time poll results. Instructors can begin by commenting on which set of strategies students most commonly used in their own lives and asking students to describe their experiences using them, including the nature of the stressor and their emotional and physical state during and after using that coping strategy. Instructors might also take the time to ask students what resilience means to them. In our experience, students will generate a number of different definitions of resilience, demonstrating that this concept is multi-faceted and can encompass a multitude of well-being indices. Instructors can use students' varying definitions of resilience to begin a discussion about how resilience is defined differently by various fields, subdisciplines, and scholars. Southwick et al. (2014) provided an accessible overview of this issue and summarize how resilience is conceptualized by different fields such as psychiatry, developmental psychology, clinical psychology, and anthropology.

The topic of divergent definitions of resilience may also be an effective entry point for introducing the concept of person–situation–strategy fit and the context-dependent nature of resilience (e.g., Bonanno & Burton, 2013; Haines et al., 2016; Lazarus & Folkman, 1987). Instructors can describe how the ability of a given coping strategy to maintain well-being and boost resilience can depend on its suitability for both the person (e.g., age, personality, socioeconomic status) and the situation (e.g., controllable vs. uncontrollable). For example, individuals higher in extraversion may benefit more from receiving social support than more introverted individuals (e.g., Connor-Smith & Flachsbart, 2007), and emotion-focused coping strategies (e.g., positive reappraisal) may be more adaptive for uncontrollable than for controllable situations (e.g., Aldwin, 1994). Furthermore, cultural factors such as norms, values, and beliefs also influence the types of coping strategies people use and their suitability and effectiveness; for example, seeking guidance and support from family is a commonly used coping strategy in collectivistic cultures that is distinct from more general social support and is associated with better coping outcomes within those populations (e.g., Heppner et al., 2006; Lazarus & Folkman, 1984). These discussion topics emphasize the importance of moving beyond a one-size-fits-all approach to coping and underscore why amassing a diverse repertoire of coping strategies at one's disposal may confer greater adaptability and, thus, greater resilience. Through these discussion topics, students can develop a deeper understanding of the nuances of coping and resilience in real-world situations.

To ensure that this exercise is both educational and enjoyable for students, we recommend emphasizing the sharing component of the activity and advising students to select their examples accordingly. We have found that students are much more comfortable when they are informed prior to completing the worksheet that they will be asked to discuss their reflections with a partner so they do not discuss overly personal examples. Although students are welcome to share personal information as part of this activity, many may wish to focus on surface-level coping experiences, especially when talking with a classmate they may not have met before. For a similar reason, we have also found that students prefer to discuss their reflections in pairs rather than small groups because they are often more comfortable sharing their experiences with only one person. If instructors wish to assign students to share their reflections in small groups, we recommend instructing students to discuss the effectiveness of the strategies more generally with limited focus on personal details. Finally, the worksheet itself is a useful reflective activity for students, so if time is limited, it may still be beneficial to include this in your course with a short discussion/debrief without the think-pair-share component. As a final point for class discussions, it may be helpful to highlight for students that the list of coping strategies on the worksheet is not comprehensive and that coping takes many more forms than are listed.

APPENDIX 29.1: Resilience and Coping Worksheet

RESILIENCE AND COPING WORKSHEET (SIDE A)

Think of a recent time in your life when you felt moderately stressed and were resilient—that is, a time when you were stressed but able to recover and adapt positively to the situation. With that situation in mind, answer the following questions:

1. What was the situation? Describe what caused you to experience stress (please choose an example that you would feel comfortable discussing with a classmate).

2. How did you cope with this situation? Describe the cognitive and/or behavioral actions you took in response to this situation.

3. How did you feel while you were coping with the situation? Did you experience any emotional (e.g., happy, sad, anxious) or physical changes (e.g., heart pounding, muscles relaxing)?

4. In your opinion, why were you able to be resilient in this situation? What factors contributed to your resilience?

RESILIENCE AND COPING WORKSHEET (SIDE B)

Think of a recent time in your life when you felt moderately stressed and were NOT resilient—that is, a time when you were stressed and your well-being was negatively impacted by the experience. With that situation in mind, answer the following questions:

1. What was the situation? Describe what caused you to experience stress (please choose an example that you would feel comfortable discussing with a classmate).

2. How did you cope with this situation? Describe the cognitive and/or behavioral actions you took in response to this situation.

3. How did you feel while you were coping with the situation? Did you experience any emotional (e.g., happy, sad, anxious) or physical changes (e.g., heart pounding, muscles relaxing)?

4. In your opinion, why were you *not* able to be resilient in this situation? What factors undermined your resilience?

A printable version of this appendix can be downloaded from the APA website at https://www.apa.org/pubs/books/more-activities-teaching-positive-psychology.

APPENDIX 29.2: Resilience-Boosting Coping Strategies Handout

Please review the following coping strategies and check off each one that you have ever used to manage stress:

☐ Positive reappraisal/benefit finding: Reinterpreting a negative event by focusing on the "silver lining" or something positive that came from the experience.

☐ Problem solving: Taking efforts to resolve the problem or situation that is causing stress as a way to alleviate it.

☐ Acceptance: Coming to terms with the reality of what happened and that it cannot be changed or undone.

☐ Humor/laughter: Using funny content (e.g., TV shows, comedy specials, books) to amuse and possibly distract yourself.

☐ Practicing gratitude: Reflecting on aspects of your life for which you feel grateful through any activity (e.g., gratitude journal, writing a letter of gratitude to a loved one).

☐ Meditation/mindfulness: Focusing your awareness on the present moment and experiencing any thoughts, feelings, or sensations that arise without judgment.

☐ Self-compassion: Being kind to yourself in difficult moments and accepting that being imperfect is part of being human.

☐ Seeking social support: Reaching out to family, friends, or others for help, comfort, or assistance.

☐ Exercising: Engaging in some form of physical activity (e.g., walking, running, lifting weights, yoga).

☐ Engaging in a fun hobby: Spending time doing something that you enjoy (e.g., reading, cooking, making art, watching movies).

INTERESTED IN LEARNING MORE?

Check out these helpful guides from the American Psychological Association on how to reduce stress and boost resilience using these strategies!

* 11 healthy ways to handle life's stressors: https://www.apa.org/topics/stress/tips
* Building your resilience: https://www.apa.org/topics/resilience/building-your-resilience

A printable version of this appendix can be downloaded from the APA website at https://www.apa.org/pubs/books/more-activities-teaching-positive-psychology.

REFERENCES

Aldwin, C. (1994). *Stress, coping, and development.* Guilford Press.

Bolier, L., Haverman, M., Westerhof, G. J., Riper, H., Smit, F., & Bohlmeijer, E. (2013). Positive psychology interventions: A meta-analysis of randomized controlled studies. *BMC Public Health, 13*(1), Article 119. https://doi.org/10.1186/1471-2458-13-119

Bonanno, G. A. (2004). Loss, trauma, and human resilience: Have we underestimated the human capacity to thrive after extremely aversive events? *American Psychologist, 59*(1), 20–28. https://doi.org/10.1037/0003-066X.59.1.20

Bonanno, G. A., & Burton, C. L. (2013). Regulatory flexibility: An individual differences perspective on coping and emotion regulation. *Perspectives on Psychological Science, 8*(6), 591–612. https://doi.org/10.1177/1745691613504116

Charles, S. T., Piazza, J. R., Mogle, J., Sliwinski, M. J., & Almeida, D. M. (2013). The wear and tear of daily stressors on mental health. *Psychological Science, 24*(5), 733–741. https://doi.org/10.1177/0956797612462222

Connor-Smith, J. K., & Flachsbart, C. (2007). Relations between personality and coping: A meta-analysis. *Journal of Personality and Social Psychology, 93*(6), 1080–1107. https://doi.org/10.1037/0022-3514.93.6.1080

Feder, A., Fred-Torres, S., Southwick, S. M., & Charney, D. S. (2019). The biology of human resilience: Opportunities for enhancing resilience across the life span. *Society of Biological Psychiatry, 86*(6), 443–453. https://doi.org/10.1016/j.biopsych.2019.07.012

Fletcher, D., & Sarkar, M. (2013). Psychological resilience: A review and critique of definitions, concepts, and theory. *European Psychologist, 18*(1), 12–23. https://doi.org/10.1027/1016-9040/a000124

Folkman, S., Lazarus, R. S., Gruen, R. J., & DeLongis, A. (1986). Appraisal, coping, health status, and psychological symptoms. *Journal of Personality and Social Psychology, 50*(3), 571–579. https://doi.org/10.1037/0022-3514.50.3.571

Folkman, S., & Moskowitz, J. T. (2004). Coping: Pitfalls and promise. *Annual Review of Psychology, 55*(1), 745–774. https://doi.org/10.1146/annurev.psych.55.090902.141456

Fredrickson, B. L., Tugade, M. M., Waugh, C. E., & Larkin, G. R. (2003). What good are positive emotions in crises? A prospective study of resilience and emotions following the terrorist attacks on the United States on September 11th, 2001. *Journal of Personality and Social Psychology, 84*(2), 365–376. https://doi.org/10.1037/0022-3514.84.2.365

Haines, S. J., Gleeson, J., Kuppens, P., Hollenstein, T., Ciarrochi, J., Labuschagne, I., Grace, C., & Koval, P. (2016). The wisdom to know the difference: Strategy–situation fit in emotion regulation in daily life is associated with well-being. *Psychological Science, 27*(12), 1651–1659. https://doi.org/10.1177/0956797616669086

Heppner, P. P., Heppner, M. J., Lee, D., Wang, Y., Park, H., & Wang, L. (2006). Development and validation of a collectivist coping styles inventory. *Journal of Counseling Psychology, 53*(1), 107–125. https://doi.org/10.1037/0022-0167.53.1.107

Kalisch, R., Müller, M. B., & Tüscher, O. (2015). A conceptual framework for the neurobiological study of resilience. *Behavioral and Brain Sciences, 38*, Article e92. https://doi.org/10.1017/S0140525X1400082X

Lazarus, R. S., & Folkman, S. (1984). *Stress, appraisal, and coping.* Springer.

Lazarus, R. S., & Folkman, S. (1987). Transactional theory and research on emotions and coping. *European Journal of Personality, 1*(3), 141–169. https://doi.org/10.1002/per.2410010304

Lucas, R. E. (2007). Adaptation and the set-point model for subjective well-being. *Current Directions in Psychological Science, 16*(2), 75–79. https://doi.org/10.1111/j.1467-8721.2007.00479.x

Luhmann, M., Hofmann, W., Eid, M., & Lucas, R. E. (2012). Subjective well-being and adaptation to life events: A meta-analysis. *Journal of Personality and Social Psychology, 102*(3), 592–615. https://doi.org/10.1037/a0025948

Luthar, S. S., Crossman, E. J., & Small, P. J. (2015). Resilience and adversity. In R. Lerner (Ed.), *Handbook of child psychology and developmental science* (Vol. 3, pp. 247–386). Wiley. https://doi.org/10.1002/9781118963418.childpsy307

Naragon-Gainey, K., McMahon, T. P., & Chacko, T. P. (2017). The structure of common emotion regulation strategies: A meta-analytic examination. *Psychological Bulletin, 143*(4), 384–427. https://doi.org/10.1037/bul0000093

Park, C. L. (2010). Making sense of the meaning literature: An integrative review of meaning making and its effects on adjustment to stressful life events. *Psychological Bulletin, 136*(2), 257–301. https://doi.org/10.1037/a0018301

Ryff, C. D. (2014). Psychological well-being revisited: Advances in the science and practice of eudaimonia. *Psychotherapy and Psychosomatics, 83*(1), 10–28. https://doi.org/10.1159/000353263

Southwick, S. M., Bonanno, G. A., Masten, A. S., Panter-Brick, C., & Yehuda, R. (2014). Resilience definitions, theory, and challenges: Interdisciplinary perspectives. *European Journal of Psychotraumatology, 5*(1), Article 25338. https://doi.org/10.3402/ejpt.v5.25338

Taylor, S. E., & Stanton, A. L. (2007). Coping resources, coping processes, and mental health. *Annual Review of Clinical Psychology, 3*(1), 377–401. https://doi.org/10.1146/annurev.clinpsy.3.022806.091520

Tugade, M. M., & Fredrickson, B. L. (2004). Resilient individuals use positive emotions to bounce back from negative emotional experiences. *Journal of Personality and Social Psychology, 86*(2), 320–333. https://doi.org/10.1037/0022-3514.86.2.320

Tugade, M. M., & Fredrickson, B. L. (2007). Regulation of positive emotions: Emotion regulation strategies that promote resilience. *Journal of Happiness Studies, 8*(3), 311–333. https://doi.org/10.1007/s10902-006-9015-4

Waters, L., Algoe, S. B., Dutton, J., Emmons, R., Fredrickson, B. L., Heaphy, E., Moskowitz, J. T., Neff, K., Niemiec, R., Pury, C., & Steger, M. (2022). Positive psychology in a pandemic: Buffering, bolstering, and building mental health. *The Journal of Positive Psychology, 17*(3), 303–323. https://doi.org/10.1080/17439760.2021.1871945

30

Healthy Foods for Happiness

A Mini-Intervention

Tamlin S. Conner and Jack R. H. Cooper

This activity involves increasing fruit and vegetable intake and monitoring the associated improvements in well-being.

CONCEPT

The purpose of this activity is to do a mini-intervention to increase the number of servings of fruits and vegetables eaten to five or more servings per day for 1 week and to measure how participants feel before and after this change. The goal is to see whether increasing fruit and vegetable intake results in well-being improvements. Participants will be asked to reflect on their usual intake of fruits and vegetables and to challenge themselves to see if they can increase that during the 1-week mini-intervention. This activity illustrates how positive health behaviors can have a positive influence on mental well-being.

MATERIALS NEEDED

- Printouts or slides of the well-being scale with scoring instructions for measuring before and after the intervention (see Appendix 30.1).

- Printouts or slides of the fruit and vegetable scale for measuring before and after the intervention (see Appendix 30.2).

https://doi.org/10.1037/0000417-030
More Activities for Teaching Positive Psychology: A Guide for Instructors, S. D. Pressman and A. C. Parks (Editors)

- Optional: A digital device (smartphone, tablet, or laptop) for each student to record their daily fruit and vegetable intake to track goal progress during the intervention. Suggested applications include MyFitnessPal and the See How You Eat (SHYE) food diary. Both are free and offer flexible ways of logging food, ranging from scanning barcodes for accurate nutritional information to uploading photos of food as a more visual record of meals.

- Optional: You could also set up the well-being and fruits and vegetables scales using Qualtrics, SurveyMonkey, or similar technology.

ACTIVITY SETTING

This activity can be done in person or entirely remotely across a 1-week period. There is a briefer option that can be completed in 24 hours. The introduction to the activity can be done in person or online, synchronously or asynchronously. The intervention part of the activity will take place in students' daily lives around meals and snack times and can be done equally well online or offline asynchronously (logging fruit and vegetable intake at the time it occurs—either via an app or on paper—or recording intake at the end of each day). The discussion at the end of the activity is best done in person or online. This activity could be run alongside lessons focused on positive psychology interventions, mind–body connections, the intersection between health and well-being, health psychology, and models of well-being, such as how diet contributes to the PERMA model of well-being (positive emotions, engagement, relationships, meaning, accomplishment; Seligman, 2018) via positive emotions.

ACTIVITY DURATION

This activity will occur over 1 week. This format would require 15 minutes for an introduction (in class, remote, or recorded) to complete baseline measures (Day 1), then 5 minutes a day outside of class for 6 days of tracking fruit and vegetable intake (Days 2–7), followed by 30 to 60 minutes in class or online to complete follow-up measures and engage in discussion (Day 8). This format runs from one day of the week to the next week to fit within a weekly class session (e.g., Wednesday to Wednesday).

Alternatively, the 24-hour intervention would require 15 minutes for an introduction to complete baseline measures (Day 1), then 5 to 10 minutes of increased fruit and vegetable intake outside of class, followed by 30 to 60 minutes in class or online to complete follow-up measures and engage in discussion (Day 2).

RECOMMENDED READINGS

Although instructors can review these readings ahead of time, students should probably read them after the activity is completed to reduce expectancy effects, where beliefs about the hypotheses bias the results of the experiment. The first recommended reading would be "The Contribution of Food Consumption to Well-Being" (Holder, 2019), which provides a brief review of how dietary patterns, including fruit and vegetable intake, relate to aspects of well-being and positive psychology constructs. After this, we suggest reading "Let Them Eat Fruit!" (Conner et al., 2017), which is one of the earliest intervention trials that randomized people to eat more fruits and vegetables to test the effects on well-being. It is an example of a randomized controlled trial (RCT), which is the strongest form of evidence in establishing causal patterns. There is also an interesting archived Reddit thread discussing "Let Them Eat Fruit!" to stimulate further interest.

- Holder (2019)
- Conner et al. (2017)
- Reddit thread discussing "Let Them Eat Fruit!": https://tinyurl.com/MATPPch30-reddit

BACKGROUND AND INSTRUCTIONS

Popular positive psychology activities focus on changing feelings through psychological interventions such as practicing gratitude, giving to others, and mindfulness meditation (see various chapters in this book). Another potent way to change feelings is through altering health behaviors. Changing healthy habits, for instance, getting more exercise (Penedo & Dahn, 2005), prioritizing high-quality sleep (Steptoe et al., 2008), and improving diet (Rooney et al., 2013) may be equally as powerful as psychological interventions, yet they are often not discussed in positive psychology textbooks nor are they considered part of the usual positive psychology arsenal. We wish to change that by introducing one health psychology intervention—a fruit and vegetable (FV) dietary intervention—that research suggests may boost well-being.

You probably know that healthy habits like eating nutritious foods are important for physical well-being. However, healthy eating may be important for mental well-being, too. One cornerstone of a healthy diet is the consumption of nutrient-rich fruits and vegetables—colorful foods from the rainbow—like apples, beets/beetroot, carrots, bananas, mangos, kiwifruit, spinach, kale, blueberries, and blackberries. Research at the intersection of positive psychology and nutrition has shown that higher intake of FVs predicts greater happiness (Mujcic & Oswald, 2016), well-being (Conner et al., 2015), and vitality or zest for life (Conner et al., 2020). In a systematic review of cross-sectional, correlational, and longitudinal research, higher intake of FVs was associated with a range of positive mental states, including quality of life, sleep quality, life satisfaction, flourishing, mood, curiosity, creativity, optimism, and self-efficacy (Głąbska et al., 2020; see also Rooney et al., 2013). One study run in New Zealand and the United States found that the top 10 raw FVs related to better well-being included carrots, bananas, apples, and dark leafy salad greens (Figure 30.1; Brookie et al., 2018). Moreover, intervention research suggests a causal effect

FIGURE 30.1. A Diagram Showing the Top 10 Raw Fruits and Vegetables Related to Better Well-Being

of increasing FV intake on improvements in positive mental states (Conner et al., 2017, 2020). As shown in Conner et al. (2017), young adults provided with two extra servings of fruits and vegetables per day (carrots and oranges or kiwifruit) showed a 10.5% increase in well-being after a 2-week intervention relative to control participants who did not alter their diet.

Interestingly, the sweet spot appears to be eating five to seven total servings of fruits and vegetables daily to achieve gains in well-being (Blanchflower et al., 2013; Brookie et al., 2018; Głąbska et al., 2020). This number range is close to the recommended "5+ a day" public health messaging reflecting physical health benefits (Centers for Disease Control and Prevention, 2005; Multicultural Health Communication Service, 2007). However, a majority of adolescents, young adults, and older adults do not achieve this 5+ a day, putting them at risk for poorer physical and mental well-being. Worse still, adolescents and young adults consume the fewest fruits and vegetables of all age groups (Albani et al., 2017; Lange et al., 2021; Lee, 2022; Nicklett & Kadell, 2013).

The goal of this activity is to increase FV intake for 1 week (or if a shorter time period is needed, 24 hours) and to test its effects on well-being. Prior research suggests that consuming 5+ servings of FV a day will result in improved well-being, such as greater happiness, positive mood, and feelings of zest for life. The activity does not specify which types of fruits and vegetables people· should choose—this will be dependent on culture, preferences, availability, and affordability. Aim for nutrient-dense fruits and vegetables that are minimally processed. Figure 30.1 shows some of the fruits and vegetables linked to well-being in the United States and New Zealand. Other nutrient-dense fruits and vegetables from diverse geographic areas include tomatoes, arugula, olives, and figs (Mediterranean); beets, radishes, eggplant, cherries, and apricots (Eastern Europe); onions, peppers, okra, pineapples, and citrus fruits (African nations); eggplant, squash, okra, pomegranates, and dates (Middle East); Chinese cabbage, bok choy, mushrooms, durian, lychee, dragon fruit, jackfruit, and rambutan (Asia); taro, cassava, sweet potato, papaya, mango, coconuts (Polynesia); avocado, green beans, peppers, papaya, and passionfruit (South America).

Instructions: One-Week Intervention

- Step 1: Orient students to the activity.
  - Explain what this intervention is and how it differs from more popular positive psychology interventions. Popular positive psychology interventions are often psychological in nature and focus on activities such as expressing gratitude, giving to others, interacting with others, or practicing mindfulness in order to boost feelings of well-being. This activity aims to see whether we can boost well-being through an alternative pathway—by changing a health behavior—specifically the amount of FVs eaten in a day. Explain that eating 5+ servings of FVs a day is known to benefit physical well-being but that we want to test whether eating 5+ a day may also benefit mental well-being.
  - Next, tell the participants that they will participate in a "real-life mini-intervention" and explain the intervention to them. Namely, tell them the experiment will take 1 week.
    - On Day 1, they will complete the well-being scale and report their recent FV intake.
    - On Days 2 to 7, they will attempt to eat as close to the 5+ daily servings of fruits and vegetables recommendation as they can. This means five or more combined servings of FVs each day, ideally with at least three servings of vegetables and two servings of fruit. People already eating 5+ a day should challenge themselves to eat at least two more servings per day than they normally do. As an option, people could aim to record their FV intake to keep on track of the goal. Each night before going to bed, participants can write down their fruit intake, vegetable intake, and total FV intake for that day to keep track of their progress. Alternatively, they could use a diet-tracking app like MyFitnessPal or SHYE. If you do the optional diet tracking, spend some time going over different serving sizes of FVs so that students know how to record this correctly. Appendix 30.2 describes a serving size. You can also refer to online resources for images of serving sizes:
      - https://www.nhs.uk/live-well/eat-well/5-a-day-portion-sizes/
      - https://www.health.govt.nz/your-health/healthy-living/food-activity-and-sleep/healthy-eating/four-food-groups
      - https://www.heart.org/en/healthy-living/healthy-eating/add-color/fruits-and-vegetables-serving-sizes

■ Finally, in class on Day 8, have students complete the well-being scale again and record their change in FV intake. Compare their baseline scores with their follow-up scores to see if a difference was detected.

- Step 2: Complete baseline measures (Day 1).

  – Show the well-being scale and the fruit and vegetable scale via computer or distribute printouts. Alternatively, you could set up a survey in Qualtrics, SurveyMonkey, or another survey tool to collect data in real time and to visualize the results during the debriefing component for greater student interaction.

  – Have students complete the well-being scale and the fruit and vegetable scale and compute their total scores for each (see Appendices for scoring). These are their baseline measures (preintervention measures). They should either write down their scores or keep the printouts as a record. Remind students to bring these scores to the debriefing session if they are completing them on paper.

- Step 3: Complete the intervention for 6 days (Days 2–7).

  – Starting the next day, participants should aim to increase their FV intake to the goal of 5+ a day, ideally consisting of three servings of vegetables and two servings of fruit, preferably in less processed forms (not fried foods, more fresh foods, and not juices or dried fruits; FVs blended into smoothies is okay). If participants are already getting 5+ servings daily, they should try to increase their usual consumption by two servings per day.

  – Optional tracking: At the end of each day, participants should write down the date and the number of servings of fruit, vegetables, and combined FVs. They can either record this on a piece of paper, in their smartphone notes, or use a specialized app such as MyFitnessPal or SHYE. This will allow them to keep track of their goal progress (optional).

- Step 4: Complete follow-up (postintervention) measures (Day 8).

  – Provide students with the well-being scale and the fruit and vegetable scale via computer and projected screen or distribute printouts.

  – Have students complete the follow-up well-being scale and the fruit and vegetable scale (optional: use their paper records, smartphone records, or app data to aid memory) and then compute their total well-being score and total FV score. These are their follow-up scores.

- Step 5: Interpret, present, and discuss findings (Day 8).

  – At a minimum, students should observe whether they were able to increase their FV intake and whether their well-being scores increased, decreased, or stayed the same. Advanced students could be asked to compute percent change scores for well-being (and FV intake) using this formula: % change score = [(post − pre)/pre] × 100. For example, if a person's well-being score was 40 before the intervention and 50 after the intervention, this would equate to a 25% increase [(50 − 40)/40 = .25 × 100 = 25%)]. If a person's total FV intake was two servings per day before the intervention and four servings per day after the intervention, this would equate to a 100% increase [(4 − 2/2 = 1 × 100 = 100%].

- Findings can be presented in several ways while maintaining anonymity. One option is to count the total number of students in class, have all students raise their hands, and say, "Keep your hand up if your well-being increased following the intervention"; then count the number of hands remaining and express this as a percentage (e.g., 20 out of 30 people showed improvement, reflecting 67% of the class). You can use the same process to see what percentage of students increased their FV intake compared with baseline. Another option is to use a spreadsheet to present findings. You could have students write their scores anonymously on a sheet of paper (pre- and postscores), have students enter their scores anonymously into a collaborative Google Sheets spreadsheet (one column for pre and one column for post) and graph the difference, or utilize the robust data visualization features of Qualtrics if you created a survey for this activity.

- Initiate discussion (see the Discussion section).

Instructions: Alternative 24-Hour Intervention Option

- Step 1: Explain the activity. The main difference from the 1-week activity is that students will be asked to increase their FV intake for a 24-hour period (that night and the following day) and report their well-being before and after the intervention.

- Step 2: Complete baseline well-being measure (Day 1). Have participants complete the baseline well-being measure but modify it so they report experiences "over the past day" (instead of the past week).

- Step 3: Complete the intervention for the next 24 hours. Starting that day, participants should aim to increase their FV intake as much as they can over the next 24 hours, ideally getting their 5+ servings a day (Days 1–2).

- Step 4: Complete follow-up well-being measure (Day 2). Have participants complete the follow-up well-being measure; again, modify it so students report experiences over the past day (instead of the past week).

- Step 5: Interpret and discuss findings (Day 2). Have participants compare their well-being scores before and after the intervention—did their scores change? Ask participants to reflect on how they feel emotionally after eating more fruits and vegetables—did they notice any changes? If so, what? How successful were they at eating more fruits and vegetables? See the Discussion section for further talking points.

DISCUSSION

Here are some questions to raise with the class:
Discussion Point 1: Did you eat more fruits and vegetables?

• Ask the class whether they were able to increase their FV intake to the target 5+ servings a day.

  – How was their 5+ a day distributed? Did they eat two servings of fruit and three servings of vegetables? Was one easier for them to do than the other?

• What were the barriers to increasing FV intake?

  – This is a great opportunity for students to discuss a range of challenges or barriers to increasing their FV intake, whether personal (dislike the taste of vegetables, forgot, too busy, not motivated), financial (cost/expense), and/ or situational (lack of time, inconvenient, no access/availability, family/ roommates/flatmates not cooperative; see also Livingstone et al., 2020). Prior qualitative research also shows that there are significant barriers to understanding and adhering to the 5+ a day guidelines, with young adults citing the following as their main barriers (Rooney et al., 2017):

    ▪ Confusion over what "5+ FV a day" means (e.g., Five combined servings of fruits and vegetables? Five servings of each? Five different types?)

    ▪ Difficulty easily/accurately estimating FV intake "on the go" (e.g., How much does a salad in a sandwich from a cafe count as?)

    ▪ Lack of standardized portion/serving information (e.g., wishing for food packaging to state how much the food contributed to an FV serving).

    ▪ Not realizing what counts toward their FV intake (e.g., Do the tomatoes in a pizza base count?)

You could ask participants whether they experienced these barriers or other ones entirely.

  – You could initiate discussion of the wider societal issues of access to FVs given the importance of these foods to optimal physical and mental health, and the role of structural inequalities in achieving the 5+ a day recommendation (socioeconomic factors, *food deserts*, where poor neighborhoods have fewer outlets for fresh FVs, cost of produce).

  – You could also initiate discussion of the types of FVs eaten. How much is this influenced by culture? Family and peers?

Discussion Point 2: Did well-being change from this intervention?

• How did student well-being scores change from baseline to follow-up?

• Prior research would predict that well-being scores should increase following the intervention, provided participants increased their FV intake. You could start the discussion by reflecting on what percentage of the class improved their well-being.

- You could also reflect on the size of the percentage changes in well-being, which tend to be small but consistent—about 2%–15% improvement.

- You could have students brainstorm why FV intake might boost well-being. A variety of biological mechanisms have been proposed to underlie this relationship (Rooney et al., 2013). FVs are nutrient-dense foods that contain a broad range of vitamins and minerals necessary for gut health, brain health, and neurotransmitter function, all of which affect how we feel emotionally. FVs contain (a) antioxidants, such as vitamin C, which are important for many bodily and brain processes that underlie mood; (b) complex carbohydrates, which stabilize blood sugar and balance mood; and (c) B vitamins, like folate, which boost serotonin production and mood (Rooney et al., 2013). There is probably not just one mechanism but multiple mechanisms. There may also be psychological pathways, for instance, feeling good about sticking to a goal or doing something healthy for oneself.

Discussion Point 3: Was there variability in the intervention effect?

- All interventions have individual variability in the findings—some people respond more favorably to the intervention, others may not respond at all, and others might even get worse after the intervention. Did you have variability? What might some of the reasons be for this variability? Brainstorm those factors as a class.

  - This could lead to an interesting discussion about how diet is only one factor that influences well-being. The inputs to well-being are complex and include personal dispositions/personality (whether someone is optimistic vs. pessimistic), social relationships (in person and online), social media complexities (and social comparison), and other health behaviors like getting high-quality sleep and sufficient physical exercise.

  - In fact, a cross-sectional study compared the big three health behaviors of sleep, exercise, and diet and found that the top predictor of well-being was better sleep quality, followed by exercise and FV intake, which tied for second place (Wickham et al., 2020). Therefore, some of the variation in the intervention effects could be tied to these other factors—such as how well people slept during the intervention and whether they exercised.

  - Some students may suggest that their well-being may have improved for other reasons. For example, perhaps they took a more active role in their health, leading to increased self-efficacy and a better mood, or perhaps they showed improved well-being because they anticipated the intervention hypothesis ahead of time.

- You may discuss with students the third variable problem, namely where a relationship between two variables (e.g., increasing FV intake and well-being) can be explained by a third variable that influences both (e.g., taking a more active role in one's health or meeting a goal). Ask participants how they might design an experiment that would avoid this issue. One possibility is an experiment where participants are simply given 5+ servings of fruits and vegetables to eat each day by the experimenters instead of relying on them to do it themselves. This would prevent participants from being involved in their own health, and as such, the results would be purely from the increased FV intake (this leads to Discussion Point 4).

- Similarly, students may have experienced *expectancy effects*, where if someone expects a given result, they will alter their actions and behavior to achieve this outcome. For example, students may have expected to have greater well-being by the end of the intervention (especially if they completed the readings ahead of time and anticipated the hypotheses). Some people might believe there is a stronger link between their diet and well-being, and this could have influenced the results. This is why, in experimental research, it is important to tell participants about the hypotheses after the end of the study, during debriefing. It is also why researchers include a range of survey items in their studies so that participants cannot guess the specific hypotheses. That is a weakness of this mini-intervention: It is easy to see that the goal is to test whether increasing FV intake improves well-being. Perhaps students can design their own mini-intervention that could circumvent these issues, which, again, leads to Discussion Point 4.

Discussion Point 4: How would you improve the intervention next time?

- Part of scientific research is learning to do a "postmortem" on a project—reflecting on what was successful or not successful and then deciding whether and how to proceed in the next stage of this research.

- How would you design a more effective intervention?
  - One key thing missing from this activity is a control group and randomization to either the intervention or control group. That will tell you how people change over the week without any intervention to isolate the intervention effects better.

- What other aspects would you change?
  - For example, you might suggest doing the intervention over a longer period, such as 2 weeks or a month.

- What new challenges might a longer intervention present?
  - How would you overcome the significant costs or barriers to eating healthfully for a whole month? These are just some things to consider when designing future directions in this research area.

Conclusion

Finally, it is a great idea to give students context for how this activity fits into the wider fields of positive psychology and health psychology, the future of this type of research, and, most importantly, why it matters. Instructors can walk students through some or all of these points:

- This activity connects two subfields of psychology—positive psychology and health psychology. Positive psychology aims to achieve "a scientific understanding and effective interventions to build thriving in individuals, families, and communities" (Seligman & Csikszentmihalyi, 2000, p. 13). Health psychology studies the connections between psychological processes and health (American Psychological Association, 2014). Whereas the majority of positive psychology interventions are more psychological in nature—focusing on changing attitudes, deepening feelings of gratitude, cultivating relationships, and practicing mindfulness—the mini-intervention featured in this chapter reflects a health psychology focus: changing a physical health behavior to impact well-being. Health psychologists have learned there is a close connection between the body and the mind and that intervening to improve the body can have flow-on effects on the mind (and vice versa). Interestingly, the majority of health psychology intervention research still focuses on the deficit model of mental health, which focuses on changing behaviors to alleviate suffering (i.e., reduce depression or anxiety). Although alleviation of suffering is important, it does not mean a person is therefore flourishing. Relatively less research in health psychology focuses on changing behaviors to improve flourishing. Physical health interventions reflect an untapped area for positive psychology intervention research. In fact, there may be other health behavior interventions that could improve well-being, for instance, those related to sleep (improving sleep quality), movement and exercise (physical activity, yoga, tai chi), body synergy (breathing and parasympathetic nervous system activation), other positive dietary changes (reducing unhealthy foods, increasing probiotic and fiber intake), and others yet to be discovered. What kinds of health behaviors do you think will improve well-being?

- This mini-intervention could be discussed in the context of models of well-being such as the PERMA model (Seligman, 2018). The PERMA model of well-being was developed by one of the cofounders of positive psychology, Martin Seligman, to better explain and define well-being. According to the PERMA model, well-being includes experiencing positive emotion (e.g., happiness, satisfaction, peacefulness), engagement (flow, where challenge and skills synergize), relationships (positive connections that make you feel loved and supported), meaning (feelings of purpose and worth), and accomplishment/achievements (success with important goals). One thing that is possibly missing from the PERMA model is feelings of physical vitality and health, which could also be considered a cornerstone of well-being. How would you change this model to include physical health (PERMA*P* or PERMA*H*, perhaps)? Also, the mini-intervention discussed in this chapter only captures one or two elements of the PERMA model—positive emotion and accomplishment (via achieving goals). It would be interesting to design a health psychology intervention that tapped into more elements of the PERMA model, including engagement and relationships. How could this be done? Would interventions that tap into more elements of the PERMA model be more effective than interventions that only tap into one or two elements?

- You could also discuss future research on the links between food and well-being. From our perspective, future research needs to prioritize testing the causal pathways and possible mechanisms. There is still a need for more RCTs where participants are randomized to increase their FV intake (e.g., via experimenter-controlled nutrition plans), and their well-being is tracked over time and compared against a control group. Longer term RCTs would help confirm a causal relationship between FV intake and well-being and allow for more definitive statements regarding causality. In addition, more work is needed on the mechanisms that account for the relationship between FV and well-being, such as dietary fiber, which can improve gut function; carbohydrates; and vitamins and minerals like vitamin C, carotenoids, and B vitamins (Rooney et al., 2013). Finally, more research is needed in diverse countries, including non-WEIRD countries (western, educated, industrialized, rich, and democratic), including those from the global south. One such study found that higher fruit consumption among adults living in non-Western developing countries was associated with better quality of life and less depression, whereas vegetable consumption was unrelated to these indicators in developing countries (Gehlich et al., 2019).

- Last, you could discuss the "so what" question of this research. Why is it important? We think this work is important because it gives people another tool—their diet—to help improve mental well-being. Improving well-being is important given the flow-on benefits to other areas in one's life. Research in positive psychology shows that higher well-being is associated with a myriad of benefits, including increased creativity, increased productivity, more prosocial behaviors, and positive relationships (Ruggeri et al., 2020). There are also positive health benefits from experiencing greater positive affect, including stronger immune function, better cardiovascular health, and even greater longevity (Pressman & Cohen, 2005; Pressman et al., 2019). So, eat your 5+ a day for better well-being and a happier, healthier life!

ASSIGNMENT

As an additional optional assignment, have each student write up a brief one- to two-page report about their experiences with this intervention, consisting of three parts:

- First, describe the activity they undertook and why; that is, what prior evidence justifies investigating the effect of increasing FV intake on well-being?

- Second, reflect on their changes in FV intake; for example, were they able to achieve the 5+ servings-per-day goal for the week? What were the barriers to achieving daily FV goals? Were they already eating healthfully, or did they have a long way to go to reach the 5+ servings a day?

- Third, have them write about how their well-being scores changed from before to after the intervention. Is this change consistent with the hypothesized effect (that increasing FV intake would increase well-being)? If not, what factors might have accounted for the patterns? How do the background readings help explain the patterns and why?

APPENDIX 30.1: Well-Being Scale (Baseline and Follow-Up)

Code Name: _____ Date: _____

Time (circle): Baseline or Follow-Up

Instructions: Below are some statements about feelings and thoughts. Please tick the box that best describes your experience of each over the past week.

Statement	None of the time 1	Rarely 2	Some of the time 3	Often 4	All of the time 5
1. I've been feeling optimistic about the future.					
2. I've been feeling useful.					
3. I've been feeling relaxed.					
4. I've been feeling interested in other people.					
5. I've had energy to spare.					
6. I've been dealing with problems well.					
7. I've been thinking clearly.					
8. I've been feeling good about myself.					
9. I've been feeling close to other people.					
10. I've been feeling confident.					
11. I've been able to make up my own mind about things.					
12. I've been feeling loved.					
13. I've been interested in new things.					
14. I've been feeling cheerful.					

Note. Adapted from "The Warwick–Edinburgh Mental Well-Being Scale (WEMWBS): Development and UK Validation," by R. Tennant, L. Hiller, R. Fishwick, S. Platt, S. Joseph, S. Weich, J. Parkinson, J. Secker, and S. Stewart-Brown, 2007, *Health and Quality of Life Outcomes, 5*, Article 63 (https://doi.org/10.1186/1477-7525-5-63). Copyright 2006 by University of Warwick. Adapted with permission. This is not the validated version of the WEMWBS because the timeframe of recall has been changed from the original "last 2 weeks" to "over the past week" to fit this teaching activity with the permission of the developer. The WEMWBS items are reprinted with permission for pedagogical purposes only. If using the WEMWBS in research, you must obtain a license at https://warwick.ac.uk/fac/sci/med/research/platform/wemwbs/using. Licenses are free to the public sector, but there is a charge for licenses issued to private or commercial organizations. If using the WEMWBS in research, use the validated version with the "last 2 weeks" timeframe because every validation study of the WEMWBS is based on the 2-week timeframe.

WEMWBS Scoring:

Add the responses, varying from 1 to 5, for all 14 items to get the total score. The possible range of total scores is from 14 (*lowest possible*) to 70 (*highest possible*). The median score is typically around 50 (Tennant et al., 2007). Higher total scores indicate more positive psychological functioning.

Total score: _____

A printable version of this appendix can be downloaded from the APA website at https://www.apa.org/pubs/books/more-activities-teaching-positive-psychology.

APPENDIX 30.2: Fruit and Vegetable Scale (Baseline and Follow-Up)

Code Name: _____ Date: _____ Time (circle): Baseline or Follow-Up

Instructions: Think about your past week. Please select the response that best describes your daily consumption of fruit and vegetables in the past week.

1. How many servings of fruit (raw, frozen, or cooked) did you typically eat each day? A serving is equal to one medium apple, banana, orange, or pear; two small apricots, kiwifruits, or plums; ½ cup berries (fresh or frozen); or one cup diced or canned fruit (no added sugar). *Do not include* fruit juice or dried fruit.

Circle your answer:	0 Servings/ day	1 Serving/ day	2 Servings/ day	3 Servings/ day	4 Servings/ day	5+ Servings/ day

2. How many servings of vegetables (raw, cooked, frozen, canned, or tinned) did you typically eat each day? A serving is equal to ½ cup cooked green or orange vegetables (e.g., broccoli, spinach, carrots, or pumpkin); ½ cup cooked, dried, or canned beans, peas, or lentils; one cup green leafy or raw salad vegetables (lettuce, kale, cabbage); ½ cup corn; or ½ medium potato or other starchy vegetables. *Do not include* vegetable juice, French fries/ hot chips, or potato chips/crisps.

Circle your answer:	0 Servings/ day	1 Serving/ day	2 Servings/ day	3 Servings/ day	4 Servings/ day	5+ Servings/ day

Scoring:

Add the responses, varying from 0 to 5, for both items to get the total score. Total scores can range from 0 to 10 servings/day of fruit and vegetables (FV). The recommended total intake is five or more servings/day of FV.

Total score: _____ servings/day of FV.

A printable version of this appendix can be downloaded from the APA website at https://www.apa.org/pubs/books/more-activities-teaching-positive-psychology.

REFERENCES

Albani, V., Butler, L. T., Traill, W. B., & Kennedy, O. B. (2017). Fruit and vegetable intake: Change with age across childhood and adolescence. *British Journal of Nutrition, 117*(5), 759–765. https://doi.org/10.1017/S0007114517000599

American Psychological Association. (2014). *Health psychology promotes wellness.* https://www.apa.org/education-career/guide/subfields/health

Blanchflower, D. G., Oswald, A. J., & Stewart-Brown, S. (2013). Is psychological well-being linked to the consumption of fruit and vegetables? *Social Indicators Research, 114*(3), 785–801. https://doi.org/10.1007/s11205-012-0173-y

Brookie, K. L., Best, G. I., & Conner, T. S. (2018). Intake of raw fruits and vegetables is associated with better mental health than intake of processed fruits and vegetables. *Frontiers in Psychology, 9*, Article 487. https://doi.org/10.3389/fpsyg.2018.00487

Centers for Disease Control and Prevention. (2005). *5 a day works!* U.S. Department of Health and Human Services. https://www.cdc.gov/nccdphp/dnpa/nutrition/health_professionals/programs/5aday_works.pdf

Conner, T. S., Brookie, K. L., Carr, A. C., Mainvil, L. A., & Vissers, M. C. M. (2017). Let them eat fruit! The effect of fruit and vegetable consumption on psychological well-being in young adults: A randomized controlled trial. *PLOS ONE, 12*(2), Article e0171206. https://doi.org/10.1371/journal.pone.0171206

Conner, T. S., Brookie, K. L., Richardson, A. C., & Polak, M. A. (2015). On carrots and curiosity: Eating fruit and vegetables is associated with greater flourishing in daily life. *British Journal of Health Psychology, 20*(2), 413–427. https://doi.org/10.1111/bjhp.12113

Conner, T. S., Fletcher, B. D., Haszard, J. J., Pullar, J. M., Spencer, E., Mainvil, L. A., & Vissers, M. C. M. (2020). KiwiC for vitality: Results of a randomized placebo-controlled trial testing the effects of kiwifruit or vitamin C tablets on vitality in adults with low vitamin C levels. *Nutrients, 12*(9), Article 2898. https://doi.org/10.3390/nu12092898

Głąbska, D., Guzek, D., Groele, B., & Gutkowska, K. (2020). Fruit and vegetable intake and mental health in adults: A systematic review. *Nutrients, 12*(1), Article 115. https://doi.org/10.3390/nu12010115

Gehlich, K. H., Beller, J., Lange-Asschenfeldt, B., Köcher, W., Meinke, M. C., & Lademann, J. (2019). Fruit and vegetable consumption is associated with improved mental and cognitive health in older adults from non-Western developing countries. *Public Health Nutrition, 22*(4), 689–696. https://doi.org/10.1017/S1368980018002525

Holder, M. D. (2019). The contribution of food consumption to well-being. *Annals of Nutrition & Metabolism, 74*(Suppl. 2), 44–52. https://doi.org/10.1159/000499147

Lange, S. J., Moore, L. V., Harris, D. M., Merlo, C. L., Lee, S. H., Demissie, Z., & Galuska, D. A. (2021). Percentage of adolescents meeting federal fruit and vegetable intake recommendations—Youth risk behavior surveillance system, United States, 2017. *Morbidity and Mortality Weekly Report, 70*(3), 69–74. https://doi.org/10.15585/mmwr.mm7003a1

Lee, S. H. (2022). Adults meeting fruit and vegetable intake recommendations—United States, 2019. *Morbidity and Mortality Weekly Report, 71*(1), 1–9. https://doi.org/10.15585/mmwr.mm7101a1

Livingstone, K. M., Burton, M., Brown, A. K., & McNaughton, S. A. (2020). Exploring barriers to meeting recommendations for fruit and vegetable intake among adults in regional areas: A mixed-methods analysis of variations across socio-demographics. *Appetite, 153*, Article 104750. https://doi.org/10.1016/j.appet.2020.104750

Mujcic, R., & Oswald, A. J. (2016). Evolution of well-being and happiness after increases in consumption of fruit and vegetables. *American Journal of Public Health, 106*(8), 1504–1510. https://doi.org/10.2105/AJPH.2016.303260

Multicultural Health Communication Service. (2007). *Fitting more fruit and vegetables into your diet.* NSW Government. https://www.mhcs.health.nsw.gov.au/publications/7950/doh-7950-eng.pdf/@@display-file/file/doh-7950-eng.pdf

Nicklett, E. J., & Kadell, A. R. (2013). Fruit and vegetable intake among older adults: A scoping review. *Maturitas, 75*(4), 305–312. https://doi.org/10.1016/j.maturitas.2013.05.005

Penedo, F. J., & Dahn, J. R. (2005). Exercise and well-being: A review of mental and physical health benefits associated with physical activity. *Current Opinion in Psychiatry, 18*(2), 189–193. https://doi.org/10.1097/00001504-200503000-00013

Pressman, S. D., & Cohen, S. (2005). Does positive affect influence health? *Psychological Bulletin, 131*(6), 925–971. https://doi.org/10.1037/0033-2909.131.6.925

Pressman, S. D., Jenkins, B. N., & Moskowitz, J. T. (2019). Positive affect and health: What do we know and where next should we go? *Annual Review of Psychology, 70*(1), 627–650. https://doi.org/10.1146/annurev-psych-010418-102955

Rooney, C., McKinley, M. C., Appleton, K. M., Young, I. S., McGrath, A. J., Draffin, C. R., Hamill, L. L., & Woodside, J. V. (2017). How much is '5-a-day'? A qualitative investigation into consumer understanding of fruit and vegetable intake guidelines. *Journal of Human Nutrition and Dietetics, 30*(1), 105–113. https://doi.org/10.1111/jhn.12393

Rooney, C., McKinley, M. C., & Woodside, J. V. (2013). The potential role of fruit and vegetables in aspects of psychological well-being: A review of the literature and future directions. *The Proceedings of the Nutrition Society, 72*(4), 420–432. https://doi.org/10.1017/S0029665113003388

Ruggeri, K., Garcia-Garzon, E., Maguire, Á., Matz, S., & Huppert, F. A. (2020). Well-being is more than happiness and life satisfaction: A multidimensional analysis of 21 countries. *Health and Quality of Life Outcomes, 18*(1), Article 192. https://doi.org/10.1186/s12955-020-01423-y

Seligman, M. (2018). PERMA and the building blocks of well-being. *The Journal of Positive Psychology, 13*(4), 333–335. https://doi.org/10.1080/17439760.2018.1437466

Seligman, M., & Csikszentmihalyi, M. (2000). Positive psychology: An introduction. *American Psychologist, 55*(1), 5–14. https://doi.org/10.1037/0003-066X.55.1.5

Steptoe, A., O'Donnell, K., Marmot, M., & Wardle, J. (2008). Positive affect, psychological well-being, and good sleep. *Journal of Psychosomatic Research, 64*(4), 409–415. https://doi.org/10.1016/j.jpsychores.2007.11.008

Tennant, R., Hiller, L., Fishwick, R., Platt, S., Joseph, S., Weich, S., Parkinson, J., Secker, J., & Stewart-Brown, S. (2007). The Warwick-Edinburgh Mental Well-Being Scale (WEMWBS): Development and UK validation. *Health and Quality of Life Outcomes, 5*, Article 63. https://doi.org/10.1186/1477-7525-5-63

Wickham, S.-R., Amarasekara, N. A., Bartonicek, A., & Conner, T. S. (2020). The big three health behaviours and mental health and well-being among young adults: A cross-sectional investigation of sleep, exercise, and diet. *Frontiers in Psychology, 11*, Article 579205. https://doi.org/10.3389/fpsyg.2020.579205

INDEX

ABOUT THE EDITORS

Sarah D. Pressman, PhD, is a professor of psychological science and the associate dean of undergraduate education at the University of California, Irvine. She received her BSc in biopsychology from Mount Allison University; her MS and PhD in social, personality, and health psychology from Carnegie Mellon University; and completed postdoctoral training in cardiovascular behavioral medicine at the University of Pittsburgh. Dr. Pressman is a world expert on the interrelations between positive psychological factors, stress, and health and regularly teaches large classes in positive and health psychology. She has received numerous awards for her research and teaching contributions in these areas. Her work on positive psychology-relevant topics has been cited approximately 10,000 times (h-index 35) and has been widely featured in popular outlets. She currently serves as an editor for *Cogent Psychology* and has received grant support for her work from many agencies and foundations.

Acacia C. Parks, PhD, has made it her mission for the past 20 years to bring evidence-based, destigmatized health care to the public. As lead consultant at Liquid Amber, she is a digital health executive and scientific advisor with deep knowledge of scientific and regulatory strategy in digital therapeutics as well as clinical product design, including coaching strategy. Prior to her work in industry, she was an associate professor of psychology at Hiram College, where she taught positive psychology, abnormal psychology, research methodology, and critical writing. She earned her PhD in psychology at the University of Pennsylvania under Dr. Martin Seligman, where they developed the manual for group positive psychotherapy, testing the therapeutic positive psychology activities therein in group settings, online, and in a variety of clinical populations, including smoking cessation, schizophrenia, and osteoarthritis. Her expertise in this area is affirmed by over 6,500 citations of her articles in scientific journals (h-index 29), three (now four!) edited books, and 10 years of associate editorship at the *Journal of Positive Psychology*.